Monasteries, Shrines and Society

Buddhist and Brahmanical Religious Institutions in India in their Socio-Economic Context

Monasteries, Shrines and Society

Buddhist and Brahmanical Religious Institutions in India in their Socio-Economic Context

Edited by
Birendra Nath Prasad

MANAK
PUBLICATIONS PVT. LTD

First Edition 2011

Published by

MANAK

PUBLICATIONS PVT. LTD

B-7, Saraswati Complex, Subhash Chowk,
Laxmi Nagar, New Delhi 110092
Phone: 22453894, 22042529
E-mail : manak_publications@hotmail.com
manak.publications@gmail.com
USA Office
8145 KOLB AVE, ALLEN PARK, M.I. 48101 USA
E-mail: rahul_upma@yahoo.com

ISBN 978-81-7831-231-6

Layout by
KHUSHNUMA

Laser Typeset by
T. ALI, Hamdard Nagar, New Delhi

Printed in India by
Nice Printing Press, New Delhi

CONTENTS

SECTION 2
Brahmanical temples in interaction with other societal institutions and processes

ACKNOWLEDGEMENTS

Much of this work was visualised during my tenure at Assam Central University, Silchar, and this could not have been possible without the help and support of Prof. S.C. Saha, Prof. Tapodhir Bhattachajee and Prof. Sajal Nag. Words fail to express my gratitude to them. Later, I moved to B.B. Ambedkar Central University, Lucknow, where I had an opportunity to offer papers on social history of early Indian Religious and Buddhist revival movements in Modern India. Many of my arguments evolved during my discussions with my MA students, and, as such, they deserve my special thanks.

I take this opportunity to thank my teachers at JNU, particularly Prof. B.D. Chattopadhyaya , Prof. S. Ratnagar , Prof. Ranabir Chakravarti , Prof. Himanshu Prabha Ray, Prof. Kunal Chakravarti, Prof. Muzaffar Alam and Dr. Supriya Verma. I have also benefited from my interactions with Prof. D.K. Chakrabarti, Prof. K.T.S. Sarao, Prof. Vidula Jayaswal, Prof. R.N. Mishra, Prof. B. Labh, Prof. R. Korisettar, Dr. Vishwamohan Jha, Dr. B.C. Deotare, Dr. Rakesh Tiwari and Dr. B.R. Mani. I am sincerely thankful to all of them.

Thanks are also due to the scholars who contributed research articles to this book. Despite their hectic schedule, they responded to my proposal enthusiastically.

I also express my thanks to Prof. Ma Tian Xiang, Wuhan University, China. He was kind enough to invite me to represent India in the 'International Symposium on Buddhism Studies in the Last One Hundred Years' at Wuhan University, China. I presented a paper therein, which was subsequently published in *Buddhist Studies Review*, London (June 2008). Prof. Richard Gombrich and Prof. Peter Harvey offered penetrating comments on that paper. This paper is being reproduced in this book. I express my gratitude to them. Thanks are also due to Dr. Amarajiva Lochan, Secretary, South and Southeast Asian Association for the Study of Culture and Religion, for his permission to reproduce my research article on Samataṭa Harikela in this book. This article was originally published in *South and Southeast Asia: Culture and Religion*, Journal of South and Southeast Asian Association for the Study of Culture and Religion, 2008.

I have received great inspiration and motivation from Prof. B.Hanumaih, Vice-Chancellor, BB Ambedkar University, Lucknow. I have received valuable support from Prof. Kameshwara Chaudhury, Prof. S. Victor Babu, Dr. V.M. Ravikumar, and Mr. S.M. Basha. I express my thanks to them.

Dr. Dhirendra Bahadur Singh provided important logistical support in Delhi, which made my job much easier. I am thankful to him. At Lucknow, friends like Dr. Pawan Kumar kept me focussed on my work. I thank him.

I also thank Gauri, my wife, for her invaluable help and support. Dr. Narendra Nath Prasad, my elder brother, has been a source of support and help for years. Vasu, my nephew, has made my life colourful with his frolics. Shri Bishwanath Prasad, my father, has been a constant source of help, support and motivation. Shri Pawan Kumar, my maternal uncle, remains a source of motivation so is the memory of my late mother.

Finally, I thank Mr. Mathura Prasad Yadav of Manak Publications for accepting the manuscript for publication, and brining out the book in a nice form.

Birendra Nath Prasad

LIST OF CONTRIBUTORS

Birendra Nath Prasad is Assistant Professor, Department of History, BB Ambedkar Central University, Lucknow, and Invited Research Fellow, Centre for Chinese Buddhism and Buddhist Art Studies, Wuhan University, China. Earlier, he was Assistant Professor, Department of History, Assam Central University, Silchar. His research interests are: social history and archaeology of ancient Indian religions, and Buddhist revival movements in colonial and post-colonial India. His email address is: bp2628@yahoo.com

M.N. Rajesh is Assistant Professor, Department of History, University of Hyderabad. His email address is: mnraja@gmail.com

Rekha Pande is Professor, Department of History, and Coordinator, Centre for Women's Studies, University of Hyderabad. Her email address is : rpss@uohyd.ernet.in

Reshma Sawant is Research Fellow, Department of Archaeology, Deccan College, Pune. Her email address is: drreshma.sawant@gmail.com

S. Jeevanandam is research scholar, Centre for Women's

Studies, University of Hyderabad. His email address is: jeeandm@gmail.com

Subash Khamari is Deputy Superintending Archaeologist, Excavation Branch IV, Archaeological Survey of India, Bhubaneswar, Orissa. His email address is: subashkhamari@yahoo.com

Sudarshan Gupta is Assistant Professor, Department of History, Radhamadhav College, Silchar, Assam. His email address is: guptajnu@yahoo.com

Umakant Mishra is Assistant Professor, History Department, Ravenshaw University, Cuttack, Orissa. His areas of interest are nautical archaeology, religion and Brahmi inscriptions. His email address is: umajnu@gmail.com

1

INTRODUCTION

BIRENDRA NATH PRASAD

India, with a colourful mosaic of religious traditions, offers an interesting field for the study of religious processes. Some religions of India are practically dead, yet they have left important imprints. Some have continued as living traditions, but with continuous metamorphosis. In this context, one may recall the eventful trajectory of Indian Buddhism. Being a missionary religion form the very beginning of its life, it was also one of the earliest 'world' religions. Within India, compared to the religious institutions of Brahmanical tradition – temples and *maṭhas* – it has a history of an early institutionalisation; an earlier spread beyond the middle and upper Ganga valley in an institutionalized form; and, barring the monumental temples of early medieval South India, a greater architectural monumentality in a major part of early historic India. One may not agree with the claims of ideologues of Navayāna (neo-Buddhism in post-colonial India) that 'wherever you dig, you are likely to find some Buddhist relic'[1]; one will nonetheless find it difficult to deny that Buddhist presence in many parts of early historic and early medieval India was quite substantial. Yet, the fate of Buddhism in India is quite surprising: it is a saga of slow appropriation. Buddhism appears to have undergone a process of hopeless appropriation. Attempts of its revival and mass popularisation in the contemporary Navayāna Buddhism notwithstanding, Buddhism has yet to regain even a fraction of social influence it once used to have. Why could it happen? Was it just a doctrinal matter, or a larger failure of socialisation strategies of Buddhist monasteries, arguably the institutional nuclei of the faith?

It must be asserted that doctrinal matters could have been important factors in determining the trajectories of historical journey of Indian Buddhism; no less important were the functional roles of its monasteries. Elsewhere, I had an opportunity to emphasize the centrality of monasteries in the institutional survival of Indian Buddhism.[2] I have also argued that the causes behind the survival and expansion of Brahmanism and decline of Buddhism may be explored by enquiring into the relative functional roles of their religious institutions. For long, study of Indian religious institutions has been dominated by art historical concerns only. A more pertinent approach may be to see them as important constituents of the overall societal matrix, as institutions in dynamic interaction with other societal institutions, acting and reacting with them, influencing them and getting influenced by them in turn. That is to say, Buddhist and Brahmanical institutions must be visualised as social phenomenon, as social institutions, in dynamic interaction with other societal institutions. This book hopes to be an endeavour in that direction. It doesn't claim to cover all parts of India, nor does it claim to cover all religious traditions: Jainism is a major omission. In terms of choice of chronological boundaries as well, it is rather vague: it covers the phase from the 6th century BCE to the present. This is solely due to the limitations of the editor and contributors of this monograph.

(I)

To have a better understanding of the context of articles in this book, it is pertinent to have a brief look into the historical reconstructions of patterns of interactions between religious institutions – Buddhist monasteries and *stūpas*, and Brahmanical temples – with other societal institutions. It is important to note that societal linkages of religious institutions of Buddhist and Brahmanical traditions have not been attempted from a comparative perspective as yet. It may be due to a perceived differentiation between the societal linkages of religious institutions of these two traditions. In a significant section of Indian historiography, Buddhism is perceived to be a non-existent phenomenon beyond the monastic walls, hence utterly incapable of having any societal linkages. Within the monasteries too, it is believed to be just a soteriological system. From Max Weber[3] to N.N. Bhattacharya,[4] this view has survived stubbornly. If this is one extreme, another extreme is provided by the ideologues of Navayāna. As per their formulations, Buddhist monasteries promoted 'capitalism,' exhorted a worldview which endeavoured for a society which respected labour and mercantile entrepreneurship; so much so that the decline of Buddhist 'paramouncy' by 6th – 7th century CE became one of the causal factors in the genesis of 'Indian Feudalism.'[5] The Brahmins and their temples, on the other hands, stood for active collaborations with the oppressive kings and their feudal lords for the exploitation of the masses.[6] These two historiographical extremes, undoubtedly, are not tenable.

At the risk of oversimplification, a very brief summary of some of the functional dimensions of Indian monastic Buddhism, as tracked in a major section of Indian historiography, may be delineated as follows :

- Buddhism began as an eremitical movement in an era of expanding urbanisation and state formation in a significant part of the Ganga valley during the 6th century BCE. For Buddhism, the process of adaptation to this urban milieu involved a process of systemic metamorphosis: an eremitical, mendicant, renuciatory tradition evolving into an institutionalized monastic tradition and becoming part of the contemporary societal matrix by providing ideological support to the process of consolidation of the emerging polities, trade and urbanisation.[7] That is to say, Buddhism was a catalytic factor in the expansion of mercantile networks and consolidation of emerging polities and, later, in the imperial unification of northern India[8]; and it was in this process that it evolved into an institutionalized monastic tradition.

- The process of expansion beyond the middle and upper Ganga valley was not uniform. While 'monarchs, merchants and monasteries' matrix remained more or less true for Buddhism in a significant part of India, which ensured a concentration of monastic institutions in or around major urban centres, many monastic institutions grew-Bhārhut for example[9]– independently of any major urban centre. In such cases, alignment of trade routes appears to have been more important. At many other places, impact of mercantile patronage is not very visible. At such places, survival strategy of Buddhist monasteries and *stūpas* was much more complex, and they continued to grow even after the decline of nearby urban centres.[10]
- In a significant part of the Peninsula, Buddhist monasteries were one of the most important catalytic factors in transition to secondary state formations and consolidations of their resource base.[11] In many parts of Deccan and South India, Buddhist monasteries tended to concentrate in the 'outside space' of cities and they became pioneers in organising this space.[12] In Kuṣāṇa northern and north-western India, monasteries provided one of the institutional nuclei for promoting trade and urbanisation.[13] In many other parts of India, they had close involvements with mercantile groups, and they received patronage from a cross-section of society.[14] In a nutshell, one will

largely agree with Ronald Davidson that before the early medieval period, Buddhist monasteries had a kind of monopoly over dealing with 'the barbarians, outcastes, tribals and the foreigners.'[15]

- The Gupta period marks a narrowing down of patronage base of Buddhist monasteries. Due to diminishing mercantile patronage, it was a shift towards a dependence on exclusive royal patronage[16] which ultimately became one of the most precipitating factors in the genesis of 'Systemic Crisis' within Indian Buddhism by the end of the Gupta period.
- By the end of the Gupta period, this 'Systemic Crisis' was apparent. It had its genesis in a combination of factors: monastic failure on agrarian frontiers and in detribalisation process[17]; evaporating mercantile patronage due to decline in long distance trade and Arab domination of the high seas, rendering it increasingly dependent on royal, 'feudal' patronage; lessening participation of women in Buddhism; militant Śaiva competition; and a serious dent in the 'previous Buddhist monopoly of dealing with the barbarians, outcastes, tribals, and foreigners' by the Brahmins. To overcome this 'Systemic Crisis,' Buddhism was forced to 'feudalise' itself. This lead to the genesis of Vajrayāna.
- Vajrayāna, developing within the monasteries, was more or less a total antithesis to what the Buddha and Buddhism stood for.[18] It was an 'imitative' 'degenerate' 'corrupt' and monastery -specific phenomenon. As Vajrayāna had 'no presence' outside the monastery, Buddhism ceased to exist after the Turkic destruction of its monastic institutions. It is better to quote N.N. Bhattacharya here:

> If Buddhism declined after Pala period, what was the real condition of Buddhism? Was it not a bundle of popular cults and superstitions, which could be called in any name? True there were few monasteries, patronised by kings and landlords and also monkish culture proclaiming the world as void entity.

> But the Buddhist monks were parasites living on the financial support of kings and landlords, and as soon as this financial support was withdrawn, monks of the great monasteries at once turned into beggars for whom none was to shed tears. Had Buddhism in its later forms been an organised religion with followers among the people it could not perish all of a sudden.[19]

To sum up, in a significant section of existing Indian historiography, reconstructions of the evolving functional roles of Indian Buddhist monasteries is a saga of a pioneer in 'forging of linkages across communities for social integration' gradually turning out to be a 'social parasite.' The question, which needs to be explored, then, is: why, and how, did Buddhist monasteries loose their competitive edge to Brahmanism?

It must be asserted again that the institutionalisation of Brahmanical temples, compared to the same of the Buddhist monasteries, has a much later dating. Temples became a regular feature of religious landscape of India during the Gupta period only, though the origins of many temples could pre-date the Gupta period. To sum up; temples became a regular feature of Brahmanism only during the phase of gradual petering out of Buddhist monastic influence in a major part of India. There must have bee some inter-relationship between these two developments. That has, unfortunately, not been analysed in some detail so far.

To say that ancient Indian Buddhism could have a sustained survival without its institutional nuclei – monasteries – will be as preposterous as to say that ancient Indian Buddhism did not exist beyond the monastic walls. Buddhism, indeed, had a vibrant presence among the laity, but it is doubtful that it resulted into the evolution of an exclusive 'Buddhist' identity in a significant section of the common population of India. Religious boundaries in ancient India were quite permeable and poly-religiosity of the landscape was generally the norm rather than an exception. The question which needs to be explored, then, is: what happened to Buddhist influence in the masses when its monasteries ceased to exist? Did it herald a sudden extermination of Buddhism or a slow metamorphosis and appropriation? What was the role of Brahmanical temples in hastening this process? These issues have not been analysed in some detail so far: only some preliminary beginnings have been made.[20] If these issues are studied in some detail, we are likely to be more informed of the processes which lead to the decline of Buddhism and establishment of Brahmanical hegemony.

(II)

It is interesting to note that in some of the important models of early medieval Indian economy and society – Feudal, Segmentary and Integrative – it is the political dimensions of temples, which has attracted significant analysis. Political factors – alliance with the political elites, and the degree of patronage received by the temples from such elites – are believed to be key factors in determining the overall importance of a temple. Way back in 1977, Burton Stein – who later became one of the foremost protagonists of 'Segmentary State' model of early medieval and medieval south Indian polity – has delineated some stages in the evolution of ritual importance of a temple. Despite an acknowledgement that careers of temples may be varied due to a variety of factors – 'each of the thousands of temples has a separate past'[21] – he has no doubt that

> This past begins with its being one sacred place (*tīrtha*) among numerous others, a place of sacred performances, vows and supplications for local people as well as, in many cases, for persons of distant places. Of these sacred centres; some seize the interests of a powerful local personage, with the resources to construct moderate or magnificent shelter for the deity of the place.[22]

His attribution of such an importance to political factors in determining the overall career of a temple is difficult to defend. That, for example, does not explain the factors behind the growth and expansion of some temples even after the withdrawal or stoppage of political patronage.[23] We are trying to say that the trajectories of such a complex institution as temple cannot be properly seen through a monochromic prism.

Temples perform an important role in the 'Segmentary State' model. In this historiography, it is through providing patronage to temples and Brahmins that the 'segmentary' state controlled different 'autonomous' segments to the core areas of the state. But, sometimes, temple may serve as the institutional base for social movements – *Bhakti* movement for example - which not only contested Brahmanical ritualism, but also created a sense of community in devotees on the basis of equality, placing community above caste divisions as criteria of social acceptance. It meant emergence of parallel and counter structures.[24] M.N. Rajesh's article in this book deals with this aspect of temples of early Chola period.

In the 'Indian Feudalism' model too, political dimensions of temples find significant analysis. In earlier macro generalisations, the temple was largely believed to be an agent of feudal or feudalising state. In a recent formulation, it has been asserted that genesis of Indian feudalism was deeply related to the process of grants to the Brahmins, temples and monasteries. As per R.S. Sharma and some other scholars, feudalism in India, unlike in Europe, began with the land grants made to the Brahmins, temples and monasteries for which the epigraphic evidence begins from the first century BCE and multiplies by Gupta period when villages together with their agricultural fields and inhabitants, with fiscal, judicial and administrative privileges and immunities were granted to the religious doneees. What was abandoned step by step to the religious donees by the state was later extended to the warrior class.[25] This was one of the most important factors in the genesis of 'Indian Feudalism.' It is interesting to note that at times, even the protagonists of Integrative model of early medieval Indian polity and economy, tend to adopt a view which appears to be remarkably close to the Feudal model. Kulke, for instance, has noted that in the century following the rule of Harṣavardhana, 'the ever increasing number of land donations to temples and Brāhmaṇas and the granting of large number of immunities created socio-economic and political structures which came very close to feudalism of the early European Middle Ages.'[26]

Integrative model of early medieval Indian polity and society appears to be more systematic in its attempt to take into account historical implications of heterogeneity of the geographical space[27], and the role of temples in affecting socio-economic and cultural integration of peripheral areas of the state to the core, nuclear areas of the same. In this context, one may recall the systematic exposition of relationship between royal patronage to temples and the process of consolidation of the local and regional states by Kulke[28]; Arjun Appadurrai[29]; and B.D. Chattopadhyaya. With reference to the integrative role of the Brahmanical temples in early medieval India, Chattopadhyaya has asserted that the rapid growth in the number and network of temples in this period was closely linked, as were the Brahmin dominated *Brahmadeyas* and *agrahāras*, with the formation of sub-regional and regional kingdoms and their legitimization, consolidation of their resource base and forging of linkages across communities for social integration.[30] Epigraphic corroboration of this model has been attempted by Cynthia Talbot in the context of spatial variations in the functional role of temples of Kakatiya period Andhra Pradesh.[31] As indicated by Talbot's analysis of spatial variations in the functional roles of Kakatiya period temples, temples had to negotiate this spatial variation. For early historic and early medieval South Asian temples, archaeological studies of temples and their functional differentiations as per the variations in the geographical space have just begun[32]; but such studies in Angkor period Cambodia have shown brilliant results.[33] We need to analyse the social implications of geographical distribution patterns of Buddhist and Brahmanical religions institutions in early historic and early medieval India. So far, the general attitude has been to attribute a particular role to such institutions without attempting a micro analysis of the locale where they were emerging and functioning. If such analysis is attempted at all, it is generally on the basis of epigraphic and literary data. Archaeological fieldwork is rarely done. Even analysis of existing archaeological data is generally overlooked. Future researches on the socio-economic roles of Indian religious institutions will benefit by undertaking archaeological study of religious institutions. Their study from an archaeological perspective may confirm or contradict some of the generally held notions. It may force us to think of more pro-active roles of some temples or Buddhist monasteries in facilitating transition from one social formation to another without any apparent royal patronage in some parts of India – a thing noted in the context of temples of tribal areas of Manbhum[34] — or may highlight the functioning of some village shrines, which too functioned without any apparent royal patronage.[35] That may also help us understand the factors behind the survival of many religious institutions even after the end of political patronage.

To sum up, a large number of Indian religious institutions interacted with their socio-economic context in a variety of ways. Their interaction pattern with the same cannot be reduced to a single trajectory. Many of them could have vied for political patronage; but many others, devoid of any political mooring, could have become important solely due to their intricate linkages with the society. It was the multiplicity of their functional roles, and a plethora of patterns of interaction with societal processes, which ensured their survival and expansion. This book hopes to be an endeavour in unravelling some dimensions of this interaction.

(III)

My article on the historiography of socio-economic history of Indian monastic Buddhism is basically a survey of studies in the functional dimensions of Indian monastic Buddhism in the past one hundred years, and, as such, it does not lay any claim to be a work of original research. But it largely sets the background for the next three articles. It traces the evolving functional roles of Indian Buddhist monasteries from c.6th century BCE to c. late 13th century CE. The basic aim is to highlight the multiple roles of the monasteries, even within small sub-regions. I have argued that it was this multiplicity which ensured the survival and expansion of Buddhist monastic institutions.

Reshma Sawant's paper deals with the advent of Buddhism in Vidarbha, and traces its interactions with contemporary socio-economic milieu. Buddhism entered into Vidarbha during the Mauryan period. The rise of the Sātavāhānas in Maharashtra significantly contributed towards the formation of new set ups in political, economic, religious and social spheres. Various aspects related to the Sātavāhana dynasty and their contribution in the spread of Buddhism is well studied by scholars but the period preceding this is little neglected or lacks the fresh assessment of new developments in archaeological contexts. Her paper focuses on the period c. 700 – 100 BCE, and traces the patterns of interactions between Buddhist monastic institutions/ stūpas and other societal institutions.

My article on Samataṭa – Harikela monasteries attempts a comparative study of the roles of Buddhist monasteries and Brahmanical institutions in the areas to the east of Surma-Meghna rivers in early medieval Bengal. Elsewhere, I had an opportunity to emphasise that Bengal offers an interesting ground to understand early medieval monastic localisation and socialisation strategies as well as the decline of Indian Buddhism.[36] Within Bengal, the sub-region to be analysed more carefully is Samataṭa- Harikela (i.e. Sylhet-Comilla – Noakhali-Chittagong areas to the east of the Surma-Meghna). This sub-region was fundamentally different from other sub-regions of early medieval Bengal. This sub-region supported a kind of society which has just made transition to state –level polity, where population was relatively sparse as a significant part of land was under forest cover. Most of the local dynasties were largely the followers of Buddhism and patronage to Buddhist monasteries was one of the means for the articulation of their sovereignty. Royal patronage to Buddhist monasteries was for legitimacy as well as for achieving the integration of peripheral areas of the state to the core areas of the same.

However, a differentiation set in soon: Buddhist monasteries tended to concentrate in the core areas of the state, and conceded initiative to Brahmanical institutions in the outlying areas. This was the unmaking of Buddhist hegemony in trans-Meghna Bengal in the long run.

Umakant Mishra's article challenges many established notions regarding the functional aspects of Vajrayāna. He has developed his arguments with particular reference to early medieval Orissa. He argues that Vajrayāna was not a 'degenerate' religion. It was, rather, an instrumental religion; a manifestation of the monastic efforts to make Buddhism more *laukika* ('this-worldly'). To cater to the ritual and instrumental needs of the laity, it innovated many gods and goddesses, devised rituals and *mantras* for their worship within the monasteries as well as within household. It also devised *rites de passages* for the laity. It also initiated the custom of married monks to make the monasteries more accessible to the laity. The laity, in return, thronged to various monastic institutions. By an innovative use of archaeological data and incorporation of the results of his fieldwork on the documentation of sculptures, he argues for the case of poly-religious nature of landscape in entire Orissa, rather than Brahmanical ascendancy and Buddhist contraction in the same; impressive presence of Vajrayāna in all parts of Orissa, with major concentration in coastal Orissa; as well as continued lay patronage to, and association with, the monasteries. His article raises many questions and helps us understand the factors behind, what I have called, 'subterranean survival' of Buddhism in Orissa,[37] and its resurfacing in the 19th century Mahimā Dharma movement.

Reconstruction of socio-economic and ritual interaction, including its pilgrimage geography, of a temple is not very difficult when epigraphic and literary data associated with it are available. This kind of database, however, is a rarity in the context of many temples. In such cases, temple architecture and sculpture provide the only source in reconstructing the socio-economic linkages of such temples. But such endeavour demands a careful handling of temple architecture and sculpture as a 'social text.' This difficult task has been attempted by Sudarshan Gupta in his analysis of wider socio-economic context and interactions of pre-Ahom temples of Assam. He has attempted to see such temples in relation to the settlement pattern, community interaction, rituals and the patterns of patronage to the temple. His core hypothesis – that temples were not just religious structures, but a place meant to serve a plethora of purposes of society at large – is very interesting, so is his assertion that the Brahmaputra valley was an integral part of the larger Indian civilisation.

In the context of south Indian temples, it has been noted long back, and rightly so, that 'Hindu temples, even from pre-Muslim times, occupied a different place for South Indian Hindus than for the north Indian Hindus, because Hindus in various parts of the subcontinent perceived the shrines of their gods in essentially very different ways,'[38] the general tendency has been to neglect the evolving roles of temples. This has hampered the analysis of the transformations taking place in the nature of society, economy and religion, and their impact on the socialization patterns of temples. M.N. Rajesh has offered a substantial critique of this approach by analysing the socio-economic and ritual roles of early Chola period (c. 850-985 CE) *Śaiva* temples. This period witnessed the emergence of temple as a major institution, though the practice of temple building has already started in the Pallava period. Early Chola temple, though not capable of matching the temples of later phases in terms architectural monumentality or patronage base, nevertheless established itself as a multifunctional institution. These temples, functioning in an environment of expanding agrarian frontiers and colonization of new lands, acted as a means of consolidating local communities and integrating them to the Chola state and society by propagating the ideology of *bhakti*. The temple represented a synthesis of many elements in society and was capable of accommodating a wide range of interests. The Cholas found it politically convenient to submit to this new ideology as the servants of god. The Cholas, in fact, adopted this ideology and systematically developed it by showing a predilection to the *Śaiva* religion due to its assimilative character and popular base. The Cholas could, in turn, through the temple, intrude into peasant regions and local governance by integrating dispersed eco-zones into a single cultural unit. The expansion of the Chola resource base and the elevation of kingship through divine association gave royalty a special status.

S. Jeevanandam's paper on the sacred geography and distribution pattern of Śaiva and Vaiṣṇava temples in medieval Tamilakam, in many ways, supplements the researches of M.N. Rajesh. He has analyzed the distribution pattern of these temples by looking into references to them in the Naynar and Alvar *bhakti* poetry, which eulogized the temples of their respective sects and extolled pilgrimage to them. Popularization of the tradition of pilgrimage created a sacred geography, which spread across entire Tamilnadu. But the distribution of temples was not uniform across this sacred geography. His analysis has reveled a heavy concentration of temples in *Cholamaṇḍalama*, the core region of the Chola state. Within *Cholamaṇḍalama*, the area having the densest concentration of temples was along the banks of the Kaveri, followed by the same of the Pennai, Vaigai and the Tamrapanni. He, therefore, concludes that there was a clear connections between Tamil temples and early agricultural developments. Chola encouragement to temple construction in the core region of their state was also motivated by their desire to consolidate their control in the same. Pilgrimage to the temples, which were located in the *maṇḍalama*s other than *Cholamaṇḍalama*, on the other hands, encouraged cultural integration.

Rekha Pandey has studied the evolution of the institution of temple dancing girls, which later crystallized into a generic term – *Devadāsī* – in medieval Deccan in the backdrop of the emergence of the Brahmanical temple as one of the most important centres of power and avenue for the interplay of social hegemonies in medieval Deccan. During the Kakatiya period, temples became institutional nuclei for agrarian expansion and crystallization of many tribes into caste.

Temples received lavish land grants, and patronage to temples became one of the means of articulation of royal sovereignty. Gradually the temple became such an elaborate institution that it became homologous to the royal court. It began to maintain an elaborate administrative and service paraphernalia. Emergence of the institution of Dēvadāsī was a corollary to this process. Pandey has analyzed the class and caste background of these temple dancing girls; patterns of endowments to them; their role in temples; their relationship with, and place in, contemporary society; and factors behind their eventual transformation into common prostitutes in the backdrop of gradual decline of the wealth and social hegemony of the temple with the foundation and consolidation of the colonial rule.

Subash Khamari has traced the survival strategies of the Liṅgarāja temple complex of Bhuvanesvara. This temple was built by Somavanshi kings in the eleventh century CE, and, as revealed by epigraphic data, it received patronage from the political elites as well. This temple is a living institution and a renowned pilgrimage centre today. This temple, in a nutshell, has outlived its royal patrons by almost a millennium. In its journey spanning one thousand years or so, this temple has devised diverse strategies for its survival and growth. He argues that survival of a grand temple like Liṅgarāja did not rest solely with the patronage of kings. The Liṅgarāja, on the other hands, devised multiple strategies for its survival, accompanied by varieties of reciprocal networks: through pilgrimage; through the creation of a hierarchy of temples within the temple complex of Liṅgarāja; through the creation of *mahātmya*s which extolled the virtues of pilgrimage to this temple; through architectural modifications, additions etc.; through rituals; and through the integration of a diverse range of castes and communities in the service network of the temple; as well as through entering into a complex hierarchical relationship with other temples of Bhuvanesvara town. His concluding observation is: the temple is not a static entity, but a multilayered polymorphic structure. Each temple devises its own strategies for survival and the historical processes that go in the making of such strategies may offer an useful avenue of research for understanding the religious processes of the past. His observations are similar to my earlier stated approach that instead of seeing the socio-economic context and linkages of religious institutions through the prism of subcontinental models, a more pertinent approach may be to see an individual religious centre in its wider socio-economic and spatial context.

As readers will notice, this book has not endeavoured to analyse the evolving functional roles of Buddhist or Brahmanical religious institutions through a monochromic historiographical prism. Nor does it wish to proffer one such prism. Each contributor has his/her own perspective. Some essays in this book may seem to contradict some other essays. That is but inevitable as they are, in reflection to the multiple roles performed by Indian religious institutions, are just attempts to catch some aspects of this multiplicity. If this book generates future research, we will consider ourselves amply rewarded.

Notes

1. Gail Omvedt, *Buddhism in India, Challenging Brahmanism and Caste*, Delhi, 2003, p. X.
2. Birendra Nath Prasad, 'Major Trends and Perspectives in Studies in the Functional Dimensions of Indian Monastic Buddhism in the Past One Hundred Years: A Historiographical Survey,' *Buddhist Studies Review*, London, 25(1), 2008, pp. 54-89.
3. Max Weber, *The Religion of India: The Sociology of Hinduism and Buddhism*, edited and translated by H.H. Gerth and D. Martindale, Delhi, 1992 (reprint), pp. 193-218; 234-255.
4. N.N.Bhattacharya, *Buddhism in the History of Indian Ideas*, Delhi, 1993, p. 188.
5. Gail Omvedt, *op. cit.*, pp. 181-185.
6. Ibid., p. 173.
7. For an analysis on these lines, see Ian Mabbett & Greg Bailey, *The Sociology of Early Buddhism*, Cambridge, 2003, p. 34.
8. J. Heitzman, 'Early Buddhism, Trade and Empire,' in G.L.

Possel, K. Kennedy (eds.), *Studies in Archaeology and Palaeoanthropology of South Asia*, Delhi, 1984, pp. 121-132.

9. Jason Hawkes, 'The Wider Archaeological Contexts of the Buddhist Stupa Site of Bharhut,' in Jason Hawkes and Akira Shimada (ed.), *Buddhist Stūpas in South Asia: Recent Archaeological, Art-Historical and Historical Perspective*, Delhi 2009, p. 171.
10. In my study of urbanization at early historic Vaiśālī, I have also noted a significant concentration of Buddhist monastic sites in and around Vaiśālī, but I could not find any direct evidence of mercantile patronage to such sites. As revealed by seals and sealings from early historic Vaiśālī, Brahmanical motifs seem to be dominant among the mercantile and artisan classes and their guilds at Vaiśālī. It must also be noted that even after the decline of the city and its mercantile class, we see the emergence of new monastic centres at Vaiśālī in the post-Gupta period. Recent excavations near the Mauryan Pillar area of Kolhuā have brought to light a cluster of votive *stūpa*s, construction of bathing *ghāṭa*s, a nunnery, and a monastery. Origin of some of them could be in the Gupta period, but most of them belong to the post-Gupta period. That is to say, Buddhist monastic institutions continued (and even proliferated) in the post-Gupta period, when the city of Vaiśālī was declining. See Birendra Nath Prasad, 'Trajectories of Urbanisation: A Study of Seals and Sealings from Early Historic Vaiśālī,' *Prajna Bharati*, Journal of K.P. Jayaswal Research Institute, Patna, Vol. XIII, 2007, pp. 7-22; idem, 'Urbanization at Early Historic Vaiśālī, c. BCE 600-CE 400," *Social Science Probings*, Delhi, June 2009, pp. 21-46. At Śrāvastī as well, a similar pattern of monastic proliferation in the post-Gupta period, when the city has already declined, has been noted, with the obvious conclusion that 'the monastery at Jetavana depended on financial support for its existence not from the adjacent city of Śrāvastī, which was no longer inhabited, but from some other sources.' See Yoshinor Aboshi *et. al.*, 'Excavations at Saheth Maheth 1986-1996,' *East and West*, Vol. 49, 1-4, p. 166. It is a high time that we should think of other paradigms for monastic sustenance and survival than their total dependence on trade, towns, and mercantile and royal patronage. We need to look into the impact of lay patronage and pilgrimage on the lives of Buddhist monastic institutions and *stūpa*s.
11. H.P. Ray, *The Winds of Change: Buddhism and the Maritime Links*

of Early South Asia, Delhi, 1994, p. 122; H.P. Ray, 'Bharahut and Sanchi: Nodal Points in Commercial Exchange,' in B.M. Pande, B.D. Chattopadhyaya (eds.), *Archaeology and History: Essays in Honour of A. Ghosh,* Delhi, 1987, p.627.

12. Shimada, in his fieldwork at Nāgārjunakoṇḍā and Amarāvatī, has noted an important difference in the spatial distribution pattern of Buddhist monasteries and Brahmanical temples in and around Nāgārjunakoṇḍā. While Buddhist monasteries, megalithic burials and memorial pillars were widely intermingled (indicating that Buddhist monasteries were occupying burial grounds) and widely scattered in the eastern part of the citadel, Brahmanical temples tended to concentrate in the western side of the citadel and along the Krsihna river, placed as if avoiding Buddhist monasteries and burial sites. That is, in contrast to Brahmanical temples, Buddhist monasteries were occupying the fringe areas of the city. He calls it the 'outside' space of city. By an analysis of published archaeological data, he attempts to show that the Buddhist monasteries tended to occupy the 'outside' space of cities in the majority of sites south of the Narmada. By a combined analysis of archaeological and textual data, he endeavours to show that this 'outside' space of cities, besides accommodating Buddhist monasteries, has served two other important roles — funerary purposes and trade and exchange of goods — both functions disliked in the traditional Brahmanical value system. This 'outside' location of monasteries was not only helpful for the monks in their religious activities, but also allowed them to enter into a variety of social relationship, with the 'outside' urban components, which the Brahmanical tradition was reluctant to embrace. See Akira Shimada '*Amarāvatī* and *Dhānyakaṭaka*: Typologies of Monastic Spaces in Ancient Indian Cities' in Jason Hawkes and Akira Shimada (ed.), *op. cit.,* pp. 231-233.
13. Xin Riu Liu, *Ancient India and Ancient China,* Delhi, 1988; idem, *Silk and Religion: An Exploration in to the Material Life and Thought of the People,* AD 600-1200, Delhi, 1996. See particularly pp. 49-72.
14. Romila Thapar, 'Patronage and Community' in Barbara. S. Miller (ed.), *The Powers of Art: Patronage in Indian Culture,* Delhi, 1992, pp. 19-34; Vidya Dehejia, 'The Collective and Popular Basis of Early Buddhist Patronage: Sacred Monuments, BC 100-AD 250' in Barabara S. Miller, *op. cit.,* pp. 35-50; S.

Nagaraju, 'From Spirituality to Power: A Millennium of Buddhist Monastic Architecture as A Mirror of Social History' in K. Sankaranasayan *et. al.* (ed.), *Buddhism in India and Abroad: An Integrated Influence in Vedic and Post Vedic Perspective*, Mumbai and New Delhi, 1996, pp. 304-5.

15. Ronald M. Davidson, *Indian Esoteric Buddhism: A Social History of the Tantric Movement*, Delhi, 2004, p.85.
16. Romila Thapar, *op. cit.*, Vidya Dehejia, *op. cit.*, S. Nagaraju, *op. cit.*
17. D.D. Kosambi, 'The Decline of Buddhism in India' in D.D. Kosambi, *Exasperating Essays: Exercises in the Dialectical Method*, Pune, 1986 (reprint), p. 66; R.S. Sharma, *Urban Decay*, Delhi, 1987, p. 131.
18. Richard Gombrich appears to be one of the most articulate champions of this view. For him, genesis of the Vajrayāna tradition was the result of a massive Tantric 'invasion' on Buddhism. As such, 'Buddhist Tantra is paradoxical Buddhism' which has 'turned the Buddhist tradition on its head.' As per his analysis, this is due to the fact that for about one thousand years (i.e. till 6th-7th century CE), Buddhism in India was a religion which could be characterized as antithetical to Tanta. See Richard Gombrich, *How Buddhism Began: The Conditioned Genesis of the Early Teachings*, Delhi, 2002, p. 163.
19. N.N. Bhattacharya, *Buddhism in the History of Indian Ideas*, Delhi, 1987, p. 15.
20. For an interesting study on these lines, see Birendra Nath Prasad *et. al.*, 'Bārā: A Recently Discovered Site in Nalanda District and Its Bearings on the Decline of Indian Buddhism,' in B. Labh (ed.), *The Ocean of Buddhist Wisdom*, Vol. IV, Delhi, 2009, pp. 225-234.
21. Burton Stein, 'Introduction' to the special issue of *The Indian Economic and Social History Review* on South Indian Temples, Vol. XIV, number 1, January-March 1977, p. 2.
22. Ibid., p. 2.
23. This is a theme, which finds an elaborate treatment in S. Khamari's paper in this book.
24. R. Champaklakshmi, *The Hindu Temple*, London, 2001, p. 100.
25. D.N. Jha (ed.), *The Feudal Order: State, Society and Ideology in Early Medieval India*, Delhi, 2000, pp. 3-4.
26. H. Kulke, 'Periodization of Pre-Modern Historical Processes in India and Europe: Some Reflections,' *Indian Historical Review*,

XIX, Number 1-2, 1992-93, p. 31.

27. Way back in the 1920s, Arthur Geddes (Arthur Geddes, 'Some Geographical Factors in Indian History,' in *Man and Land in South Asia*, ed. by A.T.A. Learmonth *et. al.*, Delhi, 1982, p. 94) has emphasised the need to understand the evolution of much of Indian history in terms of interactions between its core 'grain much of lands' of the middle and upper Ganga valley, and 'grass lands' and 'forest lands' of the rest of the subcontinent. Later, Richard Eaton summarised it by stating that much of Indian history is marked by a continuous attempt by the settled agrarian population of low-lying plains to expand agrarian frontiers in the outlying jungles. In this expansion of agrarian frontiers, there was a mutual flow of cultures, but the signs and symbols associated with the agrarian population had greater appeal on the other side. See Richard M. Eaton, 'Conversion to Christianity among the Nagas, 1870-1971,' *The Indian Economic and Social History Review*, 21(1), January-March 1984, p.1. This has been recently reformulated by B.D. Chattopadhyaya through the concept of *araṇya-Janapada* continuum. See B.D. Chattopadhyaya, "State Perception of the 'Forest' and the 'Forest' as State in Early Medieval India" in B.B. Chaudhury, Arun Bandopadhyaya (eds.), *Tribes, Forests and Social Formations in Indian History*, Delhi 2004, p. 28.
28. Hermann Kulke, "The Early and Imperial Kingdom: A Processual Model for Integrative State Formation in Early Medieval India," in Hermann Kulke (ed.), *The State in India 1000-1700*, Delhi, 1995, pp. 233-262.
29. Arjun Appadurrai, in his study of tripartite relationship between kings, sectarian leaders and temples in medieval South India (c. CE 1350-1700), has offered some interesting generalisations regarding the linkages of south Indian temples with wider societal processes. He has noted important shifts in the nature of relationship between temples and kingship. In the Pallava phase, there was a shift from sacrifice based ritualism to *brahmadeyas* and temple construction. In the Chola period, *brahmadeyas* continued, but in the articulation of public display of sovereignty, temple construction began to play a peculiar and powerful role (p. 48) because the 'temples became fundamental for the maintenance of kingship' (p. 48). Under the 'military state' of Vijayanagara, the trend of serious decline in the number and importance of *brahmamdeya*, and a concomitant increase in the number and importance of temples

intensified (p. 49). Royal endowments to temples was one of the most important means for the expansion and consolidation of the resource base of Vijaynagara empire. Ultimately, a tripartite relationship developed between kings, temples and the sectarian leaders associated with the temples. The king got 'honour' and 'legitimacy' for his rule in return of his patronage to the temples and the sectarian leaders associated with the same. The sectarian leaders, associated with the temples, were 'crucial intermediaries for the introduction, extension and institutionalisation of Vijayanagara warrior control over constituencies and regions that might have otherwise proved refractory' (p.55). See Arjun Appadurrai, "Kings, Sects and Temples in South India, 1350–1700 AD," *The Indian Economic and Social History Review* 14(1), 1977, pp. 47–73.

30. B.D. Chattopadhyaya, *Studying Early India,* Delhi, 2003, p. 166.
31. Cynthia Talbot (in her *Pre-Colonial India in Practice: Society, Religion and Identity in Medieval Andhra,* Delhi, 2001) has offered some important observations in her interesting study on the socio-economic and religious dynamics of Kakatiya period Andhra, based on a *tāluqā*-wise study of distribution pattern of Kakatiya inscriptions. Her study has revealed an irreversible shift in the settlement and socio-economic focus of Andhra in the Kakatiya period. Before the rise of the Kakatiyas, geopolitics of Andhra was dominated by the powers based in the Krishna-Godavari delta, which was the core area of pre-Kakatiya Andhra. But in the Kakatiya period, there was a massive settlement expansion in the hilly, semi-arid Telangana region. In this process, temples served as the institutional nucleus for settlement expansion. The general pattern of settlement expansion centring on temples was like this: when some land was transferred for the construction and maintenance of a temple, it was accompanied by the excavation of a new tank, whose water was used for the irrigation of the land transferred to the temple. The resultant agrarian expansion ensured a rapid economic development in the semi-arid Telangana region, and the Kakatiyas were able to unify the whole of Andhra from their base in Telangana. In this transition, the expansion of temple cult 'acted as a unifying force' (p. 125). The overall result was that the erstwhile core region of Krishna–Godavari delta was irreversibly 'peripheralised' (p. 10).The general pattern of settlement shift was: Deltaic core → Telangana → Rayalsima region. In this process of settlement expansion, the

general integrative role of temples had important spatial variations. Foundations of new temples was 'motivated by devotion, but made possible by economic growth, result of forward movement of agrarian frontiers' (p.94). Thus, we see important differentiations in the rate of construction of new temples, which was closely related to variations in the expansion of agrarian frontiers. The biggest number of temples was to be found in Telangana, least in the erstwhile core (Krishna –Godavari delta); and the Rayalsima region stood between these two regions in terms of construction of new temples (p.94). Despite this apparent similarity in the 'unifying role' of temples, there were important spatial variation in terms of their functional roles and interactions with contemporary social institutions. Talbot has noted that during the period under study, Andhra had two types of temples: major temples and minor temples, and this typological division had geographical basis. 'Major' temples generally predate the Kakatiya period, are found only in the coastal areas of the Krishna-Godavari delta, and they emerged as major pilgrimage centre in the pre-Kakatiya phase itself. Their patronage came from the cross-section of the society: political elites are included as donors, but the role of the political elite is not that prominent as we see in the 'minor' temples of the interior regions of Telangana and Rayalsima (p. 125). The case with the 'minor' temples of Telangana and Rayalsima was fundamentally different. They were local institutions, commanding local patronage. Most of them were founded by the intermediary political chiefs in the Kakatiya period. Social background of donors, kind of gifts received by the temples, and the kind of people incorporated in the temples' community of worshippers, were fundamentally different in the case of 'major' and 'minor' temples. Besides, with different sorts of resources at their command, redistributive roles of the 'major' and 'minor' temples were fundamentally different (p. 111). Thus, she concludes, 'religious centres of coastal Andhra and interior Andhra were distinct: the two types of temples served different functions in their respective areas' (p. 111). We need to look for such probable differentiations in the functional roles of religious institutions in other parts of the subcontinent.

32. A beginning has been made by Anita R. and Susan Varma. See Anita R. "An Archaeological Study of Temples in Eastern Deccan" in H.P. Ray, Carla Sinopoly (eds.), *Archaeology as*

History in Early South Asia, Delhi, 2004, pp. 426-463; Susan Verma, "The Archaeology of Early Temples of Saurashtra," in H.P. Ray, Carla Sinopoly, *op. cit.*, pp. 411-425.

33. Socio-economic roles of Khmer temples have generally been reconstructed on the basis of inscriptional data, and such studies generally underline the impression that temples provided the single biggest institutional nucleus for the economic, political and cultural integration of peripheral zones of the state to the same of the core areas of the Khmer polity. The general pattern was that when a new area was conquered, the conquering chief or the king planted temples there; or simply brought the temples of that area within the network of the imperial temple of the capital city. The temples, which were planted in the newly conquered areas, were provided with the grant of marshy lands, slaves and attendant servants. These temples had to undertake agrarian expansion in the marshy areas, and thus to create a new resource base for the Khmer polity. Gradually a complex hierarchy of temples (local/village temples→regional temples→imperial temple) developed (Kenneth Hall, "The Temple-based Political Economy of Angkor Cambodia," in Nicholas Tarling (ed.), *Cambridge History of Southeast Asia*, Vol. 1, pp. 229-239). The role of temples as 'frontier integrator' has recently been corroborated by archaeological fieldwork as well. In an intensive, village to village survey and documentation of Khmer temples, with the main aim of tracing the geographical distribution pattern of temples, it has been found that the greatest concentration of temples was to be found not in the core, nuclear, areas of the Khmer state, but in the peripheral areas of the same. Thus, the inscriptional data is generally supported by archaeological data. For details, see David J. Welch, 'Archaeological Evidence of Khmer State Political and Economic Organisation,' *Bulletin of Indo-Pacific Prehistory Association*, Chiangmai Papers, Vol. 3, 1997, pp. 69-78.
34. D.K. Chakrabarti, "Pakbir: A Jaina Site in Purulia District, West Bengal," in B.D. Chattopadhyaya, B.M. Pandey (eds.), *Archaeology and History: Essays in Honour of A. Ghosh*, Delhi, 1987, pp. 335-45.
35. D.K. Chakrabarti (D.K. Chakrabarti, *Archaeological Geography of the Ganga Plains: The Lower and the Middle Ganga*, Delhi, 2001, p. 78) has, in fact, referred to one such 'village shrine' at the site of Ratan in West Dinajpur district, West Bengal. Here, the

eastern part of the mound has been dug into by the villagers, leading to the exposure of 'what was possibly the major east-facing gateway entrance to the temple,' which was built on the top of a mud platform supported by a burnt brick retaining wall around it. The temple was possibly not brick-built as it has left no traces. Chakrabarti found two *Viṣṇu* images, which, apparently, came form this temple only. This lead him to suspect that most of the lose sculptures, datable to the Pala-Sena period, which occur profusely in Bihar –Bengal area, came from 'village shrines' of this kind. (p.98). Much before Chakrabarti, Huntington, in her impressive study of the 'Pala –Sena' school of sculptures, has noted that most of the Pala-Sena period images from Bihar and Bengal are in a stele format. They were invariably made as separate images to be set into shrines or niches, presumably in brick temples which are, for the most part, now lost. Huntington has also noted that 'actual evidence of strong patronage by Pala -Sena rulers is lacking in surviving art works.' This assertion supports our argument indirectly. See Susan L. Huntington, *The 'Pala-Sena' Schools of Sculpture,* Leiden, 1984, pp. 1-2.

36. Birendra Nath Prasad, 'Major Trends and Perspectives in Studies in the Functional Dimensions of Indian Monastic Buddhism in the Past One Hundred Years: A Historiographical Survey,' *Buddhist Studies Review,* London, 25(1), 2008, p. 80.
37. Ibid., p. 78.
38. Burton Stein, 'Introduction' to the special issue of *The Indian Economic and Social History Review,* Vol. XIV, January-March 1977, p. 2.

SECTION 1

Buddhist monasteries and *stūpa*s in interaction with other societal institutions and processes

2

STUDIES IN THE SOCIO-ECONOMIC HISTORY OF INDIAN MONASTIC BUDDHISM IN THE PAST ONE HUNDRED YEARS
A Historiographical Survey[1]

Birendra Nath Prasad

Let us begin with a fundamentally important question: Buddhism or Buddhisms? To repeat Donald Lopez, can one speak of 'The Buddhist Tradition' or 'Buddhism' or are these terms better rendered in the plural, despite surprising parallels among the practices of Buddhist cultures across time and topography?[2] That is, in the context of Indian Buddhism, should we visualize Buddhism – in which monasteries served as its institutional nuclei – as a middle Gangetic Great Tradition swooping down over other parts of India and imprinting its *Dharma* on a credulous *Tabula Rasa*? To put it differently, to what extent should Buddhist monastic practices in India be regarded solely as derivations of or deviations from the injunctions of the *Vinaya* texts? In a significant section of Buddhological historiography, the preferred approach so far has been to study Buddhism through the prism of its textual tradition. But in this approach, studies in the societal linkages of Buddhism frequently flounder in the perceived disjuncture between Buddhist norms and praxis; between 'normative' Buddhism as enshrined in the texts and 'lived' Buddhism; between Buddhist 'Great Tradition' and its local mutations.[3] This perceived disjuncture between norms and praxis has recently been explained on the basis of 'Buddhist Functionalism': that underneath the apparently 'rigid' doctrines of Buddhism, a degree of inbuilt functional flexibility is discernible which enables Buddhism to present its message across the vast expanse of Asian cultural settings.[4] It has been observed, and rightly so, that Buddhism contains a hierarchy of teachings and roles and co-exists with other systems in a structured hierarchy.[5] How did the role of the Indian Buddhist monasteries mutate across the rungs of this hierarchy across time and space, especially on the 'open frontier between Buddhism and Animism'?[6] It is with these questions that one may be tempted to begin any historiographical survey of studies in the societal linkages of Indian monastic Buddhism.

Available studies in the societal linkages of Indian monastic Buddhism swing between two extremes. In a significant section of Indian historiography, Buddhism is perceived to be merely the individualistic soteriology of world renouncers and a non-existing phenomenon beyond the monastic walls, hence utterly incapable of having any societal linkage.[7] Another extreme is provided by the ideologues of Navayāna (neo-Buddhism in India). In this schema of things, Buddhist monasteries promote 'capitalism' and are the centres for organizing resistance and rebellion against political tyrannies, whereas the Brahmins and their temples stand for active collaboration with the ruling powers for the oppression of the downtrodden.[8] Should we try to explore any middle way between these two extremes?

Any attempt to survey the societal linkages of Indian monastic Buddhism may not be an easy task, given the fact that almost any book on early Indian history is likely to contain some paragraphs on Buddhism and at least some lines on Buddhist monasteries. This enormous task notwithstanding, there are actually very few studies in the societal linkages of the same. This article, based on a survey of studies in the societal linkages of Indian monastic Buddhism in the past hundred years, attempts to ask certain fundamental questions: what did Buddhist monasteries actually do in Indian socio-economic history in general, and in the institutional evolution of Indian Buddhism in particular? Can we think of Indian Buddhism without monks and monasteries? In the case of Tantric Buddhism of the Kathmandu Valley at least, this has indeed been propounded to be the case.[9] But can this be generalized for India; even when we concede that the Buddha's first two disciples were traders from Orissa;[10] the collective body of the monks, the *Saṅgha,* was a later addendum[11]; and even when contemporary 'Protestant Buddhism' is gradually rendering monasticism less central to Buddhism than it has earlier been in many Theravāda countries? The contemporary Navayāna movement in India treats monasticism as unnecessary,[12] and expects the monks to be not on their way to being 'perfected beings' but as kinds of social activist. To what extent does it reflect the earlier theory and praxis, if we concede the fact that no vision just descends from the blue but is in some way a continuation of earlier processes?

This scepticism notwithstanding, the core thesis of the present survey would treat the *Saṅgha* as the institutional nucleus of Buddhism, the very prism through which much of the history of Buddhism in India is reflected; but the *Saṅgha* not as an ideal retreat from the world to pursue nirvanic goals only, but an institution in dynamic interactions with other societal institutions, acting and reacting with them, influencing them and getting influenced by them in turn. The present article does not purport to be an all-inclusive, exhaustive and chronological survey of available literature on Indian monastic Buddhism. It would rather endeavor to see how its institutional evolution, as a consequence of its interactions with other societal institutions, has been tracked in historical 'constructs.' It will also attempt to delineate the evolving functional roles of the *Saṅgha* from around the sixth century BCE to the thirteenth or fourteenth century CE. It will end with a retrospective look at research on the functional dimensions of Indian monastic Buddhism in the past hundred years, and will try to chart some of the prospects for future research.

At the very outset, some clarifications are necessary. The present study will treat Buddhism as just one of the traditions of India, always in close interaction with other traditions, hence will frequently employ insights from studies in institutional evolutions of other religious systems of India. 'India' in this article will cover the present geographical areas of India, Pakistan and Bangladesh. Such a diverse landmass as India consisted of many ecozones, supporting diverse material and religious cultures and much of its cultural personality has crystallized as a result of the encounters between different ecozones.[13] I have noted elsewhere that cultural communications involving great cultural transformations are communications of continuums and not communications of ruptures or disjunctures.[14] Owing to this it will be difficult for us to visualize Buddhism, with its institutional nucleus in the *Saṅgha,* as a middle Gangetic Great Tradition imprinting itself across the whole of India. Rather what Lopez[15] has propounded for the process of the spread of Buddhism outside India – not so much a disembodied *Dharma* descending on another culture from above, but rather a more material movement of monks, texts, relics and icons along trade routes and across deserts, mountains and seas – can be applied to the process of the spread of Buddhism within India as well. Any study of this process will have to take into account the tremendous geographical variations within India. Long ago, Arthur Geddes visualized the unfolding of much of Indian history in terms of continuous interactions between its core 'grain land,' namely, the upper and middle Ganges valley and its 'grass lands' and 'forest lands'; with the latter two in a continuous flux as a result of interactions with the material and religious cultures of the 'grain lands.'[16] The thing to be stressed is that Buddhism appears to be the first institutional religion of the 'grain lands' to penetrate the 'grass lands' and 'forest lands' in the Indian peninsula, northwestern regions and the swampy forests of eastern India. How did the role of the *Saṅgha* mutate across this variegated space? How did it relate to the existing economic and cultic system as it moved out of its area of origin (the middle-Ganges valley)? Did it offer any economic incentive to induce this integration? In a nutshell, we need to see the roles of the *Saṅgha* beyond the monastic walls, and beyond the norms of the *Vinaya* texts. The present article is a humble attempt in this direction.

Much of the stereotypes we encounter in the perceptions of the nature, functions and evolution of Indian monastic Buddhism have their genesis in the way most of the early Buddhologists of Europe, the representatives of the post-Industrial Revolution European mind, imbued with 'Protestant ethics' and under the heavy intellectual influence of Hegel and Gibbon, have perceived the genesis and decline of Indian Buddhism.[17] With the discoveries of textual and archaeological sources of Indian Buddhism, they discovered a dead and spent tradition. Before the Indian encounter, European scholarship had already seen its institutionalized and living presence in Sri Lanka, Southeast Asia and East Asia. The more researches progressed in Indian Buddhism, unraveling its multiple mutations across time and space, the more difficult it became to classify it under the common rubric 'Buddhism.[18] Yet it was important to reconstruct a coherent history of what they believed to be 'Buddhism,' with a clear chronological beginning, maturation and decline, and some explanation for these. For the 'progressive,' triumphant, post-Industrial Revolution British intellectualism, Hinduism with its 'decrepit,' 'superstitious' paraphernalia, was the proverbial 'Other.' Buddhism was soon perceived to be something like a 'Protestant movement' in India. Soon a schema crystallized in which 'original,' 'primitive' Buddhism constituted of the teachings of the Buddha only, which, as per their perceptions, advocated eremitical mendicancy. But the eternal 'lethargy' of India found its way among the monks, leading to the birth of monasticism. This body of monastics, under further influence of existing Indian traditions, succumbed to superstitions and started worshipping the Buddha as a god in the Mahāyāna phase. Subsequent monastic 'corruption' and 'sexual profligacy' in the garb of Tantricism was a total turnaround, stimulating its assimilation within Hinduism. That is, as per their perceptions, 'true' Buddhism was asocial and eremitical, monasticism was a deviation from the teachings of the Buddha and it ultimately became a factor in the decline of Buddhism in the land of its birth.

This approach is discernible in Spence Hardy,[19] although he largely pre-dates British studies on Indian Buddhism. He landed in Sri Lanka in 1825 as a Christian missionary and began to study the texts of Buddhism – 'a religion I was trying to replace'[20] – and its institutions. Despite his limited information, he had no doubt about the overall historical character and functions of 'Eastern Monachism':

> The history of monastic institutions, notwithstanding their claims to our respect and veneration, is a confession of failures and defects. Their avowed aim has been the reformation of manners, for the accomplishment of which each successive order begins in poverty, but, gradually increasing in wealth, becomes alike corrupt, and a relaxation of discipline was the consequence. Each new institution arose from the degeneracy of its predecessor; and was an additional proof, to all who had eyes to see, or minds to understand, that the system had inherent impotency, and was utterly incapable to produce the consequences that were desired.[21]

This 'inherent impotency' of the system surfaces time and again in writings on Buddhist monasticism. Max Weber,[22] writing around fifty years after Hardy, and attributing Indian failure to undergo the transition to industrial capitalism to structural problems in Indian religions, had at least some words of praise for Hinduism for its ability to build and sustain a social whole, however 'decrepit' and 'rotten' that might be; and also for Jainism because 'it was as exclusive, or perhaps more, a merchant religion as was Judaism in the Occident.'[23] He was, though, bitterly hostile to 'asocial Buddhism, a specifically unpolitical and anti-political status religion, more precisely a "religious technology" of the wandering and intellectually-schooled mendicant monk.'[24] He was perhaps one of the earliest pioneers in relating text to context in the history of religion and, of course, very few primary materials on Buddhism were available in his time. However, one may be surprised to note his reluctance to take into account experiences of the 'lived' Buddhism during the period in which he was formulating his arguments, such as its role in the modernization of Japan[25] or the role of the *Saṅgha* in the anti-colonial struggles or modernizations in Sri Lanka and Thailand.[26] Not surprisingly, his views have been questioned repeatedly in later studies.

The genesis and institutionalization of the early *Saṅgha*: historical reconstructions

One of the earliest exhortations of the Buddha to the monks, as we are told in the Pali Canon, was that 'not two of you would go in the same way,'[27] and that eremitical ideas were very prominent in the earliest phase of Buddhism, as the followers of the Buddha were just among many *Parivrājaka* communities.[28] Gradually monasticism developed within Buddhism and became its defining feature. Generally most of the available writings on the genesis of Buddhist monasticism have stressed the key role of the institution of *Vassā-vasā*(rainy season retreat for the monks) in the evolution of later sedentarized monasteries. But the practice of rainy season retreat was not confined to Buddhist renunciants only. Why did monasticism not develop among other wandering renunciant communities of that time? Why did monasticism get institutionalized only in the case of Buddhism? Nāgasena, in his long dialogue with Milinda, stresses that monasticism ensures easy availability of the monks for the laity and thus ensures greater chances for merit-making for them, hence the need for sedentary monasticism.[29] Indeed 'demands of the laity inducing institutionalization' has been stressed by many modern scholars as well.[30] Was it that simple? If that was the case, how did the interactions of the *Saṅgha* with other societal institutions influence the trajectories of its institutional evolution?

Unfortunately, this quest is hardly visible in most of the early writings on Buddhism: in different writings of T.W. Rhys Davids (*Outlines of Buddhism: A Historical Sketch*, 1934; *Manuel of Buddhism*, 1932; *Buddhist India*,[31] 1903); J.H.C. Kern (*Manuel of Indian Buddhism*, 1896); Monier Williams (*Buddhism*, 1889); E.J. Thomas (*Life of the Buddha as Legend and History*, 1927). These scholars did immense service to Buddhological studies in its formative phases in India and elsewhere by providing a general outline of the 'Three Jewels' of Buddhism. But they could not see the institutional evolution of the *Saṅgha* as a result of its interactions with other societal institutions, perhaps due to paucity of the database. There had been some occasional highlighting of the fact that the Buddhist *Saṅgha* was modeled on the political pattern of the *Gaṇasaṅgha* states such as the Vajjian republic,[32] and in that sense, it was fully 'democratic,'[33] but there was hardly any analysis of factors inducing this alleged interface. More recently, the same attitude is visible in a compendium edited by P.V. Bapat *(2500 Years of Buddhism)* in 1972 to mark the 2500th anniversary of foundation of Buddhism. It was an attempted holistic survey of different aspects of Buddhism in its entire Asian spectrum, with contributions from acknowledged authorities. But it doesn't have a single chapter on the functional dimensions monastic Buddhism either in India or in any other country. N.N.Bhattacharya's *History of Researches on Indian Buddhism* (1981) also has the same gap and this shows the (lack of) attention monastic Buddhism enjoys in mainstream historiography.

These lacks of interest notwithstanding, there have been some remarkable attempts in this direction. Sukumar Dutt's *Early Buddhist Monachism* (1924) offers a brave departure, and therefore demands a greater discussion here. What makes his work stand apart from the earlier 'handbooks' is a very sharp understanding of the evolutionary character of the *Saṅgha* and the need to study it in conjunction with the larger societal context in interaction with which it evolved: the *Saṅgha* was not in a perpetual state of arrested progress nor were its laws like 'the laws of the Medes and Persians that altereth not.'

The Buddhist Order (the *Saṅgha*), on the other hand had a remarkable capacity for growth, development, variations, adjustments and progress.[34] Dutt has also rejected the notion that the text of the entire Pali *Vinaya Piṭaka* was composed in one go (at the Council of Vaiśālī). Its content consists in fact:

> Of much earlier and much later materials welded together by a theory. When they are arranged in their proper sequence, they will afford us evidences of an evolution of Buddhist Monachism as reflected in the (Pali) *Vinaya Piṭaka*.[35]

He has noted the tussle between the earlier prominent eremitical mendicancy and the forest monk tradition, and the emerging monasticism and has asserted that the 'earliest episode of conflict in the *Saṅgha* between the two principles is embodied in the story of Devadatta, who seems to have attempted unsuccessfully at a revival of an old (mendicant, eremitical) ideal,'[36] but he does not analyse the process or the material factors which allowed the emerging monastic tradition to supersede the earlier forest monk tradition. He has noted the growth of the Buddhist coenobium from *Vassā-vāsa,* the rainy season retreat of an individual monk, to *Āvāsa,* originally a colony staked out for the purpose of the sojournment of the monks during the rain-retreat, to *Vihāra,* originally simply lodging-places or private apartments of the individual monks, later a term used to designate the whole of a building where many monks resided.[37] Nevertheless, he again does not offer an analysis of the socio-economic factors entailing this transition. He has also noted the absence of references to Buddhist monasticism in the Greek writings on India dating until the second century CE, and has concluded that for a long time after the Macedonian invasions (fourth century BCE), Buddhist monasteries were neither numerous nor striking enough to attract the notices of foreign writers in India.[38] He has not provided any explanation for this, perhaps owing to the fact that very few primary materials on Buddhism were available to him. A similar approach is visible in the reconstruction of pre-Mahāyāna monasticism in his later and much larger book, *Buddhist Monks and Monasteries in India: Their History and their Contribution to the Indian Culture* (1962), although he used a diverse range of sources in reconstructing the same from the Mahāyāna phase onwards. In this monograph, he noted the gradual metamorphosis in the monasteries and their institutional management from the early centuries CE; their spread along trade routes to the Deccan and beyond; the mercantile and royal patronage they received; shrinkage of Buddhist space across India from the Gupta period (320–500 CE) onwards; and emergence of 'Monastic Universities' (Nālandā etc.) in the early medieval period. He has taken the support systems of the monasteries into account, but how that support increased or diminished from time to time and what were its consequences on monastic life, and also on the trajectories of Buddhism in India and its decline, has been only perfunctorily studied. That in no way reduces the importance of this work. As the earliest macro survey of the monastic experience of India, it will remain mandatory reading for any study on the societal linkages of Indian monastic Buddhism.

Reconstruction of the pre-Mahāyāna Buddhist monasticism largely on the basis of taking the injunctions of the Pali *Vinaya* to be narrative, not normative, is visible in Edward Conze (1957), Vishwanath Prasad Varma (1973) and, to some extent, Richard Gombrich. Conze and Varma hardly make any attempt to see the institutional evolution of the *Saṅgha* as a result of its interactions with other societal institutions. Both emphasize the 'asocial' nature of Buddhism in which the *Saṅgha* is perceived to have functioned as a retreat from worldly phenomena.[39] This is, no doubt, the result of a literal reading of the Pali texts and a near total neglect of the context.

Uma Chakravarti, basing her arguments on the analysis of early Pali sources for the reconstruction of social dimensions of early Buddhism, offers much more astute observations on the institutional evolution of the *Saṅgha* against the backdrop of the prevailing socio-economic milieu during the period of the Buddha. Thus she has noted that the institution of *Vassā-vāsa* came into being when peasants started complaining to the Buddha of the damage done to their newly sown crops due to the incessant movements of the monks during the rainy season.[40] It has also been asserted that despite being deeply related with the early historic urbanization of the subcontinent, agrarian similes and metaphors played an important role in the evolution of the rules of the *Saṅgha*.[41] She has also noted the differential nature of patronage in the monarchical and *Gaṇasaṅgha* polities during the period of the Buddha. In the monarchical states based on individual ownership of property, the *Saṅgha* attracted the patronage of a cross-section of society, while in the *Gaṇasaṅgha* states, which were based on the notion of collective ownership of property in the hands of the ruling *Khattiya* clan only, the *Saṅgha* could not receive any mass patronage, hence there were fewer monasteries in these regions compared to in the monarchical states.[42] As a whole, her approach is quite refreshing. She has also noted that most of the earliest entrants to the *Saṅgha* were from well-to-do families. The Brahmins formed the single largest group, followed by the *Khattiya*s. Only a few 'low born' joined the *Saṅgha*.[43] That is to say, in its formative phase, the *Saṅgha* was not an avenue for runaways.

Gombrich may be taken as the continuation of the tradition of near exclusive dependence on Pali texts for the reconstruction of the evolution of the *Saṅgha*. In one of his later writings he has noted the congenital heterogeneity of the *Saṅgha*, as the earliest converts to Buddhism came from different background and due to the rudimentary institutional structure of the *Saṅgha*, 'many members of the *Saṅgha* must have gone on using some of their former terms and concepts.'[44] In his *Theravada Buddhism*, he has focused on the missionary impulse of the *Saṅgha* from the very beginning, and its role as the institutional nucleus of Theravāda Buddhism:

> The history of Theravāda Buddhism, seen from the point of view of the tradition itself (what anthropologists call the emic view) is the history of the *Saṅgha*. The virtual identification of the fortunes of a religion with those of its professionals is alien to most religious traditions, even to some strands within Buddhism itself – not least to many Buddhists today. But in our view it constitutes the very core of Theravāda Buddhism.

> In this it is very Indian. Our view of early Indian religion and culture is mainly a brahmin view, because it is brahmins who composed and preserved texts. Similarly, Theravāda tradition is the product of texts composed by, and indeed largely for, monks and nuns.[45]

If that is not enough, he proceeds to assert:

> Though one must not push the comparison between Buddhism and Brahmanism too far, to look for a lay tradition of Theravāda Buddhism is a misunderstanding of the same kind as looking for a low-caste tradition of Brahmanism: were it lay tradition it would not be Theravāda, the 'doctrine of the elders,' i.e. of fully trained members of the *Saṅgha*.[46]

It is doubtful that any religion can be reduced to its textual tradition by a near total denial of the larger societal contexts, the role of the laity[47] and continuous interaction between the text and context; an interaction leading to continuous metamorphosis of the *Saṅgha*. And of course anthropological studies have proved that in some Theravāda countries 'doctrines of normative Buddhism only rarely constitute the Buddhism of the faithful [who] have acquired other additional forms of Buddhism which for them are equally, or nearly equally, normative.'[48] Melford Spiro has also noted that 'most Buddhists (being "worldlings") have little to do with nibbanic Buddhism, though they are aware of and genuinely believe that they ought to aspire to it,'[49] and he has noted a similar condition in many countries where Theravāda is a living tradition now – Sri Lanka, Thailand, Burma, Cambodia.[50] Besides, Buddhism has a much more mundane, 'apotropaic' form[51]; the only form which survives the institutional liquidation of the *Saṅgha* and later helps in the re-institutionalization of the same.[52] It has also been observed that the more normative and bookish the *Saṅgha* becomes, the more detached are the monasteries from the laity, hence they have greater vulnerability to decay and decline.[53]

Gombrich notes that the ever lamented 'corruption' (by which he seems to mean the accumulation of property by the monks and the *Saṅgha)* began in the lifetime of the Buddha himself,[54] that is, the norms of the Pali *Vinaya* were not followed in letter and spirit in the earliest days itself; and later the 'lay pressure to accept gifts probably accounts for most of *Saṅgha* 's (recurrent) "corruption."[55] But why was the *Saṅgha* forced to accept gifts that went beyond its 'basic doctrines' and disciplines? Gombrich does mention that 'the *Saṅgha* early had to accommodate to the facts of political power'[56] and also notes the fact that 'the *Saṅgha,* and hence Buddhism, has a particular need of political patronage if it is to flourish.'[57] His observation – 'history has shown time and again that without state support – which need not mean *exclusive* state support — the *Saṅgha* declines from this very reason'[58] – is corroborated by some other studies. Thus, it has been observed that in many countries political consolidation of the ruling elite results in ecclesiastical centralization and rigid institutionalized hierarchization of the *Saṅgha;* and the more 'galactic' the polity turns, the greater institutional disarray for the *Saṅgha.*[59] Gombrich's and S.J. Tambiah's observations are beginnings in the right direction. We need a greater contextual study of the encounters of the *Saṅgha* rules and injunctions with secular laws and regulations and the resultant mutations at both ends. But can this study be undertaken by treating the, as it appears, normative *Vinaya* as narrative? An undue emphasis on the norms of the *Vinaya* in tracing the evolution of the *Saṅgha* largely blinds us to the multiple mutations that the *Saṅgha* undergoes as a part of its localization strategy across time and space, as a part of its 'translation into local idioms'; a common feature of the localization strategy of any world religion.[60]

Charles Prebish's study of early Buddhist monasticism, based largely on the work of Sukumar Dutt, is important for his advocacy of a 'middle way' regarding the significance of the *Vinaya* texts in the institutional evolution of the *Saṅgha,* between the two extremes propounded by Andre Bareau and A.C. Banarjee: the first holding that only doctrinal matters were responsible for the emergence of sects and schools, and the latter holding that there was hardly any difference regarding the interpretation of the *Dharma,* and it was differential interpretation of the *Vinaya* injunctions which led to the emergence of divisions in the *Saṅgha.* While Prebish advocates a middle way, he has a propensity towards accepting a greater significance of the *Vinaya* in the institutional evolution of the *Saṅgha.* He has noted that 'it cannot be mere coincidence that the schools with the most developed *Vinayas* have prospered while the others have dissipated.'[61] But what is the co-relation between different *Vinayas*, and what is the interaction of the text with the context? He has translated the Sanskrit *Vinayas* of the *Sarvāstivādins* and *Mūlasarvāstivādins* in the same book, but it could have been immensely more illuminating had he offered their textual and contextual differences or the lack of these, and factors behind these, in comparison with the Pali *Vinaya.*

The interrelationship between different *Vinayas*, their similarities and dissimilarities have invited rigorous research. As early as 1951, Erich Frauwallner, noting the close similarity between the *Vinayas* of different schools, opined that an original 'Proto-text' of the extant *Vinaya*s must have existed during the earliest days of the *Saṅgha.*[62] Étienne Lamotte has largely corroborated this theory.[63] It has also been observed that similarity is only between the *Vinayas* of the individual schools of the two sects of the first schism (*Sthaviravāda* and the *Mahāsāṅghika*) and not across the sects[64] : that is the *Vinaya*s of the five main schools of the *Sthaviravāda* sect (*Sarvāstivāda, Mūlasarvāstivāda, Theravāda, Dharmaguptaka* and *Mahīśāsaka*) are remarkably similar in the general structure and organization of the material and they treat much the same range of topics. But, according to shayne clarke, the *Vinaya* of the *Mahāsāṅghika* sect is radically different from these,[65] Largely the same thing has been observed in the rules prescribed for the *Uposatha* ceremony in the *Vinaya*s of various schools of the same sect.[66] While Clarke's construction of 'radical' difference between the *Sthaviravāda* and the *Mahāsāṅghika* sects might be misplaced, as Jan Nattier and Prebish have shown that these two 'sects' agree in condemning the 10 'lax practices' discussed at the council of Vaiśālī,[67] that is not our prime concern here. It can be agreed that at the level of normative Great Tradition, uniformity has been envisaged across schools and, to some extent, maybe also across sects. But how does that translate into practice?

It may be asserted that despite these brilliant studies on the *Vinayas* and the reconstruction of early Buddhist monastic practices in India as per the norms of the *Vinayas*, there is hardly any study of the process by which monasticism emerges among an eremitical monk community. Mention must be made of Robin Coningham's brilliant study of the institutionalization process of the *Saṅgha* in Sri Lanka.[68] He has noted that the transition from a cave-dwelling forest monk tradition to an institutionalized, sedentary and 'domesticated' monasticism was closely related with the process of transition from chiefdom polities to that of a loosely centralized polity with a paramount sovereign ruling over the whole of Sri Lanka[69]; a process rendering the *Saṅgha* and the state increasingly interdependent. At a later stage, the more centralized the polity became, the greater the temporal assets of the *Saṅgha*, ultimately leading to the development of monastic landlordism.[70] A similar process of the monastic tradition supplanting the 'original,' forest tradition of the formative phases of Indian Buddhism has indeed been noted by Reginald Ray[71] but without analyzing the factors and the processes behind the gradual establishment of monasticism as the 'authentic' tradition. He begins with a critique of traditional monastery-centric Buddhist historiography in India in which the 'monasteries form the prism through which much of history of Indian Buddhism is cast.'[72] This has entailed the construction of a 'two-tiered model' of Indian Buddhism, in which the monastics occupy the upper tier and practice a 'Buddhism of emulation,' that is, taking the Buddha as a role model rather than as a an object of devotion and veneration; whereas the laity form the lower tier, practicing a 'Buddhism of devotion,' that is, devotion and reverence to the Buddha and the *Saṅgha*.[73] The primary aim of the book is to 'amplify the voice of forest Buddhism by focusing upon the Forest Saint,'[74] but in the process he offers certain interesting observations on the nature and functions of monastic Buddhism in India, particularly its interaction with the laity and with the forest monks. For him, the forest monk tradition is the 'original Buddhism,' which has been suppressed or at least obscured by settled monasticism. Thus monastic Buddhism was 'institutionalized,' 'regulated' and 'ordered' Buddhism[75] and was the seat for the maintenance and contemplations of the textual tradition.[76] Its proximity to and dependence on the social, economic and political establishment often compelled it to accept and reinforce the status quo of the societal context.[77] In fact 'by its emphasis on order, regulation and scholasticism, monasticism reflects just as or perhaps even more so a Brahmanization of the earliest Buddhism.'[78] Despite these castigations, he could not deny the interdependence between monastic Buddhism and forest Buddhism. The forest produced the saints but could not retain them; they had to come back to the settled world of monasticism, and become part of the monastic life.[79] Excessive institutionalization and scholasticism on the other hand compelled some of the monastics to the forest.[80]

Ray undoubtedly displays remarkable scholarship yet he chooses to overlook certain important things. Despite his denials, a substantial influence of S.J. Tambiah's and Michael Carrithers's study of forest monk traditions of Thailand and Sri Lanka respectively[81] is quite discernible. Both Tambiah and Carrithers have visualized that the state, the *Grāmavāsina/Nagaravāsina* (village/town) monasteries and the *Araṇyavāsina* ('forest dwelling') monasteries together formed a functional matrix, on the models of the 'core–periphery' dialectic; the state and the *Grāmavāsina/Nagaravāsina* monasteries together forming the 'core.' In this schema of things, the forest monk tradition functions as the repository of doctrinal and meditational purity, hence the fountainhead of legitimacy whenever the state faces any grave internal or external crisis. That is to say, the forest monk tradition functions as the institutional balancing factor *vis-à-vis* the 'domesticated' *Grāmavāsina/Nagaravāsina Saṅgha* and, for this reason, receives substantial royal patronage. Should we visualize a similar role for the forest monk tradition in Indian Buddhism as well? Moreover when a *Grāmavāsina/Nagaravāsina* monk chooses to go to the forest, what is the impact of this migration on the forest society? Does he transmit the ideas and praxis of the settled agrarian world or just enter into ever-higher forms of meditation in total aloofness from the surrounding world? Ray does not address these questions; he is content only with the ritual (and spiritual) aspects of this complex matrix.

The institutional consolidation and spread beyond the middle Ganges valley: the 'monarchs, monasteries and trade' matrix and departures from this paradigm.

The linkages between the genesis of early Buddhism and early historic urbanization of the upper and middle Ganges valley are well documented.[82] But the impact of this urbanization on the institutional evolution of the *Saṅgha* has scarcely been analysed in these studies. Nor do they offer much analysis of the process of the spread of monastic Buddhism beyond the middle Ganges valley.

At this juncture, it is important to mention a fundamentally important work, *The Sociology of Early Buddhism*, by Ian Mabbett and Greg Bailey. They have pointed out the significance of a strange coincidence: the emergence of Buddhism as a renunciatory movement in around 500 BCE in an environment of growing urbanization, expanding economic and agricultural networks and political consolidation. This book largely explains how and why monks were able to exploit the social and political conditions of the mid-first millennium BCE mid-Ganges valley in such a way as to ensure the growth of Buddhism into a major world religion. For Buddhism, the process of adaptation to this urban milieu involved a process of systemic metamorphosis: an eremitical, mendicant, renuciatory tradition evolving into an institutionalized monastic tradition and becoming part of the contemporary societal matrix. Summarizing Mabbett and Bailey[83]:

1. Buddhism in its original conception had distinctive characteristics that were not congruent with the process of urbanization and state formation.
2. Buddhism came to terms with the rise of cities and kingdoms, adapting to the changing society and

changing itself in the process of adaptation. At the latter end of any process of adaptation, an institution becomes more or less integrated into, and comes to serve the purpose of, the social structure in which it is lodged.

3. Thus Buddhism acquired characteristics that were wholly congruent with the culture of city-based regional kingdoms. That is to say, Buddhism was a catalytic factor in the expansion of mercantile networks and consolidation of emerging polities and, later, in the imperial unification of northern India; and it was in this process that it evolved into an institutionalized monastic tradition.

Now it is generally accepted that evolution and growth of Buddhist monasticism was deeply embedded with the process of early historic urbanization, state formation and evolution of a centralized empire. No wonder the functional relationship between Buddhist monasteries and the processes of early historic urbanization and crystallization of empire has invited a sustained scholarly research. George Erdosy's article, 'Early Historical Cities of North India' (1987), is illuminating in this aspect. He has pointed out the dependence of the monasteries on the cities and towns. He has convincingly shown that from the sixth century BCE onwards it was only the largest towns and cities, more often the capital city of emerging polities in the Ganges valley, which were able to support the monasteries.[84] He has noted the spatial distribution pattern of the monasteries: (a) on the trade routes connecting these cities and towns; (b) just outside the cities (as was the case with Sāñcī, near Besanagar, and Sārnāth, near Benares); (c) just inside the city (as was the case with Pāṭaliputra and Kauśāmbī); or (d) a rather diffused type, without any obvious concentration but dotting the entire landscape (as was the case with Vaiśālī, Rajagṛha, Mathurā, Ahichhatra and Tilaurākot).[85] That is, as per his analysis, early Buddhism and its monastic sites were totally dependent on the resources of the towns and cities. D. K. Chakrabarti has also noted a similar pattern in the locational analysis of early monastic sites.[86]

James Heitzman, in 'Early Buddhism, Trade and Empire,' is much more systematic in the analysis of the relationship between the location of the monastic sites, trade and empire and the role played by this triad in the spread of the *Saṅgha* beyond the mid-Ganges valley. He has noted that the foundation of the Mauryan Empire (c. 320-185 BCE) and the resultant political and administrative unification of the larger part of the subcontinent resulted in the flourishing of long distance trade. Thus in an environment of expanding trade linkages and crystallizing state power, Buddhist monasteries, dependent on royal and mercantile patronage, flourished in or around important towns or along the trade routes linking them. Based on the analysis of the locational pattern of the monasteries, he has rejected the earlier model of D.D. Kosambi of direct participation of the monasteries in trade; nonetheless their indirect contribution to trade has been recognized. He has noted that the monasteries provided ideological support to their royal and mercantile patrons, and the three together formed a mutually supportive matrix.[87] Heitzman largely explains the process of the spread of the *Saṅgha* beyond its middle Gangetic core to the outlying areas: a process in which trade and traders seems to have played no less important a role than the enthusiastic missionary impulse of Aśoka. Indeed in a brilliant article exploring the nature and extent of Aśokan engagements and interventions in the *Saṅgha*, Herman Tieken has observed that in the Schism Edicts (at Kauśāmbī, Sāñcī and Sārnāth), Aśoka is not concerned with the schism in the Buddhist Church (the Universal *Saṅgha* of the Four Quarters) but divisions within local individual *Saṅgha*s. This was in line with the contemporary realities, as at that time, the level of organization in Buddhism did not go beyond individual *Saṅghas*.[88] But here too, trade had a role in the Aśoka's concerns of preventing the *Saṅghabheda*; 'as a result of the schism many new competing *Saṅghas* could have come into being and a possible source of conflict, which in turn might interrupt the smooth flow of trade.'[89]

The role of trade in influencing the location of the monasteries has been documented in the context of early historic Deccan as well, a theme we shall turn to now. In the early 1950s, Kosambi, based on his observations of direct participation of the Chinese Buddhist monasteries in trade, propounded a similar monastic participation in India in general and early historic Deccan in particular. In his approach, monasteries became totally dependent on trade and commerce, and enquiries into their other roles were largely neglected. H.P. Ray has largely built on his model, although with fundamental modifications, in advocating a more dynamic pattern of monastic interactions with the society and economy in early historic Deccan. Her different writings on the functional role of monasteries, over the past twenty years or so, show a remarkable transition: from the earlier emphasis on the dominance of the material factors (trade, agrarian expansion, secondary state formation process in the tribal areas of the Deccan) to the internal dynamics of religion and pilgrimage in determining the fate of monasteries.

The first approach is visible in her *Monastery and Guild*, in which she has emphasized the catalytic role of the monasteries in facilitating the transition from tribal chiefdoms to institutional state in the Deccan. She has noted the location of the monasteries in the fertile upper Godavari and Bhima river valleys and their role in both agriculture and trade,[90] as well as the chronological evolution of the functional role of the Sātavāhana period (c. 230 BCE–220 CE) monasteries. Thus in their earliest phase in the Deccan (around the first century BCE), they probably acted as 'pioneers and as centers providing information on cropping patterns, distant markets, organization of village settlement and trade'[91] as well as agents for the integrations of the frontier areas for the emerging polities by assisting in the 'establishment of channels of communications in the newly colonized regions and these channels could be then used by the state to enforce its authority,'[92] and also by 'providing anchorage in an environment characterized by changing alignment of social ties.'[93] She has also noted that with increasing trade and commerce, the monasteries could have got involved directly in trade and could have accumulated wealth.[94] Changes in the rock cut architecture in western Deccan and the shift to exclusive royal patronage in the Gupta-Vākāṭaka period (c.250–510 CE) has also been noted and she has stressed the need to see these changes against the background of socio-economic mutations and a probable realignment in the balance of power between the state, the monasteries and laity.[95] Her approach of rejecting any unilinear and *a priori* fixed role of the monasteries is indeed a laudable effort, as well as her approach of seeing the continuous mutations in their roles as result of their interactions with the other societal institutions.

Largely similar arguments have been rearticulated in some of her later writings. Her analysis of functional dimensions of the monastic complexes at Sāñcī and Bhārhut follows her earlier model of 'frontier integration offered by the monasteries' and their close linkages with the trade routes. She has argued that the Mauryan line of control of minerally rich Deccan passed through these regions. Attempts of the Mauryan state to get the cooperation of the tribal communities of the Deccan perhaps led to the evolution of a triangular relationship between the state, these tribal communities and the monasteries which represented the most institutionally developed form of religion that time.[96] She indeed has provided some hints regarding the evolving autonomy of the monasteries *vis-à-vis* trade and towns. It has been noted that initially the monasteries had to be located in either rich agricultural areas or along trade routes where surplus was available to support the monks. Later there was a considerable change: the simple redistributive and reciprocal relationship between the monasteries and the hinterlands altered with the monasteries constantly acquiring greater wealth and evolving into independent socio-economic institution; a parallel order in society.[97] This helps us understand why some monasteries survived and prospered even after the decline of trade and towns, by becoming deeply embedded in the agrarian structure of a given region.

In her *Winds of Change*, Ray has attempted some bold sub-continental generalizations regarding the functional role of the monasteries, although the focus is of course on the peninsula. She has noted the support provided by the monasteries, at different levels, in the phenomenal expansion of trade and commerce in the early historical period (*c.* BCE 600–CE 400). At the ideological level, she argues, Buddhism exhorted the accumulation and reinvestment of wealth in trade and commerce; at the societal level, Buddhist monasteries provided status to the traders and other occupational groups; while at the economic level, the monasteries were repositories of information and necessary skills such as writing and medicine.[98] She has noted the role played by the monasteries in agrarian expansion in the Sātavāhana Deccan where, except for one land grant to the Brahmins, all other land grants are in favour of the monasteries. In her subcontinental analysis of the location of the monastic centres, she has noted their concentration along the trade routes or near important towns; although she has assigned the absence of the structural remains of monasteries or *stūpas* in areas such as Bengal, Tamilnadu and Kerala to the problems in generating agrarian surplus capable of supporting resident population of monks.[99] In a nutshell, she has been largely successful in reconstructing the multiple roles of the monasteries and their diverse linkages with the wider societal processes.

A fundamental paradigm shift is visible in her study of the monastic complex of Kanheri, located near a suburb of modern Bombay. In contrast to other monastic sites of western Deccan, Kanheri shows a continuous occupation from the first century CE to the tenth century CE. She has probed two fundamental questions in this article: the position of Kanheri within the monasteries of Western Deccan, and factors behind the continued occupation of Kanheri when other sites in the same region show signs of decline after the fifth century CE.[100] Based on a study of the votive inscriptions, copper plates and votive *stūpas* built by the pilgrims, she has pointed out that a combination of two fortuitous factors were responsible for the continued prosperity of Kanheri in contrast to other monastic sites of western Deccan: (a) the location of important port towns in the close vicinity of Kanheri (Chaul, Sopora, Kalyan etc.), which made possible the continuous flow of mercantile patronage, and (b) its widespread pilgrimage networks, attracting pilgrims from such far off places as Sindh and Bengal.[101] Thus maritime trade was important for the fortunes of the site but the role of pilgrimage was not less important.

The autonomy of the monastic centres, *vis-à-vis* trade and towns has been reaffirmed in her recent writings. It has been observed that in the coastal Andhra where most of the early historic monastic sites have been found, only a few urban centres have been identified in archaeological records, and here pilgrimage provided an alternative strategy of mobilization of resources for the monasteries.[102] She has also attempted to construct a hierarchy within the peninsular monasteries on the basis of their size and longevity, but she has largely ignored their spatial linkages with the landscape.[103] That notwithstanding, it is a brave departure. Such hierarchizations have been attempted in the study of Buddhist monasteries outside India,[104] and even in the case of Brahmanical temples within India,[105] but this has been a rarity in studies of Indian monastic Buddhism. Hopefully her attempt would inspire further researches in this area as well as in the reconstruction of the pilgrimage geography of major and minor monasteries.

Let us come back to the lower Krishna Godavari delta and examine an important study by H. Sarkar on the emergence and growth of Buddhist monasteries in the same and their linkages with the process of urbanization. The article begins with a fundamentally important observation that the Buddhist monasteries and *stūpas* formed part of a larger social and economic matrix and should not be studied in isolation.[106] He could visualize diverse subsistence bases of the monasteries and their differential strategies in different landscapes in the micro region of Krishna Godavari delta. Thus some monasteries were located near 'agrarian cities' such as Bhattiporulu[107] and depended more on agrarian resources; some were located near port towns and depended more on mercantile patronage; some, such as Nāgārjunakoṇḍā, were located near royal centres, and were built and patronized by the ruling strata; and significantly at such centres Buddhist monasteries shared sacred space with the Brahmanical temples and the monasteries were just one of the institutions from which the ruling strata derived its legitimacy.[108] The core conclusion is: even within a micro region, the monasteries had differential roles across time and space.

As noted earlier, we have a flood of literature on the monastic art and architecture, but hardly any study on their societal implications. S. Nagaraju's study of monastic art and architecture in western Deccan offers a brilliant contrast. He has analysed the phases of monastic architecture in the region and their societal implications. In the earliest phase, monastic architecture consisted of some isolated cells, with hardly any water storage structure. As these monasteries were located in the drier regions of western Deccan, they had to store water for the use of monks in the non-rainy seasons of the years. Absence of water storage structures has been perceived to represent the phase of *Vassā–vāsa*.[109] In the second phase, from around the second century BCE to the third/fourth century CE, both architecture and water cisterns were more developed, being made with lay patronage. With this increased availability of water for the resident monks, greater sedentarization developed. In this period, monasteries attracted the patronage of a cross-section of the society – traders, farmers, artisans as well as royal patrons – and this wide base of patronage was reflected in architectural vibrancy.[110] In the next phase (fourth to seventh centuries CE), a gradual narrowing down of the patronage base and exclusive dependence on royal patronage has been noted. Based on the study of cell architecture within the monasteries, emergence of hierarchy within the monk community as well as the functioning of some of the monasteries as educational centres has been postulated.[111] In the fourth phase, from the seventh century CE onwards, the pattern was fundamentally different: total dependence on royal patronage; emergence of monasteries as owners of big landed property; further increase in their role as education centres; and, within the monastic complex, further differentiation within the monks, with some of them getting deified and sharing the same precinct with the Buddha.[112] His concluding observations are very remarkable:

> with land, money, spiritual leadership of the monks and emergence of monasteries as centres for learning we come to a phase in which the Buddhist monasteries began to act as a competitor for power with other sections of the society. We wonder whether this ambition to exercise power without the necessary backing of the social and ideological equipments was responsible for the gradual decline of Buddhism in western India, nay India in general. With the loss of royal patronage as a result of competition in the power game and the consequent depletion of number of clergy, Buddhism simply disappeared from the scene and the laity gradually assimilated themselves in other religious denominations.[113]

This is fundamentally important for us in perceiving a more pro-active role of the monasteries: not merely a recipient of social patronage but also a source or centre for the interplay of social hegemonies, with monasteries as an institution themselves exercising hegemony, however rudimentary that may be, rather than merely bestowing it to their patrons.

But why was it that only some monasteries could attract royal patronage while others failed to do so? Richard Cohen's study of the Ajantā complex is important in this context, although the article appears to be primarily concerned with a much larger issue: the localization strategy of the *Saṅgha* when it is trying to establish itself a new area; a process by which the 'Buddha becomes "of the place" by resolving uniquely local problems.'[114] At Ajantā, the *Saṅgha* worked at two levels simultaneously. The Ajantā monastic complex acted as a stabilizing factor on the troubled frontier region of the Vākāṭaka regime (c. 250–510 CE) hence received a substantial Vākāṭaka patronage.[115] At the cultic level, it offered an avenue for the Buddhist cultic integration of the animistic *Nāga* cult[116]; another example of what has been earlier referred to as the 'open frontier between Buddhism and animism,' a phenomenon that has started being documented in studies of Indian Buddhism.[117]

In the context of early historic India, societal networks

and interactions of Buddhist monasteries have been studied mostly in terms of the patronage they attracted and the return which they provided to their patrons; a return which is supposed to be legitimacy and social status. A changing patronage base has also been noted as well as its impact on the fortune of the *Saṅgha*. Thus both Romila Thapar[118] and Vidya Dehejia[119] have noted that in the early historic period, the main support base of North Indian monasteries came from the individual traders, merchants, artisans, farmers, monks and nuns, and (in the context of Sāñcī) collective patronage from some villages. Royal patronage was of course not absent, but was not so significant. Both have noted a dissipating social base of patronage by the beginning of the Gupta period, and both have attributed the decline of Buddhism to this factor.[120]

Xinriu Liu has brilliantly depicted the dynamic relationship between the monasteries and the laity in the Kuṣāṇa period (c. 30–225 CE) in North and North West India in her *Ancient India and Ancient China*. Two chapters of the book, 'The Monasteries and the Laity in Kuṣāṇa India' and 'Further Changes in the Indian Buddhist Monasteries' are greatly helpful in illuminating the diverse engagements of monasteries with society and economy, as well as the role of these linkages in doctrinal evolution and institutional innovations in Buddhism. Thus it has been noted that due to thriving trade and commerce and resultant increase in the practice of donation to the *Saṅgha*, the *Saṅgha* got involved in the social economy,[121] leading to many innovations. Thus monks owned property and offered donations to the *Saṅgha*[122] and, like individual monks, monasteries too accumulated and owned property: not from the land grants by the ruling dynasty (as was the case in Sātavāhana Deccan) but probably through the patronage of the mercantile community or even through direct participation in trade,[123] although she has provided no direct evidence for that. As the value of donations to the *Saṅgha* by the laity increased, donors came to expect more in return, leading to the emergence of the concept of transfer of merit, and ultimately to the evolution of Mahāyāna.[124] She has also noted the transition to exclusive royal patronage to the *Saṅgha* in the Gupta period, lessening monastic interactions with the laity compared to the earlier period, and the monastic attempt to maintain the relationship with the laity by the organization of rituals, ceremonies and their public performances and lay participation in the same.[125] In her writings a core argument of near total dependence of the *Saṅgha* on trade and commerce is discernible.[126] But what about their role in the agrarian sector? For Sātavāhana Deccan, monastic involvement with both trade and agriculture has already been discussed. It may not be improper to look for a similar role the monasteries in some other parts of India.

As far as the reconstructions of functional relations of the monasteries with the wider societal processes and institutions are concerned, some fundamental paradigm shifts are discernible in recent years. Mention may be made of the works of Gregory Schopen, Julia Shaw and Lars Fogelin. Each of them has unsettled many sacred cows in many ways. While Schopen has formulated his generalizations on the basis of a combined use of archaeological, epigraphical and textual data from Sanskrit *Vinaya* literature, with a greater propensity towards the use of votive inscriptions, Shaw and Fogelin are primarily interested in the archaeological landscape of monasteries to formulate certain micro generalizations regarding the functional relationship between the monastery and the countryside.

Mention must be made of Schopen's forceful criticism of scholarly obsession with the Pali *Vinaya* and a near total exclusion of all other sources in the study of monastic Buddhism in India. Scholarly preferences for textual sources, he tries to show, is influenced by the 'Protestant presupposition' that 'true religion is to be found only in the Scriptures.' If archaeological and epigraphical data show a contrary picture, they are to be regarded as 'perversion,' 'decadence' or 'exception.'[127] In the context of early Buddhological scholarly discourse, he has tried to prove this with specific examples of sustained continuation of certain perceptions based on textual sources even when well-known archaeological findings have proved them to be wrong. Textual sources will lead us to expect that monks were to observe strict poverty (a perception propagated by Rhys Davids *et. al.*). Schopen, through an in-depth analysis of votive inscriptions, coin and coin mould finds from monasteries, has tried to show that the monks not only inherited their ancestral property[128] – a theme he amplifies in another article[129] – but were also themselves one of the biggest donors to the *Saṅgha.* Basing his article on a combined use of archaeological and textual data, he attempts to show that:

> all of the *Vinayas* as we have them fall squarely in the middle period of Indian Buddhism, between the beginnings of the Common Era and the Year 500 AD. They can not, and do not, tell us what monastic Buddhism 'originally' was, but they do provide almost an overwhelming amount of detail about what it had become by that time.[130]

Of course, hardly anybody will have any problem in accepting the notion that two to three centuries might have elapsed between the preaching of the Buddha and final codification of the Pali *Vinaya*, but it is difficult to agree with his assertion that all *Vinayas* fall squarely to the middle period of Indian Buddhism. In another article,[131] he adds a new formulation: it is the *Mūlasarvāstivāda Vinaya* which is likely to be the mainstream Indian *Vinaya* as it is the *Vinaya* which shows a greater interaction with Brahmanical, larger Indian concerns. By an analysis of votive inscriptions, he has shown that, contrary to the canonical injunctions (in some *Vinayas*), it was mainly the monks and nuns, and not the laity, who sponsored the production of cultic images. Thus 'from the very appearance in the inscriptions, Mahāyāna was a monk-dominated movement,'[132] and 'not only was the image cult an overwhelmingly a monastic concern, it was also, on the basis of available sources, a monastically initiated cult.'[133] If his formulations are corroborated by future researches, we can think of a more diversified world of monastic activities: direct participation in trade; lending of the monastic money on interest and preparing written contracts for the same; greater complexities in the management of monasteries, arising out of the interface between the ecclesiastical laws and the secular laws; and the problems of management of landed estates of monasteries, which Schopen has shown to have begun rather earlier than the generally accepted early medieval phase (c. sixth century CE – early thirteenth century CE), and so on. In that case, early medieval mutations in Indian monastic Buddhism will not appear as 'feudal decadence' but as natural evolution of an enduring continuum.

Application of landscape archaeology in understanding the localization strategies of the *Saṅgha* in a particular area has brought certain refreshing paradigm shifts regarding the functional role of the monasteries. Here, mention must be made of the works of Shaw and Fogelin. Around the monastic complex of Sāñcī, John Marshall and Alexander Cunningham have earlier noted a network of dams, but these dams have not been studied in relation to the monastic sites. In her earlier articles,[134] based on her archaeological survey in the twenty kilometre radius of the monastic complex, Shaw has analyzed the relative positioning of the monasteries, dams and contemporary settlements and cult spots, to gauge the degree of interaction of the monastic sites with the countryside, particularly their role in irrigation and wet rice agriculture. It has been postulated that the introduction of wet rice agriculture was a concomitant result of the introduction of Buddhism in the Sāñcī area, and the monasteries might have taken the pioneering role in making this possible by their active involvement in the construction of the irrigation devices, from the third/second century BCE onwards. In her next article, Shaw has offered some ambitious generalizations for the process of religious change for the whole of South Asia. Based on a comparative study of the active role of monasteries in hydraulic management at Sāñcī, the Junagarh complex in Gujarat and dry zones of Sri Lanka, it has been asserted that 'the control of water harvesting and irrigational facilities was not only a means of political legitimacy for local rulers, but also formed a central component of the Buddhist *Saṅgha*'s propagation strategies.'[135] This can be largely corroborated for the dry Trans-Vindhyan regions. In the context of the Ganges valley, her theory can be accepted only in the sense of a more active role of the *Saṅgha* on agrarian frontiers.

Fogelin, in his survey of archaeological landscape of the Thotlakonda monastery, has noted that a single monastery performed multiple roles: functioning as a place for retreats for the monks, and offering economic engagements with the mercantile community and religious engagements with the laity. Such religious engagement was not in terms of the Buddhist doctrines but in the practice and conduct of daily, mundane ritual.[136] Needless to repeat, Shaw and Fogelin largely provide the models for future studies on Indian monastic Buddhism. Our focus should not be on grand generalizations but on the localization strategy of individual monasteries, or a group of monasteries, in a select sub-region.

Early medieval mutations: reconstructions of the history of an etiolating tradition

It is rather amazing to see the turnaround in Indian Buddhism in the early medieval period (*c.* sixth to early thirteenth centuries CE). For Indian Buddhism, it was a period of contradictory developments: a period when *mahāvihāra*s such as Nālandā, Somapura, Vikramaśilā and Ratnāgiri emerged and attained monumentality, while the same period was marked by a general retraction of Buddhist space across India. It was a period when Indian missionaries largely conquered China, Tibet and parts of Southeast Asia, yet also when, as we are informed by Xuan Zang, Indian Buddhist communities were convinced of the impending disappearance of the faith from India and were anxiously expecting the impending doom of Buddhism: a phenomenon which led to the emergence of 'central Buddhist realms' in many Asian countries which hardly required any spiritual legitimacy from great Buddhist centres of India.[137] For Indian Buddhism, it was also the period of the emergence of Tantric Buddhism. At the end of this period, we see the disappearance of Buddhism from a significant part of India. This disappearance was so complete that even the name of the Buddha was forgotten by an overwhelming section of Indian population. This has naturally invited sustained scholarly enquiry.

As we have noted in the preceding pages, Buddhist monasteries had diverse linkages with society and the economy in the early historic period, and they not only consumed social surplus but also directly or indirectly contributed to it; and it was owing to these diverse linkages that they survived and thrived. If we observe a crisis of bare survival in Indian Buddhism in the early medieval period, causative factors should not only be attributed to external factors such as Islamic invasions or Brahmanical hostility.[138] We see the re-appearance and prospering of Buddhist monasteries in Central Asia as late as the thirteenth century[139]; the lingering of Buddhism in Sindh until the fifteenth century[140]; and its continued survival as a living religion in Bengal,[141] the seat of the biggest Islamization east of the Sutlej. So our focus should shift from external factors to the possible faultiness in the monastic linkages with society and economy. The 'disappearance' of Buddhism cannot be attributed merely to the destruction of the monasteries and the elimination of monks. This is not to deny their role as the institutional nucleus of Buddhism. We have already noted that in the Pol Pot era in Cambodia, amidst a sustained attempt of the communist regime for the physical elimination of the monks and monasteries, Buddhism assumed an extreme apotropaic form, and after the regime changed it quickly reorganized and regrouped itself.[142] Similar was the case with Jaina temples and monasteries in medieval Gujarat.[143] Why could Indian Buddhist monasteries not regroup themselves after the initial shock and holocaust of Islamic attacks? We hear of monks educated at Nālandā going to China and Korea in the late thirteenth to early fourteenth century and offering diverse services to the state.[144] Why could they not do the same thing at home? It has also been suggested that one of the fundamental factors in the decline and disappearance of Buddhism in India was its 'social failure': that it became confined to the monasteries and offered insufficient cultivation of the laity. It has been indeed pointed out by P.S. Jaini that unlike the Jainas, the Buddhists in India hardly devised any code of conduct for its lay adherents.[145] One of the explanations for this apparent monastic apathy towards the laity has been found in the 'fact' that 'Buddhism has nothing to do with lay people and it was never a social movement.'[146] As we have seen in the previous pages, this generalization is not tenable.

With reference to the integrative role of the Brahmanical temples in early medieval India, it has been asserted that the rapid growth in the number and network of temples in this period was closely linked, as were the Brahmin dominated *Brahmadeyas* and *agrahāras*, with the formation of sub-regional and regional kingdoms and their legitimization, consolidation of their resource base and forging of linkages across communities for social integration.[147] As we have seen for the early historic phase, Buddhist monasteries were pioneers in this 'forging of linkages across communities for social integration' in a major part of India. Why did they fail to retain their lead in the early medieval period? Marxist wisdom would attribute this to their failure on the agrarian frontiers and in the detribalization process.[148] Early medieval 'parasitical monasteries consuming agrarian resources without providing anything in return,' have invited the attraction of another Marxist scholar.[149] Andre Wink has added the dimensions of long distance overland and maritime trade as well in explaining this phenomenon: that by the eleventh century CE, Islam replaced Buddhism as the 'greatest trading religion of Asia' while the agrarian world within India was gradually lost to the Brahmins by the Buddhists. This simultaneous loss of agrarian and mercantile space precipitated a systemic crisis within Indian Buddhism.[150] 'Agrarian failure' of Buddhism in early medieval India may sound surprising as, in the very same centuries, Buddhist monasteries, by virtue of their institutional management and control over irrigation systems and new agrarian technologies, controlled a significant part of the agrarian sector in Sri Lanka[151] and Burma,[152] and emerged as the biggest land owners in these two regions. In early medieval China too, it controlled a significant part of the agrarian sector.[153] The claims of Kosambi, Sharma and Wink, therefore, should be carefully assessed.

At the time of the Arab invasion (early eighth century

CE) Buddhism did assume a distinct agrarian colour in Sindh.[154] In Maitraka Gujarat, the old matrix of Buddhism and maritime trade continued at Vallabhi and these monasteries had a very close involvement with the agrarian sector.[155] In Tamilnadu, although the agrarian world was gradually lost to the Brahmins and Brahmanical temples, Buddhist monastic associations with port towns and maritime trade continued.[156] In Orissa, monasteries kept on attracting lay patronage and pilgrimage, rendering Ratnagiri 'second only to Bodhagayā as a pilgrimage centre,'[157] and there Buddhist monasteries had a 'subterranean survival,' surfacing again in the nineteenth century Mahimā Dharma movement.[158] In the case of early medieval Bengal, a very complex matrix of Buddhism, maritime trade and agrarian expansion developed[159]; though in this process, Brahmanism gradually outsmarted Buddhism, particularly on agrarian frontiers. At this juncture, it is sufficient to assert that it may be ahistorical to homogenize the functional dimensions of Indian monastic Buddhism for the early medieval period, indeed, for any period. We need micro studies, with a regional perspective, to have a better footing to understand the differential localization and socialization pattern of monasteries across the diverse landscapes.

Unfortunately, this approach is hardly visible in the available macro studies on early medieval Indian Buddhism. Thus Kanai Lal Hazra,[160] in his reconstruction of Buddhism as depicted in the writings of Chinese pilgrims, is more interested in seeing the sectarian affiliations of the monasteries, their arts and doctrines they pursued, but has hardly any concern to see the transition taking place between the periods of Fa-hsien (in India 399–413 CE) and Xuan Zang (630–44 CE) and beyond. Lal Mani Joshi begins promisingly and attempts to study certain new themes such as: evidences of royal control over ecclesiastical hierarchy of the *Saṅgha*[161]; management of their landed estates by the monasteries; and inter-monastic hierarchy, basically by drawing inferences from one monk controlling many monasteries.[162] Long before him, Sukumar Dutt had already proposed that early medieval monastic universities of Bihar and Bengal together formed a hierarchic network[163]; but neither Joshi nor Dutt had delineated a functional basis, and chronological evolution, of the same. Moreover, Joshi, by his assertion that the pattern of endowments to the monasteries as mentioned by Fa-hsien, 'could be applied in toto' in understanding the same in the seventh and eighth centuries,[164] largely refuses to recognize the institutional transitions in the *Saṅgha* as per its interactions with geographical and chronological variables.

Ronald Davidson provides a brilliant contrast. He has tried to trace the genesis and trajectory of Tantric Buddhism against the backdrop of the early medieval feudalization of Indian society.[165] In the volatile early medieval period, Davidson argues, Buddhism underwent a great distress due to diverse factors: evaporating mercantile patronage due to decline in the long distance trade and Arab domination of the high seas, rendering it increasingly dependent on royal, feudal patronage[166] lessening participation of women in Buddhism, and ultimately the disappearance of the order of the nuns within the *Saṅgha*[167]; militant *Śaiva* competition; and a serious dent in the 'previous Buddhist monopoly of dealing with the barbarians, outcastes, tribals, and foreigners' by the Brahmins who were now willing to travel great distances in search of land and patronage.[168] All this resulted in a gradual spatial shrinkage of Buddhism, and its contraction to select areas of strength. Coupled with it was a larger intellectual crisis: Buddhist intellectuals of this age developed an agenda of scepticism, and the epistemology which followed brought it dangerously close to Brahmanism.[169] Thus there was a creeping realization within the Indian Buddhist community that their faith was a 'tradition in duress'[170] and the evolution of esoteric Buddhism was the result of adaptations by a 'tradition in duress' to feudalism for its very survival. As a result of this adaptation, Buddhism was forced to feudalize itself, leading to the genesis of esoteric, Tantric Buddhism.

Davidson then proceeds to examine the differential but interrelated functions of 'institutional esoterism,' developing within the monasteries,[171] and 'non-institutional esoterism' of the *Siddhas*. In the centres of institutional esoteric Buddhism, there was a concerted attempt to forge a closer alliance with royalty so as to have greater royal patronage, and owing to this there was great internalization of feudal values and ethos, not only in the management of their landed estates but also in their very rituals and dogmas. The author has noted that there was a close resemblance between the monastic management of their landed estates, control and administration of 'branch monasteries' by the 'mega-monasteries' like Nālandā and feudal rulers' management of their landed estates and subordinate *sāmanta-maṇḍala*, that is, network of feudatories.[172] The other spectrum of Buddhist esoterism was the 'non-institutional esoterism' of the *Siddhas*, the non-conformists. The *Siddhas* gradually made their way to the monasteries and developed a symbiotic relationship with the monks. Within a remarkably short period (mid-seventh to mid-eleventh centuries), esoteric Buddhism produced a voluminous literature, and spread rapidly to Tibet, China and the rest of East Asia. Thus esoteric Buddhism was 'a tenacious success'[173] which 'stemmed the *Śaiva* tide sweeping up from the South India,' influencing Buddhist traditions beyond India.

However, it is difficult to concur with Davidson's conclusion that Tantric Buddhism, developing within the monasteries, was a 'tenacious' success. Not long after the evolution and growth of esoteric Buddhism, Buddhism did disappear from the larger parts of India, and this disappearance can not be solely blamed on 'Islamic iconoclasm.' We cannot rule out the possibility that some fundamental fault lines might have crept into the esoteric Buddhist pattern of socialization and regional adaptations. Indeed it was in the regions dominated by Tantric Buddhism in the early medieval period – East Bengal and the Swat valley – where medieval Islamization was most spectacular. It will be definitely a promising area for future research to analyse the possible fault lines in the Tantric Buddhist patterns of socialization and localization within a regional framework.

Two regions to be studied carefully to understand the early medieval monastic localization and socialization patterns are Bihar and Bengal, more especially, Bengal. Large parts of

Bengal seem to have been hardly touched by Buddhism in the early historic phase and the boundaries of the Buddhist 'middle country' (*Madhyadeśa*) ended near Rajamahal during the period immediately after the Buddha.[174] Buddhism seems to be the first institutional religion to penetrate its swampy jungles, with the monasteries forming a very complex matrix with maritime trade and agrarian expansion in the early medieval period and even earlier; yet the Delta offered the most fertile ground for Islamization in the subsequent medieval period: a period when it became an 'expanding agrarian civilization whose cultural counterpart was the growth of the cult of Allah'; in which rural mosques made of thatch and wood, 'linked politically to the state and economically to the hinterland' were functioning as a 'nucleus of integration'[175] for integrating various 'tribal' communities to the Islamic Great Tradition. In the vast landmass of South and Southeast Asia, from the Satluj to the Mekong, eastern Bengal is the only land irreversibly lost by the Indic world.[176] To what extent, if any, were Buddhist monasteries responsible for leaving this kind of socio-economic and cultural vacuum, which was later used by Islam? Yet, to our surprise, why in the whole of India, of course barring the Himalayan zone where Buddhism apparently had a different socialization strategy, has Buddhism a continued survival as a living religion only in (southeastern) Bengal?[177] Unfortunately, most available studies, of the sort 'Buddhism in Ancient Bengal' or 'Religion in Ancient Bengal,' hardly show even an awareness of this enigma. In this category, we may count the celebrated *Bangalir Itihasa: Adiparva,* by N.R. Ray,[178] Rama Chatterji[179] Pushpa Niyogi[180] and more recently Chitaranjana Patra[181] Nearly all of them are concerned with monastic art and architecture, identifications of their locations, occasionally in the land grants the monasteries received. Hardly any of them offer any analysis of the functional role of the monasteries in the society and economy. Pushpa Niyogi has also offered an analysis of land grants to the monasteries but she has not looked in to the spatial variations in the same. Hardly any of them offer any analysis of the functional role of the monasteries in the society and economy.

B.M. Morrison stands as a brilliant exception. Based on his analysis of Bengal inscriptions (c. fourth to thirteenth centuries CE), he proposes that there were four sub-regions within the Bengal Delta. Central, western and northern sectors of the Delta showed evidences of developed property relations and stratified society; in fact they 'were the heartlands of Brahmanical culture in the Delta.'[182] But in the fourth sub-region, Sylhet-Komilla-Chittagong sector (roughly the region referred to as Samataṭa in inscriptions), the pattern was fundamentally different. It was more or less a 'frontier' society with relatively sparse population and large uncultivated or forested landscape, a society that has just made the transition to state level polity. Here huge tracts of lands were granted to the Buddhist monasteries or hundreds of Brahmins.[183] Here Buddhist monasteries were acting as nuclei of integration, aiding and abetting the transition towards a more complex society. We may add here that his study forces us to leave aside macro generalizations regarding the functional role of Buddhist monasteries in the Bengal Delta, say for example between Somapura *Mahāvihāra* and the Mainamati monastic complex, as they were functioning in different locales and interacting with different socio-economic variables. In his monograph on the Mainamati complex,[184] he has offered an in-depth analysis of the functional role of the same within the Samataṭa region. He has noted the absence of any settlement site in the immediate neighbourhood of the complex or in the countryside and, in their absence, he has done a hinterland analysis of the complex on the basis of inscriptional evidences to situate it within the Samataṭa region. He proposes that it was the very hub, the very nucleus of the region. To situate it within the larger spatial context, that is, in the Bengal Delta, he has compared the Mainamati sites with other excavated sites of pre-Muslim Bengal. One may not fully agree with his method that the size of hinterland of a monastery can be estimated by dividing the distance between any two contemporary monastic centres,[185] but his approach, as a whole, is quite refreshing.

The Mainamati monastic complex demands greater

research. No doubt it was the political, economic and spiritual nucleus of the early medieval Samataṭa region. In the same region, as indicated by vase inscriptions of the eighth century CE, we see continued endowments to the monasteries by the newly Sanskritized tribal rulers,[186] that is, the monasteries were having some role in the tribal state formations and their legitimizations. In the same centuries, the maritime focus of the Bengal Delta shifts towards the east, towards the Chittagong coast.[187] And Samataṭa, unlike most other parts of South Asia, shows a continued tradition of silver coinage. What is the role of the monasteries in this complex matrix? In fact, much more intricate linkages between the early medieval Bengal monasteries and maritime connections are discernible than what we generally perceive. We see one *Mahānāvika* ('the great mariner') *Buddhagupta* of *Raktamṛtikā* monastery[188] going to Java; monasteries at the port town of Tāmralipti decline with the decline of the port[189]; whereas they crop up at an emerging inland riverine port-cum-warehousing settlement, *Vaṅgasāgarasambhāṅḍāriyaka*[190]; and Devaparavata (located somewhere near the Mainamati complex, but yet to be identified in the ground) itself functioned as a port.[191] But here is a big dilemma for us. When Samataṭa monasteries were active on the agrarian and maritime frontiers, and were acting as stabilizing factors for the emerging polities, why do we witness the biggest Islamization within Bengal in this sub-region only[192]? More importantly, why within Bengal could Buddhism survive as a living tradition in the medieval period and beyond in Samataṭa only? Hopefully future researches will unveil some aspects of this vexed problem.

Available studies on Early Medieval Monasteries in Bihar do not offer very encouraging picture. R.C. Prasad (*Archaeology of Champa and Vikramashila*, 1987), B.M. Kumar (*Archaeology of Pāṭaliputra and Nālandā*, 1987), and B.N. Mishra (*Nālandā*, 1998,in three volumes) do not leave any other impression except being compendiums of available information. This is most regretful in the context of B.N. Mishra and Brajmohan Kumar. Mishra in his monumental work has devoted two and a half volumes to the study of such themes as art and architecture, and iconography (one whole volume); reminding us once again the prophetic words of D.K. Chakrabarti:

> One should not entertain the idea that nothing more needs to be done at Nālandā. No attempt has been done to study Nālandā as an ancient settlement of which the famous monastery was only a part.[193]

Hopefully this type of study will provide some insights into the functional relationship between the monastic complex of Nālandā and its immediate neighbourhood.[194] That will also be useful in charting out the trajectories of cultural negotiations in the immediate neighbourhood of this great monastery. That will help us understand some of the factors behind the decline of Buddhism in the area.[195]

R.K. Chaudhury (*The University of Vikramashila*, 1975) has indeed offered some interesting details about the role of the monks of Vikramaśilā *Mahāvihāra* in the conversion of Tibet to Buddhism, but he has not analysed the support system of the monastery or its interactions with the wider socio-economic processes.

This contrasts sharply with Thakur's study of Tabo monastery (2001). This monastery had its beginnings in the ninth to tenth centuries and it is continuing as a living institution in the high altitude Lahaul and Spiti region of Himachal Pradesh. He has brilliantly analysed the alignment of trans-Himalayan trade routes and the monastic involvement with the trade passing through them; the pattern of land grants to the monastery and its participation in the peasant economy; and the role played by the monastery in the cultic integration of the pre-Buddhist Bon religion. He has been largely successful in tracing the variegated functions performed by the monastery, a multiplicity which ensures its continued survival. We need more studies of individual monasteries in other parts of India.

Conclusion

Needless to say, what has been attempted in the previous pages is indeed a bird's eye overview of studies, in the past hundred years, in the societal linkages of Indian monastic Buddhism. It may not be a good idea to offer any grand generalization on the basis of this. However, some suggestions can of course be proffered. It is time to acknowledge that Buddhist monastic practices in India cannot be reduced to the injunctions of different *Vinaya* texts. To analyse the trajectories of the complex functional matrix that monasteries created or were a part thereof, a better approach may be to see the interaction between text and context. Buddhism was one of the earliest world religions, yet it has developed remarkable local colours across the vast landmass of Asia. This 'localization' process, what has been earlier referred to as 'translation in the local idiom,' has been well documented in the case of many Asian countries, but it has barely begun for India. Future researches on the functional dimensions of Indian monastic Buddhism will have to negotiate one core issue: how does the *Saṅgha* localize at a particular place, yet retain its supra-local character? To analyse the twists and turns of this supralocal–local dialectic, shifting the focus away from the *Āryacaturdiśa-bhikṣu-Saṅgha,* ('Universal) Noble *Saṅgha of the Four Quarters,* to the individual monastery in its spatial context may not be a bad idea. This will entail a greater use of archaeological data and archaeological fieldwork. Archaeology provides an important method for investigating the broader societal context of monastic Buddhism. But the trick is, as earlier pointed out by Lars Fogelin, to study the monasteries by looking beyond them by examining the smaller, non-monastic archaeological sites that surround the monastery; and seeing the monastic interactions and engagements with them.[196] This may be combined with an analysis of important inscriptional and textual records associated with that particular monastery. That will provide a clue to the immediate local context of a single monastery as well as its place in the wider Buddhist world. That will enable us to have a micro understanding of the process by which the Buddhist monastic tradition localizes at any particular place; the monastic pattern of resource mobilization and other survival strategies; and also of factors behind the decay and disappearance of monastic tradition from that place.

Notes

1. This article was first published as 'Major Trends and Perspectives in Studies in the Functional Dimensions of Indian Monastic Buddhism in the Past One Hundred Years: A Historiographical Survey' in *Buddhist Studies Review*, Journal of the UK Association for Buddhist Studies, London, Vol. 25, No. 1, 2008, pp. 54-89.
2. Donald S. Lopez, Jr. (ed.), *Buddhism in Practice*, New Jersey, 1995, p. 3.
3. In fact, the very title of the first chapter of Spiro's impressive study, 'Theravada Buddhism: An Anthropological Problem,' highlights this disjuncture between normative Buddhism and 'lived' Buddhism. He has shown that the five 'core principles' of normative Buddhism, which he rather debatably, in some cases, labels materialism, atheism, nihilism, pessimism and renunciation, are rarely reflected in the lay Buddhist practices. See M. Spiro, *Buddhism and Society; A Great Tradition and its Burmese Vicissitudes*, London,1971, pp. 7–13.
4. David Scott, 'Buddhist Functionalism: Instrumentality Reaffirmed,' *Asian Philosophy*, 5, 2, 1995, pp. 127-149
5. David N. Gellner, 'What Is Anthropology of Buddhism About' in David N.Gellner, *The Anthropology of Buddhism and Hinduism, Weberian Themes*, Delhi, 2003, p. 51.
6. Trevor Ling, *Buddha, Marx and God*, London, 1979, p. 74. For some recent observations on the complex relationship between different animistic spirit cults and Buddhism, and the role of the *Saṅgha* in assimilating these cults, see Robert Decoroli, *Haunting the Buddha: Indian Popular Religions and the Formation of Buddhism*, New York, 2004. Decoroli has asserted that the inclusion of different spirit cults within the *Saṅgha* was 'far from being marginal concession to the public' as 'spirit deities played a central role in the development and growth of Buddhism in all of its contexts and in all of its forms' (p. 187).
7. N.N. Bhattacharya, *Buddhism in the History of Indian Ideas*, Delhi, 1993, p. 188.
8. Gail Omvedt, *Buddhism in India: Challenging Brahmanism and Caste*, Delhi, 2003, p. 173.
9. M.R. Allen, 'Buddhism without Monks: The Vajrayana Religion

of the Newars of the Kathamandu Valley,' *South Asia*, 1973, Vol. 2, pp. 1-14.
10. Vin. I 4.
11. One of the earliest scholars treating the *Saṅgha* as (perhaps undesirable) addenda to 'original lay Buddhism' was C.A.F. Rhys Davids, *Sakya or Buddhist Origins*, London, 1931.
12. Omvedt, *op. cit.*, p. 4; E. Zelliot, *From Untouchable to Dalit: Essays on the Ambedkar Movement*. Delhi, 1992, pp. 187–96, 222–48. For a review of Omvedt's approach, see my 'Dilemmas of Revival of Buddhism in India,' *Indian International Journal of Buddhist Studies*, 7, 2006, pp. 171–175.
13. G.D. Sontheimer, *Pastoral Deities in Western India*, Delhi, 1993, p. VII. Also see, idem, 'The *Vana* and the *Kshetra*: The Tribal Background of some famous cults' in G.C. Tripathy, H. Kulke (eds.), *Religion and Society in Eastern India*, Delhi, 1994, pp. 117-164; B.D. Chattopadhyaya, *Aspects of Rural Settlements and Rural Society in Early Medieval India*, Calcutta, 1990, Introduction; idem, 'Reappearance of the Goddess or Brahmanical Mode of Appropriation: Some Early Epigraphical Data Bearing on Goddess Cult' in *Studying Early India*, Delhi, 2002, p. 186.
14. Birendra Nath Prasad, 'Cultural Communications in Early Medieval India: Some Preliminary Observations,' in *Prajna Bharati*, Journal of K.P. Jayaswal Research Institute, Patna, Vol. XII, 2006, pp. 27-49.
15. Donald S. Lopez, Jr. (ed.), *Buddhism in Practice*, New Jersey, 1995, p. 8.
16. Arthur Geddes, 'Some Geographical Factors in Indian History,' in A.T.A. Learmonth *et. al.* (ed.), *Man and Land in South Asia*, Delhi, 1982, p. 94.
17. For an interesting analysis of this whole process, see Christian K. Wedemeyer, 'Tropes, Typologies and Turnarounds: A Brief Genealogy of Tantric Buddhism,' *History of Religions*, Vol. 41, 2001, p. 224.
18. For a critical analysis, see Philip Almond, *The British Discovery of Buddhism*, Cambridge, 1988, especially Chapter 1.
19. R. Spence Hardy, *Eastern Monachism: An Account of the Origin, Laws, Discipline, Sacred Writings, Mysterious Rites, Religious Ceremonies and Present Circumstances of the Order of Mendicants Founded by the Buddha*, London, 1860. Reprint, Delhi, 1989. All references are from the reprint edition.
20. Ibid., p. VI in Preface.
21. Ibid., p. 453.

22. Max Weber, *The Religion of India: The Sociology of Hinduism and Buddhism,* edited and translated by H.H. Gerth and D. Martindale, Delhi, 1992 (reprint).
23. Ibid., p. 193.
24. Ibid., p. 206.
25. See Winston Davis, 'Buddhism and the modernization of Japan,' *History of Religions,* 28, 4, May 1989, pp. 304-339.
26. See Somboon Suksamran (edited with an Introduction by Trevor O. Ling), *Political Buddhism in South East Asia: The Role of the Saṅgha in the Modernization of Thailand,* London, 1977.
27. Vin. I. 21.
28. S. Dutt, *Early Buddhist Monachism,* Delhi, 1984 (reprint), p. 12.
29. S. Dutt, *op. cit.,* p. 98.
30. S. Dutt, *op. cit.,* p. 99, Richard Gombrich, *op. cit.,* p. 115., B.G. Gokhale, *op. cit.,* pp. 13-24.
31. T.W. Rhys Davids's *Buddhist India* was an interpretation of ancient Indian socio-economic history from a Buddhist perspective, which, incidentally, does not contain a single line on the role and place of monasteries in the socio-economic life of ancient India.
32. Jayaswal has noted long ago that the 'birth of Buddhism was the birth of organized monasticism in the world.' See K.P. Jayaswal, *Hindu Polity,* 3rd edition, Bangalore, 1955, p. 42. It has been re-asserted recently by Richard Gombrich (*op. cit.,* p. 19) that "in all the *Śramaṇa* traditions of India, it was only the Buddhists who invented monastic life." For a similar conclusion, also see, S. Dutt, *op. cit.,* p. 110.
33. Gokuldas De, *Democracy in the Buddhist Saṅgha,* Calcutta, 1955, p. 5.
34. S. Dutt, *op. cit.,* p. 7.
35. Ibid., p. 11.
36. Ibid., p. 96.
37. Ibid., pp. 99-100.
38. Ibid., p. 98.
39. E. Conze, *Buddhism: Its Essence and Development,* Delhi, 1994, (reprint), p. 54; V.P. Varma, *Early Buddhism and its Origins,* New Delhi, 1973, pp. 379-382.
40. Uma Chakravarty, *The Social Dimensions of Early Buddhism,* Delhi, 1996, p. 82,
41. Ibid., pp. 18-19.
42. Ibid., pp. 90-92.
43. Ibid., pp. pp. 122–49.

44. Richard Gombrich, *How Buddhism Began: The Conditioned Genesis of Early Teachings,* Delhi, 2002 (second edition), p. 19.
45. Richard Gombrich, *Theravada Buddhism,* p. 87.
46. Ibid., p. 87.
47. The role of the laity in shaping the trajectories of evolution of the *Saṅgha,* particularly lay demands leading to the deliberation of injunctions of the *Vinaya* has been sharply pointed out by B.G. Gokhale in 'The *Saṅgha* and the Laity,' in his *New Light on Early Buddhism,* Bombay, 1994, pp. 13-24. Recently, the notion of inherent ritual 'superiority' of monks over laity has been questioned, forcing us to think of a new paradigm for monastery-laity interaction. See Robert Bluck, ' The Path of the Householder: Buddhist Lay Disciple in the Pali Canon,' *Buddhist Studies Review,* 19,(1), 2002, pp. 1-18. T. Ling (T. Ling, *The Buddha: Buddhist Civilisation in India and Ceylon,* London, 1973, pp. 133-135) has already noted that "between the common people and the *Saṅgha,* there exist one important relationship, not of reciprocity exactly, but of complementariness." This is the line of argument which would be pursued in my Essay.
48. M. Spiro, *op. cit.,* p.11.
49. Ibid., p. 13.
50. Ibid., p. 13.
51. Ibid., pp. 12–13
52. In a brilliant study of the process of re-emergence of the *Saṅgha* in Cambodia after its virtual institutional elimination by the demolition of larger numbers of monasteries and physical elimination of the majority of monks during the Khmer Rogue era (1975-78), it has been observed that under the conditions of such extreme persecution, the *Saṅgha* ' reverted to most basic apotropaic form' (p. 74); and it survived this calamity by the secret performance of magic, traditional rites to comfort the sick, the bereaved and the terrified by the defrocked monks(p. 74), and after the Civil War, the *Saṅgha* rapidly re-grouped itself by adjusting to the new regime. See Ian Harris, 'Buddhist *Saṅgha* Groupings in Cambodia,' *Buddhist Studies Review,* 18, 1, 2001, p. 74.
53. Richard A. O'Connor, 'Interpreting the Thai Religious Change: Temples, *Saṅgha* Reform and Social Change,' *Journal of South East Asian Studies,* 24, 2, 1993, pp. 330-339. He has brilliantly observed that as a consequence of the attempts of the Bangkok political elites to promote a strictly Textual (strictly Pali

Canonical Theravāda), normative Buddhism, 'today *Wat* (the temple cum monastic complex) is less Thai and more Buddhist' (p. 335), entailing a 'continuous tension between the *Wat* as an agent of village solidarity and the *Wat* as an agent of the national state,' thus disrupting its centuries long function of joining the lay and monastic communities (p. 335); 'a long term institutional shift rendering it peripheral to the society,' (p. 336).

54. Richard Gombrich, *Theravada Buddhism*, p.93.
55. Ibid., p. 115.
56. Ibid., p. 115.
57. Ibid., p. 116.
58. Ibid., p. 116.
59. J. Tambiah, *The World Conqueror and the World Renouncer: A Study of Buddhism and Polity in Thailand against a Historical Background*, Cambridge, 1976, p. 189.
60. It has been rightly observed that, 'if external ideas are ever to have any meaning, they must connect in some way with the pre-existing ideas and understandings: only then when they have undergone the process of "translation" in the local idiom, can they begin to have effect' (G.A. Oddie, *Religious Transformations in South Asia: Interactions and Change*, Surrey, 1998, p. 6). It is high time that we explore differential localization strategies of the *Saṅgha* across time and space.
61. Charls S.Prebish, *Buddhist Monastic Discipline*, Delhi, 2002, p. 28.
62. E. Frauwallner, *The Earliest Vinaya and the Beginnings of the Vinaya Literature*, Rome, 1956, pp. 205-207.
63. E. Lamottee, *History of Indian Buddhism: From the Origins to the Saka Era.* English translation by S. Webb Boin, Louvain-la-neuve, 1988, p. 179.
64. Shayne Clarke, 'Vinaya Matṛkā: Mother of All Monastic Codes or Just Another Set of Lists? A Response to Frauwallner's Handling of the Mahāsāṇghika Vinaya,' *Indo-Iranian Journal*, 47, 2004, pp. 80, 115.
65. Ibid., p. 78.
66. Jayeeta Gangopadhyaya, *Uposatha Ceremony: The Earliest Traditions and Later Developments, Mainly from the Vinaya Traditions Preserved in Chinese*, Varanasi and Delhi, 1986, p. 51.
67. J.J. Nattier & C.S. Prebish, '*Mahāsāṅghika* Origins,' *History of Religions*, 1976–7, 16: 237–72.
68. Robin, A.E. Coninghum, 'Monks, Caves and Kings: A

Reassessment of the Nature of Early Buddhism in Sri Lanka,' *World Archaeology*, 27(2), 1995, pp. 222-242.

69. Ibid., p. 221.
70. Ibid., p. 238. For a similar study of interdependence of the Sri Lankan Crown and Sri Lankan *Saṅgha*, see S.M. Haladhar, 'The Robe and the Throne: An Analysis of the Symbiotic Relationship between Buddhism and the State in Ancient Srilanka,' *Indian Historical Review*, XXXI, No. 1-2, January- July 2004, pp. 18-30.
71. Reginald A. Ray, *Buddhist Saints in India: A Study in Buddhist Values and Orientations*, New York, 1994.
72. Ibid., p. vii.
73. Ibid., p. 20.
74. Ibid., p. viii
75. Ibid., p. 436.
76. For a similar argument, see David McMohan, 'Orality, Writing and Authority in South Asian Buddhism: Visionary Literature and the Struggle for Legitimacy in Mahayana,' *History of Religions*, 37.3, February 1998, pp. 249-274.
77. Reginald Ray, *op. cit.*, p. 439.
78. Ibid., p. 447.
79. Ibid., p. 446.
80. Ibid., p. 441.
81. S.J. Tambiah,, *Buddhist Saints of Forests and the Cult of Amulets*, 1984; Michael Carrithers, *The Forest Monks of Sri Lanka: An Anthropological and Historical Study*, Delhi, 1983.
82. The relations between the genesis of early Buddhism and urbanisation of upper and middle Ganga valley are well analyzed. See particularly, G.C. Pande, *Studies in the Origins of Buddhism*, Allahabad, 1957, pp. 313-15; Max Weber, *The Religion of India: The Sociology of Hinduism and Buddhism*, edited and translated by H.H. Gerth and D. Martindale, Delhi, 1992 (reprint) p. 204; T.W. Rhys Davids, *Buddhist India*, Delhi, 2005 (reprint), pp. 63-85; R.S. Sharma, *Material Culture and Social Formation in Ancient India*, Delhi, 1983, pp. 122–28; K.T.S. Sarao, *Urban Centres and Urbanisation as Reflected in Pali Vinaya and Sutta Pitakas*, Delhi, 1990; B.G. Gokhale, 'Early Buddhism and Urban Revolution,' reprinted in his *New Light on Early Buddhism*, Bombay, 1994, pp. 43-57. Also see D.K. Chakrabarti, 'Location of Buddhist Sites as Influenced by Political and Economic Factors,' *World Archaeology*, 27(2), 1995, pp. 185-202. Chakrabarti has noted three major stages of growth and

expansion of Buddhism, (6th century BCE, 2nd century CE, and 1st- 3rd century CE). Each stage was 'closely linked to the successive growth and expansion of urban base in India,' (p. 185).

83. Ian Mabbett & Greg Bailey, *The Sociology of Early Buddhism*, Cambridge, 2003, p. 34.
84. G. Erdosy, 'Early Historical Cities of North India,' *South Asian Studies*, 3, 1987, p. 10.
85. Ibid., p. 10.
86. D.K. Chakrabarti, *op.cit.*, p. 194.
87. J. Heitzman, 'Early Buddhism, Trade and Empire,' in G.L. Possel, K. Kennedy (ed.), *Studies in Archaeology and Palaeoanthropology of South Asia*, Delhi, 1984, pp. 121-132.
88. Herman Tieken, ' Aśoka and the Buddhist *Saṅgha*: A Study of Aśoka's Schism Edicts and Minor Rock Edicts, *Bulletin of School of Oriental and African Studies*, London, 2000, p. 1.
89. Ibid., p. 27.
90. Ibid., p. 207.
91. Ibid., p. 207.
92. Ibid., p. 207. For a similar use of the Buddhist monasteries in the pacification and integration of turbulent Central Asian frontier regions by the Chinese State, see Antony Forte, 'Chinese State Monasteries in the Seventh and Eight Centuries' in Kuwayama Shoshin (ed.), *EchOo Go Tenjiku den Kenkyu*, Kyoto, 1990, pp. 214-258. For the similar integrative role of the Thai *Saṅgha* in the tribal northwestern frontier regions of Thailand, see Sanit Wongs Prasert, 'Impact of the Dhammacarika Bhikku's Programme on the Hill Tribes of Thailand,' in K.M. Desilva *et.al.* (ed.), *Ethnic Conflict in the Buddhist Societies: Srilanka, Burma and Thailand*, London, 1988, pp. 126-137. This article is immensely important for our purpose. It analyses the three pronged strategy of the state sponsored Dhammacarika Bhikkhu's Programme (DBP) in the traditionally shifting cultivation, tribal areas. As part of their integrative strategies, at the individual and household level, monks provide primary health care and help villagers and hill tribes to deal with local administration in matters such as taxes, registration for birth and deaths and so on (p. 129). At the community level, their main task is to impart new agrarian technologies, particularly that of wet rice agriculture (p. 129). Besides they encourage pilgrimage to local and national Buddhist pilgrimage centres by these hill tribes (p. 129). It has

been noted that among those tribes who have been taught at DBP schools, around 85% of them have already adopted wet rice agriculture (p. 130). In India, role of Brahmanical temples in the integration of the turbulent frontier regions is well documented. Buddhist monasteries, apparently, had similar roles in different parts of India and that should also be explored.

93. Ibid., p. 207.
94. Ibid., p. 208.
95. Ibid., p. 210.
96. H.P. Ray, 'Bharahut and Sanchi: Nodal Points in Commercial Exchange,' in B.M. Pande, B.D. Chattopadhyaya (ed.), *Archaeology and History: Essays in Honour of A. Ghosh*, Delhi, 1987, p. 627.
97. Ibid., p. 621. For a similar analysis of functional autonomy of the Sanchi monastic complex vis-à-vis the nearby urban centres, see Upinder Singh, 'Sanchi: The History of Patronage of an Ancient Buddhist Establishment,' *The Indian Economic and Social History Review*, 33(1996), pp. 1-35.
98. H.P. Ray, *The Winds of Change: Buddhism and the Maritime Links of Early South Asia*, Delhi, 1994, p. 122. Also see, Kenneth G. Zysk, *Asceticism and Healing in Ancient India: Medicine in the Buddhist Monastery*, Delhi 1991. Zysk has noted the key role played by Buddhism in the advancement of Indian medicine through its institutionalization of medicine in the Buddhist monastery and its role in entailing the transition in Indian Medicine from 'magico-religious system' of the Vedic Ages to the subsequent 'empirico-rational system' of the later ages. See particularly, Chapter III, 'Medicine and Buddhist Monasticism."
99. H.P. Ray, *Winds of Change*, Delhi, 1994, p. 143.
100. H.P. Ray, 'Kanheri: The Archaeology of an Early Buddhist Pilgrimage Site in Western India,' *World Archaeology*, 26(1), 1994, p. 37.
101. Ibid., p. 39.
102. H.P. Ray, *The Archaeology of Sea Faring in Ancient South Asia*, Cambridge, 2003, p. 264.
103. Ibid., p. 260.
104. Robert James Miller, *Monasteries and Cultural Change in Inner Mongolia*, Weisbaden, 1959, pp. 11-23. Also see David N. Gellner, 'The Newar Buddhist Monastery: An Anthropological and Historical Typology' in his *The Anthropology of Buddhism and Hinduism*, Delhi, 2003, pp. 134-138.

105. James J. Preston, 'Sacred Centres and Symbolic Networks in India,' in S. Mahapatra (ed.), *The Realm of the Sacred,* Delhi, 1992, pp. 79-112.
106. H. Sarkar, 'Emergence and Growth of Urban Centers in Early Historic āndhradeśa' in B.M. Pande, B.D. Chattopadhyaya (ed.), *op. cit.*, p. 632.
107. Ibid., p. 635.
108. Ibid., p. 639.
109. S. Nagaraju, 'From Spirituality to Power: A Millennium of Buddhist Monastic Architecture as A Mirror of Social History' in K.Sankaranasayan *et. al.*, (ed.), *Buddhism in India and Abroad: An Integrated influence in Vedic and Post-Vedic Perspective,* Mumbai and New Delhi, 1996, p. 302.
110. Ibid., pp. 304-305.
111. Ibid., p. 306.
112. Ibid., p. 307.
113. Ibid., p. 308.
114. Richard S. Cohen, 'Naga, Yakshini, the Buddha: Local Deities and Local Buddhism at Ajanta,' *History of Religions,* 37.4, May 1998, p. 362.
115. Ibid., p. 370. For a different perspective, i.e. total dependence of the Ajantā complex on the Vākāṭaka patronage for its very survival, see Walter M. Spink, 'Before the Fall: Pride and Pity at Ajantā' in Barbara S. Miller, *The Powers of Art: Patronage in Indian Culture,* Delhi, 1992, pp. 65-77.
116. Richard S. Cohen, *op.cit.*, pp. 366-368.
117. Yogendra Singh, 'Influence of Naga Worship in Buddhist Art,' in R.C. Sharma (ed.), *Interactions between Buddhist and Brahmanical Art,* New Delhi, 2003, pp. 30-35.
118. Romila Thapar, 'Patronage and Community' in Barbara. S. Miller (ed.), *The Powers of Art: Patronage in Indian Culture,* Delhi, 1992, pp. 19-34.
119. Vidya Dehejia, 'The Collective and Popular Basis of Early Buddhist Patronage: Sacred Monuments, BC 100-AD 250' in Barabara S. Miller, *op. cit.*, pp. 35-50.
120. Romila Thapar, *op. cit.*, p. 30; Vidya Dehejia, *op. cit.*, pp. 44-45.
121. Xinriu Liu, *Ancient India and Ancient China: Trade and Religious Exchange, AD 1-600,* Delhi, 1988, p. 104.
122. Ibid., p. 105.
123. Ibid., p. 107.
124. Ibid., p. 108.
125. Ibid., p. 133.

126. This approach has been further expanded in her next book, *Silk and Religion: An Exploration into the Material Life and Thought of the People, AD 600-1200,* Delhi, 1996. See particularly pp. 49-72.
127. Gregory Schopen, 'Archaeology and Protestant Presuppositions in the Study of Indian Buddhism,' *History of Religions,* 31.1, 1991, p. 4.
128. Gregory Schopen, 'Monastic Law Meets the Real World: A Monk's continuous Right to Inherit Family Property in Classical India,' *History of Religions,* 35.2, November 1995, p. 108.
129. Gregory Schopen, 'Deaths, Funerals and Division of Property in a Monastic Code,' in Donald S. Lopez (ed.), *Buddhism in Practice,* New Jersey, 1995, pp. 473-502.
130. Ibid., p. 476.
131. G. Schopen, 'Doing Business for the Lord: Lending on Interest and Written Loan Contracts in the Mūlasarvāstivādin Vinaya,' *Journal of American Oriental Society,* Vol. 114, No. 4, 1994, pp. 527-554.
132. G. Schopen, *Bones, Stones and Tools: Collected Papers on the Archaeology, Epigraphy and Text of Monastic Buddhism in India,* Honolulu, 1997, p. 32.
133. Ibid., p. 32.
134. Julia Shaw, J. Suitclif, 'Ancient Irrigation Works in the Sanchi Area: An Archaeological and Hydrological Investigation,' *South Asian Studies,* London, Vol. 17, 2001, pp. 55-75; Julia Shaw, 'Sanchi and its Archaeological Landscape; Buddhist Monasteries, Settlements and Irrigation Work in Central India,' *Antiquity,* Vol. 74, 2000, pp. 775- 796.
135. Julia Shaw and J. Suitclif, 'Water Management, Patronage Networks and Religious Change: New Evidence from the Sanchi Dam Complex and Counterparts in Gujarat and Srilanka,' *South Asian Studies,* London, 19, 2003, p. 75.
136. Lars Fogelin, 'Sacred Architecture, Sacred Landscape: Early Buddhism in North Coastal Andhra Pradesh,' in H.P. Ray, Carla M. Sinopaly (ed.), *Archaeology as History in Early South Asia,* New Delhi, 2004, pp. 377.
137. Tanasen Sen, *Buddhism, Diplomacy and Trade: Realignment of Sino- Indian Relations, 600-1400,* Delhi, 2004, p. 56.
138. D.C. Ahir (*Buddhism Declined in India, How and Why,* Delhi, 2005) explains the decline of Indian Buddhism in terms of 'Brahmanical propaganda of hatred' and Islamic iconoclasm.

This view needs reconsideration.

139. M.L. Bhatia, 'Identifying Buddhism in Early Islamic Sources of Sindh,' *Buddhist Studies Review*, 19(2), 2002, p. 179.
140. Ibid., p. 181.
141. Hara Prasad Sastri, *Discovery of Living Buddhism in Bengal*, Calcutta, 1897; Sukomal Chaudhury, *Contemporary Buddhism in Bangladesh*, Calcutta, 1982; A.M. Khan, *The Maghs: A Buddhist Community in Bangladesh*, Dhaka, 1999; N. Ahmed, *Discover the Monuments of Bangladesh*, Dhaka, 1984. Ahmed has noted that contemporary Bangladesh has a Buddhist population of around half a million with their main concentration in Chittagong, Comilla and Dhaka districts i.e. basically in Samataṭa area (p. 45).
142. Ian Hariss, *op. cit.*, pp. 73-106.
143. P.S. Jaini, 'The Disappearance of Buddhism and the Survival of Jainism in India: A Study in Contrast,' in his *Collected Papers on Buddhist Studies*, Delhi, 2001, p. 142. Originally published in A.K.Narain (ed.) *Studies in History of Buddhism*, Delhi, 1980, pp. 81-91.
144. Arthur Waley, 'New Light on Buddhism in Medieval India,' *Melanges Chinols et bouddhiques*, 1931-32, (Full text downloaded from http/ccbs.ntu/edu.tw/Fulltext/JR-MEL/Weale.htm), p. 372. This remarkable article is based upon the translation of a 'political inscription' (1378 CE) on a *stūpa* in a Korean temple, in the memory of an Indian monk Dhyānabhadra. The inscription definitely suggests that Buddhism was a living force in the 14th century Bengal, Kānchipuram (Tamilnadu), in the Chola Kingdom, Jālandhara(the Punjab), at Dvārāvatipura (the capital of the Hoyasalas of Karnataka) and probably in Gujarat as well (p. 355). Despite these early and significant writings on the survival of Buddhism after the Turkic destruction of its great monastic centers, due to some strange reasons, the theory of the apocalysmic collapse of Buddhism has been internalized in the mainstream Indian historiography, giving us a lopsided impression that Buddhism did not exist outside the monastery.
145. P.S. Jaini, *op. cit.* He has sharply pointed out that in contrast to the Jaina clerics who have written many 'codes of conducts' for the laity, the Buddhist could manage only one such 'code' – *Upāsakajanālankāra* – and that too not until the eleventh century CE. Worse, it was not the work of any Indian monk, but was written by a Singhalese monk in South India, in the

Pali language (p. 144.)

146. N.N. Bhattacharya, *Buddhism in the History of India Ideas,* Delhi, 1993, p. 238.
147. B.D. Chattopadhyaya, *Studying Early India,* Delhi, 2003, p. 166.
148. D.D. Kosambi, 'The Decline of Buddhism in India' in his '*Exasperating Essays: Exercises in the Dialectical Method,* Pune, 1986, p. 66. This article was originally published in 1956.
149. R.S. Sharma, *Urban Decay,* Delhi, 1987, p. 131.
150. Andre Wink, *Al-Hind: The Making of the Indo-Islamic World,* Vol. II, Delhi, 1999, pp. 349-350.
151. R.A.L.H. Gunawardana, *Robe and Plough: Monasticism and Economic Interest in Early Medieval Sri Lanka,* Tucson, 1979.
152. See Kenneth R. Hall, 'Buddhism as an Economic Force in Pagan Burma,' in Nicholas Tarling (ed.), *The Cambridge History of South-East Asia,* Vol. I, Cambridge, 1992, pp. 240-245.
153. For an interesting analysis of the process of emergence of monastic landlordism and monastic control over a significant sector of the agrarian sector, so much so that it started to eat into the resource base of the Chinese state, see Jacques Gernet, *Buddhism in Chinese Society: An Economic History from the 5th to 10th Centuries AD,* New York, 1995.
154. M.L. Bhatia, *op.cit.,* p. 164.
155. Nandini Sinha, 'Early Maitrakas, Land Grant Charters and Regional State Formation in Early Medieval Gujarat,' *Studies in History,* 17, 2, n.s., 2001, p. 158.
156. R. Champakalakshmi, 'Buddhism in Tamilnadu: Patterns of Patronage,' in *Buddhism in Tamilnadu, Collected Papers,* Chennai, 1998, pp. 81-82.
157. Debala Mitra, *Ratnāgiri* (1958-1961), Memoir of Archaeological Survey of India, No. 80, Vol. 2, New Delhi, 1981, p. 31.
158. N.N. Vasu, *Modern Buddhism and its Followers in Orissa,* Calcutta, 1911, pp. 174-175.
159. For an analysis of this process see Rila Mukharjee, 'Rice Culture,' pp. 49–58. She has noted the continued survival of Buddhist maritime network in the northern Bay of Bengal until at least the twelfth century CE (p. 56). Also see Rila Mukharjee, *Strange Riches: Bengal in the Mercantile Map of South Asia,* Delhi, 2006, p. 25. For a similar analysis of this matrix, with particular reference to southeast Bengal, see Birendra Nath Prasad, "Monarchs, Monasteries and Trade on an 'Agrarian Frontier': Early Medieval Samatata – Harikela Region, Bangladesh" *South and Southeast Asia, Religion and Culture,* Vol. 3, 2008, pp.

160-177. For an analysis of the continued presence of Buddhist maritime networks in the Bay of Bengal until the twelfth century CE, see Umakant Mishra, *Buddhism and Maritime Networks in Early Medieval Orissa*, PhD thesis, Jawaharlal Nehru University, New Delhi, 2005.

160. K.L. Hazra, *Buddhism in India as Described by Chinese Pilgrims, A.D.399-689*, New Delhi, 1983.
161. L.M. Joshi, *Studies in the Buddhist Culture of India during the Seventh and Eight Centuries A.D.*, Delhi, 2002 (reprint), pp. 74-75.
162. Ibid., p. 75.
163. S. Dutt, *Buddhist Monks and Monasteries in India*, London, 1962, p. 353.
164. L.M. Joshi, *op. cit.*, p. 66.
165. For a review of Davidson, see Birendra Nath Prasad, 'Tantric Buddhism as Sacralised *Samanta* Feudalism in Early Medieval India,' a Review of Ronald M. Davidson's *Indian Esoteric Buddhism: A Social History of the Tantric Movement*, *Social Science Probings*, Vol. 18 (2), New Delhi, 2006, pp. 147-149.
166. Ronald M. Davidson, *Indian Esoteric Buddhism: A Social History of the Tantric Movement*, Delhi, 2004, pp. 77-83.
167. Ibid., pp. 91-98.
168. Ibid., p. 85.
169. Ibid., pp. 95-105.
170. Ibid., pp. 111-112.
171. Ibid., p. 114.
172. Ibid., p. 106.
173. Ibid., p. 339.
174. S. Dutt, *Buddhist Monks and Monasteries in India*, London, 1962, p. 103.
175. Richard Eaton, 'Who are the Bengal Muslims? Conversions and Islamisation in Bengal,' in R. Ahmed (ed.), *Understanding Bengal Muslims*, Delhi, 2001, p. 35.
176. For an analysis of factors behind this cultural rupture, see Richard Eaton, *The Rise of Islam and Bengal Frontier*, Delhi, 1994.
177. Some might wonder if the nearness of the above areas to Buddhist Burma is a relevant factor. However, Buddhism has not survived in Assam, which borders Burma, which was a Buddhist country from at least the eighth century CE. Besides, Assam also borders two regions under heavy Vajryāna influence: Bhutan and Arunachal Pradesh. Yet Assam does not have living Buddhism. Buddhism survived in Nepal but

not in the Mithila area of Bihar that borders Nepal. We should not, therefore, overemphasize the issue of geographical proximity. Had proximity to Burma been such an important factor, then trans-Meghna portions of Bengal would not have seen a rather phenomenal Islamization in the medieval period. In any case, Buddhism had a 'subterranean survival' in Orissa, with no bordering Buddhist land, where it resurfaced in the nineteenth century in the form of the Mahimā Dharma movement.

178. N.R. Ray, *History of the Bengali People,* translated by J.W. Hood, Calcutta 1994. See the chapter on religious conditions.
179. Rama Chatterji, *Religion in Bengal during Pala and Sena Times,* Calcutta, 1985.
180. Pushpa Niyogi, *Buddhism in Ancient Bengal,* Calcutta, 1967. See especially pp. 50-80 for an analysis of land-grants to the monasteries, but without considering any spatial variations.
181. Chitaranjan Patra, 'Spread of Buddhism in Bengal,' in A. Dutta (ed.), *History and Archaeology of Eastern India,* Delhi, 1998, pp. 200-212.
182. B.M. Morrisson, *Political Centres and Cultural Regions in Early Bengal,* Jaipur, 1980 *(Indian edition),* p. 38.
183. Ibid., p. 35.
184. B.M. Morrison, *Lalmai: A Cultural Centre in Early Bengal,* London and Seattle, 1974.
185. Ibid., p. 129.
186. See G. Bhattacharya, 'A Preliminary Note on the Inscribed Metal Vase from the National Museum of Bangladesh' in D. Mitra (ed.), *Explorations in the Art and Archaeology of South Asia: Essays Dedicated to N.G. Majumdar,* Calcutta, 1996. The inscription records the donation of land to Buddhist monastery by one Devātideva Bhaṭṭāraka (8th century CE), who belonged to the non-Aryan *Khasa* tribe. He had embraced Buddhism (p. 239). Also see G. Bhattacharya, 'An Inscribed Metal Vase, Most Probably from Chittagong' in A.J. Gail and G.J.R. Mevissena (ed.), *South Asian Archaeology,* 1991, pp. 323-338.
187. Ranabir Chakravarti, '*Vaṅgasāgarasaṁbhāṇḍāriyaka*: A Riverine Trade Centre in Early Medieval Bengal,' in his *Trade and Traders in Early Indian Society,* Delhi, 2002, p. 153.
188. S.R. Das, *An Interim Report on Excavations at Rajabadidanga and Terracotta Seals and Sealings,* Calcutta, 1967, pp. 57-58.
189. From the 6th-7th Century CE, the port of Tāmralipti started declining, and there is no evidence to prove that sea-faring

merchants used it for maritime adventures from 8th century CE onwards (A.Bhattacharya, 'Trade Routes of Ancient Bengal,' in A.Dutta, *op. cit.*, p. 164). This is reflected in the decreasing number of monasteries. Fa-hsien saw 22 monasteries but Xuan-Zang could see only 10 monasteries (Chitaranjana Patra, *op. cit.*, p. 203), and later records are silent about the presence of monasteries at Tāmralipti.

190. Ranabir Chakravarti, *op. cit.*, p. 153. He has convincingly identified *Vaṅgasāgarasaṁbhāṇḍāriyaka*, a riverine port with warehousing facilities with Sabhar, twenty-four kilometers northwest of Dhaka, and this place contains *stūpa* and monastery-like structures.
191. Ranabir Chakravarti, *Trade and Traders in Early Indian Society*, Delhi, 2002, p. 20.
192. Richard Eaton, *op. cit.*, p. 43; M.R. Tarafdar, 'The Cultural Identity of Bengali Muslims as Reflected in Medieval Bengali Literature,' in Perween Hasan and M. Islam (eds.), *Essays in Memory of M.R. Tarafdar*, Dhaka, 1999, p. 445.
193. D.K. Chakrabarti, *Issues in East Indian Archaeology*, Delhi, 1998, p. 97.
194. For an analysis of relationship of Nālandā *Mahāvihāra* with its immediate landscape, see Birendra Nath Prasad, "Nalanda – 'the Greatest Centre for Buddhist Learning – in a Poly-religious Landscape: An Interpretation of Archaeology of Religious Transformation in Early Medieval Bihar," forthcoming. I have undertaken an archaeological survey in the ten kilometer radius of the *Mahāvihāra* to situate it in its immediate neighbourhood.
195. Nālandā *Mahāvihāra* offers a unique opportunity to understand some aspects of socialisation strategies of early medieval Buddhist monasteries in India and decline of Indian Buddhism. This is due to the availability of a particular kind of database. Hirananda Sastri's excavations at Nālandā have brought to light hundreds of seals and sealings, which, among other seals, also include the seals of various villages and *jānapadas* ('village corporations'). Income from these villages and *jānapadas* was earmarked for the exclusive use of the *Mahāvihāra*. (H. Sastri, *Nalanda and its Epigraphic Material*, Memoirs of the Archaeological Survey of India, No. 66, Delhi, 1942, p. 32.) An archaeological study of such identified villages and 'village corporations' offers one of the most important avenues for understanding the socialisation strategy of the

Mahāvihāra. What are the cultic affiliations of these villages? What kind of socio-economic organisation prevailed in them, and how did it impact the resource mobilisation pattern of the *Mahāvihāra*? Were these aspects of such villages finding their ways into the *Mahāvihāra*? My archaeological survey was also motivated by the need to understand these issues. During survey, I came across a village, called Bārā (under Silao Police Station; Block Ben in Nālandā district), which is situated at a distance of approximately seven kilometers to the southwest of the *Mahāvihāra*. I identified it with *Vārakīya –grāma-jānapadasya* ('village corporation of *Vārakīya*') mentioned in the Nālandā seals. This village, containing a big mound, is studded with Red Ware. In terms of general texture, this ware is quite similar to the Red Ware found within the *Mahāvihāra* in the post-Gupta phase. Early historic occupation is indicated by the presence of Northern Black Polished Ware, Black- and – Red Ware and ringwells. Early historic occupation pattern of the site appears to be impressive, and we see a further expansion of the settlement during the early medieval phase. If this kind of prosperous villages were granted to the *Mahāvihāra*, we can easily imagine the wealth flowing to the same. This village has an extant *stūpa*; an early Pala period image of *Tārā* in *abhayamudrā*; and miniature images of the Buddha and some other miniature sculptures in the niches of the *stūpa*. This image of Tārā is under active worship now, and her tiara is covered with a thick layer of vermillion. Due to this factor, I could not have a proper identification of the *Dhyānī* Buddha present in her tiara. As such, I could not be sure of which particular form of Tārā this sculpture represented. I also came across some mature Pala period images of *Viṣṇu*, *Gaṇeśa* and *Sūrya* in the village. This village provides some important insights in understanding the religious negotiations in a village formally 'tied' (*pratibaddha*) to the *Mahāvihāra*. Even in a village, whose revenue was meant for the exclusive use of the *Mahāvihāra*, landscape was polyreligious. Buddhism was living under the shadow of well-entrenched Brahmanism. The same villagers, who catered to some of the material needs of the *Mahāvihāra* and worshipped *Tārā* and other Buddhist deities, also paid their homage to different Brahmanical deities. Both religions were present in the landscape and they competed for space within the same. Yet Brahmanism survived in the long run, and Buddhism could not. Some clues to this perplexing phenomenon may be found in the trajectories of subsequent history of the *stūpa* and the image of *Tārā* of Bārā. It must be asserted that this cult spot is still called "*Ugratārā* temple" by local villagers. Name of the goddess – *Ugratārā* – continued, but in a Hinduised form. This site gradually became an exclusive Hindu site, and the image of *Tārā* is being worshipped as a Hindu goddess now. A Brahmin priest takes care of daily rituals. This metamorphosis is the result of the extinction of Buddhist monasteries. Till the monasteries were active, Buddhism was able to retain its institutional distinctiveness. With the collapse of the monasteries, nothing was left to resist the irreversible slide of Buddhism into various folk and Brahmanical cults. This is the inference I deduced in the case of Bārā. This inference may or may not be true for other parts of India. We need more micro studies to confirm or contradict this inference. For a detailed analysis of data from Bārā, see Birendra Nath Prasad, *et.al.*, 'Bārā: A Recently Discovered Site in Nalanda District and Its Bearings on the Decline of Indian Buddhism,' in B. Labh (ed.),*The Ocean of Buddhist Wisdom*, Vol. 4, Delhi, 2009, pp. 225-234.

196. Lars Fogelin, *op. cit.*, p. 377.

3

BUDDHISM IN A REGIONAL PERSPECTIVE
A Glance at Early Historic Vidarbha

RESHMA SAWANT

Maharashtra can be divided, archaeologically, into two zones– (a) Vidarbha (extreme eastern part of the state of Maharashtra) and, (b) Rest of Maharashtra.[1] In Vidarbha protohistoric human settlement began around the beginning of first millennium BCE at the Chalcolithic levels, as evidenced at sites like Tulajapur Garhi,[2] Adam,[3] Arambha,[4] and Shirkanda.[5] But at majority of sites of Vidarbha, human occupation started from Iron Age period characterized by megalithic burial. In rest of Maharashtra, after the decline of Chalcolithic cultures, early historical habitation began during the Mauryan period but majority of known sites belong to the Sātavāhana period.

The Vidarbha region forms the eastern part of Maharashtra and presently comprises eleven districts of Maharashtra, viz., Buldhana, Akola, Washim, Amaravati, Yevatmal, Wardha, Nagpur, Bhandara, Chandrapur, Gondia and Gadchiroli (Fig. 1). The river Wardha forms a natural line of division for Vidarbha, creating two zones, viz. the Western Vidarbha and the Eastern Vidarbha. Western zone includes the districts of Amravati, Buldhana, Yevatmal and Akola. This zone has considerably high plains and hills, except in the nuclear portion of the Purna valley. The Eastern Vidarbha comprising the remaining districts primarily has a landscape of low elevation and irregular hills and slow-moving streams.

Previous Researches

The excavated sites from Vidarbha, for which published data is available, are Kaundinyapur,[6] Paunar,[7] Takalaghat–Khapa,[8] Pauni,[9] Mahurjhari,[10] Mandhal,[11] Nagara,[12] Khairwada,[13] Naikund,[14] Bhagimohari,[15] Tharsa,[16] Arni,[17] Arambha,[18] Adam,[19] Shirkhand,[20] Pachkheri,[21] Bhawar,[22] Hamlapuri,[23] Mansar,[24] Bramhapuri (district Chandrapur),[25] Bhon[26] (district Buldhana), Kholapur[27] (district Amaravti) and others. As far as Buddhist presence in Vidarbha is concerned, which is the main focus of this paper, excavations at Pauni[28] (Bhandara district), Adam[29] (Nagpur district), Mansar,[30] and recently at the site of Bhon[31] (Buldana district) have unearthed the evidence of *stupa* structures. New discoveries in the form of Buddhist sculptures or rock-cut caves have also been reported.[32] These studies notwithstanding, Buddhism in early historic Vidarbha has never been a main object of any detailed study. But a few researches are worth mentioning, such as, an article by S.B. Deo[33] focusing on Hīnayāna Buddhism in Vidarbha. Pradeep Meshram[34] has also looked into various aspects such as the architecture of Buddhist caves, sculpture, and reading of inscriptions.

Before the advent of Buddhism: Early Iron Age Megalithic culture (700 - 300 BCE)

Vidarbha is located on a very strategic position forming a link between northern and southern India. This locational advantage seems to have proved very useful for cultural diffusion from north and south in Vidarbha. Numerous cultural currents passed through Vidarbha which cultivated reciprocal relationship and induced developments in various fields. This brought Vidarbha in political orbit of India from the very early stages of historical period. It has also been observed that the

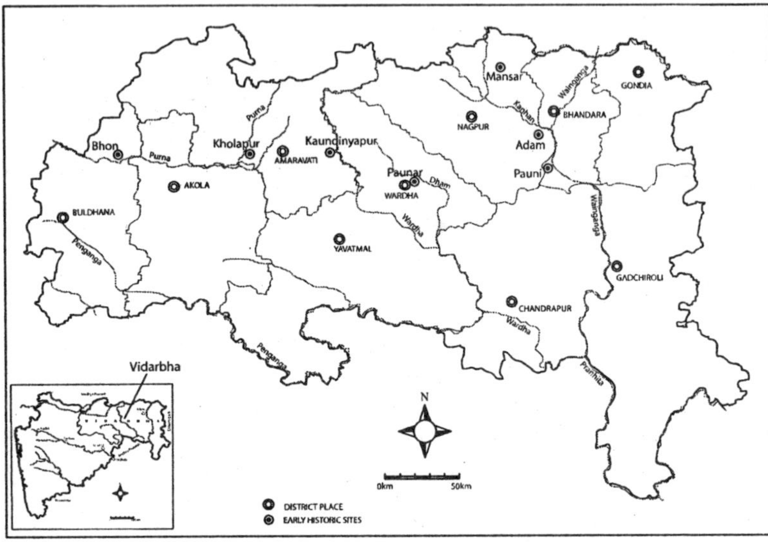

Fig. 1: Vidarbha region and important Early Historic Sites

Chalcolithic and the early Iron Age-Megalithic sites are located in the districts of Nagpur, Chandrapur, Bhandara and Gadchiroli. A very large number of megalithic burials (burial types: stone circles, menhirs, and sarcophagus) as well as habitation sites occur in the eastern part of Vidarbha from 7th - 6th centuries BCE onward. Within Vidarbha, a particular heavy concentrations of sites with numerous megaliths are noticed in the district of Nagpur. Most of the sites are located in a 50km radius from Nagpur city. They include Kamptee (21° 14 N; 71° 15′E), Junapani (21° 12′ N; 79° 00′ E), Mahurjhari (21° 14′N; 79° 30′E), Takalaghata Khapa (20° 54′ 40″ N; 78° 56′ 30″ E), Naikund (21° 20′ N; 79° 10′ E), Borgaon (21° 20′N; 78° 55′ E), and Bhagimahari (21° 24′ N; 78° 51′ E), Raipur (21° 5′N; 78° 58′ E), excavated in varying degrees over the years. Of these, Takalaghata-Khapa, Naikund, Bhagimahari, and Mahurjhari have habitational mounds. The rest are exclusively burial sites. Some sites are only habitation sites: Kaundinyapur (20° 55′ N; 78° 05′ E), Arni (20° 4′ N; 78° 57′ E), and Tharsa (21° 15′ N; 21° 15′ E). The dates for the middle levels of megalithic habitations at Takalaghat[35] are 615 $\pm$ 105 BCE and 465 $\pm$ 90

BCE. They, thus, help in assigning the Megaliths and habitations to a period between 7th and 5th centuries BCE.

The early Iron Age in Vidarbha witnessed a great progress in craft specialization in metal art, lapidary or pottery. The relative progress in the use of metals suggests that the need for these was becoming quite considerable and the reason behind this may be related to either military, agricultural, or increasing exchange needs. The same phenomenon applies to the period of early Iron Age in Vidarbha. The wide range of iron and copper implements and variety of ornaments in gold, lapidary art of excellent artistic skill support this observation. The grave goods associated with megalithic burials of the early Iron Age of Vidarbha exhibits their artist's skill. On the basis of numerous and variety of artifacts, there seem to be distinct classes of artisans and craftsmen like blacksmith, coppersmith, goldsmith, potter, cobbler, carpenter, highly skilled craftsmen in lapidaries, etc. It is interesting to note that at Naikund three copper bells are recovered from one of the stone circle having domical body which is made out of thick sheets of copper, and the clappers of iron riveted to them internally. In another instance, the copper tongue has been attached with iron rivets.[36] This bimetal technological advancement in craftsmanship is noteworthy.

Apart from craft specialization, the archaeozoological evidences furnished use of cattle, sheep and a unique evidence of horse (as status symbol/ transportation facility), which show significant importance of animal husbandry. Along with this, a few more important developments are noticed at the sites like Adam and Bhagimohari, indicating agricultural intensification. Bhagimohari, a burial-cum-habitation site of Iron Age, has yielded cultivated species like barley, lentil, common pea and grass pea as winter crop and rice, common bean, horse gram, and black gram among the monsoon (summer) crop, suggesting that the early Iron Age inhabitants not only knew and developed the agricultural skill, but also carried out their farming operations during both summer (*kharif*) and winter (*rabbi*) seasons. Rice had perhaps become the commonest ingredient of the staple during the 1st millennium BCE.[37] The site of Adam yielded domestic rice, grass pea, leguminous cotyledons, weed species, Indian jujube, beleric myrabolan, etc. from the early Iron Age levels. Of the two early Iron Age megalithic sites, Naikund and Khairwada, the former has yielded evidence for rice, wheat, barley, black gram and Indian jujube and latter furnished the evidence for rice, weeds of cultivation.[38] These evidences definitely indicate fairly developed agricultural economy during the early Iron Age period. The gradual spread of iron technology is given as the one of the reasons for intensification of agriculture which also made it possible the necessary surplus for the production of commodities for exchange.[39]

The wide range of iron implements found in the burials and the habitation sites and the discovery of iron-smelting furnace led the scholars to experiment and to check whether Naikund was producing iron implements and had exchange with other sites. It yielded an interesting results suggesting that the iron objects from Mahurjhari, Khapa, Gangapur, and Borgaon had been produced at Naikund.[40] The site of Mahurjhari has yielded a large-scale carnelian, jasper, and agate beads of different varieties. This site is regarded as a bead manufacturing centre of early Iron Age. Similarly the site of Raipur is also labeled as a bead making centre, but not as big as that of Mahurjhari. The study also put forward that the bead-making centres referred above possibly had exchange mechanism with other centres like Takalaghat-Khapa, Naikund and Khairwada.[41] A few gold objects are also reported from megalithic sites. Since no known source for gold is traceable in nearby region, tentatively it is assumed that gold came from Kolar mines of Karnataka. It has been observed that the Chalcolithic communities of western Deccan were using marine shell. The presence of these shells especially *Turbinella pyrum* or sacred conch shell at the Chalcolithic sites, majority of them in the form of bangles, was probably result of long distance trade or through contact with coastal communities. The *Turbinella pyrum* species are found on coral reef areas in Gulf of Kachchh on the Gujarat coast, Gulf of Khambhat, Palk of Bay and Gulf of Mannar.[42] Similar exploitation and use of shells has been observed during early historical period of western Deccan.[43] Though shell remains from excavated sites of the protohistoric and early historical period from Vidarbha are not studied in specific, the archaeological evidences from these sites indicate similar nature of procurement of shells by the communities. The sites like Adam,[44] Shirkanda,[45] and Bramhapuri[46] have yielded the evidence of marine shell objects in the form of bangles or beads, indicating long distance exchange.

The period of circa 500-300 BCE witnessed the use of punch-marked coins in limited scale as very few coins are reported from Vidarbha region. Coins are reported from: unknown place in Vidarbha[47]; Bramhapuri[48] (district Chandrapur); Akola, Bhandara and Yevatmal[49]; Umrer[50] (district Nagpur) etc.

In my doctoral research, I have attempted to show that Aśmaka *mahājanapada* was situated in the Wardha–Winganga valley and its cultural material can be identified with early Iron Age-Megalithic culture of Vidarbha.[51] This period is marked by agro-pastoral economy with craft specialization; extensive and creative use of metals like iron and copper; use of horse and horse ornaments; intra-regional exchange/trade; and a widespread ideology of erecting megaliths over the dead.

Thus, during c. 7th–3rd centuries BCE, when north India was experiencing the emergence of urbanization, Vidarbha witnessed a coexistence of agro-pastoral way of life in the form of *Janapada* formation and interwoven community of megalithic builders.

Advent of Buddhism: Mauryan and pre-Sātavāhana period (300 BCE - 100 BCE)

Vidarbha region gradually evolved from the early Iron Age pre-literate society to early historic literate society, which set new path for development. This has been observed in the Mauryan and pre-Sātavāhana period (c. 300-100BCE). The interaction with northern India amplified as Magadha based dynasties turned towards southern India as a part of their

Table 3.1

Details of excavated sites which have yielded Mauryan and pre-Sātavāhana deposits

Site	*Cultural Material*	*References*
Adam (*tehsil*: Kuhi, district: Nagpur)	Excavation has yielded burnt brick structures; remains of public drainage system. Pottery consists of micaceous red and black-and-red wares, besides a solitary example of Northern Black Polished Ware. Other important antiquities are: punch-marked coins; hand-made figurines, both human and animals, some with appliquÈ features; few etched carnelian beads; beads of crystal, agate and terracotta; iron implements, etc. A stupa was also discovered.	IAR 1988-89: 50-62; 1990-91: 45-50; 1991-92: 63-68; Nath 1992: 69-79
Arambha (*tehsil*: Samudrapur, district: Wardha)	Black-and-red ware bowls and dishes and a tiny Northern Black Polished sherd of a bowl are reported. Fragments of bangle, crystal bead, whetstone and fragment of iron rod are also reported.	IAR 1991-92: 73-74 IAR 1978-79: 71-72; 1984-85: 55-56
Arni (*tehsil*: Arni, district: Yevatmal)	Northern Black Polished sherd. No other details are available.	
Bhawar (district: Bhandara)	Pottery assemblage consists of red ware, which continued with certain innovations in the form of micaceous red ware with application of red and brown slip. The ceramic shapes included storage jars and vases, basins, dish-on-stand, huge bowls with inverted rims. Some of the important antiquities are grinding stone, iron knives, points, rods and few terracotta beads, etc.	IAR 1992-93: 55-62
Bhon (district Buldhana)	The excavation has yielded large scale structural activity in the form of — Brick *stūpa*, brick wells and terracotta ring wells,	

	residential as well as commercial structures, irrigation canal, etc. Few sherds of NBP are reported. Other important antiquities are beads of terracotta, carnelian, quartz, jasper; copper antimony rods; carnelian finger ring etc. (stupa structure will be discussed in later paragraphs)	Deotare *et al.* 2007, 2008
Bramhapuri (*tehsil*: Bramhapuri, district: Chandrapur)	Pottery of this period consists of black-and-red ware, slipped and unslipped red ware. The important antiquities are: *Janapada* silver punch-marked coin; copper punch-marked coin; two terracotta animal figurines; and beads.	Sawant 2006
Kaundinyapura (*tehsil*: Chandur, district: Amaravati)	Three sherds of NBP are found. Other important antiquities are: eye bead; earplugs of jasper, glass and terracotta; spindle whorls in terracotta; small arrow head; part of javelin; chisel of iron; miniature bell; antimony rod; punch-marked coins etc.	Dikshit 1968
Kholapur (district: Amaravati)	Two pieces of jet black Northern Black Polished (NBP) ware and punch-marked coin of locally issued type are reported.	Deotare 2008
Mansar (*tehsil*: Ramtek, district: Nagpur)	Pottery type of this period include micaceous red ware, slipped and unslipped red ware and large number of red polished ware particularly spouted vessels and sprinklers, etc. Antiquities include: beads of semi-precious stone and terracotta; bangles; iron objects— pestles, mullers and grinders, etc.; a *trinetra* Parvati; a turbaned male head; and Siva-Parvati with bull. A stupa structure was also discovered.	Joshi and Sharma 2005
Pachkheri (*tehsil*: Kuhi, district:	The Mauryan layers (6-5) brought to light a few associated red wares showing vases of Ahicchatra 10A type and black-and-red ware	

Site	*Cultural Material*	*References*
Nagpur)	bowls, which generally occur in the NBPW cultural horizon in the Gangetic plains. The ceramic traditions include a coarse dull red ware and micaceous red ware. Important antiquities are iron sickle, ring fastener, terracotta annular bead and an earstud.	IAR 1991-92: 64-73
Pauni (district: Bhandara)	The second phase of rampart was constructed during this period. The pottery of this period included a few NBP sherds besides the black-and-red and red wares. Beads of stone, ivory and terracotta, besides bone comb, points and copper bangles and a silver punch-marked coin were recovered. The structural remains like ring wells and mud floors are exposed during āunga Period (Period III) along with some important antiquities such as stone, glass and terracotta beads, copper antimony rod, bone stylus, terracotta wheels and skin rubbers, an etched carnelian bead and well carved ivory hair pin, etc. Few terracotta figurines of typical āunga style are also reported. These are made of single moulds showing plaques with flat back, displaying typical āunga attire and ornamentation. A stupa structure was also discovered.	Nath 1998

expansionist policy. This resulted in number of changes in social, economic, political and religious fields. These changes are quite evident from available archaeological and literary data. However, the most important change was the arrival of Buddhism in this land during the Mauryan period. The most important visible outcome of this penetration is the remains of *stūpa* structure at various sites. Before dealing with this aspect, we will take a review of excavated sites of Vidarbha region which have yielded Mauryan and pre-Sātavāhana habitation.

Stūpa sites from Vidarbha

A legend has been furnished by Hiuen Tsang (also spelt as Yuan Chwang) that Aśoka constructed 84000 *stūpas* or topes are generally said to have been for the distribution of the Buddhas relics taken for the purpose by the king from seven of the eight topes erected by the original recipients.[52] Whether to believe in this legend is difficult to answer, but one may definitely state that during Aśoka's time Buddhism attained new heights. The religious establishments at Pauni,[53] Ter,[54] Bhon,[55] Amaravati,[56] Nagarjunkonda,[57] Bhattiprolu,[58] and Jaggayyapeta[59] could have been the direct or indirect consequences of Aśoka's full-hearted encouragement to Buddhism in Deccan. An early spread of Buddhism down the south and western Deccan was probably routed through Vidarbha. The region of Vidarbha produced four sites with *stūpa* structures. They are discussed in following paragraphs with their chronological appearance.

Pauni

The site of Pauni (20° 48'N; 79° 39'E) (district Bhandara, Maharashtra) is 82 km due southeast of Nagpur. It was excavated by Nagpur University in collaboration with the Archaeological Survey of India.[60] The site was excavated for two seasons (1969 and 1970). One of the locality known as Jagannatha Tekdi yielded remains of *stūpa* complex. The structural phases of *stūpa* broadly fall into three phases.[61] (Fig. 2):

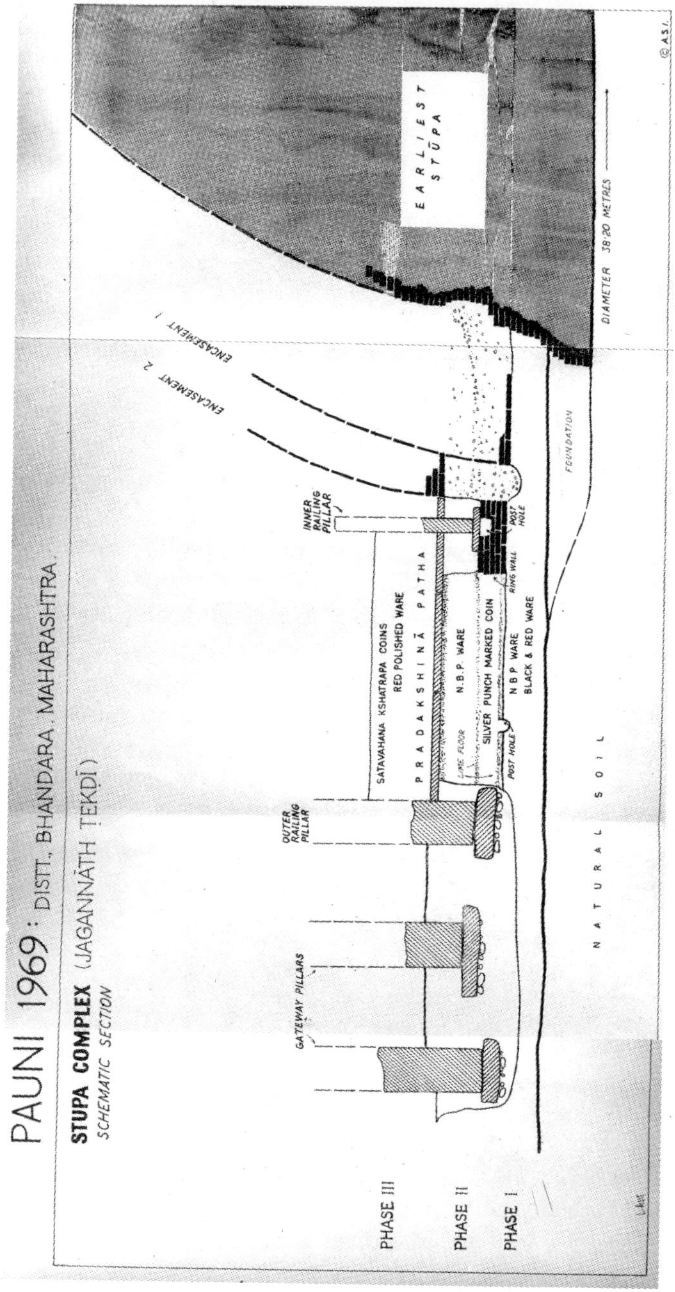

Fig. 2: Plan of Pauni *Stūpa* (after Deo and Joshi 1972)

Phase I Mauryan	i. Original *stūpa* (original diameter 38.20 mt, brick size 40 x 37 x 10 cm)
Phase II Śunga	ii. The first encasement,
	iii. The lime *Pradakṣhiṇā patha* with wooden railing,
	iv. Five course brick ring with wooden ring
	v. Stone stump railing,
	vi. *Pradakṣhiṇā patha* (maximum width 2.78 mt) withtonelabs, outer railing, gateways, pillar Phase III Sātavāhana-Kṣatrapa
	vii. Repairs and renovations on a limited scale

This excavation has yielded number of inscriptions on coping stone, octagonal pillars of the outer railing, *sucis* or horizontal bars etc. Most of the them are of one line and they record donations made by individuals. None of these inscriptions refer, even indirectly, to any king, royal officers or any member of the royal family. That forces us to conclude that these structures were able to survive and expand due to their intricate linkages with the common population.

Various sculptural remains are also reported in the form of anthropomorphic (human, *yakṣa*) floral, geometric, and religious motifs.[62]

Bhon

The site of Bhon (20° 55′ N; 76° 39′ E) is situated on the right bank of the river Purna in Sangrampur *taluka* of Buldhana district, Maharashtra. This site was excavated by Deccan College for five seasons (2003 to 2007). The excavation has unearthed brick built *stūpa* remains (Fig. 3). The diameter of *stūpa* is 14 m including *Pradakṣhiṇā patha*. The dome is completely absent. The *Pradakṣhiṇā patha* is around 1.75 m in breadth forming five rows of bricks. The brick sizes are restricted to

Fig. 3: Remains of *Stūpa* at Bhon (Courtesy: Dr. B.C. Deotare)

two dimensions i.e. 40 x 26 x 22 x 8 cm and 52 x 28 x 24 x 8 cm. The outermost brick row of *Pradakṣhiṇā patha* has peculiar symbols incised on it. Post-holes are also noted on the outermost row of *Pradakṣhiṇā patha,* which probably indicates the existence of wooden railing around the *stūpa*. No relic casket has been found but bottommost levels of *stūpa* yielded few potsherds, a bone point and lot of charcoal. This charcoal is dated to 2180±90 years BP. According to the excavator, the structural *stūpa* at Bhon is of 3rd century BCE. It is likely to be the earliest *stūpa* in Maharashtra.[63]

Mansar

The site of Mansar (21° 24′ N; 79° 17′ E) (*tehsil*: Ramtek, district: Nagpur) was excavated by the Archaeological Survey of India. At the locality called Hidimba Tekdi of Mansar, at the depth of 3.90m built right over bed rock, portion of a brick built *stūpa,* having diameter of 8m, was exposed. The size of bricks used for the *stūpa* is 46 x 22 x 7cm. The nature of evidence of fallen debris in a particular fashion indicates that this *stūpa* was destroyed by an earthquake. Immediately after the destruction of original *stūpa* (*stūpa* I) in period IB another *stūpa* was built, this time by creating boxes which were filled up with small boulders, brick bats and earth. In one of the boxes, thirty-four courses of bricks measuring 42 x 22 x 8cm were exposed. The base and knob of a lime stone relic casket were recovered from the area of *stūpa*. These two *stūpas* were constructed during the late Maurya and the early Śunga period. Also of this period, on the south-eastern corner of Hidimba Tekdi, a brick built oblong *chaitya* has been exposed.[64]

Adam

The site of Adam (21° 00′ N; 79° 28′ E) was excavated by the Archaeological Survey of India. A locality called Devi Hudki (ADM - 2) yielded remains of a *stūpa*. The earthen *stūpa* was built over with two distinct phases of construction. Circular on plan, the *stūpa* consisted of drum (*medhi*) (radius 17.30m) and dome (*aṇḍa*) (radius 10.30m) which atop the basal remains of a square *harmikā* (3.50m); in the centre of it was noticed a ring stone once supporting the *yas?i* of a *chhatrāvali*. This *stūpa* did not yield any relic casket. It is dated to c. 1st century CE on the basis of coins. According to the excavators, 'assigned to two phases of period V the *stūpa* of earlier phase was built over layer (5) whereas towards the later phase the restoration took place on the top layer (4). In earlier phase a L-shaped pathway (9.80 x 0.40 m) leading to the *stūpa* was demarcated with a single coursed shale stone wall whereas in the later phase the same was indicated by a brick wall (22.20 x 1.20 m); mud as mortar remained common to both the phases.'[65]

Epigraphic Data

On the basis of available evidences the spread of Buddhism in the region of Vidarbha can be traced back to Mauryan period, especially during Aśoka's reign. The Ceylonese Chronicle *Mahāvamsa* contributes to our knowledge regarding the third Buddhist Council, which met during the reign of Aśoka at his capital Pāṭaliputra. According to the text, the Council dispatched missionaries for propagating Buddhism in various countries. Some of the missionaries and related regions are listed here. They are: *Majjhantika* to Kashmir and Gāndhāra, *Mahādeva* to Mahiṣa-Maṇḍala, *Rakṣita* to Vanavāsi, *Dharmarakṣita* to Aparantaka, *Maharakshita* to Yavana country, *Sona* and *Uttara* to Suvarṇabhūmi, *Majjhima* to Himavata region and *Mahendra* and others to Lanka. *Mahādhamarakṣita* was sent to the region of Maharashtra.[66] Even though there is no direct mention by Aśoka having sent a missionary to the region of Vidarbha as such, but some recent evidences testifies to the Buddhist contacts with this region such as Deotek stone slab inscription of Mauryan period.

Deotek Inscription

Deotek is a small village in Chandrapur district, about 50 miles southeast of Nagpur. It contains an old temple in a decaying condition and a large stone slab bearing two epigraphs. Out of the two inscriptions, one dates back to the time of *Aśoka*[67] and the other to that of the Vākāṭakas. The inscription dated to Mauryan period is a four line inscription with characters of the early Brahmi alphabet resembling in many cases to those of the Girnar edicts of Aśoka. The language is early Prakrit; similar to the one used in the Girnar edicts. The object of inscription was to record the command of some lord (*Sāmi*) prohibiting the capture and slaughter (evidently of some animals in certain seasons as in Aśoka's Fifth pillar edict, or may be throughout the year) and declaring some punishment for those who dared to disobey it. The third line mentions executive officers (*amācha = amātyah*) whose duty might have been to enforce these orders. The last line contains the date 14, denoting probably the regnal year in which the record was incised. In some of his inscriptions (e.g. Rupanath Rock Inscription) Aśoka ordered his officers to get his edicts engraved on stone pillars, rocks and stone slabs throughout the districts in their charge. The Deotek inscription probably is the only instance of its kind. According to V.V. Mirashi,[68] the present edict may have been issued by a *Dharmamahāmātra* in the 14th year after the coronation of *Aśoka*.

Other Miscellaneous Inscriptions

At Pauni, remains of a very flourishing Hīnayāna Buddhist establishment have been brought to light. In terms of antiquity, this establishment could go back to late Mauryan and early Śunga period. This establishment comprised of two *stūpas* (one at Jagannath mound and the other at Chandkapura, which is about a mile due south of Pauni) and the remains of possible brick-built monastery in the regions adjacent to these *Stūpa*. Inscriptions associated with these *stūpas* do not mention any king or any other royal person. People, mostly from the merchant community, seem to have donated for the upkeep of the *stūpa*. It is apparent that such a magnificent centre patronized on a grand scale by the trading community must have attracted a large community of *bhikkhus* from different parts of Vidarbha and elsewhere.[69]

Some rock-cut caves are located about six miles from the village of Mandhal about forty miles due east of Nagpur.

Inscription recorded here are dated to c. 2nd century BCE. These are so far the earliest caves with inscriptions in the Vidarbha region. There are two inscribed records: one is longer and in two lines, the other is short and of one word only. Inscribed lines are:

".... sa Vandalaka putasa
Apalasa matikamam"

Meaning: '... (the cave is) the work of Apala, the son of Vandalaka.....'

It is interesting to note some resembling names are found in inscriptions elsewhere in Vidarbha. Pradeep Meshram[70] of Nagpur University discovered Brahmi inscription of *c.* 1st century BCE at Pullar in Bhiwapur *tehsil* in Nagpur district. The inscription founded engraved on a stone pillar lying in the fields near a rock cut cave, contains four letters and reads: *"Vandalasa"*

Also at Pauni, inscription no. 30, which is on fragmentary stone, reads-

"Nadana gahapatino putasa
Valanakasa pasado"

This refers to the gift by Valanaka, who was the son of the householder (*gahapati*) Nandana. Incidentally, this is the only record at Pauni, which refers specifically to the "*gahapati.*"[71] On the basis of the evidence in the excavations at Pauni and explorations of the rock-cut caves in the Chandala forest, it may be stated that the Vidarbha region came under influence of Hīnayāna Buddhism in the Maurya period.[72] Recently, Maharashtra State Department of Archaeology and Ancient Indian History, Culture and Archaeology department of Nagpur University jointly read the stone inscription of the period of Aśoka near Bhivkund (3 km from Adam) near Mandhal. This Brahmi inscription is on the ceiling of the Pandava caves. Inscription reads- '*ea ta ma va cchi.*'[73]

(IV)

Mauryas in Vidarbha: Sphere of Influence

According to the Purāṇas, the founder of the Nanda dynasty Mahāpadma Nanda exterminated the entire Kṣatriya race. The Kṣatriya dynasties which were uprooted by him were Aikshvāku, Pānchāla, Kāśī, Haihaya, Kalinga, Kuru, Mithilā, Surasena, Vitihotra and Aśmaka.[74] Therefore the annexation of *Aśmaka mahājanapadạ* by the Nandas probably brought Vidarbha under the influence of Magadha based empires.[75] The existence of a city called *Navananda Dehra* (modern Nanded) on the Godavari has been pointed out by scholars to indicate Nanda supremacy over considerable parts of the Deccan.[76] One may think as to why Nanda rulers felt it necessary to annex this region. It is likely that the growing Magadhan Empire must have experienced resource crunch. The Mauryas faced a similar situation later. As a result of this, probably the Magadha rulers were attracted towards South India and Vidarbha. Probably what had attracted the Nandas in early age and the Mauryas at a later stage were the large scale iron ore deposit and mineral sources in Vidarbha and other lucrative sources of far south for which they had to cross through Vidarbha, therefore, bringing this area under their influence was essential. Mahāpadma Nanda annexed Aśmaka and other areas for extermination of Kṣatriyas. Probably expansion of Magadhan empire for rich resources must have been the concealed reason behind his expansionist policy. Same strategy seems to have adopted by the Mauryas. The widened trade orbit and increasing demands of their own state had forced the Mauryas to search for resources of raw material, minerals and lucrative objects in neighboring areas where they could satisfy their needs without imposing direct, centralized rule over the same. Therefore, as S. Seneviratne appropriately described, Mauryas maintained relations with bordering areas as "power to collect homage and tribute" and "not the power to organize all political affairs of a large and in principle precisely delimitable area."[77]

What this period reflects is the absence of any significant

known power in Vidarbha. The Aśmakas, though literally got annexed by the Nandas, but the possibility of its survival in submissive nature cannot be denied. Probably some other local chiefs also must have been getting heavy hands over the conditions and trying to establish a small rule. There is no evidence of direct rule of Mauryas, but there are evidences of long distance trade which required some local administrative functionary to carry it efficiently. Archaeological evidences support long distance trade in the form of Punch-marked coins of Magadha-Maurya, Ujjain-Eran coins, cast coins of Taxila, etc. Some antiquities having Mauryan influence like eye bead, decorated legged quern, structural developments like Stupa, ring-wells (indicating development of urban traits) cannot exist without an active role of local powers in Vidarbha. Therefore this period has been labeled as 'Sphere of Influence' which reflects the active role of the Mauryas in the region of Vidarbha but without disturbing or interfering local political set up. The Mauryan presence has been recognized by the presence of things like NBPW, punch-marked coin, spread of Buddhist institutions (*stūpa*), typical Mauryan antiquities like eye beads, etc., which had come through the trade orbit expanded by the Mauryas. The subsequent period saw the emergence of powerful local powers in the Vidarbha after the collapse of the Mauryan Empire.

Period of decentralization of power: Emergence of local rulers and city states

After the disintegration of Mauryan Empire India underwent many political changes. This period witnessed the emergence of new local powers in different parts of India, which can be therefore named as the 'Period of Decentralization of Power.' As far as Vidarbha is concerned, we see the emergence of local powers. Circa 2nd century BCE onwards, we get coins of Bhadra, Mitra and coins of unknown local rulers (e.g. from Bhon) along with coins issued by some cities (e.g. Bhadravati). But this emergence of local rulers proved favorable for the development of Vidarbha in general. Earlier period (Mauryan period) was marked by an absence of any significant local ruler in this region. During the pre-Sātavāhana period there are considerable number of coin issues by local rulers, showing change and development in authority level which subsequently hastened such developments as regional and long distance trade (coin evidences from Bhon and Adam), general increase in standard of living in the form of structural developments (such as, widespread use of ring well, good quality bricks for houses, etc.) and material culture (evidences from Adam and Bhon) showing progressive urban traits. The pre-Sātavāhana period was a step further towards the state formation process and full-fledged urbanization. Subsequent period, i.e. the Sātavāhana period, experienced further development in state formation and urbanization process due to changes in various fields religious, social, economic, and political.

Megaliths, Buddhism and the Mauryas: Change in economic set up and expansion of trade

Undoubtedly, during the protohistoric and historic periods, the Vidarbha region, being a significant resource base, had its own importance. Moreover the strategic position of the region constituted a connecting link between northern and southern India. In early historic period political unity established by the Mauryas boosted trade. The trade with south India also intensified during this period, which is more visible if one looks the locations of Aśokan edicts which occur in large number in the peninsula and in the north India along routes leading to the peninsula.[78] As it is mentioned in *Arthaśāstra* (7.12.22-24), southern route was regarded as more profitable as gold, pearls, diamonds, semiprecious stones, and gems came from there.[79] South India, particularly gold bearing region of Karnataka, pearl producers like coastal Andhra Pradesh, and Gulf of Mannar, ivory, spices, semiprecious stones etc. provided lucrative resources for increasing Mauryan trade (regional and inter-continental). Vidarbha worked as gateway toward extreme south for Mauryas not only in religious mission but more importantly in trade mechanism.

The importance of the Vidarbha region as a significant

resource area was recognized during the protohistoric and historic times. In the *Arthaśāstra* (2.11.37) *Sabharashtraka* comes as place from where diamonds could be obtained.[80] And *Sabharashtraka* is identified with Vidarbha in Bhattaswamin's commentary on the *Arthaśāstra*.[81] *Bṛhatsaṁhitā of* Varāhamihira mentions Vidarbha (XIV.8) as a region in south-eastern direction, which included modern Berar and the tract between the rivers Varada and Wainganga. The people of Vidarbha are referred to as Vaidarbha (IX.27). There is a mention of the river Vena (XVI.9) (modern Wainganga), a tributary of Godavari. Varāhamihira refers to its banks (IV.26), which were celebrated for diamond industry (LXXIX.6).[82] The Chandrapur Gazetteer mentions a place called Wairagad situated at the confluence of Kophragarhi and Sathatas in the Gadchiroli *tehsil* (now in Gadchiroli district). It is recorded that Wairagad once possessed diamond mines and are referred to in the 'Ain-i-Akabari' of Abul Fazal.[83] The importance of Wairagad (corrupted form of Vajragarh; Vajra means diamond) is reflected in some early South Indian Inscription.[84] Vajra or Vayiragaram is mentioned in Tamil literature and inscription. The earliest reference is perhaps in Tamil poem entitled *'Silappadigaram'* which is believed to have been written between 110 and 140 CE. It is stated in this poem that the Chola king Karikala was on terms of friendship with the Kings of Vajra, Magadha, and Avanti.[85] It is also noteworthy that the chief queen of Chedi King Kharavela was from Vajragadh.[86] It seems that because of strong political entity and producer of such valuable trading commodity(diamond), Vajragadh had very important role to play in contemporary trade. Apart from such items of trade mentioned in the literature, there might be following goods available for trade:

Thus, on the whole it is surmised that Vidarbha might have played an important role in the widening trade orbit during Mauryan period with its resources described above.

C] Religio-cultural aspects

The period before the arrival of Buddhism in Vidarbha has witnessed Megalithic culture which saw large scale

Table 3.2
Possible export items of trade from Vidarbha and South India

District	Possible items for export for inter-regional and long distance trade
1. Bhandara	Spices, lac, teak wood, silk (wild), raw iron as well as iron objects, food grains, bamboo objects and other forest products, etc.
2. Chandrapur and Gadchiroli	Iron, mica, ochre, pottery, diamond, silk (wild), lime and forest products, etc.
3. Nagpur	Copper, coal, gold, iron, lead, limestone, mica, gems and semi-precious stone (raw material or finished beads), bamboo objects, etc.
4. South India	Gold, diamond, pearls, salt, shells, semi-precious stones (raw material or finished beads), coral, spices, ivory, etc.

construction of megalithic burials in the form of circles, menhirs, and sarcophagus. Other than these ritualistic buildings over the dead, we have very less or negligible data available about religious beliefs of the people of this period. With the advent of Buddhism in Vidarbha the scenario changed since it brought with it a whole new idea of philosophy, new religious structural settings, new contacts with varied groups of population (monks, traders, royal officials from the north etc.), and probably the new way of living or some developed concepts of urbanization from northern India.

Spread of ideas: Manifestation of Buddhist Symbolism

The interaction between different regions during Mauryan and subsequent periods significantly contributed to the spread of various ideas (artistic, religious, material, technology etc.) which recurrently occurred at various sites in early historic India. Some of the examples are given here.

The foremost example of spread of idea is the construction of *stūpa*. With the spread of tenets of Buddhism and the efforts of Aśoka, the concept of building of *stūpa* also spread all over

Indian subcontinent. The visible result is remains of *stūpa* structures, of mud or brick, small or big, all over India. The *stūpa* sites in Vidarbha are already discussed above.

The sites like Nasik, Adam, Bahal, Bhon, Pauni (all in Maharashtra), Kakarehta (Madhya Pradesh), Karvan (Gujarat), Panch-Pahari (Bihar), Sonkh (Uttar Pradesh), Taxila (Pakistan), have yielded few legged querns decorated with auspicious Buddhist symbols like *triratna, nandipāda, swastika, dharmachakra,* pair of fish (*mīn-yugma*), triangle-headed standard etc.[87] (Fig. 4). The provenance of this object from Maharashtra to Taxila, and up to Uttar Pradesh and Bihar signifies the popularity of this object. Though its function is not clear to us today. Only speculations can be made. The presence of auspicious symbols on these querns perhaps indicates ritualistic usage of these legged querns in the past.

Another very interesting feature has been noted at the site of Bhon. The outermost brick row of *Pradakṣhiṇā patha* of *stūpa* has three peculiar symbols, i.e. Brahmi *'ma,'* second is present day devanagari 'ṭa'; and third symbol somewhat looks like a *stūpa* structure, engraved on it (Fig. 5). Similar type of engraving on bricks is noted at the site of Navdatoli. The bricks of drum portion of Navdatoli *stūpa* bear some Brahmi letters (details about symbols are not published in report).[88] Few engraving on the bricks is also reported from the site of Kasrawad, however they are regarded as 'some irregular marks of the brick makers,'[89] but the possibility can not be ruled out of these being marks some letters or Buddhist symbols. The similarity in using the same idea, i.e. engraving symbols on bricks of *Pradakṣhiṇā patha,* is striking as these places are geographically quite far from one another. Hence interaction between these areas (due to trade contact or any other reason) must have played some role in imparting a similarity in these engraved decorations.

Third example is that of the *triratna* symbol. *Triratna* symbol represents the three important tenets of Buddhism, the Buddha, the *Dhamma,* and the *Saṅgha.* This symbol has been profusely and very artistically depicted not only on the *stūpa* decoration (from Sanchi, Bharhut to Nagarjunkonda) but

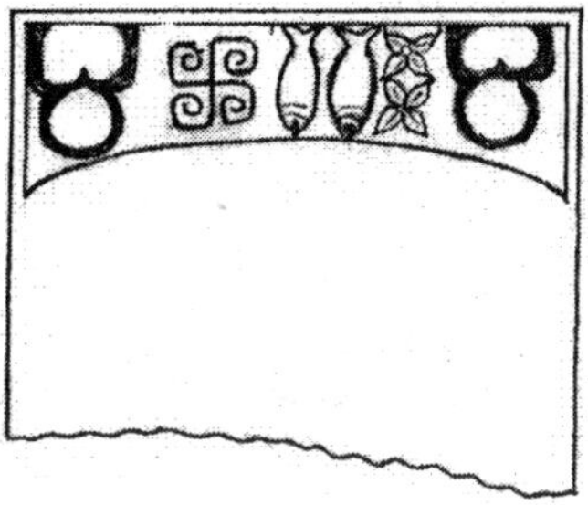

A. Bhon specimen

B. Nasik specimen

C. Taxila specimen

Fig. 4: Decorated legged querns from Nasik, Bhon and Taxila

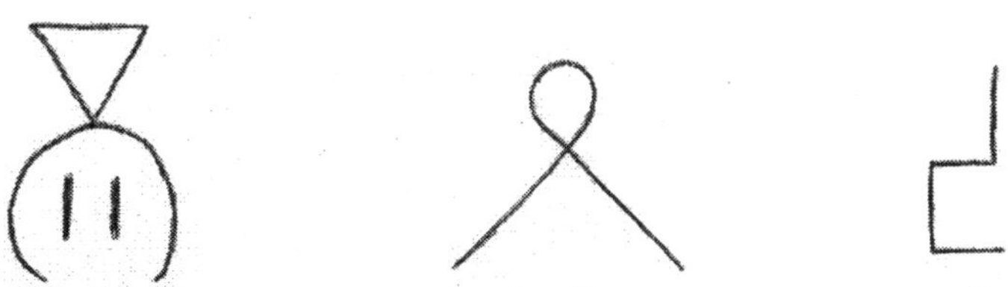

1. 2. 3.

Fig. 5: Symbols engraved on bricks of *Pradakshiṇāpatha*, Bhon
(Courtesy: Dr. B.C. Deotare)

Fig. 6a: From Bhon

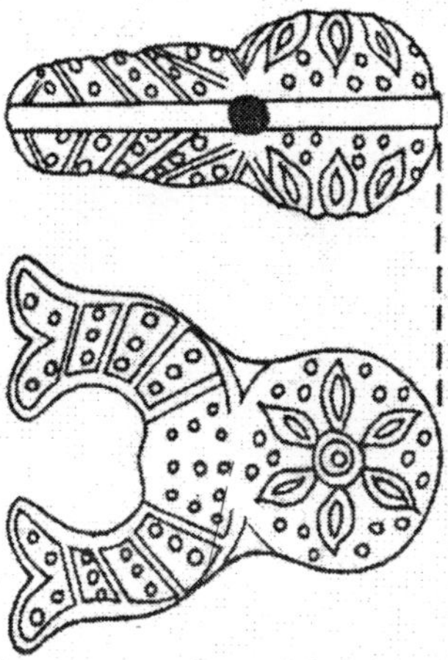

Fig. 6b: From Bhokardan

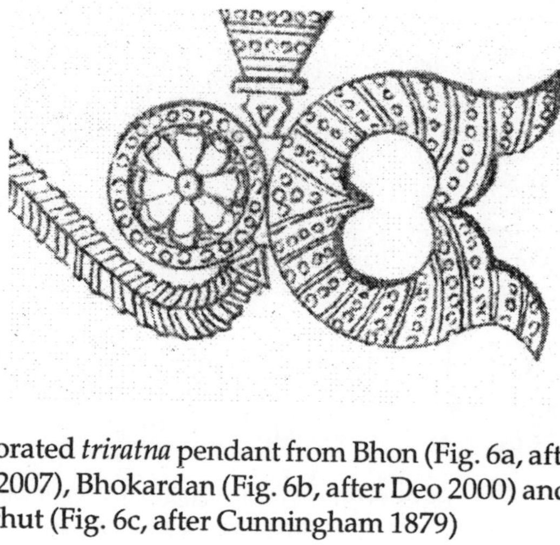

Fig. 6c: From Bharhut

Fig. 6a-6c: Decorated *triratna* pendant from Bhon (Fig. 6a, after Deotare *et al.* 2007), Bhokardan (Fig. 6b, after Deo 2000) and Bharhut (Fig. 6c, after Cunningham 1879) on various early historic objects like pottery, decorated legged querns, pendants, household objects, seals and sealings etc. The site of Bhon yielded almost twenty-five *triratna* pendants out of that, four pendants are highly decorated, similar to those exhibited in Bharhut panels (Fig. 6a-6c).

These are some representative examples of Buddhist symbolism manifested through various modes of expression in early historic period in Vidarbha along with the rest of Indian subcontinent. The spread of Buddhist ideology with unique similarities in artistic expression is outstanding in spatial and temporal context.

Patterns of patronage to Buddhist institutions

In western Maharashtra there are various groups of Buddhist monuments (caves, *stūpa*, vihāras), important are Bhaja, Karle, Bedase, Kuda, Kanheri, Pitalkhora, Junnar, Nasik, Ajanta etc. Majority of monastic structures received donations from traders (i.e. perfumer), guilds, professionals (i.e. physician), common people etc. The caves of Nasik (some 20 in number) owed their existence to the Sātavāhanas and the Kṣatrapas.[90] It is generally assumed that big religious establishments needed royal or mercantile backing to flourish. Interestingly, in the case of *stūpa* establishment at Pauni, it seems that this establishment was supported by the common population. Votive inscriptions from Pauni do not refer, even indirectly, to any kind of royal patronage. Even the names of any royal official do not figure as donor. So we may conclude that the Pauni *stūpa* was a monument revered and nourished by the common population.

Similarly the archaeological material from the site of Bhon is a good example of patronage provided by the royalty as well as the commoners. The *stūpa* structure, *triratna* pendants, *triratna* symbols on pottery, legged querns (decorated with auspicious Buddhist symbols), and symbols depicted on coins (i.e. tree-in-railing, wheel) are various forms through which an ideology of Buddhism recurrently comes in forefront.

Summing up

The development of Megalithic culture of early Iron Age in Vidarbha, Karnataka and Andhra Pradesh; the penetration of the Mauryan economy and administration on one hand and Buddhism on the other, have induced social changes. Increase in trade, extent of trade network, trader class, and ultimately change in economical background, may have accelerated changes towards the emergence of guild organization and their participation in donation activity for the benefit and spread of Buddhism. It was an important and visible change during this period. Buddhism, owing to its relatively liberal rules regarding social status and the counting of wealth, provided a suitable environment for facilitating long-distance trade. The enlarged trade orbit and encouraging religious policies under the Mauryas helped to spread Buddhism in south and the region of Vidarbha contributed its fair role in the contemporary scenario.

Acknowledgment

I am deeply grateful to Dr. B.C. Deotare, Deccan College, for giving me permission to attend the excavations of the site of Bhon, to study its material for my doctoral research and to use few illustrations for the present paper.

Notes

1. M.K. Dhavalikar, *Historical Archaeology of India*, New Delhi, 1999, p. 60.
2. B.P. Bopardikar, *Excavations at Tuljapur Garhi 1984-85 (Vidarbha, Maharashtra)*, New Delhi, 1996.
3. *IAR* 1990-91, 1991-92.
4. *IAR* 1991-92.
5. *IAR* 1991-92.
6. M.G. Dikshit, *Excavations at Kaundinyapur*, Bombay, 1968; S. Mishra, *et. al.*, '2000-2001 Excavations at Kaundinyapur, Wardha Valley,' *Proceedings of National seminar on Megalithic Tradition in Ethnography and Archaeology in India*, held by Indira

Gandhi Rashtriya Manav Sangrahalaya, Bhopal during 28th -30th Nov. 2005.

7. S.B. Deo and M.K. Dhavalikar, 'Report of Paunar Excavation (1967),' *Nagpur University Journal (Humanities)*, Vol. XVIII, Nos. 3 & 3, 1968.
8. S.B. Deo, *Excavations at Takalaghat and Khapa*, Nagpur, 1970.
9. S.B. Deo and J.P. Joshi, *Pauni Excavation (1969-70)*, Nagpur, 1972; A. Nath, *Further Excavations at Pauni*, New Delhi, 1998.
10. S.B. Deo, *Mahurjhari Excavations 1970-72*, Nagpur, 1973.
11. A.M. Shastri, 'Mandhal Utkhanan' (in Hindi), *Vidarbha Sanshodhan Mandal Varshik*, 20, 1978, pp. 142-174.
12. *IAR* 1979-80.
13. *IAR* 1981-82.
14. S.B. Deo and A.P. Jamkhedkar, *Excavations at Naikund 1978-80*, Bombay, 1982.
15. *IAR* 1982-83; 1983-84.
16. *IAR* 1989-90.
17. *IAR* 1984-85.
18. *IAR* 1991-92.
19. *IAR* 1989-90, 1990-91, 1991-92.
20. *IAR* 1991-92.
21. *IAR* 1991-92.
22. *IAR* 1992-93.
23. Chetan Sali, 'Vakataka Culture: Archaeological Perspective,' *Sanshodhak*, 1998, pp. 3-38.
24. *IAR* 1994-95; J.P. Joshi and A.K. Sharma, 'Excavation at Mansar, District Nagpur, Maharashtra – 1997-2000,' *Puratattva* 30, 2000, pp. 127-131; J.P. Joshi and A.K. Sharma, 'Mansar Excavation 1998-2004: The Discovery of Pravarapur,' *Puramanthan* (Pravarapur special) 3, 2005, pp. 1-26.
25. S.R. Walimbe, 'Excavations at the Early historic Site of Kahali-Bramhapuri,' *Deccan College Annual Report* (2001-2002), Pune, 2003, pp. 39-40.
26. B.C Deotare, Gurudas Shete, Reshma Sawant, Vaishali Kathale, S. Naik, 'Discovery of Structural Stupa at Bhon, District Buldana, Maharashtra,' *Puratattva*, 37, 2007, pp. 177-185; B.C Deotare, Gurudas Shete, Reshma Sawant and S. Naik, 'Ancient Irrigation Canal: Evidence from the Purna basin, Vidarbha Region of Maharashtra,' *Puratattva* 38, 2008, 210-216.
27. B.C. Deotare, 'Excavations at Kholapur, District Amravati, Maharashtra,' *Deccan College Annual Report* (2007-08), Pune, 2008.

28. S.B. Deo and J.P. Joshi, *Pauni Excavation (1969-70)*, Nagpur, 1972.
29. A. Nath, 'Archaeology of the Wardha Wainganga Divide,' *Puratattva* 20, 1989, pp. 93-98; A.Nath, 'Adam – an Index to Vidarbha Archaeology,' in B.U. Nayak and N. C. Ghosh (eds.), *New Trends in Indian Art and Archaeology*, Vol. I, New Delhi, 1992, pp. 69-79.
30. J.P. Joshi and A.K. Sharma, 'Mansar Excavation 1998-2004: the Discovery of Pravarapur,' *Puramanthan* (Pravarapur special) 3, 2005, pp. 1-26.
31. B.C Deotare, Gurudas Shete, Reshma Sawant, Vaishali Kathale, S. Naik, 'Discovery of Structural Stupa at Bhon, District Buldana, Maharashtra,' *Puratattva*, 37, 2007, pp. 177-185.
32. IAR 1994-95, p. 58; Pradeep Meshram, 'Vidarbhat Alikade Milalele Kahi Bauddha Puravashesha,' *Vidarbha Samshodhana Mandal* 1995, 38, pp. 155-166.
33. S.B. Deo, 'New Evidence of Hinayana Buddhism in Vidarbha,' *Puratattva*, 6, 1972-73, pp. 84-86.
34. Pradeep Meshram, *Vidarbhatil Buddha Dharmacha Itihaas*, Nagpur, 1993; Pradeep Meshram, *Vidarbhatil Bauddha Dharmakshetra- Pauni*, Yavatmal, 1994; Pradeep Meshram *et. al.*, *Kshitij Vaidarbhiya Paryatanache, Bhatala – Ek Upekshit Shilpgram*, Nagpur, 2005.
35. S.B.Deo, *Recent Researches on the Chalcolithic and Megalithic Cultures of the Deccan*, Madras, 1982, p. 37.
36. S.B. Deo and A.P. Jamkhedkar, *op. cit.*
37. M.D. Kajale, 'Archaeobotanical Investigation on Megalithic Bhagimohari and its Significance for Ancient Indian Agricultural System,' *Man and Environment*, Vol.XIII, 1989, pp. 87- 92.
38. M.D. Kajale, 'Archaeobotanical Investigation on Megalithic Bhagimohari and its Significance for Ancient Indian Agricultural System,' *Man and Environment* Vol. XIII, 1989, pp. 87-100; M.D. Kajale, 'Archaeobotanical Investigations on a Multicultural Site at Adam, Maharashtra, with Special Reference to the Development of Tropical Agriculture in Parts of India,' in J.G. Hather (ed.), *Tropical Archaeobotany: Applications and New Developments*, 1994, pp. 34-50.
39. S.Seneviratne,. 'The Mauryan State,' in H.J.M. Claessen and P. Skalnlk (ed.), *The Early State*, the Hague, 1978, p. 382.
40. V.D. Gogte, *et. al.*, '14 MeV Neutron Activation Analysis of Megalithic Iron Objects,' *Bulletin of Deccan College Research*

Institute 43, 1984, pp. 49-52.

41. P.S. Joshi, *The Vidarbha Megaliths: A Cultural Study*. Unpublished Ph.D. Dissertation submitted to University of Poona, Department of Archaeology, 1993, pp. 207-208.
42. J.M. Kenoyer, 'Shell Working at Mohenjo-daro Pakistan,' in J. Schotsmans and M. Taddei (ed.), *South Asian Archaeology* 1983, Naples, 1985, pp. 301; Arati Deshpande – Mukherjee, 'Marine shell utilization by the chalcolithic societies of Western Deccan region of India,' in Daniella E. Bar, Yoser Mayer (ed.), *Archaeomalacology*, Proceedings of the 9th conference of the international council of Archaeozoology, Durham, 2002, pp. 174-184.
43. See Arati Deshpande – Mukherjee, *op. cit.*, pp. 174-184.
44. *IAR* 1990-91, pp. 89-90.
45. *IAR* 1991-92, pp. 68-69.
46. S.R. Walimbe, 'Excavations at the Early Historic Site of Kahali-Bramhapuri,' *Deccan Collage Annual Report* (2001-2002), Pune, 2003, pp. 39-40.
47. D. Rajgor, *Punch-marked Coins of Early Historic India*, California, 2001. Coin Type no. 479, 494.
48. Reshma Sawant, '*Aśmaka Mahājanapada:* A New Perspective,' *Man and Environment*, XXVII (2), 2003, pp. 9-20.
49. D. Rajgor, *Punch-marked Coins of Early Historic India*, California, 2001. Coin Type no. 479, 494.
50. A. Ramteke, 'Coins of Vidarbha Janapada: A Revolutionary Discovery,' *Indian Coin Society Newsletter*, no. 40, July-September 2006, pp.68-87.
51. For details, see Reshma Sawant, *Vidarbha: An Archaeo-Historical Approach*, Unpublished Ph.D. thesis submitted to Deccan College, Pune, 2006.
52. Thomas Watters, *On Yuan Chwang's Travels in India (629-645 A.D.)*, Vol. II, New Delhi, 1988, p. 91.
53. S.B. Deo and J.P. Joshi, *Pauni Excavation (1969-70)*, Nagpur, 1972.
54. B.N. Chapekar, *Report on the Excavation at Ter (1958)*, Poona, 1969.
55. B.C. Deotare, Gurudas Shete, Reshma Sawant, Vaishali Kathale and S. Naik, 'Discovery of Structural Stupa at Bhon, District Buldana, Maharashtra,' *Puratattva* 37, 2007, pp. 177-185.
56. Amita Ray, *Life and Art of Early Āndhradeśa*, Delhi, 1983.
57. Ibid.
58. A. Rea, *South Indian Buddhist Antiquities*, Madras, 1894.

59. Ibid.
60. S.B. Deo and J.P. Joshi, *Pauni Excavation (1969-70)*, Nagpur, 1972.
61. S.B. Deo and J.P. Joshi, *op. cit.*, pp. 22, 25-30.
62. S.B. Deo and J.P. Joshi, *op. cit.*, pp. 37-43, 44-56.
63. B.C. Deotare, *et.al.*, 'Discovery of Structural Stupa at Bhon, District Buldana, Maharashtra,' *Puratattva*, 37, 2007, pp. 177-185.
64. J.P. Joshi and A.K. Sharma, 'Mansar Excavation 1998-2004: The Discovery of Pravarapur,' *Puramanthan* (Pravarapur special), 3, 2005, 1-16.
65. A. Nath, 'Archaeology of the Wardha Wainganga Divide,' *Puratattva*, 20, 1989, p. 97.
66. P.V. Kane, 'Ancient Geography and Civilization of Maharashtra,' *Journal of Bombay Branch of Royal Asiatic Society* Vol. XXIV (1914-17), 1917, p. 621; A.M. Shastri, *An Outline of Early Buddhism*, Varanasi, 1965, p. 57; S.B. Deo, 'New Evidence of Hinayana Buddhism in Vidarbha,' *Puratattva*, 1972-73, 6, p. 84.
67. V.V. Mirashi, 'New Light on Deotek Inscriptions,' in *Studies in Indology*, Vol. I, Nagpur, 1968, pp. 125-134.
68. Ibid., pp. 125-134.
69. S.B. Deo and J.P. Joshi, *Pauni Excavation (1969-70)*, Nagpur, 1972; S.B. Deo, 'New Evidence of Hinayana Buddhism in Vidarbha,' *Puratattva*, 1972-73, 6, pp. 53-60.
70. *IAR*, 1994-95, p. 58.
71. S.B. Deo and J.P. Joshi, *Pauni Excavation (1969-70)*, Nagpur, 1972, pp. 41-42.
72. S.B. Deo, 'New Evidence of Hinayana Buddhism in Vidarbha,' *Puratattva*, 1972-73, 6, pp. 84-86.
73. *Lokamat*, Hello Nagpur, 6th January 2008.
74. H.C. Raychaudhury, *Political History of Ancient India*. Calcutta, 1950, p. 156.
75. In my Doctoral thesis, I have identified *Aśmaka Mahājanapada* period with the period of early Iron Age Megalithic culture of Vidarbha.
76. P.L. Gupta, *The Amaravati Hoard of Silver Punch-marked Coins*, Hyderabad, 1963, p. 150.
77. S. Seneviratne, 'Kalinga and Andhra: the Process of Secondary State Formation in Early India,' *The Indian Historical Review*, VII, 1981, p. 62.
78. Romila Thapar, *Cultural Past – Essays in Early Indian History*,

New Delhi, 2002, pp. 428-430.
79. R.P. Kangle, *The Kautiliya Arthaśāstra*, Part II, Bombay, 1963, p. 179.
80. Shamashastry, *Kautilya's Arthaśāstra*, Mysore, 1929, p. 78.
81. K.P. Jayaswal and R.D. Banerji 'The Hathigumpha Inscription of Kharavela,' *Epigraphia Indica*, XX (1929-30), 1933, pp. 71-89.
82. A.M. Shastri, *India As Seen in the Bṛhatsaṁhitā of Varāhamihira*, Delhi, 1969, p. 106.
83. *Chandrapur District Gazetteers*, 1973, (second revised edition), p. 782.
84. Hiralal, 'Kuruspal Stone Inscription of Somesvaradeva,' *Epigraphia Indica*, Vol. X, 1909-10, pp. 25-28.
85. Ibid., pp. 25-28.
86. K.P. Jayaswal and R.D. Banerji, *op. cit.*, p. 71.
87. Reshma Sawant, *Historical Archaeology of Vidarbha* (forthcoming).
88. H.D. Sankalia, S. Subbarao and S.B. Deo, *The Excavations at Maheshwar and Navdatoli 1952-53*, Pune, 1955, pp. 29-30.
89. D.B. Diskalkar, 'Excavations at Kasrawad,' *Indian Historical Quarterly*, 25, 1949, pp. 2-3.
90. B.G. Gokhale, *Buddhism in Maharashtra*, Bombay, 1976.

4

MONARCHS, MONASTERIES AND TRADE ON AN 'AGRARIAN FRONTIER'
Early Medieval Samataṭa–Harikela, Bangladesh, c. 400 CE-1250 CE.*

BIRENDRA NATH PRASAD

Introduction: genesis of 'systemic crisis' in early medieval South Asian Buddhism

In this paper, an attempt would be made to understand the decline of South Asian Buddhism through the vantage point of Samataṭa-Harikela (i.e. Sylhet-Comilla-Noakhali-Chittagong sector of modern Bangladesh). Aim is to have a micro understanding of the processes behind the decline

* This article was first published as "Monarchs, Monasteries and Trade on an 'Agrarian Frontier': Early Medieval Samaaṭa-Harikela Region, Bangladesh", in *South and Southeast Asia: Culture and Religion*, Journal of South and South-East Asian Association for the Study of Culture and Religion, Vol. 3, 2008, pp. 160-177.

within a regional framework. We will also try to situate it within the larger theoretical debate regarding the decline of Buddhism in South Asia. In the mainstream Indian historiography, it is generally believed that survival and flourishing of Buddhism in India depended on the strength of its monasteries[1] and not on a well-integrated community of lay worshippers.[2] Of course this theory is not much different from the earlier theories emphasizing the social and ritual 'failure' of Buddhism in explaining the decline and disappearance of the faith from India.[3] A significant section of Indian Marxist scholarship attributes this decline to an alleged Buddhist failure on agrarian frontiers.[4] Andre Wink has added the dimensions of long distance overland and maritime trade in explaining this phenomenon: by 11th Century CE, Islam replaced Buddhism as the 'greatest trading religion of Asia' while the agrarian world within India was gradually lost to the Brahmins by the Buddhist; and it was this simultaneous loss of agrarian and mercantile space that has precipitated a 'systemic crisis' within Indian Buddhism.[5] To what extent this is true for Bengal in general and Samataṭa – Harikela area in particular, given the fact that Buddhist monasteries in this part of Bengal seems to have been active on agrarian and maritime frontiers? Is there any inherent link between monastic patterns of socialization in the early medieval phase and the medieval Islamisation of eastern Bengal in general and trans-Meghna Bengal in particular?

Introducing trans-Meghna Bengal: Cultural shifts in a 'frontier' society

Studies in cultural dynamics of pre-modern Bengal in general and east Bengal in particular (today's Bangladesh) frequently flounder in explaining the cultural shift – mass conversion to Islam – in the medieval period. Medieval Islamisation has been such a phenomenal success in Bengal that 'today the Bengalis constitute the second largest group in the rank of Islam after the Arabs'[6]; rendering Bangladesh to be 'an island of Muslim majority in a sea of Hinduism.'[7] Medieval Islamisation is most spectacular in eastern Bengal in general and trans-Meghna Bengal in particular. Factors behind this cultural shift in eastern Bengal have been attributed to the 'frontier' character of the landscape and Islamic negotiations[8] and resolutions of the same.[9] Such formulations will expect us to believe that Islam wrote its script on a credulous *Tabula Rasa* by expounding its message of wet rice agriculture to a 'tribal' population. However, early medieval Samataṭa –Hārikela does not appear to be a blank space. Home to various 'minor' dynasties – the Khaḍgas (c.650-700 CE) the Rātas (c.700-750 CE), the Devas (C.750-800CE) and the Chandras (900-1040CE) – nearly all of them being Buddhist in affiliation, and proving the generally accepted idiom that 'Buddhism was the dominant vehicle through which kingship and state formation was articulated in early medieval Bengal'[10] — it was also the area where Xuan Zang saw the largest number of Buddhist monasteries in entire Bengal.[11] It is also the area of a massive Buddhist monastic complex on the Lalmai-Mainamati ridge in Comilla district.[12] Besides, this is the only area in entire South Asia where Buddhism has survived as a living religion.[13] Yet Samataṭa –Harikela has offered the single biggest seat for medieval Islamisation in the entire Indian subcontinent to the east of the Satluj river. Buddhist pattern of socialization in the early medieval phase and subsequent Islamisation could not have been unrelated. Obviously the issue is much more complex than what we generally tend to believe. In this paper, an attempt will be made to understand some aspects of this complexity.

At this juncture, to have a better understanding of the uniqueness of trans-Meghna tracts within early medieval Bengal, it is important to underline the geographical and cultural heterogeneity of early medieval Bengal. In a brilliant study of Political Geography of early medieval Bengal, Morrison has found that Bengal Delta had at least four sub-regions[14]: (1) Vārendra (covering the areas of north Bengal) (2) Dacca- Faridpur region (roughly the historical Vaṅga), (3) Bhagirathi-Hughali areas (Rāḍha) and (4) Sylhet- Comilla-Chittagong sector (variously referred to as Samataṭa or Harikela). In Vārendra, from the very beginning, land was transferred in favour of individuals and extent of the transferred land was always small. The same pattern was more or less visible in Dacca-Faridpur area as well as in the Bhagirathi-Hughali areas.[15] But the pattern was fundamentally different in the Sylhet-Comilla-Chittagong sector. In this sector, land was always granted to institutions: Buddhist monasteries or Brahmanical temples or to a group of large number of Brahmins, and the size of the land grant was very large compared to the same in other sectors of Bengal. Within this sector too, there were important variations. Compared to Comilla or Chittagong area, size of land grants was larger in Sylhet area.[16] His conclusions are obvious: in central, northern and western sectors of Bengal, property relations were fully developed, and culturally they were more or less integrated with the same of the middle Ganga valley. In fact, they were the 'heartlands of Brahmanical culture in the Delta.'[17] Samataṭa- Harikela had different orientations: economically, politically and even culturally. It was a society of relatively sparse population, lacking a long history of individual property rights; hence land grants to the institutions or large congregation of the Brahmins. Within the Delta, 'Buddhism had not attracted a major following anywhere except in the lands lying east of the Meghna where it continued to receive benefactions in the thirteenth century.'[18] Early medieval Samataṭa also displays the evidence of continued minting of high quality metallic coinage and biggest concentration of brick built architecture in the Delta *viz.* the Mainamati monastic complex.[19] We should not have any problem in conceding to his observations that 'the land that now lies in the modern Sylhet-Comilla-Chittagong districts was the home of people with a culture different from those found elsewhere in the Delta.'[20] This Sylhet-Comilla-Chittagong sector, as per Eaton, was the ultimate 'frontier' won by Islam through agrarian expansion centering upon rural mosques, made of thatch and wood and 'linked politically to the state and economically to the hinterland' and acting as 'nucleus of integration in an expanding agrarian civilization whose cultural counterpart was the growth of cult of Allah.'[21] If that is the case, what can be visualized regarding the monastic pattern of socialization in early medieval Samataṭa-Harikela, particularly the role of the Buddhist monasteries on agrarian frontiers? What was their relationship with contemporary political and economic processes? It is with these questions in mind that we will begin our study by focusing upon the societal linkages of Buddhist monasteries in early medieval Samataṭa-Harikela. Much of our analysis will be based on the study of land grant inscriptions engraved on copper plates, recording the donation of land to Buddhist monasteries and Brahmanical institutions.

State formation in early medieval Samataṭa-Harikela, its legitimization and consolidation process, and the role of Buddhist monasteries in this matrix

One of the characteristic features of early medieval South Asia was the 'emergence of regions with their distinct cultural personalities'[22] or the 'emergence of nationalities.'[23] 'Indian Feudalism' school of historiography tends to see it as a 'feudal' imposition from above, but it appears to be a case of developments from below. It was inextricably linked with the process of local state formation. To quote Kulke:

> The overwhelming majority of the early medieval states of India emerged from a process of continuous agrarian expansion and political integration. This development took place in those areas of South Asian subcontinent that had lain at the periphery or even outside the core areas of ancient Indian state formations. This process started from local nuclei of early socio-economic and political developments and increasingly came to include their hinterlands.[24]

This paradigm is fundamentally important for us. In the early historic period, Samataṭa was, no doubt, a peripheral region. In the *Prayāga Praśasti* of Samudragupta, it has been referred to as one of the *pratyānta* (frontier) kingdoms defeated by the Emperor. We may safely deduce that by this period, formation of a local state has already taken place in Samataṭa or it was in the offing. Later it could have become a part of the Gupta Empire but convincing proofs for this are lacking as most of the Gupta period copper plates are confined to Vārendra area. However, as attested by archaeology, Comilla district does not appear to be in cultural backwaters in the early historic period. It has been observed that in terms of number and concentration of early historic archaeological sites, modern Comilla district was second only to Bogra district, the early historical heartland of Bengal.[25] We may safely suggest that modern Comilla district must have been the 'local nuclei of early socio-economic and political developments.' It is likely to be the core region of various local states of Samataṭa. From this base, they could have adopted different means to integrate their peripheral regions in the process of consolidation and expansion of their resource base. It has been proved beyond doubt that the core area of the Rāta dynasty and the Khadga Dynasty was in modern Comilla district only. The Chandras, originally hailing from Rohitagiri (Rosangi in Arakan), had their earlier political centre in the modern Comilla district only; only later they moved to the more centrally located Vikramapura area from where they could have controlled larger parts of Bengal. For these dynasties, land grants to Brahmins and Brahmanical temples, and, of course, to Buddhist monasteries, appear to have been an important instrument for affecting economic and cultural integration of peripheral areas to the nuclear areas of their domain. This is a theme we shall turn to later. Let us turn to another important variable of this complex matrix: trade.

For early medieval Samataṭa, significance of trade should not be overlooked, as it could have a fundamental impact on the political economy of various local dynasties as well as on the socialization patterns of Samataṭa monasteries. 7th century CE onwards, port cities of Western Delta – Tāmralipti and Chandraketugarh – began to decline due to diverse factors. There is no evidence to prove that sea-faring merchants used it for maritime adventures 8th century CE onwards.[26] Decline of port activities at Tāmralipti was also reflected in the dwindling number of Buddhist monasteries in this port town.[27] An important consequence of this was the gradual shift of the maritime focus of the Delta towards the east, towards the

Chittagong coast.[28] Archeological or literary evidences for any port in Western Delta not forthcoming for the early medieval period, it may not be unreasonable to assume that Samataṭa could have provided the main opening to the sea for entire Bengal. It is important to mention that, compared to other parts of Bengal, early medieval Samataṭa offers a remarkable contrast in terms of continuation of high quality metallic coinage. Excavations at the Mainamati monastic complex have lead to the discovery of around 350 coins in gold, copper and silver.[29] This could have been due to developed trading contacts of the region. Samataṭa-Harikela region was, no doubt, well -connected with neighboring regions by overland and maritime routes. The political and cultural centre of Mainamati – Devaparvata too appears to have been well-connected with the hinterland by rivers. These riverine routes could have been useful in channelising resources as well as merchandise. In fact, it has been suggested that Mainamati- Devaparvata complex was the most important riverine port in Samataṭa from the second half of the 7th Century to the first quarter in 10th Century CE.[30] Discovery of coins of Abbasid Caliphs at Kutila Mura in Mainamati monastic complex suggests that Southeastern Bengal was well connected to the Arab maritime network stretching from Africa and Europe in the west to China in the east.[31] This is also reflected in the intimate knowledge of the southeastern coast of Bengal in the Arab maritime literature[32] as well as in growing Arab presence at the Chittagong coast, 8th-9th centuries CE onwards.[33] This is not to suggest that Buddhist network in the Bay of Bengal has collapsed by this time.[34] It is generally believed that Indian Ocean witnessed a 'trade revolution' in the 11th century CE[35] and Samataṭa rulers could have benefited from this.[36] But the absence of indigenous currency in these centuries remains a puzzle.[37] A general absence of references to merchants and other mercantile groups in Samataṭa inscriptions – a situation fundamentally different form Gupta period North Bengal where merchants were accorded important place in *Viṣaya* administration – renders this theory plausible that much of the Samataṭa maritime trade could have been in the foreign hands. Samataṭa monasteries benefited from this trade as a portion of wealth from this maritime trade, as indicated by the discovery of Abbasid and indigenous coins from Mainamati complex, could have flown to the monasteries. This may be one of the factors behind the flourishing of monasteries at Mainamati. However in the absence of a strong indigenous mercantile class, the overall impact of foreign trade on economy could not have been significant; nor could it have provided a stable resource base for Samataṭa monasteries. Tarafdar has rightly pointed out that the kind of commercial activities, as evidenced in early medieval Samataṭa, could hardly originate a process of urbanization that might bring into being a stable commercial middle class, for profits form trade were either appropriated by feudal lords or establishments. Capital formation under these conditions could have been impossible and the ruralisation resulting from a predominantly agrarian economy perhaps remained unaffected by trade and money economy.[38] This absence of a 'commercial middle class' had implications for the Buddhist monasteries as well. We do not have evidences for direct mercantile patronage to Samataṭa monasteries in the way we see in the cases of early medieval Kanheri,[39] Brahmanical *maṭhas* of Konkan,[40] and early medieval temples of Rajasthan.[41] Due to this factor, dependence of Samataṭa monasteries on royal patronage appears to have been greater.

At this juncture, it must be emphasized that a mono-causal or unilinear approach may not be useful in understanding the monastic survival strategies as they assume differential shapes across time and topography.[42] In the case of early historic western Deccan, it has been seen that in their earliest phase, Buddhist monasteries had greater involvement with the agrarian sector. It was much later that, with increasing trade and commerce, monasteries could have got involved directly in trade and could have accumulated wealth.[43] Should we visualize a similar chronological evolution in the role of Samataṭa monasteries as well? Should we believe that initially they had greater involvement with the agrarian sector and it was only later that they depended more on wealth from foreign trade? Where do they stand vis -à -vis Brahmanical institutions in this regard? And why did they lose hegemony to the Brahmins? Any analysis of this issue will naturally entail an analysis of land grant inscriptions of early medieval Samataṭa. That will give us some ideas about the milieu in which these monasteries were interacting with other societal institutions. That will also be useful in comparing the role of Buddhist monasteries with the same of Brahmanical institutions on agrarian frontiers.

Buddhist monasteries on agrarian frontiers: the Samataṭa-Harikela experience

The earliest dating copper plate inscription discovered so far in the Samataṭa-Harikela region is the Gunaighar copper plate of Mahārāja Vainyagupta (507 CE), discovered at Gunaighar village (18 miles northeast of Comilla town); recording the donation of 11 *pāṭaka* of *Khila* (uncultivated) land in the village of *Kantedadaka* to a Buddhist monastery built by Ācārya Śāntideva.[44] This monastery was dedicated to Ā*rya Avalokiteśvara*.[45] References to *Gunāikragāhara* (obviously modern Gunaighar) occur in this inscription; hence it may be reasonably assumed that donated land was located in the vicinity of modern Gunaighar itself. A careful analysis of this inscription will lead us to three important inferences: the poly-religious character of the locality (which appears to be well-settled) in which Buddhist monasteries had a privileged place; monastic alliance with the state; as well as evidences of evolution of hierarchy among monasteries in this area. Significance of evolution of hierarchy among Buddhist monasteries in Samataṭa at such an early date is yet to be worked out. This monastery was granted low-lying, water logged and marshy land.[46] Obviously the monastery was expected to undertake agrarian expansion in the donated land. Landscape surrounding this donated land was poly-religious. Besides being bordered by cultivated fields belonging to various individuals, it was bordered by an earlier Brahmanical *agarahāra* settlement in the east[47]; a *rājavihāra-kṣetra* (i.e. cultivated fields belonging to the 'royal monastery') in the south[48] ;and also the cultivated fields belonging to the Buddhist monastery headed by Ācārya Jitsena in south.[49] In the western side, it was bordered by cultivated fields belonging to the temple of *Pradyumneśvara*, a Brahmanical deity.[50] Frequent references to various water channels and boat parking stations in this inscription will naturally make us think that the locality in which land was granted bordered some river and it was low lying and marshy. Here religious institutions (Buddhist monasteries, Brahmanical temples and *agrahāras*) seem to have been institutional bases for agrarian expansion and 'forging of linkages across space for social integration.' This could have been helpful in the consolidation and expansion of material and ideological resource base of emerging local states in the trans-Meghna areas. Another important inference is that at such an early date, hierachisation has developed among Samataṭa monasteries. This inscription attests to the presence of at least three monasteries in or around Gunaighara: the monastery headed by Ācārya Jitsena, the monastery built or headed by Ācārya Śāntideva (to which land was transferred in this inscription), and a 'royal monastery' (*rājavihāra*). Obviously the *rājavihāra* stood at the top of hierarchy and patronage to Buddhist monasteries, thus, seems to have important role in royal legitimization. It has been asserted that 'Buddhism was the dominant vehicle through which kingship and state formation was articulated in early Bengal."[51] Gunaighar inscription proves that this was largely true for 6th CE century Samataṭa as well. This tendency of direct royal association with particular monasteries later culminated in the evolution of monasteries named after individual kings, such as Bhavadeva Vihāra and Ānanda Vihara in the Mainamati Complex. At a later date, it led to the practice of naming important temples and *agrahāras* such as Laḍaha-Mahādeva-Bhaṭṭāraka,[52] Chandrapur-Brāhmaṇapura[53] etc. on the name of the kings who created or patronized them. Clearly, patronage to such institutions constituted an important element in the articulation of royal sovereignty.

Political pattern in Samataṭa in late 6th and 7th centuries CE is not very claer. This period is marked by the emergence of a powerful, semi-independent *Sāmanta* stratum, owing nominal allegiance to the paramount ruler of Samataṭa (*Samataṭeśvara*). This stratum, for the consolidation and expansion of its resource base, or for legitimacy, patronized Buddhist monasteries or Brahmanical institutions. However, it is also from this period only that a differentiation emerged in the pattern of land grants to the Buddhist monasteries and Brahmanical institutions. Besides the Nidhanapur copper plate of Kāmrūpa king Bhāṣkaravarmana, which informs us the creation of *Mayuraśālmala-agrahāra* in *Chandrapuri Viṣaya* (presumably in Sylhet district) for settling hundreds of Brahmins by granting them a large tract of uncultivated land as per the principle of *bhūmichhidra Nyāya*; three more 6th-7th century copper plates have come to light from trans—Meghna areas: (1) Kailan copper plate of *Pañca-Mahāśabdaprāpta Śrīdharaṇa Rāṯa*, (2) Tippera copper plate of *Sāmanta* Lokanātha and (3) Kalapur copper plate of Sāmanta Maruṇḍanātha. Any study of these copper plates will have to take into account the remarkable similarity in their seals. Seals attached to all the three plates refer to *Kumāramātyādhikaraṇa.* In the next line, they record the name of the individual donors: *Śrīdharaṇa Rāta, Lokanātha* and *Maruṇḍanātha* respectively. D.C. Sircar has rightly opined that these seals actually belonged to the *adhikaraṇa* (Office of the Board of Administrators) attached to the *Kumāramātya* (the Administrative Officer, who was enjoying the status of a prince of royal blood) who was usually the ruler of a *Viṣaya* or its subdivision.[54] The names of *Lokanātha, Srīdharana Rāta,* and *Maruṇḍanātha* were written on the seals, apparently to indicate that they had countersigned the original document, which was afterwards incised on the copper plates, and the importance given to them will suggest that they had risen to semi-independent status.[55]

Let us begin with the Tippera copper plate (c.564 CE), discovered in the old Tippera district (modern Comilla district). In this copper plate, we are informed that at the request of *Mahāsamanta Pradoṣaśarmana,* an orthodox Brahmin, forested lands (*āṭavi bhukhaṇḍa*) were granted in the *Suvvuṅga Viṣaya* for providing *bali-satra-caru* (roughly translated:

worship, hospitality and offerings) to the temple of the Brahmanical deity *Ananta Narāyaṇa;* as well as for the support of a community of some two hundred Brahmins.[56] As the tract was granted without any reference to its boundaries, it appears to have been very large. The distinct non- Sanskritic name of the *Viṣaya* (*Suvvuṅga*) in which land was granted might suggest that it was located on the remote frontiers, probably in a tribal region.[57] Obviously this is a case of attempted expansion of agrarian and cultural frontiers in which temple and the Brahmanical *agrahāras* acted as nuclei of integration. A similar attempt is visible in the Kalapur copper plate of *Sāmanta Maruṇḍanātha* (second half of 6th century CE). This grant seems to have been made on the request of a Brahmin Jayaswāmina, who had earlier received one *paṭaka* of land and built a *maṭha* and installed therein an image of *Bhagavata Ananta Narāyaṇa.*[58] Kalapur copper plate records the donation of one *pāṭaka* and two *dronas* of jungle land (*āṭavi bhūkhaṇḍa*) for providing *bali, satra* and *caru* at this *maṭha,* as well as for the maintenance of Brahmins attached to the same. Location of the donated land has satisfactorily been identified in the Srimangala Police Station area of Sylhet district, on the borders of hills of Tripura.[59] Tipperah and Kalapur copper plates prove beyond doubt that Brahmanical institutions were pioneers in advancing agrarian and cultural frontiers in the forested tracts of Comilla and Sylhet districts as well as in the adjoining districts of Assam and Tripura.

This contrasts sharply with the Kailan copper plate of Śrīdharaṇa Rāta (c.575 CE), found at the village of Kailan, 18 miles southwest of Comilla town. This plate was issued from Devaparvata (i.e. Lalmai Hills) recording the transfer of 25 *pāṭakas* of land at the request of *Mahāsandhivigrahika* Jayanātha. Part of this tract was donated to a congregation of 13 Brahmins; Jayanātha himself retained part of the land; whereas five *pāṭakas* were granted to a Buddhist monastery.[60] Location of the donated land could not be exactly identified so far, though it may be assumed that it could have been somewhere near the find spot of the copper plate.[61] A developed agrarian structure is discernible in this plate and Buddhist monastic preference for concentration in Comilla district, arguably the heartland of early medieval Samataṭa, becomes more pronounced in the coming centuries. That makes us think that royal legitimization, and not agrarian expansion, was the main motive behind grant of land to the monasteries in Comilla district.

This tendency of monastic concentration in relatively well-settled Comilla district, and surviving mainly by appropriating agrarian resources of well-settled villages instead of attempting agrarian expansion in outlying areas, is discernible in two Asharafpur copper plates (c.665 CE). They have been found at Asharafpur village (30 miles to the northeast of Dacca city) and location of donated land has satisfactorily been proved to be either in the eastern portions of Dacca district or in the western portions of Comilla district.[62] In the first plate, king Devakhaḍga donated 9 *pāṭaka*s and 10 *drona*s of cultivated land to Ācārya Saṅghamitra, for the use of a Buddhist monastery.[63] In the second plate, Rājarājā, son of Devakhaḍga, donated 6 *pāṭaka*s and 10 *drona*s of cultivated land to the same monastery. These plates suggest that some monasteries got deeply enmeshed in the agrarian relations of contemporary society. They throw valuable light on the position of some peasants who cultivated the land granted to this monastery. The first copper plate speaks of some land 'enjoyed' by a certain *Sarvatantra*, but cultivated by a certain *mahattara Śekhara* and others.[64] In the second copper plate, mention is made of some land 'enjoyed' by *Sulabdha* and others, but cultivated by *Durggata* and *Rājatasa*.[65] But the plots mentioned in these copper plates were actually owned by the king and the crown prince, who took them away from the 'enjoyers' of the same and donated the land to the monasteries. It appears that the peasants, who tilled the land under the previous landlords, continued to do so even after it became the property of the *Vihāra*s. Obviously when such a well settled land was granted to the monasteries, main motive could not have been agrarian expansion, but royal legitimization. Of course, it may be argued that in the western portions of Comilla district, concerted attempts of agrarian expansion of the type we see in Sylhet district might not have been required. But that does not explain why the monasteries conceded space to Brahmanical institutions in Sylhet district. At the present state of our knowledge, we don't know why we don't have much evidence for monastic presence in Sylhet district.

In the Devaparvata copper plate of Bhavadeva (8th century CE),we see the transfer of 7.5 *pāṭakas* of cultivated land in favour of *Vendamati Vihārikā*. Donated land was scattered in four villages in *Vendamati* within *Peranāṭaṇa Viṣaya*. [66] Donated land was probably located in modern Comilla or Noakhali district.[67] The same inference, as noted in the context of Asharafapur inscriptions, is applicable here as well.

However, that should not be taken to mean that Buddhist monasteries were totally inactive on the tribal frontiers. In fact, in some of the copper plates, we see that patronage to Buddhist monasteries was the medium though which some of the tribes, which were undergoing the transition to state polity, sought their legitimacy and stability.[68] That is, Buddhist monasteries were having a catalytic role in the tribal state formations and their legitimizations. This aspect seems to be most marked in Chittagong area.

This process, however, is not discernible in Sylhet area. In the Paschimabhag copper plate (first half of 10th Century CE), a process of colonization of a huge, uncultivated area spread over three *Viṣaya*s, centering upon Brahmanical institutions is visible.[69] A similar attempt is visible in two Bhatera copper plates of 11th Century CE. In the Mainamati plates of Laḍahamādhavacandra and Vīradhara Deva, we see that idioms have turned more and more Brahmanical. That may indicate a gradual loss of Buddhist hegemony in Samataṭa.[70] Though Buddhist monasteries received patronage from local rulers even after the foundation of the Muslim rule in the Bengal,[71] that does not negate a gradual erosion of Buddhist influence in Samataṭa region in the previous centuries. This erosion is despite continued trumpeting of *Parama Saugata* appellation in their inscriptions by the rulers of Samataṭa-Harikela.

Summing up: implications of monastic reluctance to engage agrarian frontiers

One important impression, which was highlighted in the previous pages, was the apparent heterogeneity in the trans-Meghna portions of Bengal. Elements of similarity could not have been absent in the swamps and forests of low lying Sylhet plains, fertile Comilla-Noakhali districts and plains of Chittagong coast, where maritime activities could have a greater significance. Yet, elements of dissimilarity appear to have been more profound. Obviously spatial linkages of religious institutions – Buddhist monasteries and Brahmanical temples or *maṭhas*- had differentiations across this variegated space. It has been noted in the previous pages that the areas, which constitute Comilla and Noakhali districts today, appear to be the 'local nuclei of early socio-economic and political developments.' From this core, various dynasties attempted to integrate two 'frontiers' – Sylhet and Chittagong districts – by extending patronage to Buddhist monasteries and Brahmanical institutions. A portion of the wealth accruing from maritime trade could have flown to the monasteries, but in the absence of a strong indigenous mercantile class, it could not have very durable. Their major resource base seems to have been agrarian. However, as we have seen in the previous pages, most of land grants to Buddhist monasteries took place in a very limited area: in the Sadar area of Comilla district. Land grant to Buddhist monasteries in this area was motivated primarily by the urge for royal legitimization. Of course this is not to suggest that they were not present on the agrarian frontiers of Sylhet or Chittagong, but, as a whole, this is a saga of gradual loss of space to the Brahmins. In a nutshell, Brahmanical institutions outsmarted Buddhist monasteries on agrarian frontiers in early medieval Samataṭa. That seems to be the unmaking of Buddhist hegemony in trans-Meghna Bengal in the long run. Yet we are not fully sure that the apparent matrix – "Samataṭa rulers making money from maritime trade and patronizing Buddhist monasteries with a portion of this money and land grants for royal legitimacy; and relying primarily on Brahmanical institutions for advancing agrarian frontiers"– explains the dynamics of early medieval Samataṭa- Harikela in totality. Further researches are required to unveil aspects of this complexity.

Notes

1. Andre Wink, *Al-Hind: The Making of the Indo-Islamic World*, Vol. II, Delhi, 1999, pp. 335-336.
2. Ibid., p. 335.
3. P.S. Jaini, 'The Disappearance of Buddhism and the Survival of Jainism in India: A Study in Contrast,' in his *Collected Papers on Buddhist Studies*, Delhi, 2001, p. 142.
4. D.D. Kosambi, 'The Decline of Buddhism in India' in his *'Exasperating Essays: Exercises in the Dialectical Method*, Pune, 1986, p. 66; R.S. Sharma, *Urban Decay*, Delhi, 1987, p. 131.
5. Andre Wink, *Al-Hind: The Making of the Indo-Islamic World*, Vol. II, Delhi, 1999, pp. 349-350.
6. Akabar Ali Khan, *Discovery of Bangladesh: Explorations in the Dynamics of a Hidden Nation*, Dhaka, 2001, p. 18.
7. Richard M. Eaton, 'Who are the Bengal Muslims? Conversions and Islamisation in Bengal' in R. Ahmed (ed.), *Understanding Bengal Muslims*, Delhi, 2001, p. 34.
8. Richard M. Eaton, *op.cit.*, p. 36.
9. Ralph Nicholas, 'Vaisnavism and Islam in the Environs of Rural Bengal' in Rafiuddin Ahmed (ed.), *Understanding Bengal Muslims*, Delhi, 2001.He has analyzed the sectarian affiliations of social stratification in pre-1947 Bengal Delta. He found that Bengal peasantry adhered either to Islam or Vaisnavism, may be due to the fact that 'Bengal Delta was a kind of slowly opening frontier which was gradually settled agriculturally, in which Islam and Vaisanavism are likely to have functioned to provide authority in an anarchic frontier society through their loosely constituted religious organizations, *millat* and *maṇḍali* respectively.' (p. 66)
10. Rila Mukharjee, 'Rice Culture of Divine Right in a Celestially Ordered Zone: A Case Study of South Asian and South-East Asian Ideologies and Hegemonies from c.2000 BC. to c. 1800 AD with Specific Reference to Bengal,' *Revista Lusofona de Ciencias Sociais*, Lisbon, 2004, p. 55.
11. T. Watters, *On Yuan Chwang's Travels in India, AD 629-645*, Vol.

2, Delhi, 1996 (reprint), p. 187.

12. In terms of extent, Mainamati Complex appears to be one of the largest Monastic Complexes in South Asia. The entire area (approximately 18 kilometer in length and at times 5 kilometer wide) was studded with large number of monasteries built over a period of six to seven hundred years, under the patronage of different Samataṭa dynasties. At least 55 archeological sites have been identified so far, each representing the remains of one monastery or other; except Charapatra Mura, which appears to be a Brahmanical shrine. In recent years, many monographs dealing with the art and architecture of Mainamati Complex have come. See particularly F.A. Khan, *Mainamati*, Karachi, 1963; B.M. Morrison, *Lalmai: A Cultural Centre in Early Bengal*, London and Seattle, 1974; A.K.M. Shamshul Alam, *Mainamati*, Dacca,1982(second edition); A.B.M. Hussain (ed.), *Mainamati-Devaparvata*, Dhaka, 1997; Abu Imam, 'Samataṭa- Mainamati: Some Observations' in G. Sengupta, S. Panja (eds.), *Archeology of Eastern India: New Perspectives*, Kolkata, 2002, pp. 613-629.
13. For the practices of living Buddhism in Southeastern Bengal see Sukomal Chaudhury, *Contemporary Buddhism in Bangladesh*, Calcutta,1982; A.M. Khan, *The Maghs: A Buddhist Community in Bangladesh*, Dhaka, 1999. Also see N. Ahmed, *Discover the Monuments of Bangladesh*, Dhaka, 1984. Ahmed has noted that contemporary Bangladesh has a Buddhist population of around half a million with their main concentration in Chittagong, Comilla and Dhaka districts, that is, basically in Samataṭa area (p. 45).
14. B.M. Morrison, *Political Centres and Cultural Regions in Early Bengal*, Jaipur, 1980 (Indian edition), p. 38.
15. Ibid., p. 38.
16. Ibid., p. 38.
17. Ibid., p. 38.
18. Ibid., p. 154.
19. Ibid., p. 153.
20. Ibid., p. 119.
21. Richard M. Eaton, 'Who are the Bengal Muslims? Conversions and Islamisation in Bengal' in R. Ahmed (ed.), *Understanding Bengal Muslims*, Delhi, 2001, p. 35.
22. B.D. Chattopadhyaya, *The Making of Early Medieval India*, Delhi, 1994, p. 35.
23. R.S. Sharma, 'The Problem of Transition from Ancient to

Medieval in Indian History,' *The Indian Historical Review*, 1, 1974, p. 8.

24. Hermann Kulke, 'The Early and Imperial Kingdom: A Processual Model for Integrative State Formation in Early Medieval India,' in Hermann Kulke (ed.), *The State in India 1000-1700*, Delhi, 1995, p. 250.
25. M.M. Hoque, Seema Hoque, 'Ancient Human Settlement Pattern of Bangladesh: A Preliminary Study,' *Journal of Bengal Art*, Dhaka, Vol. 2 (1997), p. 289.
26. A. Bhattacharya, 'Trade Routes in Ancient Bengal,' in A. Dutta (ed.) *History and Archaeology of Eastern India*, Delhi, 1998, p. 64.
27. At Tamralipti, Fa-hsien saw 22 monasteries but Xuan Zang could see only 10 monasteries (Chitaranjana Patra, 'Spread of Buddhism in Bengal,' in A. Dutta, *op. cit.*, p. 203), and later records are silent about the presence of monasteries at Tāmralipti.
28. Ranabir Chakravarti, 'Maritime Trade and Voyages in Ancient Bengal,' in his *Trade and Traders in Early Indian Society*, Delhi, 2002, p. 135.
29. M.R. Tarafdar, 'Trade and Society in Early Medieval Bengal,' in his *Trade, Technology and Society in Medieval Bengal*, Dhaka, 1995, p. 13.
30. Ranabir Chakravarti, '*Vaṅgsāgarasambhāṇḍāriyaka*: A Riverine Trade Centre in Early Medieval Bengal,' in his *Trade and Traders in Early Indian Society*, Delhi, 2002, p. 152.
31. M.R. Tarafdar, *op. cit.*, p. 15.
32. Ibid., p. 16.
33. Ibid., p. 18.
34. Rila Mukharjee, ' Rice Culture of Divine Right in a Celestially Ordered Zone,'p. 56; Idem, *Strange Riches: Bengal in the Mercantile Map of South Asia*, Delhi, 2006, p. 25.
35. Hermann Kulke, 'Rivalry and Competition in the Bay of Bengal in the Eleventh Century and its Bearing on Indian Ocean Studies' in Om Prakash and Denys Lombard (eds.), *Commerce and Culture in the Bay of Bengal 1500-1800*, New Delhi, 1999, pp. 17-35.
36. Rila Mukherjee in her 'Rice Culture' has taken this argument to another extreme. She asserts that there were two sectors in the Bengal Delta: the western Delta and the eastern Delta. Western Delta relied primarily on wet rice agriculture and its society was overwhelmingly agrarian. Despite having evidences for expansion of agrarian frontiers, eastern Delta

was primarily maritime in orientation. After the 10th Century CE, the eastern Delta (Samataṭa) engaged more in trade and less in agriculture. She has related this phenomenon to the Indian Ocean "trade revolution" of 11th-12th Centuries CE (p. 60). However she fails to explain the puzzling absence of indigenous coinage and references to native mercantile groups in Samataṭa-Harikela copper plate inscriptions during these centuries.

37. M.R. Tarafdar, *op. cit.*, p. 16.
38. Ibid., p. 26.
39. In fact Kanheri may provide a good case for comparison with the Mainamati Complex. Like Mainamati, it was also benefiting form maritime trade. Unlike some other monastic sites on the Maharashtra coast, which declined and disappeared after 400 CE, Kanheri displays the evidences of flourishing occupation till 10th-11th Centuries CE. Location of important port towns in the close vicinity of Kanheri (Chaul, Sopora, Kalyan etc.) which made possible the continuous flow of mercantile patronage and its wide spread pilgrimage networks- attracting pilgrims from such far off places like Sindh and Gauḍa (Bengal) – ensured its survival and growth despite the apparent lack of royal patronage during these centuries. See H.P.Ray, 'Kanheri: The Archaeology of an Early Buddhist Pilgrimage Site in Western India,' *World Archaeology*, 26(1), 1994, p. 37. Right now, we don't have anything to visualize the nature of mercantile patronage to the Mainamati Complex, if any. Similarly, we don't know why we don't have many evidences for local and supra-local pilgrimage at Mainamati complex.
40. For an interesting analysis of the impact of commercial rivalries between the local merchants of early medieval Konkan and the merchants coming from north India (Rajasthan etc.) on the fortunes of a *Maṭha*, see Ranabir Chakravarti, 'Monarchs, Merchants and a *Maṭha* in Northern Konkan, c. 900-1053AD,' *The Indian Economic and Social History Review*, 27,2, 1990, pp. 189-208.
41. For an analysis of comparative impact of royal and mercantile patronages on the fortunes of temples of early medieval Rajasthan, see Shanta Sharma, 'Rulers, Urban Milieu and Temple Patronage: Shifting Contours in Rajasthan, c. AD 700-1000,' *History Today*, 4, 2003, pp. 9-21.
42. For a historiographical review of evolving functional roles of ancient Indian Buddhist monasteries, see Birendra Nath

Prasad, 'Major Trends and Perspectives in Studies in the Functional Dimensions of Indian Monastic Buddhism in the Past One Hundred Years: A Historiographical Survey,' *Buddhist Studies Review*, Journal of the UK Association for Buddhist Studies, London, Vol. 25(1), 2008, pp. 54- 89.

43. H.P. Ray, *Monastery and Guild: Commerce under the Satavahanas*, Delhi, 1986, p. 208.
44. R.R. Mukherjee, S.K.Maity (ed.), 'Gunaighar Copper Plate of Vainyagupta,' in *Corpus of Bengal Inscriptions Bearing on History and Civilization of Bengal*, Calcutta, 1967, p. 65
45. Ibid., p. 65.
46. R.R. Mukherjee, S.K. Maity, *op.cit.*, p. 67.
47. Ibid., p. 67.
48. Ibid.
49. Ibid., lines 30-31.
50. Ibid., p. 67.
51. Rila Mukherjee, ' Rice Culture of Divine Right in a Celestially Ordered Zone,' p. 55.
52. This temple is mentioned in the Mainamati Plates of Laḍahcandra, regnal year 6 (i.e., c.1005 CE). See D.C. Sircar, *op.cit.*, pp. 40-57.
53. Mentioned in the Paschimabhaga Copper Plate of Śrīchandra, regnal year 5 (i.e. c. 935 CE). See D.C. Sircar, *op.cit.*, pp. 19-40 for an analysis of this Inscription.
54. D.C. Sircar, *op.cit.*, p. 15.
55. Ibid., p.15.
56. D.C. Sircar, *Indian Historical Quarterly*, XXIII, p. 224.
57. *Suvvuṅga Viṣaya* has been identified with the Cachar district of south Assam. See N.K.Bhattasali, 'New Light on the History of Assam,' *Indian Historical Quarterly*, XXI, 1945, p. 28. Recently it has been asserted that it could have included the southern extremes of the North Cachar Hills district of Assam. See J.B. Bhattacharjee, *Barak Upatykar Itihaser Ruparekha* (in Bengali), Shillong, 1992, pp. 135-144.
58. D.C. Sircar, *Epigraphic Discoveries in East Pakistan*, Calcutta, 1973, p. 16.
59. K.K. Gupta, *Copper Plates of Sylhet*, Vol. 1, (7th –11th Centuries AD), Sylhet, 1967, p. 80.
60. *Indian Historical Quarterly*, XIII, 19, pp. 221-240.
61. B.M. Morrison, *Political Centers and Cultural Regions in Early Bengal*, Jaipur, 1980, p. 33.
62. Ibid., p. 37.

63. *Epigraphia Indica*, XV, p. 3.
64. *Journal of Asiatic Society of Bengal*, 1, No. 1, 1905, pp. 89-90, 116-118.
65. Ibid., pp. 90-91, 116-117.
66. D.C. Sircar, *Journal of Asiatic Society, Letters*, Vol. XVII, 1951, pp. 83-94.
67. B.M. Morrison, *op. cit.*, p. 39.
68. See G. Bhattacharya, 'A Preliminary Note on the Inscribed Metal Vase from the National Museum of Bangladesh' in D. Mitra (ed.), *Explorations in the Art and Archaeology of South Asia: Essays Dedicated to N.G. Majumdar*, Calcutta, 1996. This inscription records the donation of land to a Buddhist monastery by one Devātideva Bhaṭṭāraka (8th century CE), who belonged to the *Khasa* tribe. He had embraced Buddhism (p. 239). Also see G. Bhattacharya, 'An Inscribed Metal Vase, Most Probably from Chittagong,' in A.J. Gail and G.J.R. Mevissena (eds.), *South Asian Archaeology*, 1991, pp. 323-338.
69. For an analysis of this inscription, see D.C. Sircr, *op. cit.*, pp. 19-40.
70. See D.C. Sircr, *op. cit.*, pp. 41-59, for an analysis of these inscription.
71. See Mainamati Plate of Raṇavaṅkamalla Harikāladeva, c.1220 CE (D.C. Bhattacharya, *Indian History Quarterly*, IX, pp. 282-89) recording the donation of 20 *pāṭaka* of land in favor of the monastery dedicated to a Buddhist goddess *Durgottara*. This monastery was located in the city of Paṭṭikera, somewhere near the Mainamati Complex.

5

VAJRAYĀNA BUDDHISM AS A RELIGION OF THE LAITY IN EARLY MEDIEVAL ORISSA (INDIA)

UMAKANT MISHRA

Vajrayāna arose in eastern India in 5th century CE and found substantial presence for about seven centuries. However existing historiography on the religions of India regards this form of Buddhism as 'degenerate.' In such historical reconstructions, it is reduced to psychosexual practises. It is also claimed that it had little or no resemblance with the 'Nibbanic Buddhism' of Buddha's times or the devotional bodhisattvahood of Mahāyāna. It is also regarded as imitative, and a phenomenon largely confined to the monasteries, without any social base. Therefore, it is generally argued that Vajrayāna became extinct after royal patronage was withdrawn to the monasteries.[1]

It is also believed that there was hardly any difference between Brahmanical religions and Vajrayāna Buddhism, as Vajrayāna was 'imitative.' This 'imitative' character was one of the most important factors in facilitating its assimilation into an octopus Brahmanism. Here, it is worth quoting Kunal

Chakrabarti:

> "In popular understanding Buddhist and Brahmanical icons came to perform the same function. Even in the realm of underlying metaphysical premises Tantricism brought the Buddhist and Brahmanical ways of worship close. When both the religions began to receive royal patronage irrespective of the personal faiths of the rulers it carried the universal message that the differences between them, if any, were marginal and that both were entitled to be venerated in almost equal manner.[2]

The present paper contests all the above three characterisations of Buddhism. It argues that Vajrayāna was not a degenerate religion; rather it was culmination of attempts to make a monastic religion more instrumental, social and this-worldly. As a social and instrumental religion for laity, Vajrayāna innovated many gods and goddesses, created *mantras* and rituals for their worship within the households. Secondly, it was not imitative but distinctive with its own identity and worked within the normative tradition of Buddhism. Vajrayāna texts regard Buddhism as *Ekayāna* (One Way) and Vajrayāna as an extension of Mahāyāna. Thirdly, it was not confined to monastic complexes only. On the other hand archaeological excavations and explorations have brought to light numerous Buddhist sculptures from hundreds of sites in Orissa, which shows the horizontal spread of Buddhism in Orissa. If we accept these contestations, it raises several questions about the religious landscape of Orissa between 5th to 12th centuries CE.

1. Archaeological evidence of horizontal and vertical spread of Buddhism in Orissa

Recent archaeological excavations and explorations have brought to light more than 100 Buddhist sites in Orissa. Most of these sites flourished between 7th to 12th centuries CE, even though the nucleus of some of these sites, like that of Ratnagiri, Langudi and Lalitgiri, go back to pre- and early centuries of the Christian era. Some of these Buddhist establishments were not only spatially vast but also showed remarkable temporal continuity for more than a millennium. From the structural point of view, the monastic complexes were huge, as compared to the medium-sized Kalinga temples, which were constructed in the same period.[3] Historical evidence indicates horizontal expansion of Buddhist sites, enlargement of few establishments and uninterrupted temporal continuity of some in the period between 5th but especially between 7th century and 12th century CE. These sites contain sculptures, of Buddhist gods and goddesses, with *dhāraṇīs* and *mantras* inscribed on them. The geographical spread of Buddhism in Orissa indicates its wide scale practice in coastal Orissa. Not all sculptures had their provenance in the immediate cultural eco-niches and some of these sculptures might have travelled from the big monastic establishment of Ratnagiri, Lalitgiri, Solampur, Kuruma, or Bhubaneswar, but the number of Buddhist sites clearly indicates that it was quite wide-spread.

1.1. Vertical spread of Buddhism

The horizontal spread of Buddhism in Orissa raises questions about the underlying nature of Buddhism. What made the religion so wide- spread in Orissa? The study of Buddhism of the period also revealed its vertical expansion. One encounters, 6th-7th century onwards, numerous Buddhas, Bodhisattvas, Buddhist gods and goddesses in numerous monasteries of Orissa. Nowhere else in India, except perhaps in Nalanda, so many varieties of gods and goddesses are found as in Orissa, clearly indicating the worship of these gods and goddesses.

One indicator of the vertical growth of Buddhism is the rich diversity in terms of the pantheon structure. Buddhism introduced numerous deities in its pantheon in order to make the religion more this-worldly. These deities were invoked and worshipped by people. The diversity in Buddhist pantheon reflects the attempt to extend the religion further by encouraging greater involvement of people in the form of worship of these deities, performing rituals, observing *Vratas* and celebrating calendrical festivals of Buddhist divinities. The following paragraphs categorises these divinities according to their different forms and places of their provenance, which indicate the spread of different cults in Orissa.

1.1.1 *Tārā*

The *Sādhanamālā* and other texts refer to different forms of Tārā divided into five on the basis of their colour. The following diagram represents various forms of Tārā, which are described in the *Sādhanamālā*. Goddess Tārā was introduced quite late-only in 6th century CE-and gained enormous popularity by 8th century CE. While *Mahāśrī* Tārā is a conflation of Saraśvatī and Lakṣmī, Siṁhanāda and Durgotāriṇī Tārā are modelled on Durgā, who is called *Durgatināśinī.*[4] Tārā in her form of saviouress from perils first appeared in cave 9 of Ellora[5]; Sarvajnanamitra wrote *Ārya-Tārā-Sragdhara-Stotra* in 8th century; and the Candi Kalasan temple in Indonesia, dated 778 CE, invokes the name of Tārā, who delivers people from the world of infinite sorrows.[6] Srī Harṣa, the author of the *Naiṣadhacarita* (7th-8th century CE) speaks of the custom of making a circle in camphor mixed with musk in the shrine of the goddess.[7] Tārā cult was very popular in Orissa. Tārā is found in the niches of 99 monolithic stūpas of Ratnagiri. Though the *Sādhanamālā* describes many forms of Tārā, the classical Tārā *mantra (Tāre Tuttāre Ture Svāhā)* is reserved only for 11 forms only. In Orissa all these forms are found except *M ṛtyuvancana Tārā* and Vaśyādhikāra Tārā. On the other hand we have evidence of *Caturbhuja Sita Tārā.*

Table 1
Tārā and her Different forms in Orissa

Different forms of Tārā	*Place*
1. Tārā in *lalitāsana, varada mudrā*	Lalitgiri, Ratnagiri, Achutarajpur, Solampur, and other places (129)
2. Standing Tārā (10)	Lalitgiri, Ratnagiri, Solampur, etc.
3. Aṣṭamahābhaya Tārā[8]	Sheragarh (1), Ratnagiri (2)– 3
4. Simhanāda Tārā[9]	Ratnagiri (3), Sheragarh (1), Bhubaneswar (1), —(5)

5. Khadiravanī Tārā[10]	Jaraka (2), Tikiria Temple in Banpur Achutarajpur, Ratnagiri, Baneswarnasi, Choudwar, Sundargram—(9)
6. Mahattarī Tārā	Ratnagiri (2), Achutarajpur, Tiadisahi, Baudh, —(6)
7. Mahāśrī Tārā	Bhubaneswar- (1)
8. Dhanada Tārā[11]	Kapilesvara Temple in Bhubaneswar, Varaha temple Jajpur, brought from Solampur, Baseli Thakurani at Bania Sahi in Cuttack, Kapila Prasad 1 – (4)
9. Four-armed Sita Tārā	Solampur – 1
10. Four-armed Durgotāriṇī Tārā	Lalitgiri, Ratnagiri (2)
11. Vajra Tārā[12]	Ajodhya, Ratnagiri (2)
12. Cintāmaṇi Tārā	Nagaspur, Adaspur-2
Total -12	178

Note: Figure in parentheses refers to number of sculptures.

1.1.2. *Avalokiteśvara*

Avalokiteśvara was the most popular *bodhisattva* in the Buddhist pantheon and his position in Buddhist countries is next to that of the Buddhas. One of the reasons for his popularity is his infinite *karuṇā*. One passage of the *Karaṇḍavyuha* characterises him as taking the shape of all gods of all religion."[13] He is the ruling divinity during the present *kalpa (bhadra kalpa)*, which started with the *Mahāparinirvāṇa* of Gautama and will continue till the advent of Maitreya. Right from the fifteen forms in the *Sādhanamālā*, *Avalokiteśvara*'s forms multiplied through centuries. In 18th century paintings in Machandar Vahal in Nepal, his 108 forms are illustrated.[14] In Ratnagiri monolithic stūpa he is the second most represented divinity after Tārā and is found in the niches of 42 monolithic *stūpas*. The scriptural justification for his numerous forms was one strategy to absorb elements of other cults. In Nepal Karuṇāmaya Matsyendranātha is identified with Kṛṣṇa. Avalokiteśvara is also identified with Śiva. Avalokita shares with Śiva the epithets *isvara, maheśvara* and *Lokeśvara*. Śiva was worshipped as a *bodhisattva* and as a form of Avalokiteśvara.[15]

Various forms of Avalokiteśvara can be conceptualised as a strategy of adaptation of elements of other cults. While Amoghapāśa, Sugatisandarúana, Nīlakaṇṭha are modelled on Śiva, Hālāhala Lokeśvara closely resembles Umā-maheśvara. On the other hand, Viṣṇu-Lokeśvara is a conflation of' Viṣṇu, and Lokeśvara; Śaṅkhanātha Avalokita has striking similarity with another form of Viṣṇu,.

Table 2
Forms of Avalokiteśvara and their Distribution Pattern in Orissa

1. Cintāmaṇicakra Avalokiteśvara[16]	Ajodhya, Ratnagiri, Siddhesvara Temple – 3
2. Cintāmaṇi Lokeśvara	Khutia temple, Ajodhya,[17] Bhubaneswar (OSM), Ratnagiri, 3
3. Khasarpaṇa Lokeśvara	In different places–17 Achutarajpur, Balasore, Bhainchua, Baneswarnasi, Ranibandha, Mudupur, etc.
4. Lokanātha	Udayagiri (3), Jajpur, Kapila, Solampur, Bhubaneswar, Ramesvara in Baudh, Lalitgiri – 9
5. Harihara (?) Lokeśvara/ Avalokita in Dharmacakra-mudrā	Kolanagiri, Balasore, Choudwar – 4
6. Vajradharma/ Rakta Lokeśvara	Siddhesvara Temple in Jajpur, Ratnagiri, Achutarajpur, Aragarh –
7. Saḍakṣarī	Ratnagiri – 2
8. Jaṭāmukuṭa	In different places -38
9. Śaṅkhanātha	Baudh, Udayagiri now in San Francisco Museum, Mudgala 1 –4
10. Amoghapāśa Lokeśvara	Solampur, Udayagiri, Ratnagiri (4) –6

11.	Sugatisandarśana Lokeśvara	Udayagiri (Patna Museum), Cuttack, Dharmasala – 3
12.	Hālāhala Lokeśvara	Achutarajpur, Meghesvara Temple[18] in Bhubaneswar –2
13.	Standing Lokeśvara and Seated Lokeśvara in conventional mode	In different places –37
14.	Viṣṇu-Lokeśvara	Siddhesvara temple at Jajpur – 1
15.	Simhanātha Avalokiteśvara	Baneswarnasi 1
	Total (14)	**130**

Note: Figure in parentheses refers to number of sculptures.

1.1.3 Forms of Mañjuśrī

Mañjuúrī is the Buddhist god of wisdom and knowledge, and hence is represented in sculpture holding a sword and *Prajñāpāramitā* book. The sword, called *Prajñākhaḍga* in some *sādhanas*, invariably in his right hand, is intended to cut asunder all ignorance, while the book, in his left hand, is the means of attaining transcendental wisdom. As bodhisattva of wisdom he is some times identified with ultimate substance *dharmadhātu.* In fact it is to one of the forms of Mañjuúrī, Dharmadhātu Vāgīśvara that the most common sacred object after *caitya* i.e. *dharmadhātu* is dedicated in Nepal. Sylvain Levi in the context of Nepal records that *dharmadhātu* is dedicated to Dharmadhātuvāgīśvara Mañjuśrī and if a *Vajra* is kept on the top, it is called Vajradhātu, which is dedicated to Vairocana.[19] Thus Mañjuśrī, particularly *dharma* variety is always identified with ultimate essence. The *Niṣpannayogāvalī* refers to *Dharmadhātuvāgīśvara maṇḍala. Dharmaśaṅkhasamādhi* Mañjuśrī of Ratnagiri corresponds iconographically to Vajrarāga Mañjuśrī or Vairocana, according to the traditions of Amoghavajra (who took *Vajradhātu maṇḍala* to China) and the Tibetan version of *Mahāvairocanasambodhi.*[20] Mallman and Van kooij observe that some sort of unification took place between Mañjuśrī and Vairocana and other Buddhas.[21] The *Sādhanamālā* describes 13 forms of Mañjuśrī.

Table 3
Forms of Mañjuśrī and their distribution pattern in Orissa

1.	Siddhaikavīra	Ratnagiri (bronze) –1
2.	Dharmaśaṅkhasamadhi	Ratnagiri – 3
3.	Dharmadhātu Vāgīśvara	Aragarh –1
4.	Arapacana Mañjuśrī	Ratnagiri 2, Achutarajpur 1, Kusinga 1, Khiching (Baripada Museum) 1 –5
5.	Mañjuvajra	Amarprasadgarh[22] –1
6.	Mañjuvara	Ratnagiri (5), Khiching (3), Nagaspur (1), Vajragiri (1), Kalyanpur (1) – 11
7.	Mañjughoṣa	Ratnagiri monolithic stūpa –1
8.	Mahārājalīlā Mañjuśrī	Ratnagiri (3), OSM (1), Paschimesvara Śiva temple in Talcher (1) –5
9.	Vajrarāga	On the back slab of Akṣobhya and Amitābha image at SDO- compound Museum –2
10.	Two-armed with book on *utpala* and *varada mudrā* (non-textual) – both standing and seating	Ratnagiri monolithic stūpa – 29, other images at Ratnagiri –12, Lalitgiri –1, Brahmavana –1, Vajragiri (OSM) –1, Udayagiri – as attendant deity in various *maṇḍalas* as well as the central image in the rock-cut MaÚjuúrī *maṇḍalas* – 8, Solampur –2, Dihakula –1, Achutarajpur –3 – 58
	Total 10	88

Note: Figure in parentheses refers to number of sculptures.

Table 4
Cult of Eight Bodhisattvas and other Bodhisattvas: Distribution pattern of such sculptures in Orissa

1.	Sāmantabhadra	Lalitgiri (I) 3, Udayagiri-6, Solampur(s)1, Ratnagiri(s) 3 – 13
2	Maitreya	Ratnagiri(s &i) 4, Udayagiri 7 (s), Lalitgiri 4 (i), Achutarajpur (i) 2, Solampur(s) 1 Khiching (s) 1, Baud 1 – 20

3. Lokeśvara	In many places
4. Kṣitigarbha	Lalitgiri (i&ii) 2, Ratnagiri (s) 3, Udayagiri(s) 7, Achutarajpur (I) 1, Solampur (s) 1 Khiching (s) 1– 15
5. Vajrapāṇi	Ratnagiri (s&i) 4, Vajragiri (i) 1, Lalitgiri (i) 1, Achutarajpur (i) 1, Solampur(s) 1, Udayagiri (s) 5, Khiching (s)
6. Ākāśagarbha	Lalitgiri (i) 2, and at other places under Vajrapā?i section
7. Mañjuśrī	In many places
8. Sarvaṇivarṇaviskambhī	Lalitgiri (i &s) 2, Ratnagiri 3 Udayagiri (s) 8
Other Bodhisattvas	
1. Candraprabha	Lalitgiri 1

Note: Figure in parentheses refers to the number of sculptures.

It is to be noted that independent, freestanding Bodhisattvas as part of a *maṇḍala* is found exclusively at Lalitgiri. Given the size of these *bodhisattvas* one can surmise the extensiveness of *Tathāgata maṇḍala* in Lalitgiri, of which Donaldson has identified five.

1.1.4. Pañca Buddha and their emanations in Orissa: Akṣobhya

In the absence of elephant or *vajra* symbols by which Akṣobhya is identified, the recognition is mainly made on the basis of the absence or presence of attendant Bodhisattvas and specific *mudrā,* in Akṣobhya's case it is the earth-touching *(bhūmisparśamudrā).* His image is found in many places but the largest is found in Udayagiri where there are at least four Akṣobhya *maṇḍalas*. The following table represents his emanation.

Amoghasiddhi

The following table represents gods and goddesses of *Amoghasiddhi* family.

Table 5
Emanations of *Akṣobhya* and Distribution pattern of such Sculptures in Orissa

Gods	*Places where Scul*	*Goddesses*	*Places*
Caṇḍaroṣaṇa	Ratnagiri		
Heruka	Ratnagiri, Achutarajpur, Choudwar Kuruma	*Mahācīna Tārā*	———
Hayagrīva	As attendant of Lokanātha he is found all over Orissa	*Jāṅgulī*	Haripur, Kuruma
Kṛṣṇayamāri	Ersama, Ratnagiri (as an attendant of Avalokita	*Parṇaśabarī*	Ratnagiri
Jambhala	In Numerous places	*Vasudharā*	Udayagiri, Ratnagiri, Dharmasala, Lalitgiri
Trailokyavijaya	Achutarajpur, Ratnagiri	*Nairātmā*	Trivienisvara temple, Tiruna
Samvara	Ratnagiri		

Amitābha Family

Similarly the following gods and goddesses of Amitābha family are found in Orissa. The *Sādhanamālā* refers to *Mahābala* and *Saptaśatika*. I have not come across any image of *Saptaśatika Hayagrīva*, who is described as holding *vajra* and *daṇḍa* in his two hands and has a horse face. At Lalitgiri, I found an image of *Hayagrīva* having horse face, but his two other cognisances are absent. On the other hand, Hayagrīva in *vandanavinayi-mudrā* is found in *Khasarpaṇa* and *Jaṭāmukuṭa Lokeśvara* images of Orissa. Mahābala also figures as an attendant deity on *Jaṭāmukuṭa Lokeśvara* image. Among the goddesses, different varieties of *Kurukullā* and *Bhṛkutī* are found in Orissa. On the other hand, I have not come across any *Mahāsitavati* image.

Table 6
Emanation of *Amoghasiddhi* and distribution pattern of such Sculptures in Orissa

Goddesses	*Places*
Khadiravanī Tārā	See different forms of Tārā
Sita Tārā	
Dhanada Tārā	
Parṇaśabarī	Ratnagiri, Dharmasala and *Udayagiri*
Mahāmāyūrī	Kosangarh, Badasahi, Ratnagiri

* Vajrāmṛta is the sole god in *Amoghasiddhi* family, and is not found in Orissa.

Kurukullā: There are three different forms of *Kurukullā*, namely *Śukla, Uḍḍiyāṇa* and *Tārodbhava Kurukullā*. The second one suggests the popularity of the god in *Uḍḍiyāṇa*. *Tārodbhava Kurukullā* variety is found at Ratnagiri II monastery area, Udayagiri rock-cut image, *Candana Mandapa* in Kakatpur, now worshipped as goddess Narāyaṇī. *Uḍḍiyāṇa Kurukullā* is found from Achutarajpur bronze hoard. On the other hand *Bhṛkutīis* are found as attendant deity in *Jaṭāmukuṭa* and *Khasarpaṇa Lokeśvara* images of Orissa and also occur independently.

Vairocana family

While Vairocana image is found in many places including at Lalitgiri, Ratnagiri and Udayagiri, his *Prajñā Locanā* is discovered from Ratnagiri, Gardeipancana and possibly a three-headed Devi image near the Raghunatha temple at Solampur. The three-headed Devi holds a lotus on her left and a sword on her right. Vairocana's male emanations, Nāmasaṇgīti is not found in Orissa. Out of eight goddesses of Vairocana family, six are found from Orissa. They are Mārīcī, (Uṣṇiṣavijayā), Sitapatra Aparājitā, Vajravārāhī and Cuṇḍā.

The Buddhist counterpart of Sūrya is found all over Orissa attesting the popularity of the goddess in Orissa. Aśokakāntā Mārīcī is found from the bronze hoard of Achutarajpur, Ratnagiri and many other places. Eight-handed standing Mārīcī, called Mārīcīvupa, who is without any companion, is found from numerous places. Also found are eight-armed standing Mārīcī with companion called Samkṣīpta Mārīcī and Uḍḍiyāṇa Mārīcī from Mārīcīpur and Odosingoda in Jajpur district.

Table 7

Emanation of Vairocana and distribution pattern of such sculptures in Orissa

Goddess	*Place*
Mārīcī	In many places
Uṣṇiṣavijayā	Ratnagiri
Vajravārāhī	Choudwar, Baseli Thakurani, Badagaon
Cundā	Ratnagiri, OSM, Udayagiri, now in Patna Museum, Achutarajpur and other places
Aparājitā	Lalitgiri, Udayagiri and Ratnagiri

While *Jambhala* and *Ucchuṣma Jambhala* belong to *Ratnasambhava* family, *Vajra Tārā, Vajrayoginī, Vasudharā, Mahāpratisarā and Prasanna Tārā* belong to *Ratneśa* family. *Aparājitā* image is found from Lalitgiri, Ratnagiri and Udayagiri but in no image is she trampling on *Gaṇeśa* as is enjoined in the text. On the other hand in Orissan images, she is represented trampling on an elephant. *Vasudharā* images with ear of corns are found in many places (Lalitgiri, Ratnagiri, Udayagiri, etc.)

Images associated with great events of the life of the Buddha

While Buddha images of different postures are found all over Orissa, there are only few images, which depict the life of Buddha. Most important from iconographic point of view is the eight-*mahāpratihārya* image from Solampur, which is now affixed to the back wall of the Raghunatha temple. Descent of the Buddha from Lalitgiri, Brahma and Indra as parasol bearers of Buddha from Udayagiri, *Mucalinda* image from Lalitgiri, Ganiapalli and G. Udayagiri (OSM) are other sculptures which deal with Gautama' life.

2. Vajrayāna as religion of the laity

The widespread presence of various gods, goddesses and Bodhisattvas underlies the vibrancy of the Buddhism in Orissa. In our opinion, the worship of these goddesses was clearly social and instrumental in nature. Instrumental actions are those behaviours, which are oriented "to changing the state of the world as a means to the end of one's subjective experience."[23] If a prayer, a spell, in its correct formulation tends to achieve the purpose for which it was recited, will be characterised as instrumental. To take an instance, if a childless woman goes to Hārītī and worships her in the correct manner, performs the enjoined rituals, we will conclude that the prayer is an instrumental mean to achieve the desired end i.e. to get a child. The desired goal (getting a child) leads to change in one's subjective experience. Prayer or performance of rituals in this situation will be considered as instrumental means while the deity performs an instrumental role.

Vajrayāna Buddhism catered to the devotional and this-worldly needs of the masses. Here one finds numerous Buddha, *Bodhisattvas*, gods and goddesses, both in peaceful and wrathful moods. Each god and goddess was assigned an instrumental role to fulfil the everyday needs and aspirations of the masses. The germ syllable (*bījamantra*) of each deity was believed to possess magical powers and recitations of these *mantras* guarantee fulfilment of desires. It also incorporated other elements of the period, *viz.*, incorporation of deities from Brahmanical religion, incorporation of motifs and symbols from it, incorporating tribal and Tantric-goddess tradition to its fold. It developed an elaborate ritual structure as well.

In a way the innovation of multitude gods and goddesses could be seen as a culmination of the process of making Buddhism more instrumental. The soteriolgy of Vajrayāna is the attainment of *śūnyatā*, which can be achieved by esoteric means, but as an exoteric religion, it is more akin to Srāvakayāna and Mahāyāna. The similarities with Srāvakayāna and Mahāyāna were the worship of Buddha, chanting of *mantra*, monastic ritual like *Caityavandanā*, etc. Gellner has shown in his studies of Newar Buddhism that in practice, Newar Buddhists (who are mainly Vajrayāna follower) rites are Srāvakayāna during the rites themselves, but bracketed by an inoffensive exoteric version of the Vajrayāna. The *Samvarodaya Tantra*[24] had described the characteristics of a *vajra* master, which include the ideas of Theravāda, Mahāyāna and Vajrayāna.[25]

In the exoteric form of Vajrayāna the male deities appear without their female partner. Unlike Vajrayāna texts, in Orissa not a single image of a male deity is found embracing his *Prajñā*. This tradition of observing *srāvaka* practices in a limited context within a framework of Vajrayāna is characterised as Mahāyāna in Nepal.[26] Buddhism in practice was closer to this form in Orissa during 7th-12th centuries CE. There are two reasons to support such a formulation. First, there is not a single Buddhist male god found embracing his *Prajñā*, which is an integral part of Vajrayāna ritual. This suggests that rituals were more *Srāvakayāna* in its form. The second evidence to support such a formulation is that Vajrayāna Buddhism was not restricted to serious practitioners but had wider appeal. This is borne from the niches of numerous votive *stūpas*. The votive *stūpas* contain in their niches many deities introduced during Vajrayāna phase and reveal the cult preference of the pilgrims. None of these depict any embracing pose. Even though Vajrayāna Buddhism as soteriology was esoteric, as an exoteric religion it is highly unlikely that monastic organisations of early medieval India, which had established economic interests, would have preferred the open display of such antinomian practices of esoteric Buddhism. In fact, the Buddhist *tantras* betray traces of a process of routinisation of these extreme practices. In fact, some important Vajrayāna texts, like the *Hevajra Tantra*, betray an attempt to routinise many esoteric Tantric practices. It says,

> first the precepts should be given, then the ten. Then he should teach *Vaibhāsya*, then the *Sautāntrika* After that he should teach *Yogācāra*, then the *Mādhyamika*. After he knows levels of the ways of Mantras then he should begin on *Hevajra*. The pupil who lays holds with zeal will succeed. There is no doubt.[27]

Kanhapada's commentary on this passage prescribes a process from exotericism to esotericism rather than outright display of antinomian behaviour.

Moreover, it is to be noted that many of the Buddhist deities who trample on Hindu divinities are largely absent in Orissa. This seems to be a conscious decision by the Buddhists. On the other hand, Buddhism developed an elaborate pantheon structure and rituals for the laity. Such a structure requires the need of a specialist because these divinities that were invested with powers to solve specific problems required a particular mode of worship as well as a set of rituals.[28] For the average populace, who constituted the base of a widely spread religion, the saliency of existential wants predominated over other objectives. The Buddhist deities seem to cater to these needs. A poor man could pray to Vasudharā to give him plenty. An infertile lady could worship *Hārītī* for getting children. Vajrayāna Buddhism developed a vast structure of pantheon, from Buddhas to *ḍākinī*, who fulfil these existential needs of people. The *Sādhanamālā* and other texts refer to instrumental functions of each deity. The following table represents instrumental functions of these deities.

Table 8

Instrumental functions of Buddhist divinities

Category	*Buddhist deities*	*Instrumental Function*
Buddhas	*Dipankara*	Islanders' deity favouring merchants
	Bhaiṣajyaguru	Healer Buddha; worshipped for curing illness
	Vajrapāṇi	God of Rain (ii) provide elixir of life (iii) to cure snake
	Avalokiteśvara	Saviours. As savours he saves from eight or eleven fears
	Avalokiteśvara in feminine form	Worshipped by woman
	Mañjuśrī	(i) For learning (ii) destroys ignorance (iii) god of Agriculture
	Sankhananga Mañjuśrī	for bewitching woman

Category	Buddhist deities	Instrumental Function
Bodhisattvas	*Ārogyaśālī Lokeśvara*	God of healing
	Simhanāda Lokeśvara	Invoked to cure leprosy
	Cintāmaṇi Lokeśvara	God of Wealth
	Kṣitigarbha	Master of six world of Desire (ii) God of Death
	Ākāśagarbha	God of Wealth
Goddesses	*Harītī*	Goddess of fecundity, prevents small pox, protects kitchen
	Aparājitā	Goddesses of ghosts
	Trailokyavijaya	Conqueror of evil spirit
	Aṣṭamahābhaya Tārā	Saviouress
	Jāṅgulī	Cure snake-bite
	Kurukullā	For bewitching lovers
	Vajra-Sarasvatī	Goddess of wealth, learning
	Vasudharā	Goddess of abundance
	Parnaśabarī	Small pox
	Uṣṇīṣavijayā	Goddess of transcendental wisdom
	Mahāmāyūrī	Invoked in snake bite
	Prajñāpāramitā	Goddess of Intelligence
Gods	*Yamāntaka*	Invoked to conquer death
	Hayagrīva	God of horse traders
	Mahākāla	God of wealth and hearth
	Jambhala	God of Wealth

2.1. Priesthood and Rituals

Two other aspects of Vajrayāna also contributed to the expansion of Buddhism. Of course, the Vajrayāna texts were highly metaphysical in their meaning but many of the idioms and expressions provide an indication of the way it tried to reach out to different groups. In many texts and *caryāpadas* there are reference to lower-caste women like *ḍoma, hadi etc.* The Tantric *yogins* themselves have occasionally gone out of their way to emphasise the low social status of their preferred partners, specifying on occasions that the ideal consort was a sixteen year female partner of the despised *ḍoma* caste. The societal implication of such a position is difficult to ascertain because it is difficult to know how far the gender polarities that existed in Buddhist Tantric circles had anything to do with the conventional gender role. However, it is certain that the inferior position accorded to women within the monastic establishment was somewhat retrieved by Vajrayāna by according an important position to feminine principle. Further, women were accorded religious authority on the basis of religious realisation and the timely display of their magical power.

More important aspect is the implication of female principle and the need of a *guru* for initiation to Vajrayāna. Initiation into Vajrayāna, both for laity and monk, required ritual. A *guru* who is an accomplished one can do this. An accomplished one in Vajrayāna traditions requires various practices including the need of a female partnership. Through this logic Vajrayāna established a married priest system, who could act as *guru*, to initiate the new to its fold. Dumont summarises this process thus:

> An individualistic soteriolgy is in fact used to define another hereditary group. Tantricism combined mysticism and ritual to great effect. It gave value to the individual. Yet at the same time, the emphasis on secrecy, the necessity of a *guru* and the importance of sexual partner and therefore, marriage, Tantricism also provided a Sanskritic idiom for the religion of the group.[29]

2.1.1 Rituals

The Vajrayāna rituals are not Tantric in their entirety. The Vajrayāna form treats not only the tantric rites but also the Mahāyāna rituals like the erection of *stūpa*, setting up of images, *stotras*, and daily rituals. The *Kriyātantra* deals with ceremonies at the building of images, erection of images of Buddhist divinities. The *Caryā-tantras* deals with the cults of daily practice. In the category of *Kriyātantra*, the *ādikarmapradīpa* was the most important. The *Kriyāsamgraha pañjikā*, which is catalogued in the Brahmanical manual of rituals category in the *Asiatic Society of Bengal* Manuscript section[30] is actually a Buddhist text. It describes the ceremonies and religious rituals, which the *Adikarma Bodhisattvas* i.e. the adherents of Mahāyāna had to perform. The work consists of a *sutra* text with a running commentary and contains precepts on the initiation ceremony for disciple (which can be a layman or monk). They include sprinkling of water, washing and prayers, rules for rinsing mouth, morning and evening devotion, offering of water to departed, alms giving, worshipping of Buddha at various times of the day. The Jayarampur plate of Sri Gopacandra (5th century CE) records that the grant of villages was made in order to make provisions for *bali* (offering to all creatures), *caru* (offerings to the ancestors), *gaḍdha* (sandal paste), *puṣpa* (flowers), for *haviṣa* (oblations), *pātra* (the pots for offering oblations).[31]

The *Aṣṭamīvrata-vidhāna* contains the rules for the ceremonies to be held on every eighth day of the first half of the month, dedicated to *Mañjuśrī*.[32] Śrī Harṣa in the *Naiṣadhacarita* speaks of the custom of making a circle of camphor mixed with musk in the shrine of the goddess.[33] I-tsing refers to many customs, which were practiced by the people in 7th century CE. These customs vary from bathing of deities to offerings to various deities.[34]

2.1.2 Vajrayāna as a religion of magical protection

The ontological explanation on the identity of *nirvāṇa* and *samsāra* is the philosophical basis of magic of Vajrayāna. The absolute is the only reality and pervades the entire universe. Each thought, action and word is in its true essence an activity of the Absolute. As its manifestation, this phenomenal world contains all the mysteries of reality and its hidden forces can be used for salvation. As a reflex of the Absolute, the universe everywhere reflects, manifest and reveal this Absolute Unity. If all things are fundamentally one pure spirit, all cosmic phenomena is linked to each other in a thread; each word, action and thought is somehow connected with the Eternal Ground of the world. Magic is this unity. If the thought is the only reality, the thought condensed to *mantras* have powers over material thing. The *śūnya*, in turn, form of a god or goddess in whose power the magician can share by identification.

Even before this philosophical justification of magic Buddhism had developed a number of rituals which are now considered to be Vajrayanist – recitation of spells, worship of images, performances of rites, etc. Theravāda Buddhism, in response to psychophysical needs, had developed a number of non-soteriological goals within the domain of legitimate Buddhist concerns.

The Buddhists used magical formulas as shields to protect themselves from physical dangers from the very beginning. Buddha himself believed in supernatural powers and was ascribed to have classified four kinds of *iddhipadas* (supernatural power) – will, effort, thought, and investigation. The early Mahayanists used the *sūtras* as protective spells and called them *dhāraṇīs*.[35] Fa-hien recited the *Surāngama sūtra* as a *dhāraṇī* in his journey, while crossing the Gobi desert, Xuanzang recited the *Hṛdaya sūtra* (*sūtra* of the Heart of Perfect Wisdom) by calling for the aid of Hwan-yin (a form of *Avalokiteśvara*), who had taught this *sūtra*.[36] The use of *dhāraṇīs* (*dhārayati anaya iti*– by which something is sustained) as protective spells was very popular in this period. Numerous *dhāraṇīs* in clay seals are found from Ratnagiri. Vasubandhu in the *Bodhisattvabhūmi* categorised four kinds of *dhāraṇīs* – *dharma dhāraṇī, arthadhāraṇī, mantradhāraṇī* and the *Bodhisattvakshantilābha dhāraṇī*.[37] From 5th century CE onwards, independent *sūtras* of Vajrayāna were composed and they were credited with powers, which could lead to salvation. In many *stūpas* of Orissa, one finds *dhāraṇīs* being inserted inside a *stūpa*. An inscription, now in the Orissa State Museum (OSM), Bhubaneswar, states that the construction of a single *caitya* (*stūpa*) with a deposit of a *dhāraṇī* inside it confers on the donor the merit of one *lakh* of *Tathāgata caityas*.[38] The following table gives a list of some *dhāraṇīs* and their functions.

Table 9
Various Dhāraṇīs and their Functions

Dhāraṇīs	*Function*
1. The *sūtra* on the *dhāraṇīs* for protecting children	1. For the protection of children
2. (i) *Mahāpratisarā dhāraṇīs* Mahā-pratyangira- dhāraṇī (i) Vasundharā dhāraṇī	2. Invoked for longevity
3. Mahā Pratyangira-dhāraṇī	3. Invoked to ward off evil and endow with all powers to do good to the devotees
4. Maniratna sūtra dhāraṇī	4. Recited to dispel diseases and disaster
5. Pancarakṣā (five Protective spell) dhāraṇī (i) Mahāpratisarā (ii) Mahasahasra Pramardini (iii) Mahāmāyūrī (iv) Mahā–sitavatī (v) Mahārakṣā-mantranusārini	5. For protection against sin, disease and other evils
6. Uṣṇīṣavijayā dhāraṇī	6. Efficacious in curing diseases and prolonging life
7. *Vajravidarananama-dhāraṇī*	7. To ensure robust health
8. *Piśāchi Parṇasavarināma-dhāraṇī*	8. to ward off disease

Vratas and litanies

R.L. Mitra in his book *The Sanskrit Buddhist Literature* cites many *Vratas* and *avadānas*, which are popular among the Newari Buddhists. These *Vratas* and *Avadānas* are important for they allude to the number of rituals and fasts practised by the lay Buddhists. In one of his writings on why Buddhism died out in India where as Jainism continued to exist in few pockets, Jaini concludes that one of the most crucial factors for the decline of Buddhism in India was the relative absence of specially Buddhist observances for the laity.[39] A careful analysis, however, will give a different picture. Fasting on holy days of *Eight Precepts* (*Aṣṭamivrata*) was one of the ancient *Vratas* for the laity.[40] Amoghapāśa Lokeśvāra is worshipped during *Aṣṭamivrata*. Many Sanskrit manuscripts, copied in the *Nepal Samvat*, describe these *Vratas* and *Avadānas*. But most of them belong to the 18th century. Some of these rituals are associated with the worship of stūpas. The *Uposadha Avadāna* deals with *uposatha* ceremony during *Aṣṭamī vrata*, which was celebrated on the eighth of waning moon. A hut was erected with five kinds of sacred wood in which Lokeśvāra was worshipped. The performer observes the purification of the eight members of the body before after it for week.[41] The *Suchandravadāna* (NS 245) was dedicated to Vasudharā, the Buddhist counterpart of Lakṣmī. The rite should be undertaken on the 3rd of the waning moon in the month of *bhadra*. The rite consisted of bathing in a river, putting on clean clothes filling a pitcher with pure water over which the *mantra* of Vasudharā is repeated. The *Chaitya pungava (Nepal Samvat* 905 i.e. 1894 CE) is a rite of the adoration of *caityas* and rituals and merits there of. The *caitya* is to be made of pure clay mixed with the five products of the cow, the five nectars (*sic*), the five jewels and five aromatics. The mixture is then to be kneaded seven times while repeating *Sāmantabhadra mantra*.[42] I-tsing refers to popularity of *caityas* thus;

> the priest and laymen in India make *caityas* or images with earth or impress the Buddha's image on silk or paper. Sometimes they build stūpas of the Buddhas by making a pile and surrounding it with bricks. The *Kathinavadāna*describes on the merit of chastity, abstinence, etc. during the period of Buddhist lent *kathina*. This period extends to thirty days from the first of the new moon in the month of *āsvina*. Gift to monks and recitals of the stories in praise of charity are the principal observances.[43]

The *Tārā- sata-nāma stotra* is a collection of 108 epithets strung together in the form of a hymn in praise of a goddess Ekajaṭā Ārya Tārā. The hymn is alleged to have been imported by Avalokiteśvara to Vajrapāṇi and is intended to be worn as amulet to avert evils proceeding from thieves, war, fire, lions, waters, elephants, tigers.[44] Table 2 (on page 158) represents some of the *stotras*.

Table 2
Important Stotras dedicated to Buddhist Deities

Stotras	*Nature and dedicated to*	*Author*	*Ref. Winterniz 1983: 362-386)*
Suprabhāta - stotra	A morning hymn in praise of Buddha in twenty-four verses	Harṣa	
Aṣṭamahā-śrī caitya-stotra	A hymn in praise of the eight great shrines in five stanzas	Ascribed to Harsa	———
Lokeśvara śataka	Hundred stanzas in praise of *Lokeśvara*	Vajradatta in Devapala's reign (9th century)	———
Paramārtha nāma sangiti	A litany of an enume ration of names and laudatory epithets of Buddha	?	Mitra 1981:185
Ārya -Tārā sragdhara stotra	A *stotra* in *sragdhara* metre in praise of *Tārā* in thirty-seven verses	*Sarvajñānamitra* of Kashmir(8th- 9th century)	Winternitz vol. II
Ekavimsati strotra	Hymn dedicated to *Tārā* in twenty-one verses	?	Wayman 1959: 36-43
Ārya Tārā nāmastottra -śataka-stotra	Long of praise consisting of 108 names of the goddess *Ekajatā* ārya Tārā	?	Mitra 1981: 259-60
Vasudharā sattotatTārā-satanāma	108 epithets forming a hymn in praise of *Vasudharā*	?	Mitra:1981: 274
Sapta-buddha stotra	Praises of the seven *Mānuṣī* Buddha	?	Winternitz

There are other protective *mantras* in Buddhism as well. The classic *mantra* of *Avalokitśvara Padmapāṇi 'Om Maṇipadma Hum'* is one of the most important *mantras* of *Avalokiteśvara* and is widely popular in Tibet. The surest protection from physical danger is the love and graciousness of *Tārā*. In sculpture as in the *Aṣṭamahābhaya Tārā* image of Ratnagiri, *Tārā* is depicted as guarding her devotees from the eight great perils. Similarly *Avalokiteśvara* emerges as eight different deities to free from eight fears as acolytes of *Aśṭabhaya-trāṇa-Ekādaśamukha Avalokiteśvara*.[45] The short *mantra* of *Tārā 'Om* Tāre *Tuttāre Ture Svāhā,'* when recited properly, is believed to confer many boons and is highly efficacious. The power of these *mantras* is derived from their "consecration by the Buddha, which exerts upon them a deep and inconceivable influence."[46]

3. Other evidences of social base of Buddhism: votive *stūpas*, plaques, terracotta amulets

The above evidences clearly point out that Vajrayāna Buddhism addressed to the instrumental needs of the laity and therefore, innovated gods and goddesses, created rituals and mode of worships for them, thus clearly negating the argument that it was bundle of superstitions and psychosocial practices confined to monks only. The worship of such gods and goddesses was not limited to monks alone. Their worship by the lay worshippers in Orissa was attested by number of votive *stūpas* at the Buddhist sites of Orissa, which carry in their niches, these gods and goddesses indicating the cult preference of the pilgrims.[47] Laypersons and monks donated a huge number of votive *stūpas* in various Buddhist pilgrim centres. In Orissa as well as in other Buddhist sites of India a number of sacred objects like votive *stūpas*, terracotta plaques, seals and *dhāraṇīs* and terracotta amulets have been found. These sacred objects, sacralised by a ritual process, carry forward and contain the power and charisma of the Buddha himself. They are as sacred and potent as the Buddha himself.

In normative and popular Buddhist literature the Buddha was represented as radiant, full of energy and powerful under whom the Brahmanical gods served as attendant deities. After his death his *cetiyas* was imbued with potency and considered to be beneficial to those who worship these symbols. With the conception of primordial Buddha, god and *dharma-kāya* in Mahāyāna Buddhism originated the ideas of infinite Buddhas. The *Saddharmapuṇḍarīka* says that when the Buddha sat in meditation rays of light burst forth from his hair, between his eyebrows and illuminated 18 hundred thousand Buddha lands down to great hell, *Avici,* and up to the limit of existence.[48] The notion of radiance and fierce energy and potency associated with the Buddha were carried to his *cetiyas* and further to sacred Buddhist objects and words through a process of ritual sacralisation.

This three-stage transformation of potency and radiance – from the Buddha to his *cetiyas* to other sacred objects has resulted in the proliferation of votive *stūpas,* terracotta images, amulets and other sacred objects. These sacred objects were imbued with indexicality after a certain ritual process. These indexical symbols represent both continuities and transformation simultaneously. For instance, the votive *stūpas* of *śārīrika* variety remind, on the one hand, the *śārīrika cetiyas* of the Buddha, and hence indicate the continuities of the tradition of the Buddha's *cetiyas*. On the other hand, the *śārīrika stūpas* underwent transformation in the sense that the *śārīrika cetiyas* of other historical Buddhist saints, by virtue of the continuation of a tradition going back to the Buddha, can also be considered as having potency to provide benefits to their worshippers. As Tambiah says:

> The amulets as objectification of charisma are shown to have double presence: they embody memories past historical traditions and heroes, and they are linked to present-day living saints who are in contact with followers and disciples to whom they radiate their saintly virtue.[49]

The votive and other structural *stūpas* provided a dynamic linkage between the local populace, who venerated these small *stūpas* of the local monks and the monastic establishment. It also reinforced the existing practice of worshipping *cetiyas* associated with the Buddha.[50]

Apart from the *śārīrika stūpas*, the other popular objects of veneration were votive *stūpas*, terracotta amulets, seals, sealing and *dhāraṇīs*. Clay seals and sealing as well clay *stūpas* are found in large numbers in many Buddhist establishments of India and elsewhere. The large store of terracotta seals with the creed-and-deer symbol stamped on them and the diminutive clay *stūpas*, with small seals found in the monasteries of Saranath are Buddhist memorabilia which pilgrims would take away from the Buddhist sites to their respective places or, to deposit at their village shrines. At the temple of Pagan and elsewhere in Burma, many such terracotta tablets and seals have been found, which, from the designs on them, have been thought to have come from India, and to have been brought by the Burmese pilgrims returning from Saranath and Bodh Gaya.[51] Hundreds of these tiny clay stūpas are found in 1924 at Pejeng on the island of Bali and in 1935 from Jongke in Java, seven kilometre north of Jog Jakarta. Further clay tablet and stūpas were found from Kedah and Borobodur respectively.[52]

Terracotta seals and sealings of monastery and private monks and lay people have been found in plenty in Ratnagiri, Nalanda and Bodh Gaya, etc. The short inscriptions on these seals and sealing refer to the donor, his socio-economic status, place to which he belongs to and other details which point out the wide support base of early medieval Buddhism. In fact, these seals and sealing of different persons prove that early medieval Buddhism, far from being confined to monastic establishment and its esoteric secret practices, enjoyed wider social support.

Terracotta amulets of different postures of the Buddha – in *bhūmisparśa*, *dharmacakra-pravartana* and other *mudrās* – provide another basis to understand social base of Buddhism in our period of study. Used as pendant and believed to have efficacy, these small terracotta amulets were worn by devotees. Amulets of different categories have been a subject of a fascinating anthropological study by Tambiah in the context of Thai Buddhism.[53] Though there is no evidence of terracotta amulets of famous Buddhist monks in India (main thrust of Tambiah's work), the amulets of Buddha alone indicate that these were popular objects, worn and used by devotees of far and wide.

From 7th-8th century onwards, the Buddhist *dhāraṇīs* replaced *Pratītya-samutpāda* in dedicatory *stūpas*.[54] *Dhāraṇīs* were Buddhist magical words believed to power and efficacy. These *dhāraṇīs* when placed inside a votive *stūpa*, are believed to have suffused the latter with energy, like a sort of electrical charge, and can be immensely beneficial. An inscription of Orissa, dated to the 10th century CE, states that the construction of a single *caitya* (*stūpa*) with a deposit of a *dhāraṇīs* inside it confers on the donor the merit of the erection of one lakh of *Tathāgata caitya*.[55] I-tsing echoes this prevalent belief when he testifies that the people when construct a *stūpa* put in the *caityas* two kind of *śarīras*: (1) the relic of the Great Teacher; (2) the *Gāthā* of causation. If these two are put in the image or *caitya*, the blessing derived from them are abundant.[56] Ratnagiri, Lalitgiri and other sites have yielded *stūpas* having *dhāraṇīs* in them.

Therefore these material artefacts – *śārīrika stūpa*, votive *stūpas*, votive *stūpas* with *dhāraṇīs* in them, terracotta amulets, plaques, seals and sealing – attest to a more general and popular support base of Buddhism. These material objects, along with the Buddhist iconography provide true index of the popularity of Buddhism and accruing support base that went beyond royal patronage, so much emphasised as vital for the growth of a religion.

The votive *stūpas* can be categorised into three types: structural, monolithic and clay votive *stūpas*. In Orissa, one

Votive *stūpas*. Inset A Lalitgiri *Chhatravalī* converted to a Tulsi Pedestal. Inset B: Votives *stūpas* at Udayagiri. Inset C: votive *stūpas* near *mahāstūpa*, Ratnagiri

finds the first two varieties while clay votive *stūpas* have been found from the archaeological excavation of Saranath and Maha Bodhi. The monolithic *stūpas* can be classified into two further categories: *śārīrika* and purely votive. The *śārīrika stūpas* have small socket at the base to put the *dhātu*. However, the overwhelming numbers of the monolithic *stūpas* are votive. The excavator of Ratnagiri has divided the monolithic *stūpas* of Ratnagiri into following categories on the basis of surface treatment.

1. Plain or slightly decorated *stūpas* without any image; plain *stūpas* with relief of *āyaka* pillars;
2. Plain or decorated *stūpas* with a slight projection on the one side of the drum and dome meant for carved into a niche for an image
3. Plain *pañcāyatana stūpa* the four smaller *stūpas* being fashioned on the top corner of the platform;
4 *Pañcāyatana stūpas* relieved with an image within a niche; plain or decorated *stūpas* with a niche on one side for a detachable image; plain or decorated *stūpas* relieved with an image inside a niche, in one specimen two images within separate niches.

When Cunningham excavated Mahābodhi area, he found, "*stūpas*, monolithic *stūpas*, clay *stūpas*, both baked and unbaked from two three inches in height to the size of walnut. Scores of small *stūpas* are found inside the large *stūpas* enclosing small seals. This observation is an echo of what Xuanzang saw at Bodh Gaya in 7th century:

> Here there are *stūpas*, in another places *vihāras*. The kings, the princes and other great personages throughout Jambudvīpa who have accepted the bequeathed teachings as handed down to them have erected these monuments as memorials.[57]

I-tsing referred to the popularisation of *stūpa* cult thus,

> The priests and laymen in India make *caitya* (*stūpa*) or images with earth or the Buddha's image on silk or paper and worship it with offering wherever they so. Sometimes they build stūpas of the Buddha by making a pile and surrounding with bricks. They sometimes form these *stūpas* in lonely field and leave

> them to fall in ruins.[58]

Xuanzang also referred to the popularity of stūpa worship:

> It is a custom in India to make little stūpas their height is about six or seven inches. This, then, was the occupation of Jayasena; with his mouth he declared the excellent law, whilst with his hand he constructed these *stūpas*. Thus he acquired highest and most excellent religious merit.[59]

Votive *stūpas* of these varieties exhibit a great amount of variations. In sheer number the votive *stūpas* of Ratnagiri even outnumber the same of Bodh Gaya. While some of these monolithic votive *stūpas* are elaborately decorated and have images in their niches – either in relief or sculptural- the others are quite simple. Most of these votive *stūpas* contain in their niches images of different Buddhist divinities. In some votive *stūpas* of Ratnagiri, one finds elaborate sculptural *maṇḍala*s as in the *Jambhala maṇḍala* in votive *stūpa* no. 37 of Ratnagiri, or monolithic *stūpa* with *Prajñā*s of four *Dhyānī Buddha* on four corner Introduction of sculptural *maṇḍala*s in *stūpas* — as in Udayagiri main *stūpa* and votive *stūpas* of Ratnagiri — mark a decisive advance in *stūpa* worship, as *maṇḍala* form of *stūpa* represent a complex stage of Buddhism.

In Ratnagiri more than 700 monolithic *stūpas* have been exposed by excavation in the *mahāstūpa* area and area in front of monastery 2 alone. The number of partly visible *stūpas* scattered on hill, particularly near the banyan tree are considerable. Some of these monolithic votive *stūpas*, which are limited in number, were doubtless used for enshrining the bone relics of the departed monks. For this purpose they were provided with socket, usually at the base to hold the charred bones. The remaining *stūpas* are all votive, and were sometimes inscribed with the usual Buddhist creed formula. Several unfinished *stūpas* have been found from the area. They have projections on one side of the drum and dome. Presumably, the intention was to carve the figure of the deities into these projections according to the inclination of the devotees. Evidently, these somewhat incomplete *stūpas* were sold or dedicated during the period of heavy rush of pilgrims of varying means, and consequently had to part with these *stūpas* in place of plain decorated *stūpas,* which fell short of demand. These monolithic votive *stūpas* could not be permanently kept in the immediate vicinity of *mahāstūpa* due to their ever-increasing number as well due to the outgrowth of small structural *stūpas* around the *mahāstūpa.* Hence, these monolithic *stūpas* were dumped in the nearest available place. Some of these found place on the ruined tops of earlier structural *stūpas.* Some of these were dedicated more than once is proved by addition of an image either carved on the monolithic itself or fashioned on a separate slab or put inside a niche cut evenly in the finished body of the *stūpa* on a few *stūpas.* Thus the *stūpa* on plate LXXXI B of Ratnagiri (Vol. I) appear to be an addition, the *stūpa* itself having most probably been originally a *śārīrika* memorial.[60] This rededication around the *mahāstūpa* indicates the heavy inflow of pilgrims who were cheated by the workmen. The workmen probably removed the earlier votive *stūpas* secretly to their workshop to make little redesigning before they were sold to pilgrims. The sheer number, rededication and dumping around the *mahāstūpa* indicate that Ratnagiri attracted a heavy flow of pilgrims, at least in some seasons.

The plain or decorated *stūpas* with image in their niches numbering 270 constitute the largest group among the monolithic votive *stūpas* of Ratnagiri. Among the Buddhist divinities in these niches, *Tārā* outnumbers others. The other deities in descending order are various Buddhas, *Avalokiteśvara* and *Mañjuśrī* respectively. *Tārā* became quite popular from 6th century CE onwards replacing *Avalokiteśvara* as a Saviour deity. Many forms of *Tārā* have been found in Orissa. The popularity of the deity owed to the belief that she protected the devotees from many perils.

Amulets and plaques of terracotta have been found from Ratnagiri, Lalitgiri and Udayagiri and also from Buddhist sites like Bodh Gaya and Nalanda. Amulets are worn as a charm to ward off evil. While the plaques are affixed to a structure and represent a donation by the devotee they also represent memorabilia to be taken to their homes. One feature, which differentiates an amulet from the plaque, is the loop in the former to be moon as a pendent. Ratnagiri has yielded both while Bodh Gaya and Nalanda principally have plaques only. In Lalitgiri, two slate plaques of Brahmanical divinities namely *Gaṇeśa* and *Mahiṣamardini Durgā* have been unearthed apart from terracotta plaques of animals. While I noticed one terracotta Buddha figure with loop, others are usually plaques. Tambiah has classified these terracotta plaques and amulets "as sediments of power" into four categories in the anthropological context of Thai Buddhism.[61] They are:

- Amulets/plaques that are the representation of the famous and historic Buddha, which have played the role of Palladian of the Thai kingdom.
- Amulets that owe their fame to the representation of famous Buddhist monks, especially the 19th century, who sponsored their making and sacralisation. The most famous of them are called Phra Somdet and Phra kling.
- Miscellaneous amulets, a large residual alms of representatives of sods, humans, animals, birds and anomalous beings sacralised by marks and lay experts skilled in base arts.
- The contemporary amulets being blessed by the forest dwelling meditation masters, some of whom are acclaimed as saints.

To these classes should be added terracotta plaques and amulets of other Buddhist divinities and terracotta plaques having *dhāraṇīs* or *Gāthā* of causation.

In historical context of Indian Buddhism one finds no. 1, no. 3 and no. 5 types of terracotta plaques/amulets. These terracotta plaques/amulets were produced in the sites; they were either devoted by the devotees in the sacred monastic site or a after a process of sacralisation and dedication, were taken with them to their respective homes.

Ratnagiri museum displays some beautiful terracotta of Buddha in *bhūmisparśa-mudrā*. Apart from the plaques, four moulds have been discovered from Ratnagiri to produce plaques. From the impression taken for the mould, it is seen that the person responsible for the mould was a man of skill and artistic vision.[62]

While these archaeological artefacts indicate interaction between the laity and monastic establishments they do not completely reveal various dimensions of interaction. The nature of some of these interactions was obviously ritual-based, as the dedication of votive *stūpas* needed to undergo a process of ritual sacralisation before they could be dedicated in the *mahāstūpa* area. Other ritual-based interactions include sacralisation of amulets and plaques as well the seals of important monks used most probably as some sort of talisman. However the degree of interaction or the precise nature of interaction is more complex and broad-based, rather than merely confined to ritual-based actions. It is important to know: how far was the monastic establishment trying to reach out to the surrounding settlements? What are the economic and other contexts of such a reaching out? How far did they act as charmer and benefactor of boon or solver of the existential problems of the laity? What role did they play in rituals of laity, who tried to propitiate many instrumental deities for granting their wishes? How was the monastic establishment engaged with persons who were cultivating lands endowed to the monastic establishments? I-tsing wrote:

> According to the teachings of the *Vinaya*, when a cornfield is cultivated for the *Saṅgha*, a share of the product is to be given to the monastic servants or some other families by whom the actual tilling has been done. Every produce should be divided into six parts, and one-sixth should be levied by the *Saṅgha*; the *Saṅgha* has to provide the bulls as well as the ground for cultivation, while the *Saṅgha* is responsible for nothing else. Sometimes the division of the product should be modified according the seasons. Most of these monasteries in the west (India) follow the above custom, but there are some who are very avaricious, and do not divide the produce, but the priest themselves give out the work to servants, male and female, and see that the farming is properly done.[63]

4. Vajrayāna Buddhism as 'imitative'?

The geographical spread, numerous gods and goddesses,

their worship, rituals, votive *stūpasā*, plaques and amulets attest the spread of Buddhism beyond the confines of monks and monasteries and indicate its dynamism. But the innovation in pantheon structure and rituals are regarded as imitative. The characterisation of Buddhism as 'imitative' of Brahmanical religions and having no resemblance with Buddhism of Buddha's time has two connotations. First, the religion lost its original identity by imitating the practices of Brahmanical religion. Secondly, these practices are completely antithetical of the so-called original Buddhism.

Charges of corruption and degeneration originate in the assumption that religion in question was essentially egalitarian, ascetic and hostile to magic but over time, displayed characteristics contrary to these. This line of argument has three shortcomings. The scholars who formed this view (mainly 19th century European scholars) studied Pali scriptures in order to recover from them the teachings of the Buddha. But these texts contain other narratives besides Buddha's teachings, and there is no historically valid way to establish that his teachings were followed ad verbatim in the initial days of the religion. On the contrary, recent scholarship of Schopen and Huntington has questioned the basic assumptions about the nature of early Buddhism.[65] The assumptions, which Schopen has questioned on the basis of epigraphic and archaeological evidence, include the following:

- The assumption that monks did not venerate *stūpas* and images, nor perform other meritorious rituals
- They did not exercise concern about their own dead
- That the merit transference and filial piety are non-Buddhist accretion on the tradition
- That Buddha relic are totally lifeless
- That monastic practice is distinct from lay practice

On the other hand, Schopen has concluded that Indian Buddhism was more than the sum total of its "*śāstras* where monks and nuns actually surpassed laypeople as patrons and devotees of *stūpa* and image cults; where residents of monasteries not only handled but minted money and were often exceedingly rich and powerful; where the Buddha relic was virtually alive in his *stūpas*, treated as an exalted co-residents of the monasteries in which the *stūpa* existed and endowed with all the rights of regular residents there, including the ownership of property; where monks and nuns were actually quite preoccupied with the treatment of their own dead and possible evil consequence of failing therein."[66]

This deviation from Buddhist texts is only one strand of the changed paradigm. The other aspect, which is equally important, is the degree to which the Buddhist texts were actually known in later times. Epigraphic evidence, at least, does not support the idea that the Buddhist literature was widely known in actual Buddhist communities, but in fact, points in the opposite direction.[67]

The third source of the 'decline hypothesis' stems from a very little appreciation of the Vajrayāna form of Buddhism. The symbolic 'texts' were dismissed as 'imitative' and imbued with sexual symbolism. Vajrayāna literature was branded as abstruse, dense and philosophical. They needed in-depth study, and those who skimmed through them treated these texts like a 'red herring,' which provide little knowledge about the philosophical basis of Vajrayāna. Recent research has resulted in the publication of huge corpus of literature, which can now be brought into comparative relationship, both as regards to theory and practices with other religions, as well as the philosophical schools which existed at other periods. The answer to the question whether Vajrayāna Buddhism was 'Buddhist' in nature or not consists in its receiving or not receiving sufficient acceptance within the body of teaching and practise of any group who considered themselves to be Buddhists. As regards to the question of imitative, non-distinguishable character of Vajrayāna, it is worth quoting Snellgrove:

> It is indeed true that Buddhist and non-Buddhist *tantras* are based upon similar materials and that many parallels may be obvious, but one may well ask at what previous stage of the doctrine was this not true.[68]

Buddhists viewed different *Yānas* as part of a single Buddhist system. The Buddhists themselves maintained a conceptual separation between soteriology and this-worldly religion. Theravāda Buddhism or Mahayāna theoretically presuppose that all can attain salvation but they do not envisage — in spite of the changes in emphasis in Mahayāna — that all could do so in one's own life. For example, Snellgrove quotes a Mahāyāna text which prescribes generosity (i.e. almsgiving) for the lowly, the practice of morality for the middling and tranquillity for the advanced.[69] Thus, spiritual hierarchy is built into Buddhism and was so even in the time of Buddha himself.[70] The three *Yānas* of Buddhism were not merely chronological developments in the evolution of Buddhism as a religion. They also provided different *mārgas* (paths) and built up different cognitive structure and an affective belief patterns to cater to the needs of different sections of the society. The three *Yānas* are like three *mārgas* of salvation. They attempt to incorporate different philosophical traditions and practices within a Buddhist system, thereby, enriching the religion and enlarging the boundary. The three *Yānas* can be conceptualised as a totality, important according to the relative affiliation of the seeker. The three vehicles document not merely different practices and philosophical traditions, they also account for an evolving Buddhism through centuries of changes and adaptation. At the epistemological level, the three *Yānas* were seen as constituting a whole. The Buddhist, while conscious of the differences, also thought of the unity of three *Yānas*. *Tattvaratnāvalī* in *Advayavajrasamgraha* considers different vehicles as part of one single Buddhist system.[71]

Vajrayāna Buddhism was considered to be a spiritual advancement upon the earlier two forms of Buddhism. Thus a sort of hierarchy was attempted. The *Hevajra Tantra* refers to this hierarchy thus:

> First the Eight Precepts should be given, then Ten. Then he should teach the *Vaibhāsya*, then the *Sautāntrika*. After that he should teach the *Yogācāra*, then the *Mādhyamika*. After he knows all the levels of the Way of the *Mantras*, then he should begin on *Hevajra*. The pupil who lays hold with zeal will succeed, there is no doubt.[72]

Same sort of interrelationship between various *Yānas* existed at the iconographic level. One problem encountered in identifying *Vairocana* of Udayagiri *Mahāstūpa* is his close resemblance with *Dharmadhātu-samādhi Mañjuśrī*, with which he is identified in various texts. In Tantric Buddhism some sort of unification had taken place between the celestial Buddhas and *bodhisattvas*, as in case of *Vairocana* and *Mañjuśrī*.[73] When I-tsing visited India, he did not find much difference between Theravāda and Mahāyāna form of Buddhism.

Some of the religious practices of Vajrayāna were significantly different from the earlier one, but it operated within the Buddhism schema, employing distinct Buddhist terminology. The Vajrayāna texts tried to build an elaborate epistemological system to explain, accommodate and adapt certain baseline beliefs and practices.

5. Conclusion

The paper tried to argue that Vajrayana variety of Buddhism developed and achieved great saliency in Orissa. It was an instrumental and social religion and numerous innovations it made were aimed to make the religion more this worldly (*laukika*) and social. Gods and Goddesses were introduced, rituals elaborated, *stotras* and *Vratas* were written to make it more instrumental and social. These innovations made the religion widespread and laity-oriented. Different sections of the laity thronged to various Buddhist centres, donated votive *stūpas* and took away with them terracotta plaques, amulets and sealings of Buddhas, bodhisattvas, monks and monasteries. These objects transformed the spiritual energies of the Buddhas, sacred centres to the household. These innovations took place between 5th to 12th century CE at a time when the Brahmanical religions made temples, provided land grants to Brahmins, popularised *tīrthas* and wrote *sthalapurāṇas* to popularise them. Once historians accept a poly-religious rather than predominantly Purāṇic Hinduism landscape of early medieval Orissa, as the above historical evidence suggests, they need to change the angle of historical inquiry and address the question of poly-religious landscape, religious equations in a poly-religious context and dynamics of religions and society and religions in this vibrant and dynamic period of Indian history.

Notes

1. N. N. Bhattacharyya, *Buddhism in the History of Indian Ideas*, Delhi, 1987, p. 15.
2. K. Chakrabarti, *Religious process: Puranas and the Making of a Regional Tradition*, Delhi, 2001, p. 142.
3. Kalinga-style temples began to be constructed in a big way from 7th century CE onwards in Orissa. The Shatrughneswar group of temples of Bhubaneswar belongs to the earliest phase, dated to 7th century CE. By this time temple-building activity had already assumed a mature form, consolidating an earlier beginning of Kalinga-style temple architecture. For details, see K. C Panigrahi, *Archaeological Remains at Bhubaneswar*, Calcutta, 1961.
4. *Devī Mahātmya* IV, in V.S. Agrawal, *Devī Mahātmya: The Glorification of the Great Goddess*, Varanasi, 1963, p. 67.
5. The panel no. III. 2 of cave (ascribed to the middle of 7th century CE) represents *Tārā* with a stalk of a lotus in her left hand; she stands on a lotus, the stem of which is held by *nāgas*. The panel is badly damaged. Still one can recognise the dread of fire and shipwreck on the left and elephant, serpent and brigand on the right. See R. Sengupta, "A Sculptural Representation of the Buddhist Litany to *Tārā* at Ellora," *Bulletin of the Prince of Wales Museum of Western India*, No. 5, pp. 12–15.
6. The Kalasan Inscription invokes *Tārā* as a saviour thus: 'May she, who, seeing the world immersed in the sea of existence, duly deliver it through the three means.' H.B. Sarkar, *Corpus of the Inscriptions of Java*, Vol.1, Calcutta, 1971, pp. 34-40
7. K.K. Handique (Tr. and ed.), *Naiṣadhacarita*, Poona, 1965. Chapter 22: 136,
8. The idea of *Tārā* as a saviouress found several references in the epigraphic records of different places from 7th to 12th century CE. For example, in the Nalanda inscription of Vipulaśrīmitra, assigned to the first half of the 12th century CE, she was invoked as *Jagata-tāriṇī.* The more famous Kalasan inscription of Java and the Dambal inscription also invoke this saviour aspect of goddess *Tārā*.

9. While the *Sādhanamālā* and the *Niṣpannayogāvalī* do not describe this variety of *Tārā*, Getty and A K Gordon found such variety in Tibet. Gordon (A.K. Gordon, *The Iconography of Tibetan Lamaism*, Delhi, 1967, p. 75) refers to *Siṁhanāda Tārā* as green in colour, she is endowed with two hands, has one head and is seated on a lotus throne supported by a roaring lion. Alice Getty (A. Getty, *Gods of Northern Buddhism*, Oxford, 1978, p. 123) also refers to this form of *Tārā*. Mallar Ghosh (M. Ghosh, *Development of Buddhist Iconography in Eastern India: A Study of Tārā, Prajñās of Five Tathāgatas and Bhṛkuṭī*, Delhi, 1980, p. 154.) refers to a *Simhanāda Tārā* at Bhuinpara and Sheragarh.
10. The Banpur Inscription of Somavamsi king Indraratha records a donation to the temple of *Khadiravanī Tārā* of Kongoda region (K.B. Tripathy, 'Banpur Copper plate Inscriptions of Somavamsi Indraratha,' *JASB, Letters*, 1966, VIII, 4, pp. 271-76). The *Sama Tārā* image is most likely referred to in the *Aṣṭasahasrikā-Prajñāpāramitā* manuscript (CE 1015) housed in the Cambridge University Library (Debala Mitra, *Bronzes from Achutarajpur*, Delhi, 1978, pp. 27-28).
11. *Sādhana* no. 107 describes *Dhanada Tārā* as green in complexion and benign in appearance. She has the radiance of the moon and she is seated in *sattvaparyaṅkāsana*. She has four hands showing rosary, the *varada* pose, the *utpala*, and the book. She bears image of *Amoghasiddhi* on her crown and is surrounded by eight goddesses (*Sādhanamālā*: 219). On the exterior of Varaha temple of Jajpur is affixed an image of *Dhanada Tārā*, which was most likely brought from Solampur. She is seated in *vajraparyaṅkāsana* on a lotus seat holding a rosary, *nilotpala*, book in her uplifted back hand. She is flanked by six *bodhisattva*s rather than by eight goddesses, as enjoined in the *Sādhanamālā* (T. E. Donaldson, *Iconography of the Buddhist Sculptures of Orissa*, Vol. 1, Delhi, 2001, p. 253).
12. A beautiful *Vajra Tārā* image is preserved in the Uttaresvara temple of Ajodhya. The deity is seated in *vajraparyaṅkāsana* on a *viśvapadma*. Her principal right hand, upraised, wields a *vajra*, while the corresponding left displays *tarjani mudrā*. The lowered right hand holds a conch, while the other two right hands, upraised, wield a nose and a pair of arrows. On the other hand, she holds a *vajra*, *kuśa*, a bow and *nilotpala* in her four left hands. However deviating from the texts like the *Sādhanamālā* (*Sādhana* Nos. 90, 93, 97, and 110) and the *Niṣpannayogāvalī* (*Vajra Tārā maṇḍala* of the *Niṣpannayogāvalī*,

Number 16), the sculpture represents only four *pujapokaraṣas* rather than the usual ten. In the Tibetan and Japanese *maṇḍalas* the *pujāpokaraṇas* appear in *Apsarā* form. *Vajradhūpa* (Southeast), corresponding to *Akṣobhya* offers incense and therefore, holds an incense burner; *Vajrapuṣpa* (Southwest) corresponding to *Ratnasambhava* offers flowers and thus, carries a flowers in a pot; *Vajradīpa* (northwest), representing *Amitābha* family, offers a lamp and holds a candle wick in a pot while *Vajragaṅdha* of *Amoghasiddhi* family holds a pot.(Shashibala, *Comparative iconography of the Vajradhatu- Mandala and the Tattva Sangraha,* Delhi, 1989, pp. 344-355).

13. B.Bhattacharyya, *The Indian Buddhist Iconography,* Calcutta, 1968(reprint), p. 124.
14. Lokesh Chandra, *One Thousand forms of Avalokiteśvara,* Delhi, 1988.
15. E. J. Thomas, *The History of Buddhist Thought,* London, 1933, p. 193. *Avalokiteśvara* is also conceived as having thousand forms, which is influenced by the *viswarūpa* of *Viṣṇu*. Lokesh Chandra, *One Thousand forms of Avalokiteśvara,* Delhi, 1988.
16. *Cintāmaṇicakra Avalokiteśvara* as dispenser of prosperity is very rare in India. Out of the three examples in Orissa, the image in the Siddhesvara temple in the outskirt of Jajpur town, is affixed to the interior wall of the *Jagamohana* of the temple and he could be either *Viṣṇu, Lokeśvara* or *Cintāmaṇicakra Avalokiteśvara* (T.E. Donaldson, *Iconography of the Buddhist Sculptures of Orissa,* Vol. 1, Delhi, 2001, p. 185). In the *Cintāmaṇi Lokeśvara* image of Ajodhya Balaśore, *Cintāmaṇicakra Avalokiteśvara* is seated in front of the *ghaṭa,* out of which emerges the *kalpavṛkṣa*. In the niches of *stūpa* 97 in the area east of Temple number 6 at Ratnagiri is an image of *Cintāmaṇicakra Avalokiteśvara*. His right hand is in the meditation *mudrā* while the left holds the vessel from which the *kalpavṛkṣa* is sprouted. (Debala Mitra, *Ratnagiri (1958–61),* Vol. II, Pl CCLXVII, p. 333).
17. In the Khutia temple (Maricai temple) of Ajdohya, there is an image of *Cintāmaṇi Lokeśvara* who flanks the main *Mārīcī* image. *Lokeśvara* stands in a flexed pose with his right hand lowered in *varada* and the left hand, holds a lotus. He is flanked in his lower left by *Cintāmaṇicakra Avalokita,* who is seated in front of a *ghaṭa*. A *kalpavṛkṣa,* whose foliage arches to the other side of the image, is seen issuing from the *ghaṭa*. Dispersed along the meandering creeper are *saptaratnas*. Beneath the right hand are five *preta*s with their raised hands clasped to receive the jewel.

In the Badagada headless chlorite image, which is now in the OSM Bhubaneswar, the *pretas*, including *Sucimukha* are standing with their hands clasped to receive the jewels. The *kalpavṛkṣa*'s trunk is overarched.

18. Mallman has brought to light this sculpture in her article how this Buddhist deity is worshipped as *Brahmā* and *Sarasvatī* (M. T. de Mallman, *Introduction a l' iconographie du Tantrisime boudhique*, Paris, 1975, pp. 203-20). Worshipped as *Umā-Maheśvara* in the *Jagamohana* of the 12th century Meghesvara temple of Bhubaneswar, *Hālāhala Lokeśvara* is six-armed and has three heads. The trident, entwined by a serpent stands on the right back corner of the seat while the *kapāla* is at the back left corner. *Lokeśvara* is seated in *lalitāsana*. He has principal right hand in *varada*, as prescribed in the *Sādhanamālā* (*Sādhanamālā:* 65-66) whereas *Śiva* is usually depicted in *abhaya mudrā* when he is with *Pārvatī* and holds a chin of Umā and/ or a *nilotpala*. On the other hand the raised middle hand holds a rosary while the arrow in the uplifted back hand is partially obliterated. With one of his left hands, he embraces the *Prajñā* (T.E. Donaldson, *Iconography of the Buddhist Sculptures of Orissa*, Vol.1, Delhi, 2001, p. 209).
19. S. Levi, *Le Nepal: etude historique d'un royaume hindou*, Vol. II, Paris, 1905, p. 19.
20. A. Wayman and R. Tajima, *The Enlightenment of Vairocana*, Delhi, 1992, p. 37.
21. M.T. de Mallman, *Introduction a l' iconographie du Tantrisime boudhique*, Paris, 1975.
22. *Guhya Mañjuvajra* of Amarprasadgarh is wrongly identified as *Trailokyavijaya* by Sahu (N.K. Sahu, *Buddhism in Orissa*, Bhubaneswar, 1958, p. 217). The *Mañjuvajra maṇḍala* of the *Niṣpannayogāvalī (maṇḍala* No 20*)* describes six-armed *Mañjuvajra* variety to which the Amarprasadgarh image closely resembles. The six-armed deity sits in *vajraparyaṅkāsana*. His two principal hands holds a *vajra* and *ghanṭa* in *vajrahunkāra mudrā*. By the second right hand he brandishes a sword over the heads and holds an arrow in the third right while in the second and third left hands he holds a bow and a lotus. The right face exhibits loud laughter and appears ferocious while the left one shows complete absorption in meditation.
23. M. Southwold, *Buddhism in Life: The Anthropological Study of Religion and the Sinhalese Practice*, Manchester, 1983, p. 185.
24. 17.1-6

25. S. Tsuda, *The Samvarodaya-Tantra: Select Chapters*, Tokyo, 1974, p. 274.
26. D.N. Gellner, *Monk, Householder, and Tantric Priest-Newar Buddhism and its hierarchy of Rituals*, Delhi, 1996, pp. 143-144.
27. *Hevajra Tantra*, II, 90.
28. For the mode of worship and rituals involved in *Tārā* cult, see S. Beyer, *The Cult of Tārā: Magic and Ritual in Tibet*, Berkley, 1973.
29. L. Dumont, *Homo Hierarchicus: The Caste System and its Implications*, Chicago, 1980, pp. 187-191.
30. H.P. Shastri (ed.), *Advayavajrasamgraha*, Gaikwad Oriental Series, 90, Baroda, 1927, 119 ff.
31. S.N. Rajaguru, 'Jayarampur Copper-Plate Inscription of the time of Gopacandra,' *Orissa Historical Research Journal*, Vol. 11, 1962, pp. 206-29.
32. Debala Mitra, *Ratnagiri (1958–61)*, Vol. 1, Delhi, 1981.
33. *"Tarvihara-bhubi candramayim cakra; yanmandalim himabhubam mrganabhibasam; Tanaiba tanvi sukrutena mate jinasya."* K.K.Handique (tr. and ed.), *Naiṣadhacarita*, Poona, 1965, chapter 22: 136.
34. "When the laity invites a monk to a festival at his home "priests sit according to their ranks. At the upper end of the row of seats, are the images of *Arhat*s to whom offer being made first. At the lowest end of the row an offering of food is made to the holy mother, Hārītī (J. Takakusu, *A Record of the Buddhist Religion as practised in India and Malay Archipelago*, Delhi, 1966, p.37). I-tsing has also noted that " there is likewise in great monasteries in India, at the side of a pillar to the kitchen or before the porch a figure of a deity carved in wood, chair, with one foot hanging down towards the ground. Being always wiped with oil, its countenance is blackened, and the deity is called *Mahākāla*. At mealtimes those who serve in the kitchen offer light and incense and arrange all kinds of prepared food before the deity. (p. 38). I-tsing has also recorded the rules of decorum in cleansing the sacred object of worship.
35. Some formulas expressing the four noble truths in Dravidian languages were used as a sort of *dhāraṇīs* by the *Sarvāstivādinas* owing to the belief in *satkriyā*, which was supposed to be effective. F.Bernard, *"Zur Entstehung erner Dhāraṇī," Zeitschrift der Deuschen Morgen Landischen Gesellschaft*, Leipzig, 1967, pp. 162-63.
36. H. Nakamura, *Indian Buddhism, A Survey with Bibliographical*

Notes, Delhi, 1987, pp. 314-318.

37. M. Winternitz, *History of Indian Literature*, Delhi, 1933, pp. 380-387.
38. *Epigraphia Indica*, XXVI, 1941, pp. 171-174.
39. P.S. Jaini, 'The Disappearance of Buddhism and the survival of Jainism: A Study in contrast,' in A. K Narain (ed.), *Studies in the History of Buddhism*, Delhi, 1980, pp. 81-91.
40. D.N. Gellner, *op.cit.*, p. 220.
41. Debala Mitra, *Ratnagiri*, Vol. 1, 1981, p. 265.
42. Ibid., p. 281-282.
43. Ibid., p. 265.
44. Ibid., p. 259-260.
45. Lokesh Chandra, *Buddhist Iconography*, New Delhi, 1987, pp. 632-638.
46. *Mahāvairocana Sūtra*, Ch. IV.
47. While some monolithic *stūpas* at Ratnagiri are *śārīrika stūpas*, the overwhelming number is votive in nature. Debala Mitra, *Ratnagiri*, Vol. 1, 1981, p. 108.
48. *Saddharmapuṇḍarika Sutra*, Ch. I.
49. S.J. Tambiah, *The Buddhist Saints of the Forest and the Cult of Amulets*, Cambridge, 1984, p. 197. Tambiah's excellent study on cult of amulets and forest monks of Thailand provides the theoretical basis for the study of votive *stūpas*. Two excellent studies on votive *stūpas* are Lawson's unpublished dissertation on the clay sealings in British Museum, and Benistie's study of the votive stūpas in Ratnagiri and Bodh Gaya. See M. Benestie, *Contribution a l'etude du stūpa bouddhique indien: Les stūpas mineurs de Bodh- Gaya et Ratnagiri*, Vols. 2, Paris, 1981; D. Lawson, *A Catalogue of Indian Buddhist Clay Sealings in British Museums*," Ph.D Dissertation, University of Oxford, 1982.
50. Schopen writes about Buddhists' desire to be buried close to a holy site. G. Schopen, Bones, *Stones and Buddhist Monks: Collected Papers on the Archaeology, Epigraphy and Texts of Monastic Buddhism in India*, Honolulu, 1997, p. 225.
51. *Archaeological Survey of India Annual Report (ASIAR)*, III, p. 71.
52. J. Allen, 'An Inscribed Tablet from Kedah, Malaysia, Comparison with Earlier Finds,' *Asian Perspectives* 27(1), 1991, pp. 35–57.
53. S.J. Tambiah, *The Buddhist Saints of the Forest and the Cult of Amulets*, Cambridge, 1984.
54. *Pratītya samudapāda* is found inside many *stūpas* in Ratnagiri. I-tsing, the Chinese monk, has described this popular custom

thus: "the priest and laymen in India make *caityas* or images with earth they put in the images of *caityas* two kind of *śarīras*. (1.) the relics of the Great Teacher, and (2.) *The Gāthā of the Chain of Causation.*" J. Takakusu, (tr.) *A Record of the Buddhist Religion as practised in India and Malay Archipelago (671-695) by I-tsing,* Delhi, 1966(reprint), pp. 150-151.

55. *Epigraphia Indica,* Vol. XXXI, pp. 171–174.
56. J. Takakusu, *op. cit.,* pp. 150-151.
57. S. Beal, *Si- Yu-ki or Buddhist Records of the Western World,* London, 1958 (reprint), p. 115.
58. J. Takakusu, *op. cit.,* p. 150.
59. S. Beal, *op. cit.,* pp. 153-54.
60. Debala Mitra, *Ratnagiri,* Vol. 1, p. 138.
61. S.J. Tambiah, *The Buddhist Saints of the Forest and the Cult of Amulets,* Cambridge, 1984, p. 208.
62. Debala Mitra, *Ratnagiri,* Vol. II, pl. CCCXVI, IA
63. J. Takakusu, *op. cit.,* p. 61.
64. K. Chakrabarti, *Religious Process: Puranas and the Making of a Regional Tradition,* Delhi, 2001, p. 142.
65. S. Huntington, 'Aniconism and the Multivalence of Emblems: Another Look,' *Ars Orientalis,* Vol. 22, 1992, pp. 111-56.
66. G. Schopen, *op. cit.,* pp. 200-278.
67. G. Schopen, *op. cit.,* p. 145.
68. D. Snellgrove, *The Hevajra Tantra: A Critical Study,* Vol. II, London, 1959, p. 7.
69. D. Snellgrove, *Indo-Tibetan Buddhism: Indian Buddhists and Their Tibetan Successors,* London, 1987, p. 90.
70. R. Gombrich, *Theravāda Buddhism: A Social History from Ancient Benares to Modern Colombo,* London, 1988, pp. 73-74.
71. H.P. Shastri (ed.), *Advayavajrasamgraha,* Baroda, 1927.
72. D. Snellgrove, *The Hevajra Tantra: A Critical Study,* Vol. II, London, 1959, p. 90.
73. K.R. Van Kooji, 'The Iconography of the Buddhist Wood Carvings in a Newar Buddhist Monastery in Kathmandu (Chusya-Baha),' *Journal of the Nepal Research Centre,* 1, 1977, p. 77.

SECTION 2

Brahmanical temples in interaction with other societal institutions and processes

6

TEMPLES IN THEIR WIDER CONTEXT
A Study of Temples of Early Medieval Assam

SUDARSHAN GUPTA

There exists a strange insularity in the historiography of Assam in the sense that it never tried to view the history of Assam against the background of developments in India as a whole.[1] Not only Assam, but the whole of North-East India has a peculiar dilemma. It was seen as a mystic land[2] about which and its people rest of India had little, fragmentary or false notions. This contributed to historical marginalization of the entire North-Eastern region. O.P. Kejariwal found that there is a discernable lack of interest or information about North-East India outside North-East; so much so, that an Indian History Congress Volume categorized a paper on North-East as "Non-Indian."[3] It was in this backdrop that this research problem germinated with the necessity of locating the rich history of this region in its truest stride and correct endeavour.

It has been little more than one and a half century since the attention of the scholars has been drawn to the study of the decayed past of the history and archaeology of Assam. A major breakthrough was attained in unveiling the potentiality of the early history of Assam with the establishment of the

Kamrupa Anusandhan Samity (The Assam Research Society) in 1912. Its publication "Journal of the Assam Research Society" (JARS) carried scholarly articles. However, almost up to 1950, literary accounts were given topmost priority, which were then used, and a corroboration of them was sought in the sculptural and architectural remains. A detailed survey of the historiographical trend enables one to formulate that there has been very little work on the 'Temple Architecture of Assam' in its holistic aspect. Almost all the works are mere descriptions of the icons, sculptures, architectural remains etc. Temples in the existing studies were viewed to serve the purpose of day-to-day religious activities. No such serious attempt has been made to view the temple in its wider context, that is, the temple in relation to settlement pattern, community interaction, rituals and so on. Probably, all these facts taken into consideration would take us to a much better position to decide about the issue of patronage, which in the studies so far has been conventionally attributed to the royalty per se. As such, the objective of this work stems from the hypothesis that temples were not merely religious structures, but also a place meant to serve the plethora of purposes of the society at large. Finally, on the basis of the findings, it would enable us to justify the fact that Brahmaputra valley (or Assam, and on macro basis, the entire North-East) had its own contribution to make to the enrichment of various facets of greater Indian culture and thought. Further, a detailed discussion on regional traditions of art historical scholarship towards the end will be done to assign Brahmaputra valley as the easternmost part of the larger Indian Civilization. A discerning eye would reveal that this articles is an attempt to promote emotional integration by positioning the valley (Brahmaputra), the state (Assam) and the region (North-East) in the map of India in its truest stride.

The theme of the present work is the analysis of temple architecture of Brahmaputra Valley of Assam (from 6th century CE to 12th century CE) in its social context. The study begins with an analysis of physical background and a critical analysis of the various names of ancient Assam, which is necessary to reach a logical and valid conclusion. A very brief discussion is also included as regards the present status of the temples, icons, sculptures etc. under study. The Da-Parbatia temple at Tezpur, being the most elaborately ornamented and the most ancient existing temple in the area of this study, has been given a detailed description, of which, of course, I hardly claim any originality, but rather a work of compilation based on primary and secondary sources. However, on the basis of this material description, fresh evaluation was performed by me to view this temple in its wider context. In order to analyse the multifarious functions of the temples, a thematic description of the architectures have been done, such as, Navagraha (group of nine temples) found in various parts of the valley under study and the subsequent causes behind such constructions. Corroboration has been sought from the literary accounts to impart a holistic approach to this study. This is followed by an analysis of the 'erotic sculptures,' where I have sought to provide a critical approach to the study of eroticism and erotic art from a socio-psychological point of view with emphasis on religio-philosophic concept of erotic art. Then comes a brief description of the dancing figurines depicted in the temples, again to see the temple as an institution serving diverse functions. On the basis of these facets, an attempt is made to articulate my view point on the much debated issue of patronage and plethora of purposes served by the temples.

Ancient Assam, known as Prāgjyotiṣa is commonly associated with Lauhitya, Kāmarūpa and Kāmākhyā. B.K. Kakati suggested that the word " Prāgjyotiṣa' is Sanskritisation of Austric group of words like *pau* (= hill) + *ger* (= hill) + *jo* (= high) + *tic* (= long) = '(land of) high and long mountains.'[4] The further sought to connect Kāmarūpa and Kāmākhyā with an Austric basic word, meaning 'a grave, a corpse,' the place names being connected with the legend found in the Purāṇas of Sati's dead body being cut-up and a part of it falling in Kāmākhyā hill in Kāmarūpa.[5] Lahutiya (Brahmaputra) is evidently a Sanskritised form of the Tibeto-Burman name 'Luhit.'[6] The word Lahutiya gives a meaning in Sanskrit as 'the red river,' but is probably a Sanskritisation of the pre-Aryan, Sino- Tibetan name. It is noticed that the river takes this colour during the rainy season, when it cuts through the red-soil in the adjacent embankments.[7] The Brahmaputra means 'son of Brahmā'[8]. The Brahmaputra has numerous tributaries and is the principal river flowing from east to west through the heart of Assam, touching the districts of Nagaon, Sonitpur, Darrang, Goalpara, Kamrup, Tezpur, Sibsagar and Dibrugarh.[9]

Prāgjyotiṣapura has been taken to mean the 'city of eastern astrology or astronomy ('Prāg' means former or eastern and 'jyotiṣa' means a star, astrology, shining).[10] Prāgjyotiṣapura stood for both the country and the city. The name is interesting in connection with the romantic image conceived by the rest of the country as a land of magic and incantation and with the view that it was in Assam that the Tantric form of Hinduism originated. The interpretation of the name as a place of 'eastern astrology' does not seem to be justified though there are a number of references to its association with the solar-cult and planetary worship. According to P.C. Choudhury, the archaeological remains point to the prevalence of the solar-cult, and the existing temple of Navagraha in Guwahati and Sūrya Pahār in Goalpara justify this origin of the name of the land.[11] However, the archaeological evidence does not support the meaning of Prāgjyotiṣa as the city of eastern astrology. The solar-cult, which was already prevalent in other parts of India, moved to Assam at a late period, and the temples of Navagraha and Sūrya Pahār were built during the late medieval period.[12] The Kālikā Purāṇa states that Brahmā made the first calculation of the stars at Prāgjyotiṣa, and this points to the early importance of the place in astrology and astronomy as this work was composed in the 10th century CE or little after, whereas, the name of Prāgjyotiṣa had already been known in the Epics.[13] Hence, it could be safely postulated that there seems to be no real connection between the names Prāgjyotiṣapura or the temple of Navagraha with the reputation of Kāmarūpa as a land of magic or sorcery or as the supposed centre of origin of Tantric Buddhism.

The name of the kingdom Prāgjyotiṣapura was converted to Kāmarūpa probably during the early centuries of the

Christian era, but Prāgjyotiṣa remained as the name of the capital city of the kingdom of Kāmarūpa. References to Kāmarūpa as kingdom are made almost in all the epigraphs of this period. The earliest epigraphical document mentioning Kāmarūpa is the Allahabad Pillar Inscription of Samudragupta wherein the name of Kāmarūpa has been mentioned as one of the frontier states, outside the limits of the Gupta Empire.[14] Hiuen Tsang also mentioned Prāgjyotiṣa as Ka-mo-Lu-po.[15] In the Raghuvaṁśa of Kālidāsa and in the Kālikā Purāṇa, both the names Prāgjyotiṣa and Kāmarūpa are mentioned.[16] Rājaśekhara, the court-poet of Mahipāla, the Pratihāra king of Kanauj (910 CE-940 CE) writing in the early part of the 10th century, however, mentions Prāgjyotiṣa and not Kāmarūpa as one of the countries of Āryāvarta along with Magadha, Pauṇḍra, Tāmralipta and Sumha. On the other hand, the Arab writer Alberuni, in the 11th century, mentioned Tirhut, Mudgagiri (Monghyr), Nepal, Kāmarūpa and Bhutan among the eastern countries.[17] The epigraphic evidences like, Uttarbil and Nagaon grans of Balavarman and Bargaon and Sualkuchi grans of Ratnapal Varma Deva and other copper-plates grants mention Prāgjyotiṣa as the capital city of Naraka.[18] It therefore appears that, since the beginning of the Gupta period, down to the 10th century CE, the kingdom was known throughout Āryāvarta both as Prāgjyotiṣa and Kāmarūpa, though it's kings preferred to designate themselves as lords of Prāgjyotiṣapura down to the 12th century CE.

The history of architecture in Assam on the basis of the material available can be pushed back to the Gupta period i.e., the Varman dynasty of the Kāmarūpa, if not earlier. The epigraphical and literary evidences throw light on the construction of numerous shrines dedicated to Śiva, Sūrya, Viṣṇu, Devi and other deities. The Mārkaṇḍeya Purāṇa refers to an early temple of Sūrya built in Kāmarūpa.[19] The Chinese Pilgrim Hiuen Tsang refers to 'hundreds of Deva temples' which were extant during the time of his visit (643 CE.).[20] The Tezpur Grant of Vanamāla states that the king repaired the lofty temple dedicated to Śiva, which had fallen down.[21] According to the Guwahati grant of Ratnapāla, he "studded the earth with whitewashed temples, enshrining the idols of Śambhu."[22] Silimpur Stone Inscription Prāhsa records the erection of a Śiva temple.[23] The Gāchtal Pillar Inscription (Nagaon) mentions that the King Viśwasundaradeva ordered one *Chandrākānta* to repair a Śiva temple, which had been damaged by the Mlecchas.[24] These are just to name a few.

Unfortunately, not a single ancient temple or any other building (religious or secular) in the original form, is now preserved in this region. Wherever temple existed in that period, we see only heaps of ruins over which the Ahom-Koch temples were constructed during the later phase. The heaps of ruins are full of various broken parts of the stone temples. The scattered components of the temple and palatial remains on stylistic ground are assignable to a period ranging from Gupta period to c.12th century CE. Now, this being so, a question which will undoubtedly preoccupy one's mind is why so few architecture of the time have come down to us. The reasons of the total damage of the temples belonging to the Pre-Ahom period are more than one. According to Sir Edward Gait, the nature of the soil and the climate are mainly responsible for the destruction of the monuments.[25] Again, physical conditions give impetus to the rapid growth of jungle vegetation. The character of the country has also affected the nature of the building material used and this again has influenced the style of its architecture. Entire North-Eastern India is in earthquake prone zone. There must have been some large scale earthquakes to crumble down the beautiful temples. It is possible that in the great earthquake of 1896, some buildings and monuments fell down making them irreparable.[26] Apart from nature, man also did great damage to various structures (religious and secular) of Assam. The widespread havoc brought about by the Burmese was another potential factor for the destruction of many temples and other buildings.[27] Gait endorsed the view of religious fanaticism of the Mughal invaders; however, it is difficult to seek corroboration of this view in other literary sources. Thus, in the light of this description, it is evident that there is a great paucity of extant temples in the Brahmaputra valley during the period of this study. We have just the scattered ruins of temples and stray sculptures, from which we will have to trace and weave a regular architectural history thematically and provide a subsequent analysis the same.

The village of Da-Parbatia, three miles west of Tezpur town, possesses the glory of having the most reputed and ancient architectural ruins of the oldest temple in Assam. The ruins consist of the remains of a brick-built temple of Śiva, of the Ahom period, created upon the ruins of a stone temple of the latter Gupta period, datable to circa sixth century CE. The former collapsed during the devastating earthquake of 1897, thus revealing the stone door frame of the older structure.[28] (Fig. 1).

The mound is nearly 20 feet above the surrounding ground and is entirely covered with large rubber trees and small undergrowth. The door frames stands in front of a large block of stone with a square cavity in its centre. Historians (R.D. Banerjee, K.L. Barua and Krishna Deva) are of the view that in most probable circumstances, the older liṅga was fixed in this hole. Two door-jambs, each having four different vertical bands (*paṭṭas*) are joined with a lintel above. The pillars of the door frame are five feet three inches in height from the ground level, while its breadth, that is, the pillars are of one foot four inches. While the lintel measures five feet, nine inches in length and one feet three inches in breadth.[29] The lower part of the right jamb is occupied by the river goddess Gaṅgā's image while on the left jamb stands Yamunā (Fig. 2&3).

Behind their heads, halos are depicted indicating the heavenly nature of the two rivers. Both the rivers are standing with garlands in their hands and are attended by a number of miniature figures. The facial appearance of both the figures bears similarity with Mongoloid facial appearance, while the hair style and the ornaments represent the traditional Indian style. Therefore, from the facial appearance we may presume that these were carved and sculptured by the local artisans of this place. The outermost vertical bands of the door jambs extend beyond the lintel. The first two innermost bands are adorned with scroll (*pūtralatā* design). The second bond has

Fig. 1: Door Frame:Da-Parbatia Temple, Tezpur

the tail of a nāgī continuing horizontally on the lintel. The third band consists of ornamental foliage having a straight stem with amorini clinging to it. The fourth band is made up of four super imposed panels containing human figures and lotus buds (*Padma-Koṣas*) alternatively. The last band is a double intertwined creeper forming conventional rosettes, which is continued on the side projection of the lintel. The lintel consists of a separate piece in which the topmost horizontal band bears on it five caitya windows (Chāndrasśālā) with the figures of deities. These caitya windows are very much common in the Gupta temples at Bhumrah and Deogarh of the c. 6th CE. The

Fig. 2 Enlarged view of River Goddess Yamunā, Da-Parbatia

window in the centre of this lintel is occupied by the seated image of Śiva in the form of Lakuliśa.[30] The other images carved are of a Kṛṣṇa alike, Sūrya, Gaṇeśa, Sarasvatī. Some other figures are yet to be identified.

The Da-Parabatia temple door frame is not connected with any inscription. So, in this situation various other methodologies had to be adopted to place it in the time frame,

Fig. 3: Enlarged view of River Goddess Gangā, Da-Parbatia

such as, the architectural style, techniques of terracotta plaques and last but not the least from the ceramic finds. R.D. Banerjee is of the view that, "the artists' sense of proportion, the beautiful symmetry of the figures and ornamental devices and the excellence of execution tend to prove that this door lintel belong to the same period as the great schools of sculptures which existed at Pāṭaliputra and Benaras in the 5th and 6th centuries A.D."[31] N.D. Choudhury is also of the view that, "The exposed brick structures of the temple in their general layout are more akin to a typical Gupta temple rather than to that of an Ahom temple. Among the existing Gupta brick temples, the Bhitargaon temple (near Kanpur) is probably the earliest, which is, dated to the later part of 6th century AD and the Da-Parbatia may go back to the 6th century AD."[32]

However, Krishna Deva assigns it to 7th century CE on the same basic of the style of architecture.[33] The Da-Parbatia temple is brick built and the simplest in general lay-out, and followed the Gupta principles of squares, designs and dimensions, all of which prove its early origin during the 6th century CE. During the clearance of the ruins of this temple a number of terracotta plaques, showing a seated human figure in each were discovered, the moulding of the torso and the general techniques proves beyond doubt that these plaques cannot be later in date than the 6th century CE. Two of these plaques reveal the existence of a modified form of the acanthus motif in Assam in this early age. This device has been noticed in some of the Gupta temples of other parts of northern India, notably at Bhumra and Nachna Kuthara.[34]

At Da-Parbatia, potsherds have been found on the surface. A shallow bowl, jars etc. were discovered below the plinth of pots in broken condition. The entire ancient pottery is wheel turned. The fabric of pottery from Da- Parbatia is fine, pots are made of well levigated clay, free from impurities and mostly fired uniformly. No painted designs have been noticed except incised designs. The ancient ceramic industry of the Brahmaputra Valley known from Da-Parbatia, Mayang and Mahadeosal (Nagaon district) is represented by Red Ware only.[35] Technologically on the basis of the fabric, surface treatment and differential firing resulting in different shades of the same colour, the Red Ware can be broadly sub-divided into three categories: (a) Red-Slipped -Ware (b) Buff Ware (c) Pinkish Coarse Ware.[36]

At Da-Parbatia, only Red-Slipped- Ware has been found. The original surface of this ware was red slipped. Due to stagnation of water, the slips have mostly vanished. The core is not gritty and shows particles of mixed mica. The following shapes occur in Red-Slipped Ware: (i) Jars of different sizes

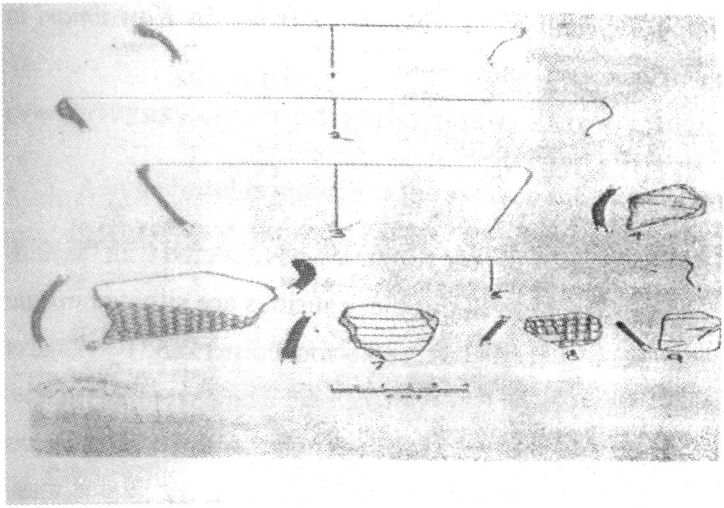

Fig. 4 : Pottery from Da-Parbatia

and shapes (ii) Bowls (iii) Basins[37] (Fig. 4).

On the basis of fabric and shape, the date of the ceramic industry of Da-Parabatia is assigned to circa 6th century CE or a little earlier. Thus, on the basis of the above, it can be safely asserted that architectural activities reached its perfection in Prāgjyotiṣa- Kāmarūpa in the 6th century CE and the techniques and style was in conformity with those of the Madhyadeśa.

We come across many sites in the Brahmaputra Valley where the group of temples numbering nine has been noticed. The sites mainly are: Bamuni Pahar, Devasthan (Maudangā, Mikir-Ati, Gosainjuri, Rajbari (Jugijān) and Na-Naththan. Probably in Kawaimari and Singri there were also nine temples.[38]

The Bamuni Hill, near Tezpur town is covered with the ruins of a group of nine temples. Six of these shrines are situated in a large rectangular enclosure, one in each of its four comers and two large ones in the centre, the seventh stands to the east. The pavements inside the garbhag? has of both the larger shrines in the middle of the enclosure are still intact. One of the central temples is slightly smaller than the other. There is a controversy regarding the identification of the other two shrines in this place due to the nature of the ruins. (Fig. 5)

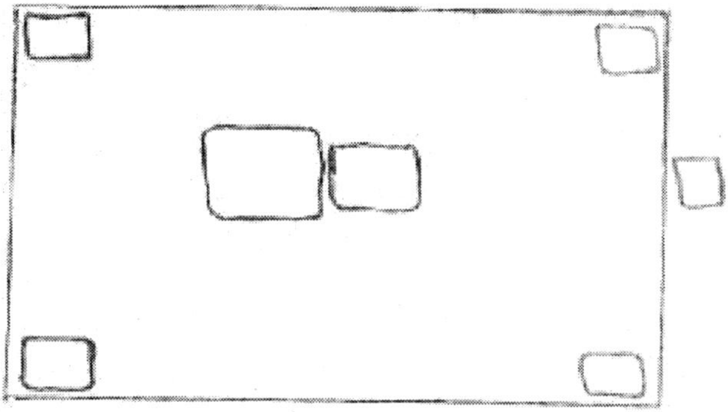

Fig. 5: Sketch of Nine Temples: Bamuni Hills
(Controversy about two sites due to the nature of the ruins)

A huge lintel is noticed in the site. All the niches contain the figure of deities, probably Navagrahas, one in each. A Viṣṇu avatāra pillar (164x72x47cms) have also been found with the images of Narasimha, Paraśurāma, Balarāma, Varāha and Rāma, the incarnations of Viṣṇu. An image of Naṭarāja measuring two feet one inches in height and one feet six inches in breadth, with one head and six hands were discovered among the ruins. Other images found are of Brahmā (*sthānaka* figure) and Sūrya. The temples of this site were attributed to different gods like Viṣṇu, Sūrya, Śiva, Durgā etc. Stylistically, the ruin of this site has been placed between 9th and 10th century CE by scholars.

At Gosainjuri, district Nagaon, there are nine small mounds containing ruins of temples, close to each other facing each other, in parallel lines. The last mound is comparatively bigger with abundant bricks on it. Door lintels and a broken sculpture of Viṣṇu, (height: 77 centimeter) have been discovered. The second mound is small containing a gneiss door sill and a liner of block stone (168 x 38 cms.) with a carved lotus on it in the centre (Fig. 6).

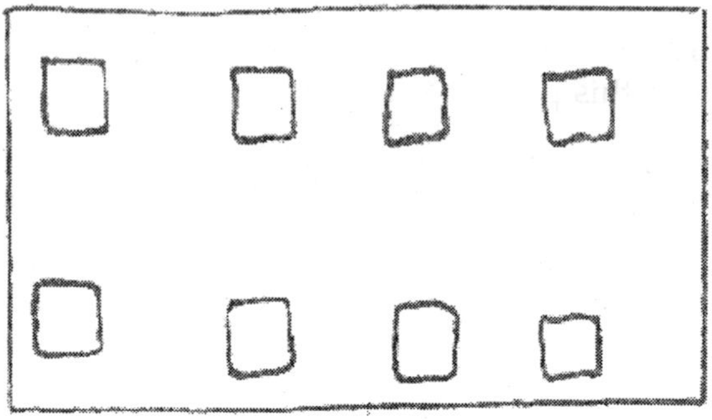

Fig. 6: Sketch of Nine Temples: Gosainjuri (Nagaon)
(Controversy about one temple due to
the nature of the ruins)

At Mikirati near Dabki (district Nagaon), there are nine mounds existing in three rows at equal distance. The central one is the biggest and the others are small in size. The central one reveals brick structures and a pedestal of grey soap-stone (Fig. 7). On the north east comer of the group of shrines, one Śiva-linga with Yonipaṭṭa has been found. Images of Umā- Maheśvara and Viṣṇu, are noticed at the site. A heap of ruins of a stone Śiva temple is seen at a little distance of these group of temples.

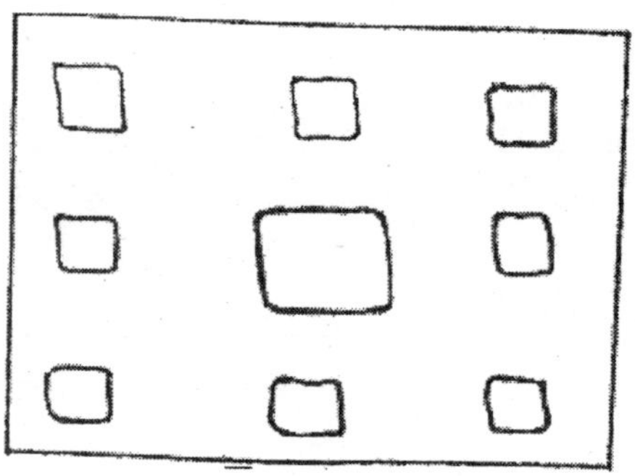

Fig. 7: Sketch of Nine Temples
Mikirati, near Davoka (Nagaon)

At a place called Rājbari in Jugijan (district Nagaon), there are nine mounds containing ruins of stone temples of gneiss stone lying scattered. The nine temples stand in three rows; instead of the central one, the middle of the first row is the biggest one (Fig.8). The temples were probably dedicated to Śiva, as the Śiva lingas are still intact in some of the ruins. In a small modem shrine in the site, an image of Umā-Maheśvara is installed which has been discovered from the nearby river bed.

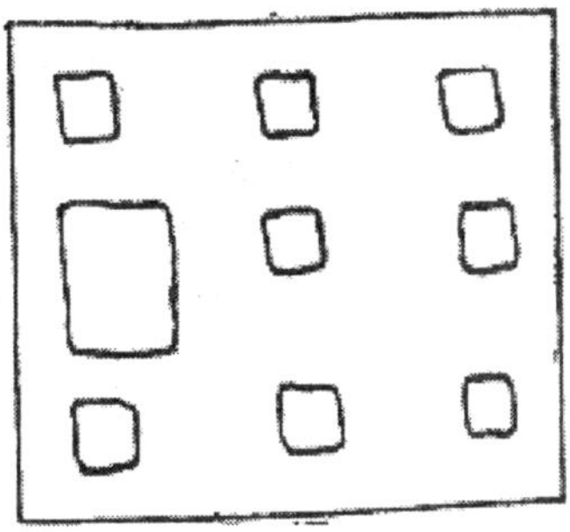

Fig.7: Sketch of Nine Temples
Rajbari in Jugijan (Nagaon)

Traces of a group of temples, probably nine in number, showing the biggest one in the centre, have been noticed in Kawaimari (district Nagaon) (Fig. 8). The temples were made of hard gneiss stone. Amidst the ruins, there is a door jamb (95x29 cms.) bearing the figures of Daśāvatāras of Viṣṇu; a lintel having three raised panels containing the figures of Viṣṇu, Śiva and Sūrya respectively with other attendants on both sides and the space between then occupied by other deities.

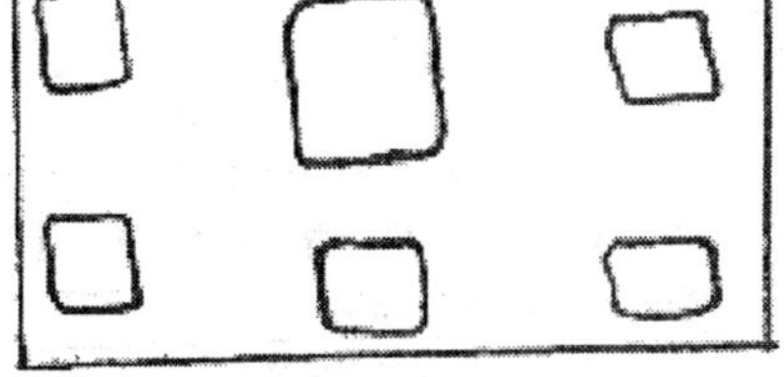

Fig.8 Sketch of Nine Temples: Kawaimari (Nagaon)

At a place called Devasthān (Maudanga), about 3 kms. from Howraghat, there are nine mounds, containing ruins of temples. Eight mounds are seen in two rows facing each other and the ninth one is in one corner. (Fig. 9) The ruins consist of doorjambs, lintels, stray images, Śivalingas with pedestal and carved stones. A frieze (162x91 cms.) bearing an image of Umā-Maheśvara in the centre of the lower panel with a lion and a bull at the feet and on the upper panel is the image of Gaja-Lakṣmī; on the right side is Viṣṇu, and Gaṇeṣa is on the farthest end. All are in sitting posture. A beautiful Śiva -lingam schist stone is found intact, seated not on the usual Yonipaṭṭa, put on a beautiful pedestal.

Fig. 9. Sketch of Nine Temples
Devasthān (Maudanga)

References are not found as to why the nine temples were erected in one place. The temples dedicated to the gods and goddesses are Viṣṇu, Śiva, Sūrya and Durgā. No definite evidences have been found for the Navagraha (nine planets), although certain scholars on the basis of texts have stretched this point too far and even tried to establish the fact that "zero was first formulated in Prāgjyotiṣapura."[35] In some lintels, figures of the Navagrahas are noticed with the gods Viṣṇu, Śiva, Brahmā and Sūrya at Bāmunipahar, Cole Park, Singri, Kawaimari and other places. The planets could have been popular in Assam in the early medieval period. The Navagraha Temple at Guwahati is an example of this. On the basis of the nine planets, nine temples had been erected at one place.

The remains of ancient buildings, and temples as well as sculptures are scattered in the Tezpur town. Most of them are fragments and some of them are now preserved in the Cole Park. Among these objects, a huge lintel (312x78x77 cms.) having three raised panels, one in the centre and the other two in two sides is important. This lintel contains the figures of Trinity with their attendants and some Navagrahas. The extensive ruins lying at a place locally called Viṣvakarmathān in Singri, show that there were several temples. One door lintel (184x67x59 cms.) having two raised panels which are divided into two large niches in the centre with smaller one on either side is found. The left panel is occupied by a figure of Śiva in *sthānaka* attitude while the extreme right one is occupied by Viṣṇu, in the same posture. The space between the extreme left end is divided into six niches and they are separated from each other by round pilasters, and each of the niches contains one of the Navagrahas. The extreme left side of the lintel is broken.

A group of nine temples is found at Alampur in Mahboobnagar district adjoining Hyderabad. This group is popularly known as Nava-Brahmā temples; of them eight belong to the northern style and one (of Tarka Brahmā) to the southern styles.[40] According to the Arthaśāstra, shrines should be erected in the centre of the city for goddess Apājitā, Jayanta, Vaijayanta, Śiva, Vaiśravaṇa, Aśvina (divine physicians) and goddess Madira (Sri Madiragrham).[41] N.D. Choudhury is of the view that the places where the groups of temples in Brahmaputra valley are found must have been temple cities.[42] It therefore seems that the architects of the Brahmaputra valley were influenced by the rules of the Arthaśāstra and the number of temples rise up to nine for Navagraha. Most of the temples were clearly dedicated to Śiva, as the Śiva-līngas have been found inside. According to the Śilpaśāstra, the temples are classified in accordance with the number of *rathakas*. The number of *rathaka* distinguishes the classes of temples: the Brāhmana (is characterised) by nine, the Kshatriya by seven, the Vaiśya by five, and the Sūdra by three *rathakas*. Who knows that the group of temples found in various parts of the

Brahmaputra Valley which yielded less than nine temples from a single site might have been influenced by the rules laid down in the Śilpaśāstra.[43]

The worship of the *'grahas'* along with the twelve *Ādityas* came to occupy a very important place in the religious life of the Hindus, during the medieval period. The texts like Yāgnvalkyasūtra, Viṣṇudharmottara, Agni Purāṇa, *Amsumadbhedāgama* and Śilparatna describes the forms of the Navagrahas (nine planets) in different ways. The figure of Navagrahas are depicted in the lintels of the medieval temples and the earliest specimen is known from Bhubaneśwara temple, belonging to the 8th-9th centuries A.D.[47] As in the case of Brahmaputra Valley, the group of nine temples and also the depiction of the Navagrahas belong to the 9th century CE and later. The Navagrahas are Sūrya, Soma, Bhauma, Budha, Guru, Śukra, Śani, Rāhu and Ketu. J.N. Banerjee is of the view that the figure of Ketu is a latter addition. In the earlier shrines, the lintel contains only eight *grahas*, as remarked by Banerjee, citing the corroborative evidence of the shrines at Bhubaneswara.[45] In the lintel from Changchoki (Assam), only eight grahas are depicted, and Ketu is absent.

Another interesting issue is that of the erotic sculptures. The theme can be classified into three orders: the elementary erotic motifs, the three dimensional carved sculptures and figures displaying the abnormal trends. Whenever we talk about erotic sculptures depicted in the temples of the ancient period, immediately one is captivated by the sites of Puri, Bhuvaneswar, Khajuraho and Konark. Hardly anyone knows that the pre-Ahom temples in the Brahmaputra valley contain numerous such erotic depictions. It is really a mystery, how this valley of exquisite antiquities, escaped the notice of all for such a long time. In spite of this plethora of erotic depictions in Assam, we don't find mention of it in the two authoritative volumes on this issue written by D. Desai[46] and G.V. Bhaskara Reddy.[47] It is now established that many priceless images of the valley under study were either stolen by curio-hunters or by religion-duped villagers without perhaps realizing the value of the sculptures they removed.[48] In the sculptures of the valley under study, we find instances of exhibitionism, man with large erect penis; women with vulva cavernous and gaping man and women in auto eroticism; promiscuous group sexuality; and zoophilia, with animals like bull. Besides human figures, animals and birds are also noticed in copulating figures.

The Assam State Museum, houses five stone blocks, showing erotic scenes. The first block bears two scenes. The right sides of the block carry a male and a female human figure in sitting posture. Both of them are depicted in embracing, kissing and copulating posture. This posture can be identified with the type of embrace entitled 'kshiranira,' described by Vātsāyana in his Kāmasūtra.[49] The next sculpture on the same block of stone shows a male figure seated cross-legged and on the lap of the figure seats a female. They are seated facing each other. The next slab of stone shows a male and female in standing posture. Here the female is seen feeling a little shy or ashamed while the male is seen taking initiative. The fifth scene is depicted in another slab of stone which, in all, bears six different scenes. The six scenes depict three masturbating, one dancing and two copulating scenes. All the sculptures of this slab are smaller in size than the other erotic sculptures described above. Another slab has two erotic scenes. The first represents a female human figure engaged in sexual union with a bull (Zoophilia). The first of these two sculptures is exactly similar to the scene in the first slab, while in the last scene; the male is shown sitting and raising his right leg upto the shoulder of the female who with her right hand holds the feet of the leg behind her head.[50]

An erotic scene is noticed in a stone slab from Singri ruins. Two niches are divided by circular pilasters of the panel, and each of the niches contains four figures. The second niche contains a male and a female in similar pose. The two female attendants, one on each side are apparently trying to shut out the scene by keeping their hands over their eyes.[51] Another interesting scene is depicted on a slab from Changchaki, where the male and female figure is depicted seated on an easy chair in *mithuna*[52] pose.[53] At Kāmākhyā, a small piece of stone, bearing an erotic scene, half-hidden in the earth is noticed in a small way leading to some residents of the Paṇḍās (priests).[54]

Hardly forty kilometers away from Guwahati, the gateway of North-East, and three kilometres from Baihata Chariali on National Highway No. 52, Madan Kāmdev is an enigma, a mystery, a marvel which speaks about the ancient Kāmarūpa. Kalpa-Briksha (the tree of fulfillment), six-sided Bhairava, four headed Śiva, Demons, Serpents and men, women and animals in every conceivable erotic postures, all in ruins, ruin of gigantic proportion that is Madan Kāmdev. Every sculpture here is vibrant with fervour of joy, which transformed rocks into living, breathing and dancing beauty -a timeless dream on silent rocks. It is believed that Kāma or Madan, the god of Love was reborn in this place after being turned into ashes by angry Lord Śiva. One school believes that Madan was reborn and united to his wife Rati in this tiny hillock. Another school argues that the name Madan Kāmdev is romantic association to this place, because of the numerous erotic sculptures.[55]

Fig. 10. Erotic Sculpture, Madan Kāmdev Temple.

Department of Archeology, Assam, more or less has confirmed that the ruins of Madan Kāmdev belonged to the 10th to 12th century CE when the Pāla Dynasty ruled Kāmarūpa. The ruins are believed to be the remains of more than 20 temples consigned to Lord Śiva. The surviving portion of Madan Kāmdev shows that these were perhaps the finest medieval temples ever built in the entire Brahmaputra valley. Be it or so, otherwise Madan Kāmdev, continues to remain an archeological challenge. Madan Kāmdev ruins have yielded quite a few erotic sculptures. A slab bears two such sculptures. The first represents a female and a male in *'maithuna,'*[56] while the two attendants close their eyes by *putting* on their hands. The other scene shows a male sitting above the ground level on something keeping his legs on the ground before him. A female is shown squatting in his front and with both of her hands holding the penis of her partner. This is a rare erotic depiction found in the valley. Another slab represents zoophilia between a man and an animal which could not be identified.

At Deulgovinda, North Guwahati, a few *mithuna* figures are noticed sculptured on two pottikas. The *pottika* is an upper architectural part of a temple. R.D. Choudhury is of the view that these sculptures occurring in architectural parts of a ruined temple, seem to belong on stylistic ground to CE 9th-10th centuries. An old slab of stone, small in size, bearing two scenes,[57] is seen stuck into the basement of a modern house near Deulgovinda. Here one scene shows a male human figure applying force on a female figure to bring it closer. Probably, it is an instance of a rape scene. Besides human figures, animals and birds are noticed in copulating postures. A terracotta plaque bearing a pair of peacocks from Sadiya in amorous poses is illustrated by B.K. Barua.[58] A scene from Na-Nath-*than* is depicted on a pillar where a male deer is seated upon the back of the female deer, in the act of coition. A frieze from Deoparvat shows a royal archer shooting a deer couple when in coition.[59] All these sculptures described above, on stylistic ground may be placed in 9th-10th century A.D.[60]

Vidya Dahejia is of the view that eroticism, in art, is indeed a culturally loaded category.[61] A holistic view of the issue can be reached by psycho-analysis.[62] The psycho-analysis of eroticism is divided into three parts, viz, normal eroticism, abnormal eroticism and zoophilia. Effective adjustment of an individual to the social environment is the sign of normality. The animalism of a person depends on his mental and physical growth, social status and sex. For example, pre-play before an actual sexual intercourse is considered normal along with other sexual practices and the same is found in sculpture.[63] The propriety of erotism in Art depends mostly on the mental attitude and the degree of intellect and similarly the inner vision of the observer rather than upon the erotic representations themselves. It has already been enunciated that human personality is basically creative, and hence appreciate the sensuous gleanings.[64] In fact, every society and culture have their own norms, beliefs, customs and traditions. So the question that arises here is, that how far society of ancient period accepted the sexual life as depicted through sculpture on temple walls? The answer must positively be that the society had accepted the trend of representing such erotic practices on common places like temples.

The Agni Purāṇa enjoins that the *dvāra* of a temple should be decorated with *mithunas*.[65] The Orissan Art text of the 10th century CE *Śilpaprakāśa* lists 16 types of women who best decorate a monument[66] and these find their visual counterpart in the profusion of female images in the temple walls of Assam. Once established, a stereotype faithfully passed from one generation to another. No doubt, some sexual practices out of the depicted ones are of normal type in the sense that they are being practiced and considered qualitative, probably by majority of the people. The few more abnormal practices are being practiced by less number of people but are not at all the practices of a rarity. Zoophilia means sexual love with animals.[67] The lack of satisfaction, accompanying culture is the necessary consequence of certain peculiarities developed by the sexual instinct by the pressure of culture.[68]

Again, the idea of depicting erotic motifs in Indian art is stimulated by moods and modes of human personalities with the social background and subsidiary implications Nude worship has in the late 1980's being witnessed at Chandragutti village in Shimoga district of Karnataka in Renukamba temple.[69] Similarly, the practice of carving amorous *mithuna* motifs on door jambs might have been considered auspicious by the ancient people. These erotic sculptures have the support of the traditional practices of centuries of temple building and had been enjoined by the texts, such as the *Kāmasūtra*. Also the institution of Devadāsi originally associated with fertility purpose ultimately lost its meaning and became a means of pleasure garbed in the form of worship in the temples. In fact, temples have been made to explain the origin of religious prostitution. In Vanamala's inscription, mention is made of the numerous temples in the country. Vanamala himself rebuilt the large temple of Haṭakeśvara to which he dedicated a number of prostitutes evidently for services as Devadāsīs.[70] It might be seen as a process of appeasing the priestly class to earn legitimacy and support by the ruling class. Thus, the services of Devadāsīs became popular in the religious life of the period under study; the temples of Assam thus became centres to serve the purposes of prostitution in the garb of religion with the active support of the royalty. In the presence of such religious prostitution in the temple campus, temples seemed to have contributed a lot in the denigration of the status of the women to a great extent. Various literary texts describes that *bhoga* was explicitly recognized and glorified in the aristocratic society.

Another germane issue of this discourse is the worship of human generative organs, known to be prevalent throughout the course of history as the basis for procreation, propagation of the species and also for the fertility rites of nature. The worship of Yoni and Linga in the form of Śiva-liṅgam is a glaring instance for this. The magical efficacy of sex got a broader recognition in ancient Indian culture. The coalescence between primitive magic and highly evolved spiritual ideas resulted in a powerful religious sect called 'tantricism.' It incorporated folk and tribal magico-religious beliefs and rites at an organized level. It exercised considerable influence over all major religions of India, namely, Hindu, Buddhist and Jain.

So, varied indeed are the concepts of obscenity and so different are the ethical standards in various time and space, that it is not possible to have any permanent marker for obscenity down the ages. In fact, one can authentically study this serious subject with the appearance and development of human emotions at different times and at different levels in the light of objective activity.[71] Thus, these erotic sculptures were the outcome of a number of factors, such as, psycho-sexual pattern of the people, worldly interest in sensual pleasure and superstitious belief.

The temple ruins of the Brahmaputra valley also yielded sculptures depicting musical (*sangīta*)[72] activities found on stone slab fixed an the walls, panels, door jambs, lintels etc. They formed an integral part of the temple decoration. A large slab of stone representing a very interesting dance scene has come from Cole Park, Tezpur. The slab is divided into seven panels by circular pilasters, and each panel contains two figures either of males or of females, or both. Various musical activities are depicted on this slab.[73] (Fig. 11). Another dance scene is noticed on a door jamb lying near the Deputy Commissioner's residence, Tezpur. All the figures are under canopies.[74] A door sill from Baragangā depicts two lions flanked and a *ghaṭa* in the centre; and on both sides of the sill there are four panels each divided by pilasters all the panels are occupied are occupied by music parties.[75]

Fig. 11: Dancing Scene from Cole Park, Tezpur

A door jamb from Mathajahār shows an individual dancing female figure on the bottom. Another stone slab from Chartherangphargaon depicts a dancing female figure.[76] Similarly, we also find a slab depicting erotic dancing postures of a female with two attendants at Madan Kāmdev. It can be postulated on the basis of the erotic sculptures yielded from the valley of the period under study, that the Devādāsī system was also prevalent in the temples of Assam. The Devadāsīs used to be proficient in *sangīta* and therefore the various sculptures depicting musical activities on the temple was a place for these performances, thereby widening the functions of the temple.

On the basis of this material description, it would be possible to analyse the role of the temple in its wider context. For this, one needs to keep in purview the historiographical trend. George Burton Adams declared that the field of the historian was and would long remain the discovery and recording of what actually happened. This line soon found its supporters in other disciplines. J.W. Burgess wrote in the annual report of the American Historical Association that the task of the historian was true and faithful recording of the facts of human experience and political scientists would put those facts into principles of political behaviour.[77] This view of history as the record of facts was beautifully summed up by E.H. Carr as, "the common sense view of history."[78] It needs no long arguments to see that a common sense view produces only 'common sense historians' and that in an age of specialisation and specialists (micro studies), such historians will not do. Expressing his unhappiness with this trend, Carr goes on to say that in this view, "The facts are available to the historians in documents inscriptions and so on like the fish in the fish mongers slab, the historian collects them, takes them name and cooks them and serves them in whatever style appeals to him."[79] But in most cases, especially in North-East India, historians of this brand do not even take the trouble of cooking. They serve the fish raw. Our historians (a section of them) often merely lift the facts from what they call documents and publish them. This, perhaps, outlines the cause for viewing the temple merely as a structure serving the purpose of day to day religious activities by majority of the scholars of this region while ignoring the role of temple in a plethora of activities.

As already discussed, we get numerous evidences from the epigraphs, of description regarding the construction of temples by the kings of Kāmarūpa. But unfortunately in the event of lack of inscriptions at the temple site, the issue of 'patronage' has assumed a great complexity. For instance, Krishna Deva ascribed the temple of Da-Parbatia to Bhāṣkarvarmana.[80] But there is no mention of it in his inscriptions or copper-plates or in the literary sources. Whereas, the local populace believes that the temple door frame along with other remains scattered nearby belongs to the time of legendary king Bāṇa for his tutelary deity Śiva. Some of them believed that on the ruins of the old temple of Bāṇa, the then kings and rulers of this area reconstructed the temple whom they considered to be the king Nagakshya and later on by the kings of the Śālasthamba dynasty. In this respect, we may mention that the rock inscription of Harzara Barman is at a distance of about one mile east of this temple on the bank of the river Brahmaputra on a very big bolder. The memory of Harzara is so strong in the minds of the people, that they not only attribute the Da-Parbatia temple to king Harzara, but anything inscribed and designed on stone or rock is attributed to him.[81] But this does not seen to be possible as this inscription bears the date 510 Gupta era, which stands for 829 CE, whereas, the architectural pattern, sculptural styles and ceramic evidence at Da-Parbatia, place the temple at 5th - 6th centuries CE. This probably led K.L. Barua to assert that the "Da-Parbatia temple might have been built by a predecessor of Bhāṣkarvarmana."[82]

The rock inscription of Harzara Barman purports to be an ordinance regulating the plying of boats on the Brahmaputra within certain boundaries operated therein. It seems that the dispute was between fishing boats and boats belonging to the royal navy. It was ordained in the inscription that fishing boats must restrict themselves to mid-stream and that any violation of the order would be punishable with a fine of hundred cowries.[83] The order was inscribed in bold characters on a huge rock boulder on the banks of the river so that it may be visible to all boats passing up and down.[84] This testifies the strategic importance of the site being frequented by numerous boats belonging to both the fisherman and to the royal navy.[85] M.M. Sharma argues that Haṭṭapeśvara might have been the name of a deity installed in some central market place (haṭṭa) nearby.[86] Engraving a royal edict must serve the purpose of making it visible to the maximum number of viewers. It could thus be postulated that the site witnessed traffic of diverse economic activities. And the capital Harupeśwara (modem Tezpur) was no doubt a major partner in the process of commercialization. This was facilitated by the good network of the river-system of the Brahmaputra valley.[87] Thus, it could be argued that the temple in the vicinity of all these activities was no doubt a happening place and also served as a centre of diverse community interaction. It is also feasible that various communities like the merchants, fisherman, royal personnel etc. contributed generously to the temple. Hence, to assign the entire temple complex to the patronage of a single individual (i.e., king in this case)[88] demands a rethinking. It is time now for the historians to give up the traditional mentality of searching a single patron for a religious structure. They should rather try to bring the concept of multiplicity of patronage in case of the temples; for a temple serving only as a 'religious structure' seems to be an oversimplified version. Temples were ideal locations for the purpose of advocating not only religious, but economic, social, political and cultural hegemony by the 'movers and shakers' of the then society. Likewise, as regards other temples too, studies should be directed towards viewing the temple in its wider context. The conventional studies based on literary sources and epigraphs are in the trend of assigning every religious structure to the patronage of royalty. It is not so difficult to trace the psychology of these scholars. The Śaiva cult prevailed in Assam from the time of Naraka and Bhagadatta, the traditional rulers as known from the literary sources. The archaeological evidence shows that the cult became well developed in the early centuries of the Christian era. The rulers of Kāmarūpa, down to Dharmapāla patronised Śaivism and regarded the Śiva as their tutelary deity. K.L.

Barua ascribed the temple of Da-Parbatia to Bhāṣkarvar-mana.[89] Now the presiding deity of the Śiva temple where 'āmiṣabhoga' is offered is invariably the *Ardha-Nārīśvara* Śiva whose worship is conducted according to Tantric rites. The first copper-plate inscription of Dharmapāla, recorded in the third year of his reign, begins with the adoration of the *Ādi Deva* (primeval deity) *Ardha-Juvatiśwara* (*Ardha-Nārīśvara*). Further, Barua also cities Kālikā Purāṇa, which also contains the story of the origin of *Ardha-Nārīśvara*, and postulates that it was probably complied in Kāmarūpa about this time. Barua takes this to be another indication of the fact that Dharmapāla and his predecessors were the votaries of Tantricism. And on this basis, Barua concluded: "it is very probably that the temples of *Ardha-Nārīśvara* Śiva were founded by these kings."[90] There is no denying the fact that the kings might have been the donors, but to assign all the temples of the Brahmaputra valley to the royalty per se appears like reading too much from the not so written inscriptions and literary texts.

Evidence of early settlements can also be discerned around the temple sites even in the modern district of Kāmrupa. The entire Kalapahar-Narakasur complex is bounded by the idols of Gaṇeśa. All these idols are in a group of three or four generally placed in a northwest-southeast orientation. The idols at Ganesguri (Guwahati) are the largest and most prominent. Thus the occurrence of Gaṇeśa all along the periphery definitely proves that the entire complex was an early settlement. Similar occurrence of Gaṇeśa on the cardinal points of settlement is also found in other parts of Guwahati. There is also a reference in the Mārkaṇḍeya Purāṇa, which says that Gaṇeśa is to be placed around settlement as a protector and guardian deity. Stylistically dating of these icons by the Department of Archaeology, Assam has placed them in the pre-Ahom age.[91] That the site of the temples (many of them) was an important place is attested by the fact that numerous temples in the Brahmaputra Valley have been erected upon the ruins of the older temples in comparison to some others, which were relatively been abandoned. The Da-

Parbatia temple of Tezpur, which has already been discussed, is one such example. Again at Nagaon, we have the temple of Hatimuria dedicated to Mahiṣamardinī (Durgā). It was built by Gadadhar Tarun Duara Barphukan under the orders of the Ahom king Pramatta Singha in the year Śaka 1667. But scholars like R.D. Banerjee, K.L. Barua on the basis of style of the sculpture therein and on comparison of it with the similar image found in the Tezpur ruins, assign it to 9th-10th century CE.[92] According to K.L. Barua, "assigning the image to 9th-10th century A.D., it would seem that there was originally a stone temple, which was probably demolished by an earthquake and that in the 18th century A.D., Ahom king built a brick temple which still exists, though in a very dilapidated condition."[93] Such instances can be multiplied.

The sites of the temples have no doubt earned a wide reputation and must have become quite famous not only for religious functions only, but also for other activities. As already discussed, it is evident from the inscriptions that the Devadāsīs were dedicated to the temples. They, no doubt, might have been engaged in dance and music.[94] The temple ruins of the Brahmaputra valley yielded sculptures depicting musical activities. These varied sculptures might actually suggest that the temple was a place for the performance of these arts, thereby widening the functions of the temple. Again, we have numerous evidences of Kāmarūpa being a centre of Brahmanical learning and Sanskrit studies. Many kings gave land grants to the Brahmins. We have early evidence of performance of the *'samavartana'* (convocation) ceremony of a *snātaka* (graduate) after the completion of his studies under a *guru*.[95] Though it needs wide research, yet it could at least be postulated that these sorts of activities associated with learning could have taken place in the temple complex. However, the probability of this assumption is very high because during the period under study, education (Sanskrit studies, mainly religious in nature) were monopolised, that is, controlled, regulated and governed by the Brahmins. Again, we find numerous evidences of land-grants being made to the Brahmins, who had sole authority, as regards the jurisdiction of the temples. It could therefore be possibly inferred that the Brahmins would have imparted Sanskrit education in the very 'campus' of the temples, where they dwelled.

Apart from the stone architecture, tanks and fortifications have also been noticed, mostly in the vicinity of the temples. Ancient tanks are frequently found in almost all the sites of the ruins. Wells and ring-wells were not so popular in ancient time in Assam and naturally tanks were dug for the supply of water. It was probably customary to dig a tank near the temple in the pre-Ahom period as well as in the Ahom period. In Darrang district alone, there are 361 old tanks, some of which were, of course, dug during the Ahom period.[96] The biggest tank so far noticed in the Brahmaputra Valley is the Harzarapukuri in Tezpur, constructed by Harzara Varman in the 9th century CE. At the North-West of Harzarapukuri, we have another tank called Balipukhuri. At Madan Kāmdev, we have a group of more than 15 temple ruins, datable to 11th to 12th century CE. Large temples were noticed near the temples. The district of Nagoan and Kamrup also has numerous such tanks. R.D. Choudhury is of the view that tanks were dug near the temple complex because "water was very essential for deity worship in temple."[97] But here one needs to keep in mind the size of the tanks, which were quite large. The huge size of the tanks and the volume of water therein would raise a vital issue that need to be addressed, Deity worship and other everyday religious nitty-gritty would probably not require such large volume of water. It can be argued that the water of the tank was not used only for deity worship, but also for other purposes as because the temple was a site of community interaction. Again, wet rice cultivation in ancient Assam made judicious use of indigenous irrigation technologies. *Hiuen Tsang's* observation of the abundance of 'streams and tanks' in the towns may be taken as an indication of the importance of irrigation technique in the region.[98] Hence, it would not be surprising to view these tanks as providing water for irrigation in the lands in the vicinity of the temple, which probably were owned by the Brahmins of the temples.[99]

As already mentioned, the objective of the study was to analyse the temple as a place meant to serve various purposes of the society at large. And this long survey, I hope, has enabled to lift the veil from the various subtle, yet important issues interconnected with temple architecture in the Brahmaputra valley of the pre-Ahom period in Assam. In this backdrop, it really seems strange when one discovers that in the historiography of this valley, it was never tried to view its history against the backdrop of developments in India as a whole, whereas the present study reveals that the Brahmaputra valley had its own contribution to make to the enrichment of various facets of Indian life and thought. Kāmarūpa is certainly mentioned as an outlying (*pratyānta*) region in the Allahabad Pillar Inscription of Samudragupta but its isolation was far from total.[100] The Tezpur Rock Inscription of Harjara Varman, which bears the date of 510 Gupta era (829 CE) is of utmost importance in this regard. The date proves undoubtedly that Gupta era was in vogue in this part of the country also. Again, the Barganga Rock Inscription of Maharajadhiraja Bhutivarman in Mikir Hills (district Noagaon, Assam) mentions 234 Gupta era (554 CE). Bhutivarman's Prime Minister, Āryaguṇa in this inscription styles the king as *'Param Bhāgawata.'* The same is applied to the Gupta kings as evident from the coins of Chandragupta II, Kumaragupta, and Skandagupta.[101] Thus, imitation or influence went to the extent of applying their epithets to these Kāmarūpa kings. After the Gupta era fell into disuse, the Śaka era came into use. It might be that with the downfall of the Guptas, their almanac gradually became unpopular and as the Śaka era became well known by then in the neighbouring states, people of this kingdom preferred to use the same era.[102] A local era called Kāmarūpa era probably started by Bhāṣkarvarmana in 594 CE is mentioned in a later Assamese manuscript. But the inscriptions of Assam, found so far, give no clue to the existence of any such indigenous era.[103] In all probability, the local era was not such popular and it could not get royal recognition owing to wide popularity of the Gupta era and the Śaka era.

Further, the Puspabhadra grant of Dharmapāla mentions

a Brāhmana to be well versed in Śruti, Smriti, Mimāṁsa and Cānakya or Arthaśāstra.[104] The earliest specimens of Sanskrit composition may be found in the inscriptions of the rulers written in Kuṭila type of Brāhmi. Composed in both prose and poetry in stately diction and lucid style, most of these may be well compared with any other composition from other parts of India.[105]

The architecture of the period from the 6th century CE to the 12th century CE at different places in Assam indicates that the temple architecture of the valley was closely related to the general architecture and art forms developed in Madhyadeśa.[106] It is noticed that several iconographic traits, decorative motifs, architectural designs and temple sculptures had a good deal of impact from Bengal, Orissa and Central India. The Gangā and the Yamunā images at Da-Parbatia shows that the plain and imposing halo with geese-pecking on the borders is an unconventional motif that should be viewed as an independent regional innovation. One should not loose sight of oval heads and rendering of facial features which further emphasize their local variations. Similar is the case with Viṣṇu image from Mikirati belonging to the late 6th or early 7th century CE. Clearly the patronage and the craftsmanship are local but extra regional connections can be very well discerned. The inscribed Viṣṇu image from Deopani shows later Gupta influence with admixture of Mongolian features. Some images are having late Gupta or early Pāla characteristic features and also show some local characteristic traits affiliated to the Mongolian culture. The majority of Viṣṇu, and Sūrya images belong to 11th and 12th century CE, and they are having the characteristics of the Sena school, viz. long pointed Śilapaṭṭa, slim body structure wearing paridhāna of thin fabric and profusely ornamented.[107] Thus, though there were generous borrowings from northern and eastern Indian traditions, yet a regional idiom was in the process of formation in the central portion of the Brahmaputra Valley.

S. Kakati states that Assam had its indigenous school of sculpture, that is, 'Kamrupa School of Sculpture.'[108] But it cannot be taken to be entirely true. Local variations do not prove the existence of a separate school of art.[109] As in Assam, in other regions too, local variations have been noticed. Kramrisch has rightly remarked that like plasticity and naturalism, dynamic characteristics, influenced by various social factors, determined the art history of India as a whole.[110]

As one reads into the historical processes contributing to the emergence of art activities in the Brahmaputra valley of Assam during the pre-Ahom period, one becomes increasingly aware of the limitations of art historical scholarship in India. It testifies that our understanding of the regional traditions is extremely fragmentary. Regional traditions do not grow and survive in isolation and it is equally important to identify the elements that go into the making of such a tradition. Brahmaputra valley can thus be called as the easternmost part of the larger Indian civilization. All the issues discussed here points to the fundamental cultural unity of India and the understanding of this small fact may very well promote emotional integration.

Notes

1. O.P. Kejariwal, 'North-East in Indian Historiography, the Need for a Corrective,' in the *Proceedings of North-East India History Association* (*NEIHA*), Pasighat, 1987, pp. 71-84.
2. Jawaharlal Nehru, A Note by the Prime Minister on his tour of North-East Frontier Areas, October 1952, Shillong; as cited in S. Nag, 'Aspects of Historiography of North-East India,' *Proceedings of NEIHA*, 17th Annual Session, Aizawl, 1996, pp. 66-74.
3. O.P. Kejariwal, 'The Indian History Congress and Historical Research in North-East India,' in the *Proceedings of NEIHA*, Kohima, 1998, pp. 33-81.
4. B.K. Kakati, *The Mother Goddess Kamakhya*, Guwahati, 1948, p. 6.
5. Ibid., p. 6.
6. *Brahma Purāṇa*. Ch. 64; *Raghu Vaṁśa*, IV, 81; *Yoginitantra*, 22.119; as cited in N.D. Choudhury's *Historical Archaeology of Central Assam*, Delhi, 1985, p. 16.
7. Ibid. There is a mythological interpretation also, given as to

the origin of this name. It is connected with Paraśurāmakuṇḍa or Brahmakuṇḍa that the great saint Paraśurāma washed-off his blood stains after killing his mother, and regained his sainthood. Hence, the water of the river is said to have turned red.

8. Ibid. it has been mentioned in the *Yoginitantra.*
9. *G.B.D.'s General Knowledge*, Kolkata, 2006.
10. Edward Gait, *A History of Assam*, Calcutta, 1926, p. 15.
11. P.C. Choudhury, *The History of Civilisation of the People of Assam to the 12th century* A.D, Gauhati, 1966, pp. 26-27.
12. K.L. Barua, *Early History of Kamrupa*, Gauhati, 1966, pp. 9-10.
13. Ibid.
14. J.F. Fleet, *Corpus Inscriptionum Indicarum*, Vol. III, 1970, p. 14.
15. K.L. Barua, *op. cit.*, p. 7.
16. Ibid.
17. Ibid., p. 8.
18. M. Mazumdar, 'Changing Capital Cities of Ancient Assam-A Myth or Realiity' in *The Searchlight*, published by G.C. College History Forum, Silchar, Assam, Vol. I, 1995-96, pp. 3-6.
19. N.D. Choudhury, *Historical Archaeology of Central Assam*, Delhi, 1985, p. 164.
20. Ibid.
21. Ibid.
22. a. *The Tezpur Grant of Vanamala Varma Deva*, in K.L. Barna, *Early History of Kamrupa*, Gauhati, 1966, pp. lll-112.
    b. Dr. Dimbeswwar Barua, ed. *Kāmarūpaśāsanāvalī*, Publication Board, Assam, 1981.
23. (a) Ibid. (b) Ibid.
24. N.D. Choudhury, *op. cit.*, p.165.
25. Edward Gait, *op. cit.*
26. Ibid. The earthquake of 1596 threw up from below hot water, sand and ashes contributed to the collapse of many buildings (p. 98). Again, the earthquake of 1897 also records mass destruction (p. 20).
27. Ibid., p. 20.
28. a. R.D.Banerjee, *Annual Reports, Archaeological Survey of India*, 1925-26. A detailed description of this devastating earthquake can be found in this work. Reference regarding this earthquake can be also be found in the following works:
    b. Krishna Deva, 'Dah Parbatia Śiva Temple Doorway, Kāmarūpa Style, c.7th c.A.D.,' Text, Vol. II, Pt. I, pp. 215-217, Plate No. 438 in M.W. Meister (ed.), *Encyclopedia of Temple*

Architecture (in North India): Foundations of North Indian Style, Delhi, 1989.

c. K.L. Barua, *Early History of Kamrupa*, Gauhati, 1996, pp. 113-115.

29. M.C.Das, "Da-Parbatia Temple Door Frame" in the *Proceedings of NEIHA*, Aizawl, 1996, pp. 126-28.
30. 28th Incarnation of *Śiva* according to *Vāyu* and *Linga Purāṇa.*
31. R.D. Banerjee, *op. cit.*
32. N.D. Choudhury, *op. cit.*, p. 168.
33. Krishna Deva, *op. cit.*, pp. 215-217.
34. R.D. Banerjee, *op. cit.*
35. N.D. Choudhury, *op. cit.*, p.204.
36. Ibid.
37. Ibid.
38. Refer to the *Annual Reports, Archaeological Survey of India* by R.D. Banerjee, 1925-26. The description of these groups of temple can also be found in the following secondary sources:
    a. K.L. Barua, *op. cit.*
    b. N.D. Choudhury, *op. cit.*
    c. R.D. Choudhury, *Archaeology of the Brahmaputra Valley of Assam (Pre-Ahom)*, Delhi, 1985.
39. This view was articulated by V. Choudhury. He was very influenced with the *Navagraha* Temple atop the Chirasala Hill in Guwahati and thereby sought resort in the "astronomical heritage of the city called *Prāgjyotiṣapura* in ancient times." He even attributed the decimal system of calculation to have originated in *Prāgjyotiṣapura*. However, the sources on the basis of which he came to this conclusion are not mentioned properly. As such, such a simplification remains enigmatic and hence ahistorical in nature. V.Choudhury, "Astronomical Heritage of Pragjyotishpura ", in the *Proceedings of NEIHA*, Tripura University, 17th Session, 1997, pp. 80-86.
40. Krishna Deva, *Temples of Northern India*, p. 19.
41. Kautilya, *Arthaśāstra*, translated by R. Samasastry, 1929, Book II, Ch. IV, p. 54.
42. N.D. Choudhury, *op. cit.*, 1985, p. 180.
43. Bansidhar Mohanty, 'The Cultural Relations of Assam and Orissa,' in M. Neog and H.K. Barpujari, (ed.), *Professor Suryya Kumar Bhuyan Commemoration Volume*, 1996, Local Committee XXII Session, All India Oriental Conference, Guwahati, Assam, pp. 162-167. A King of Assam, Śrī Harsadeva (730-750 A.D.), is said to have tremendous influence on Orissa by virtue of his

valour: It is said that learned Brāhman Pandits of Singri near Tezpur were sent to Orissa and architects and sculptors from Orissa were recruited in large numbers in order to construct temples. In the 9th century A.D., King Harjaravarman of Assam had diplomatic contact with the Kings of Orissa.

44. J.N. Banerjee, *Development of the Hindu Iconography*, Calcutta, 1956, pp. 443-444.
45. Ibid.
46. D. Desai, *Erotic Sculptures of Ancient India*, Delhi, 1975.
47. G.V. Bhaskara Reddy, *Erotic Sculptures of Ancient India*, Delhi, 1991.
48. Official Website of *National Informatics Centre*, Kamrup District Centre (Assam) "*Places of General Interest.*"
49. a. S.C. Upadhya, *Kāmāsūtra of Vatsāyana*, 1963, p. 102.
    b. Sir Richard Burton,(Translated) The *Kāmāsūtra of Vatsāyana*, 1883.
50. For a detailed description of these sculptures, refer N.D. Choudhury, *op. cit.*, pp. 174-76.
51. For details, refer N.D. Choudhury, *op. cit.*, 190.
52. The word '*mithuna*' means a couple who may or may not be in a sexual relationship, but may be said to be erotic couples.
53. N.D. Choudhury, *op. cit.*, p. 190.
54. R.D. Choudhury, *op. cit.*, p. 177.
55. Pradip Sharma, *Temples of Assam (Places of the Pilgrimage & Worship of Assam).*
56. The term '*maithuna*' means sexual intercourse.
57. R.D. Choudhury, *op.cit.*, pp. 176-177.
58. B.K. Barua, *A Cultural History of Assam (Early Period)*, Guwahati, 1969.
59. N.D. Choudhury, *op. cit.*, p. 190.
60. This view is endorsed by B.K. Barua, R.D. Choudhury, and N.D. Choudhury.
61. Vidya Dahejia (ed.), *Representing the Body*, Delhi, 1997.
62. Psycho-analysis is a process of investigation of mental processes which are almost inaccessible in another way.
63. G.V. Bhaskara Reddy, *op. cit.*, p. 80.
64. *Ibid.*, p. 81.
65. a. N.D. Choudhury, *op. cit.*, p. 189.
    b. R.D. Choudhury, *op. cit.*, p. 174.
66. Vidya Dahejia, *op. cit.*
67. G.V. Bhaskara Reddy, *op. cit.*, p.84.
68. *Ibid.*, p. 88.

69. *Femina*, 8-22 July, 1986, p. 60.
70. K.L. Barna, *op. cit.*, 1996, p. 99.
71. Vidya Dahejia, *op. cit.*
72. Here I have preferred to use the term '*sangīta*' for dancing and other musical activities because in Indian classical music, *sangīta*' is defined as: '*Geetang badyang tatha nrityang,/Troyang sangeeta muchchota.*' That is, vocal music, instrumental music and dance, these three branches taken together is called *sangīta*'
    a. Debabrata Dutta, *Sangeet Darsika* (in Bengali), Vol. 1, 1984
    b. Nilratan Bandopodhyaya, *Sangeet Pariceeti* (in Bengali), Vol. 1, 1988, p. 22.
73. N.D. Choudhury, *op. cit.*, p. 189.
74. Ibid.
75. Ibid.
76. Ibid.
77. A.K. Barna, 'On Approaches to the Study of History,' *NEIHA*, Agartala, 1997, pp. 21-25.
78. E.H. Carr, *What is History?* Harmondsworth, 1975, p. 9.
79. *Ibid.*
80. Krishna Deva, 'Dah-Parbatia Śiva Temple Doorway,' in M.W. Meister, *op. cit.*, p. 217.
81. M.C. Das, 'Da-Parbatia Temple Door Frame,' *NEIHA*, 1996, pp. 126-128. I tried to trace the oral history prevalent in the site by talking with the local population. But this exercise seems to be futile in the light of historical studies as the information gathered was misleading and ahistorical in nature. So the use of oral tradition as a source in our case has got great limitations.
82. K.L. Barua, *op. cit.*
83. Ibid., p. 79.
84. M.C. Das, 'Harjaras Rock Inscription,' *NEIHA*, Agartala, 1997, pp. 76-79.
85. The inscription refers to the fisherman and boatman as '*Kaibarta*,' who till date are found to be associated with fishing as their profession around the banks of the rivers in Assam.
86. M.M. Sharma, *Inscriptions of Ancient Assam*, Guwahati, 1979, p. 88.
87. M. Mazumdar, 'Economic Enterprises, Industrial Products and Urban Pattern of Pragjyotisha- Kamrupa, c.4th-10th c. A.D.,' *NEIHA*, Aizawl, 1996, pp. 135-142.
88. B.S. Miller also expressed the view that it is a general tendency among the historians/art historians in India to look for an individual patron in order to explain the donor of the religious

structures. B.S. Miller, *The Powers of Art*, Delhi, 1992, p. 9.

89. K.L. Barua, *op. cit.*, p. 101.
90. Ibid.
91. Tridip Sharma, 'The Archaeology and Strategic Significance of the Kalapahar-Narakasur Hill Complex,' in *NEIHA*, 1996, pp. 130-134.
92. *JARS*, Vol. II, No. 1, April 1934, p. 12, as cited in Dr. Maheswar Neog(ed.), *Studies in the Early History of Assam*, (A Collection of Papers published in various Journals by K.L. Barua), 1973.
93. Ibid.
94. This view is endorsed by B.K. Barua, R.D. Choudhury and N.D. Choudhury.
95. Nagaon Grant of King Bala Vannana of the 9th-10th centuries CE
    *P.C. Choudhury, 'The Royal Patronage of Sanskrit Learning in Assam,' in *Professor Suryya Kumar Bhuyan Commemoration Volume*, ed. Prof. Dr. Maheswar Neog & Dr. H.K. Barpujari, 1966, pp. 168-169.
96. R.D. Choudhury, *op. cit.*
97. Ibid.
98. Gautam Sengupta, 'Brahmaputra Valley Sculpture: The Formative Period,' in Amita Ray and Amir Mukherjee (ed.), *Historical Archaeology of India*, Delhi, 1990, pp. 281-297.
99. The earliest inscription of Assam recording large-scale donation of land to *Brāhmaṇas.*
100. Gautam Sengupta, *op. cit.*, pp. 281-297.
101. Dimbeswar Neog, *Introduction to Assam*, Bombay, 1947, p. 25.
102. All together four inscriptions in Assam bearing Śaka era have been found:
     *Assam Plates of Yallabhadeva -1107 Śaka era
     *Kanaibari Inscription -1127 Śaka era
     *Gachtal Inscription -l 149 Śaka era
     *Arnbari Inscription -1154 Śaka era
     —Dr. Dimbeswar Barua, *Kāmarūpaśāsanāvali*, Publication Board, Assam, 1981.
103. Ibid.
104. P.C. Choudhury, 'The Royal Patronage of Sanskrit Learning in Assam,' in M.Neog and H.K.Barpujari (ed.), *op. cit.*, p. 169.
105. Ibid., p. 170.
106. a. Edward Gait, *op. cit.*, p. 21.
     b. N.D. Choudhury, *op. cit.*, p. 165.
107. a. N.D. Choudhury, *op. cit.*, p. 259.

b. P.D. Choudhury and M.C. Das, *Ancient Treasures of Assam.*

108. S. Kakati, *JARS*, VIII, pp. 38-43, as cited in N.D. Choudhury, *op. cit.*, p. 259. Almost similar view is also expressed by Krishna Deva. While describing Da-Parbatia Temple, Tezpur, he mentioned it as the representative of the Kamrupa style. For details, refer to M. Meister, *op. cit.*, Vol. II, Pt. I, 1989, Text. p. 215.
109. N.D. Choudhury, *op. cit.*, p. 259.
110. Stella Kramrisch, *Indian Sculpture*, London, 1933, p. 25.

7

ŚAIVA TEMPLES IN THE EARLY CHOLA PERIOD

Syncretism, Religious Trends and Tamil forms of Worship, *c.* 850 CE – 985 CE

M.N. Rajesh

Tamil *bhakti* movement has been presented as an ecstatic outpouring of the Tamil *Śaiva* and the *Vaiṣṇava* saints with little stress on the nature of religious transformation, particularly the forms of worship that complemented the theological shifts in the orthodox religions. In this paper, I seek to examine the diverse strands that contributed to the rise of the *bhakti* movement and their popular socio-cultural bases. The main theme chosen is the forms of worship, specially the altered character of religion that one finds in Tamilnadu after 7th century CE with the rise of the *bhakti* cult and its institutional base, the temple. By extension, the focus is on the emergence of new forms of worship, some of which were appropriated from the Jainas and popular folk cults. This appropriation was in the backdrop of intense sectarian rivalries; in a situation when the *Śaiva*s and the *Vaiṣṇava*s were ranged against the Jainas and the Buddhists.

The period under study (c. 850 – 985 CE) was of prime importance in Tamilnadu. The various socio-political institutions like the temple and the concept of kingship, which took definite shape during the period, anticipated later developments when the temples increased in size, grandeur and number, and become powerful institutions.

Writers like Nilakantha Sastri and others looked at the Chola period as a homogenous whole, which led to broad generalizations about the nature of society, economy and religion with no regard to changes or transformations. This unified view of the entire Chola period also obscured many of the developments that were taking place over time. Recent historiography is also not free from this constraint of looking at the Chola history of 400 years as a unified whole. This trend is also discernible in different writings of Burton Stein.

In this regard the division of Chola history under early, middle, and later periods seems to be more acceptable on the basis of significant differences in the degree of development, in the integration of an agrarian society, as well as urban growth, whose beginnings may be placed in the 9th century CE. Hence the present study focuses on the early Chola period, which saw the emergence of the temple as a major institution, although temple building was started by the Pallavas. The early Chola period temples did not achieve the grandeur of the later temples but they represented the beginning of great significance in the development of the technology of temple building in stone, the emphasis being on the structural mode of architecture. This period also witnessed a remarkable agrarian expansion and colonization of new areas. This expansion reached a saturation point by the 11th century CE.

The importance of the temple as an institution with multi-dimensional functions was also established because the temple acted as a means of consolidating local communities and integrating them into Chola society and state. This was achieved through an ideology based on the concept of *bhakti*, its popularization and dominance in all spheres of activity and in all the politico-cultural regions (such as *Cholamaṇḍalama*,

Pāṇḍyamaṇḍalama, Tondaimaṇḍalama and *Koṅgumaṇḍalama*) of the Tamil macro region.

Bhakti was developed initially as an ideal to voice protest against the exclusive Brahmin supremacy in the religious sphere and their social dominance. Hence the temple, which was a Brahmanical but *āgamic* institution combining features of Sanskritic and non-Sanskritic cultures, was constantly glorified in the *bhakti* hymns and hence became a central institution of integration with a superordinate character. Its popularity was due to many factors like the use of the Tamil language and the absorption of *Murukan* in the *Śaiva* pantheon, a factor of great importance in extending the popular base of Saivism. Thus the temple represented a synthesis of many elements in society and was capable of accommodating a wide range of interests, ranging from all the new forms of Saivism, such as the *Kālamukhas* and *Pāśupatas* and later the *Siddhas*, as well as the newly emerging peripheral and occupational groups (including craft groups) and the merchant community. Even the Cholas found it politically convenient to submit to this new ideology as the servants of god. The Cholas adopted this ideology and systematically developed it by showing a predilection to the *Śaiva* religion due to its assimilative character and popular base. In return the Cholas could, through the temple, intrude into peasant regions and local governance by integrating dispersed eco-zones into a single cultural unit. The expansion of the Chola resource base and the elevation of kingship through divine association gave royalty a special status.

The sources for the study of the early Chola period are mainly inscriptional records from temples. The spread and distribution of the inscriptions are pointers to the expansion of the temple movement. Apart from this, they also provide interesting information on the expanding economic linkages of temples and their integrative role in society. Inscriptions both in the form of copper plate records and epigraphs on stone have been used in this paper. This study is, however, confined to the inscriptions of the *Śaiva* temples, considering the fact that the addition of non-*Śaiva* inscriptions would make the study too vast. These inscriptions are scattered all over the Chola territory. Those of the early Chola period are more concise and shorter than the middle and late Chola records. Placed in the proper perspective – i.e. space and time – the contextual analysis of these inscriptions provides an interesting vision of the nature of developments.

The religious literature, i.e. the *Tēvāram* on the other hand, belongs to the previous period (seventh to ninth centuries CE) but it remarkably supplements epigraphy with the crucial information which the temple inscriptions do not provide, such as the symbolism of the *Śaiva* temple, growth of the *Śaiva* pantheon and its iconography. The *Tēvāram*, in fact, represents the main hymnal corpus of the literature, apart from its *Vaiṣṇava* counterpart and is still a living tradition forming a part of the everyday existence of the Tamil *Śaiva*s.

It would be highly difficult to understand early Chola society without simultaneously discussing the main trends in religion, which is inextricably linked to societal organization in the form of castes and communities. Beginning from the religious conflict of the days of the *Tēvāram* hymns, religious conflict was a central aspect of the developments leading to the downfall of Jainism and Buddhism and the triumph of Puranic religions, viz., Vaisnavism and Saivism. In this process the temple, its ideology and various cultural practices etc. contributed a lot through a process of appropriation of the ideals of Jainism and Buddhism on the one hand and, at the same time, the maintenance of a balance between Sanskritic and native sensibilities on the other. They together played a major role in the process of acculturation, interaction and assimilation through which *bhakti* tradition developed within Saivism and Vaisnavism. As religion was one of the dominant factors defining societal organization, the multi-dimensional aspects of religion are also analysed such as myths, motifs and legends – both Sanskritic and Tamil – and the syncretic idioms which reached down to the masses.

It is too well known to be repeated here that Tamilakam was a theatre of religious conflict between the orthodox Puranic sects and the so-called heterodox (Jaina and Buddhist) sects.

For reasons of patronage, main theatres of these conflicts were in the erstwhile capitals of the Pallavas and Pāndyas in Kancipuram and Madurai respectively and this is one of the contexts to locate the origin of *bhakti*.

This competing situation gave rise to a lot of legendary and traditional accounts regarding the debates between the two opposing religious groups, which ultimately led to the victory of orthodoxy over heterodoxy. Royal conversion was a central theme in the change from the dominance of Buddhism and Jainism to that of the Puranic religions. Far from being focused only on religion we find that there were elements of protest against the existing social hierarchy, particularly in the poems of the *Ālvārs* and the *Nāyanārs* where the protests were voiced more specifically against the elitism of the Brahmins in the religious sphere and the yearning for an emancipatory vision of salvation to all irrespective of caste. This protest even appropriated some of the ideals of the Jaina and Buddhist sects like equality before God and salvation irrespective of economic and caste status, which attracted the masses on account of their social message and simplicity. Due to its widespread popularity, it is this form of *bhakti* that the Cholas consciously adopted as their ideology. Through deliberate measures like the setting up of images, ritual singing of *bhakti* hymns and introducing rituals of a popular kind, they promoted *bhakti* movement and its institutional base viz. the temple.

During the early Chola period, Puranic religion witnessed new developments like an increasing practice of singing the *Tiruppadiyam* as well as further developments in Saivism. This was coeval with the near total disappearance of Buddhism and decline of Jainism. Earliest references of religious contestation are found in the *Mattavilāsa Prahasana*, a Sanskrit work of the Pallava period written by king Mahendravarmana, wherein many references are made to the deterioration among various sects such as the Jainas, Buddhists, *Pāśupata*s, *Kālamukha*s etc. indicating a state of tension among the various sects.[1] Reflections of this conflict were perceptible not only in the society but also in the realms of religion, philosophy and matters pertaining to everyday life. An examination of the developments in these diverse spheres of religion would help us in delineating the various socio-religious strands and help us to pinpoint the factors leading to the downfall of Jainism and Buddhism and the ascendancy of Saivism and Vaishnavism as the official religions patronised by the ruling houses, the Cholas and the Pāndyas.

The evolution of *bhakti* in Tamilakam was partly due to the challenges posed by the heterodox sects and due to the progress of Saivism and Vaishnavism through a process of acculturation and interaction with the local cults over the centuries beginning with the Sangam Age. Jaina challenge was met with in a dual way. At one level, the contestation assumed the character of an open conflict against the Jainas, their gods, and their asceticism. At another level, some aspects of Jaina religion, which struck a receptive chord among the local populace, were appropriated. Conflict and persecution appear as the main process of change from heterodoxy to orthodoxy. There is a reference by Sambandar that 8000 Jainas were impaled after they were defeated in a debate at the Pandya court.[2] Mahendravarmana, the Pallava ruler, was initially a follower of Jainism. After his conversion to Saivism, he is said to have destroyed Jain *Pallis*.[3]

Iyarpakai Nāyanār, (one of the 63 *Nāyanār*s) is said to have attacked his relatives violently, since they obstructed a Śaiva saint to whom he had given away his wife on the latter's demand.[4] This indicates that the grace of god could be obtained even through violence and is a noteworthy theme that the use of force could be sanctioned under the approval of religion. *Eripatta Nāyanār*'s story of the killing of a royal elephant as it damaged the flowers meant for Śiva's worships is another pointer in this direction.[5] Thus we see the according of religious sanction to this aspect of grace (i.e. through violence) is known as *marrakarunai*.[6]

The contestation of the Śaivas with the Jainas was taking place in all fields and at all levels though there is high visibility in the courts and the urban centers which had by now become *Śaiva* religious centers with the building of new temples and their consecration that later led to the formation of a sacred geography.

In the field of philosophy, the Buddhist view that there was no soul but rebirth and the Jaina belief of the denial of a universal god was a bit too hard for the Tamilian mind to assimilate as it went against the indigenous beliefs.[7] The heterodox sects put a great stress on the idea of transmigration but the *bhakti* sects paid only lip service to the above and stuck to the indigenous concepts of the dead. This was one strand that led to the decline of Jainism and Buddhism in Tamilnadu.[8]

It is also a truism that the *Śaiva bhakti* movement did not concentrate on mere philosophical abstraction, which would anyway not be of much relevance to the common folk. Instead, they went a step ahead of the Jainas in attracting the common folk by preaching to them in their own language and thus were composed the soul stirring hymns of the 63 Saivaite saints, the *Tēvāram,* which has attained a semi-canonical status. Incidentally the number 63 is itself said to be a holy number for the Jainas as it denoted the number of the *Śalākapuruṣas*.[9] Indigenous forms of worship were drawn from the Tamil religious practices of the early historical (Sangam) period that were current and popular. The religion of the Sangam period consisted of worship of the local gods such as *Murukan, Māyon, Korravai,* etc. whereas Vedic sacrifice was popular among the Brahmins.[10] This sacrificial cult could not reach the masses even though the royal houses of the Pallavas and the Pāndyas had adopted it.[11] This dichotomy was understood by the *bhakti* saints and thus their efforts towards integrating the various forms of worship.

Digressing a bit from the main point, it would be worthwhile to examine the socio-economic and politico-religious context during the early Chola period and their compulsions that led to the patronage to the orthodox sects, especially the institution of the temple. The early Cholas were faced with two problems: (a) the need to restructure the production process and (b) to reorganize the society on the lines of the Brahmanical social order. Along with their attempts of reorganizing the society on the lines of Brahmanical social order, they also tried to co-opt the rising social groups. Large-scale agrarian expansion took place under the institutional aegis of the temple in the early Chola period and vast tracts of the Kaveri delta were colonized. Related to this process was the peasantisation of a number of tribes, hence the need to reorganize the society on the lines of the Brahmanical pattern.

The main function of *bhakti* was to bring changes in the religious sphere in consonance with the necessities of social adjustments and at the same time asserting the supremacy of the Vedas. Thus the temple cult was the answer to it because it broke Brahmin exclusivity in religion and gave it a popular appeal.[12] This was a necessity, because in an agrarian society there was plurality of castes, each with its distinct culture that would stand in the way of integration. Thus the synthesis was achieved through the institution of the temple. Resentment among some sections of the orthodoxy to the temple cult is clear from the ascription of low caste status to the *Ādi Śaiva* Brahmins (who were priests of the *Śaiva* temples) by the more orthodox *Smārta* Brahmins.[13]

The superiority of the *bhakti* religion is clearly alluded to many times in literature and the texts. The earliest *Nāyanārs*, and Appar preached the superiority of the *Śaiva* faith in unambiguous terms.[14] Worship in any form was acceptable and earned divine grace. An examination of the mode of worship by the various persons would illustrate this point more clearly. The story of Kannappar who worshipped *Śiva* with flowers and washed the idol with water from his mouth and finally offered his own eye to the bleeding Śivali?ga is on of the oft-quoted examples.[15] A few devotees also adopted socially prohibited ways like gambling and robbery and used that wealth to propitiate *Śiva*.[16] This shows that all forms of worship got sanction if they pay obesciance to *Śiva*. This was one of the major hallmarks of the *bhakti* movement.

The multifaceted character of *bhakti* can be understood in detail when one sees the two major features of the *Śaiva* religion of this period: the grace of god and the ecstatic mode of worship. The Jaina religion held the view that women were responsible for the degeneration of moral values and thus they advocated celibacy, which was practiced by ascetics. But the *bhakti* movement stood this theory on its head and did not advocate restraint. It was, rather, in favour of harnessing several forms of worship, mainly in the form of dance and singing that was a release. This led to the view of salvation as a mystic union with god that could be achieved within the confines of human reality as worship was given a sensual character. One of the leaders of the *bhakti* movement, in characteristic detail, describes the attributes of *Pārvatī* and gives a sensual tinge when he talks of her breasts.[17] Goddess *Umādevī* is portrayed as wearing the mekalai around her hip.[18] The *Tēvāram* describes in detail about the worship of *Śiva* by dance and song[19] where women also joined singing with men.[20] *Tiruvaiyāru* was famous as a center of dance and there is a graphic description of this city with its *arangam*s or stages where dance masters taught them *Kūttu*.[21] The practice of dancing was prevalent in temples also where epigraphic references speak of grants made for maintaining dancers.[22] This could reach a wider audience and also pander to the senses. There are references to women who made a lot of noise in a playful and vibrant atmosphere while swimming in the tanks.[23] Mention is made of the sufferings of the lovelorn lady and her yearning for her beloved in vain.[24] *Cuntarar* had two wives: *Paravaiyār* and *Sangiliyar*.[25] *Tirunīlakanta Nāyanār*'s lustful dalliances with a courtesan were pardoned, as it was perceived as an act of worship to *Śiva*.[26]

Here one notes that sanctioning of emotional ways of seeking god led to instinctive modes of worship. This served as an outlet for realizing latent energy. It is strongly noticed in singing where *bhakta*s break into raptures and are taken to a point of ecstasy. As David Kinsley points out in the context of *bhakti*, the creation of the world, its preservation, destruction etc would be viewed as a play of god.[27] This aspect of *bhakti* was started by the *Ālvār*s who portrayed the *līlās* of *Kṛṣṇa*, his amorous exploits. This emotional *bhakti* of the *Ālvārs* was in fact original to Kṛṣṇaism and is found in facets in Saivism, particularly among the *Nāyanārs*.[28] The Tamil *Śaiva* saints led groups of devotees and went on long pilgrimages singing of the Lord and thus was born the concept of pilgrimage.[29] There are many references in the *Tēvāram* to singing and musical instruments, which are described in detail. There is a reference to music and dance[30] and also to the rhythm of the mulavu that accompanied these songs.[31] There are also many grants for the singers of the *Tiruppadiyam* under the early Cholas. The popularity and indispensability of singing the *Tiruppadiyam* can be gauged from the fact that the singers of *Tiruppadiyam* were paid more than the temple priests.[32]

The institution of the Devaradiyars[33] and the dancing girls, who get references in the epigraphic records, added colour and life to religious narrations by propagating religion in the form of an art which was also an entertainment and which, like literature, drew on folk themes.[34] Thus the popularity of *bhakti* among the masses was due to its rejection of ritual formalization.

Significantly, language that the *bhakti* poets used created an emotional impact and bound the worshipper to the deity.[35] One of the major features of *bhakti* movements in India is the concept of a personal god to whom the devotees could address all his yearnings and problems. It is in this context that the relation of the personal god with the devotee is examined to understanding the prevailing power relations in society. God is addressed to as *Perumān, Talaivan,* and *ālvān,* all of which are used to indicate positions of power and authority.[36] The devotee has to just surrender to the lord, and his grace will save him. *Śiva* is portrayed as merciful and forgiving.[37] This concept of god enabled the devotee to visualize god as someone who was very near and who would lend an ear to his or her problems. The poetry of the period (7th-9th centuries CE) brings this out very clearly. We have seen one segment of the poetic literature i.e. the intense psychological and emotional state of the poet saints.[38] The other segment is that of a devotee praying to the all powerful *Śiva* or *Viṣṇu,* asking for gifts and deliverance.[39]

As we have seen, the troubled state of affairs in the society (in material and emotional spheres) was an important factor behind the triumph of *bhakti,* leading it to adopt a bias towards the common man. In short the emotional *bhakti* alone could not satisfy the common man and hence his material needs were addressed to the personal god. The general character of the hymns shows the longing for a personal relationship with god and a sense of disgust in relation to this world.[40] There were not only many things that the common man could not reach out to because of lowly position that is indicted in his sense of despair. In this position there was no way except of surrendering to the God, and God always gave refuge to anyone, as *Sambandar* says in his *padigam* that even the Jainas and the Buddhists would get refuge if they submit to *Śiva*.[41] David Shulman has expounded the same view in his analysis of the *Asura* myths wherein the *Asura* too can get salvation if he submits to *Śiva*.[42] Such is the place of grace in the concept of *bhakti*. In fact the word 'path,' which is a Tamil rendering of the word *patti*, is sometimes used to signify love (*katal*), but in the works of the *Nayanārs* we find that the use of the word *arul* (grace) figures more prominently.[43]

This grace leads to salvation and demands single-minded devotion or loyalty from the devotee, which will take care of the devotee in all circumstances. There is also a warning that god would not help the insincere.[44] *Śiva* is also addressed to as *Arulālan* or the bestower of grace, and this is also seen in temples in the iconographic representation of *Śiva* in the *Andhaka Surahamurti* form.[45] *Cakkiya Nāyanār* was a Buddhist saint but when he accepted *Śiva*'s faith 'he got salvation.'[46] Another aspect of *bhakti* is the ambiguity of terms that leads to several connotations as we saw in the examples of *katal* and *Arul*. Similar are the groups to whom the messages were intended for.

The hymns of the saints speak of different types of temples (*Ilankoyil* and *Perunkoyil*) as well as different types of festivities in the same. It is only in the big temples that music and dance formed part of the daily rituals indicating a favorable economic position.

But here also some other problems emerged. The entire Tamil country was not united and there were problems of diverse gods and goddesses. There was also a problem of a stratified society with different value systems and ideals, and thus rose the problem of reconciling all these diverse interests. Further the folk traditions and festivals were strongly rooted and could not be wiped out. The incorporation of *Murukan* in the *Śaiva* pantheon as the son of *Śiva* and *Pārvatī* was one of the major factors behind the expansion of the *Śaiva* religion. *Murukan* was the earthly god of war and love. He could fit completely in the temple milieu and not remain as transcendental gods but remain deeply rooted in this world.[47] This was more of an imposition of a local cult rather than an upgradation of it due to Brahamanisation.[48] The *Tēvāram* has many references to *Murukan* and *Valli* and their marriage. They also mention his peacock and cock flag.[49] References eulogizing his twelve eyes (i.e. six faces) and his katampa garlands[50] and *Murukan* 's victory over *Curapadma*[51] are dwelt at length in a heroic genre. *Sambandar* mentions that *Murukan* was very popular among the ladies of the hilly region, who used to sing songs and worship him.[52] This is a significant feature of early Tamil worship, which continues even today. The worship of *Murukan* is described in more detail than that of any other God.

Vināyaka (*Gaṇeśa*) is also mentioned but only in some verses.[53] The mother goddesses *Umā* is mentioned at many places.[54] We also find many temples that are built for the mother goddesses in this period like the *Selliyamman Koyil, Pidāri koyil* etc.[55] An inscription mentions that there was a serious outbreak of smallpox (*Māri Jvaram*) in 808 CE, which led to out-migration from a particular village.[56] The prevalence of these diseases and the popular belief in Tamilnadu of appeasing Amman was prevalent and would also have been a contributory factor for her popularity. By the middle Chola period we find separate shrines for mother goddesses built in the temples, which was because of her increasing popularity.[57] The interpretations in the *Tēvāram* also contain references to the mother goddesses which may be taken to indicate her growing popularity and the need to take her cult into the *Śaiva* pantheon.[58] She was identified with *Umādevi*, the consort of *Śiva*, and is found in almost all sculptures along with *Śiva*, as prescribed in the *Āgamas*.

The older forms of worship such as the worship of the tree and other sacred objects like snakes and stones were not discontinued but also formed parts of the temple. We have a reference to the kadimaram and solemnization of marriage by tying the thread to the tree.[59] Even today, we find Talavirutcham, a sacred tree, in most of the Śaiva temples. At some places of religious importance like Chidambaram, Madurai, the *Talavirutcham* is taken from the local flora as in *Tiollaivanam* and *Ketampavanam*.[60] The name *Pātiripuliyūr* is given to the said centre after the name of the *Pātiri* tree.[61] Saint *Cuntarar* took his oath before being wedded to *Cankiliyar*, only under the sacred *makil* tree at *Tiruorriyur*.[62] *Sambandar* mentioned the place *Kurralām* (in Tirunelveli district) by the name of the sacred tree itself. This led to the conversion of the local shrine to a *Śaiva* shrine.[63]

Canmpantar says that all girls should observe various *Pāvai Nonbus*.[64] In the inscriptions we have references to endowments made by soldiers of various "regiments" in memory of their dead colleagues, which is reminiscent of the hero stones of the Sangam Age.[65] Thus the religion of the day made itself available to all classes of people, more so to the common man, as they had many opportunities to voice their social protest in this religion. There are references to how the vanity of the powerful was crushed.[66] The king is posed as the servant of God and not as the master of the masses.[67] In some places the Brahmins are portrayed as lacking in true understanding. An examination of the lives of all the 63 saints reveal that except a few the vast majority of them were not well versed in the Vedas and other sacred literature and their only qualification was their unstinted devotion. Besides, they belonged to all castes. There is a case of parody of a patron by *Cuntarar* who compares the king and the deity as patrons and then goes on to say that it is the temple god, who is superior.[68] The espousal of these issues pertaining to society also gave the *Śaiva* religion attractiveness to the common man. *Cuntarar*, who is described as *Śiva*'s friend, at one point asks the god for gold and says that he will not move unless he is given the same.[69]

Another feature of the Jainas that was appropriated by

the *Śaivas* was the idea of miracles. The vast majority of the people was ignorant and stepped in their own value systems and could not comprehend the various aspects of nature. To begin with *Appar*'s curbing of his colic achieved two things. Firstly, it proved that by the grace of *Śiva* anything could be set right. Secondly, it was a rebuttal of the Jaina efficacy of miracles. *Sambandar* is said to have brought a Brahmin boy back to life in *Avinācī* who was devoured by a crocodile and was missing for two years.[70] *Ninmrasir Nedumāran*, the king of Madurai, who was also called *Kun Pandyan* and was a hunchback before his conversion to Saivism, was cured by *Sambandar* after he became a *Śaiva*.[71] *Cuntarar* had lost his eyesight and could regain it only after a holy dip. The only qualification needed to secure *Śiva*'s grace was unqualified submission and unstinted devotion and loyalty.

The problem of the folk theme was tackled by the system of local Talapuranas. Even in the days of *Appar*, local *Talapuranas* connected with a particular shrine had developed. At Pullirukkuvelur, the local *Talapuranam* refers to the story of *Jatāyu*.[72] The local *Talapuranas* are merely reworking of classical Sanskritic myths in a Tamil setting where the local south Indian ideas have been absorbed. This is the case with the *Mahiśāsura* myth, where *Mahiśāsura* offers a *liṅgam* to the goddess, which is not a standard account.[73] In the temples of the early Chola period there are sculptures depicted many Puranic stories and legends of which eight legends are referred to in the *Tēvāram*. *Śiva*'s killing of *Andhakāsura* at Koval is the first.[74] Another favourite legend is how *Brahmā* and *Viṣṇu* tried to find the head and feet of *Śiva* but were unable to do so. This is sculpturally represented in the *Liṅgodbhava Mūrti*.[75] The famous legend of *Śiva* burning the *Tripuras* is said to have taken place at Tiruvadigai.[76] *Śiva*'s burning of *Kāma* with his third eye is also a favourite legend. This is said to have occurred at Kurukkai.[77] Thus each temple developed its own *Talapuurana* taking into account the local sensitivities and adapting to them, which was on of the main reasons for the spread of *bahkti* cults.

Along with the local *Talapuranas* there were also local

festivals celebrated throughout Tamilnadu. There're many references to the popularity of these festivals. In the month of *āippasi,* the *Thireuvonbam* festival was celebrated,[78] the *Kārthigai* festival in *Kārthigai,*[79] the *Apanguni Uthiram* festival,[80] which was a very popular festival like the *Tiruvādirai.*[81] The *Mahāmaham* was also a popular festival celebrated at Kudandai.[82] The epigraphs also contain many references to endowments made for these festivals indicating their popularity.[83]

The adaptation to native sensibilities by giving credence to local cults helped in localizing the action of the God and led to the popularity of the local myths as the acquaintance of the people with the above was already there. Another major feature was the rise of short-term avatar as associated with feats performed at a particular shrine, which made the gods relevant to the day-to-day life of the people. The repeated assertion by the saints that salvation could be attained even while leading a normal family life became popular as it required no extra effort and rigorous asceticism.[84]

Thus the above features were all synthesized in the temple where they could be systematized as per the Āgamic conventions. It was not possible for these features to flourish independently because of lack of patronage, a problem that the temple never faced. In the early Chola period many temples of the later Pallava period were rebuilt in stone. The temples also had *maṭhas* attached to them. It is said that *Appar* established some *maṭhas.*[85] This provided an institutional force to the temple with organized spiritual leadership. The capacity of the Śaivas to absorb into their fold radical elements like the *Pāśupatas* and the *Kāpālikas* also contributed to its popularity.[86]

Temple worship was done in the Āgamic way which is referred to in the Tēvāram[87] as well as in the inscriptions.[88] The reigning deity was worshipped with flowers to the chanting of Vedic hymns and the *Tiruppadiyam.* People propitiated the stone idol by offering sandalwood and incense to the stone idol.[89] The deity was draped in silk on ceremonial occasions like the king. Like the king the deity was also taken out in procession.[90]

In short it can be said that the growth of *bhakti* could be seen in the image worship and *devapujā*. The grace of *Śiva* was not the same for everyone and could take different forms.[91] The image of *Śiva* with *Yajñopavita,*[92] *Śiva* with malu, and the serpent in the *Visāpaharana murti,*[93] *Śiva* in *Bhikṣāṭaṇa* form[94] or the fiery *Śiva* with ash appealed to particular moods and strata of society.

The *bhakti* ideal, with its stress on the day-to-day life, was within the confines of reality and helped man to come to terms with it. The appeal to the local sensibilities and to the multiple gods forming a polytheistic pantheon in different forms and different modes of worship were its main features. In times of distress the devotee could turn to any of the gods which suited him and there was choice of the forms in the recognition of his moods and predilections, all of which were taken into account in order to appeal to the common man.

A study of the socio-religious context of the early Chola temple has shown that the temple emerged and consolidated itself as a Brahmanical and Āgamic institution. It also developed as an institutional base of the ideology for the exercise of Chola political authority. In other words it became a religio-political symbol. All this happened under the early Cholas, especially by the time of Uttama Chola (970 – 985 CE). The *Śaiva* temple movement had become the prime concern of the ruling family. In fact the result of this development are more clearly visible under the middle Chola rulers (Rājarāja I and Rājendra I: 985 – 1044 CE).This period also marks the apogee of Chola power and its socio-religious and cultural developments. This was particularly true in the context of maturation of the *Dravida* style of temple architecture, which culminated in the stupendous monuments at Tanjavur and *Gaṅgaikoṇḍacholapuram*, where various aspects of Tamil culture stood exemplified.

The wealth of the temple was next only to that of the state. The temple controlled a large part of agrarian sector, and it functioned as an unofficial 'department of agriculture' for the state. This could happen because state management of revenue administration under the early Cholas was not fully institutionalized. Revenue organization under the middle Chola period rulers did see the development of such a state department, which, in reality, acted through the temple.

To state that the temple promoted agriculture would mean that the agriculture was the only form of production and obscure all other forms of production. Yet the large number of donations of livestock and mention of manratis would point to the importance of pastoralism and integration of pastoralists into the economy of the temple which was a great consumer of pastoral products. The redistributive role played by the temple created several classes of landowners, cultivators i.e. from elite groups to labour groups. All this was institutionally linked to the Brahmin assembly or the *Sabhā,* the mercantile corporation or the *Nagaram* and the Vellalas' assembly or the *Ur* which enforced the writ of the temple in all places.

These institutions were the mainstay of the power structure of the Cholas. In addition, the links between royalty and temple was directly established by the Office of *Srikariyam,* which was held often by a royal official with the title *Muvendavelan*. This increased royal influence to a great degree. In effect the temple acted as the supreme channel of communication which was tapped by royalty and other elite groups.

The widening economy of the temple not only brought in various professional groups but also created stratification among them i.e. within each occupational group with a ritual ranking. For example the *Pattasalins* and *Kaikkolas* represent higher and lower ritual groups among the weavers. The *Pattasalins* supplied cloths to the temple and the royalty. We get references to this effect in the Madras Museum plates of Uttama Chola. But the *Kaikkolas* were lower in status as they were engaged in other types of occupations in temples. Their duties included the cultivation of temple lands as well. But it is in the case of the Brahmins, where we find a more conspicuous stratification. The *Smārta* Brahmins, who were well-versed in the Vedas, occupied the top slot in this hierarchy, followed by the *Śivabrāhmaṇas* and others, who were temple priests. At the lower levels, there were Brahmins who worked as lighters of lamps and providers of water and flowers. The absence of the *Kṣatriya Varṇa* is a conspicuous feature of South Indian society. But the royal donors assumed *Kṣatriya* status both by building temples and through a complex set of legitimating factors like genealogies and Dharmasastric rituals such as *hiraṇyagarbha* and *tulabara*.

The Vellalas seem to be the largest community of non-Brahmins, associated with agriculture. But with diversification of economic activities, they were also stratified on the basis of their economic status and occupational importance such as traders (*Nagarattaras*), weavers (*Kaikkulas*), perhaps craftsmen (*Kammalas*). The last mentioned could also have included non-Vellala groups from the tribal areas. The term *Sankarappadiyar* also indicates existence of mixed caste groups although in early Chola inscriptions they figure more as suppliers of oil.

The segregation of certain groups like the *Parayars* in the *Paraichcheri* or *Tindachecheri* (untouchable colony) is attested to by the inscriptions and religious texts. However the notion of a large religious community and that of salvation through *bhakti* would seem to have decreased differences in the religious sphere if not in the society and economy. The temple could use even the non-coercive ideology of *bhakti* to maintain a stratified society through an illusion of equality.

The Śaiva religion in the period had many facets and thus its popularity was due to the fact that it catered to all sections of society. *Bhakti* leaders propagated their messages in the language of the masses. They propounded a message which was devoid of intellectual dogma. The popularity of their teachings was enhanced more by the use of popular drama, *kuttu* or dance and music by the *devaradiyars,* who lent colour to the temple functions. Their popular appeal can be seen in the singing of the *Tiruppadiyam* hymns which was more widely understood than the Vedic rituals. This is indicated by the fact that remuneration of the *Tiruppadiyam* singers was higher than that of the priests. The *Tēvāram* also came to be called the *Tamil Veda*.

Other practices of a popular nature like worship of trees,

snakes, local festivals, pilgrimages and sacred sites were all included in the religious movement. The bulk of the inscriptions speak of endowments for this rituals and festivals. Thus *bhakti* could accommodate diverse strands from orthodoxy to radicalism as exemplified by the various forms of Saivism such as the *Kālamukhas* and the *Pāśupatas* down to the folk elements.

The royal association with the divine religious paraphernalia is evident from similar rituals used to wake the king and the deity. The etymology of the word *Koil* meaning both the temple and the palace are parallels which cannot be missed. This served to disseminate the royal ideology via the temple. The orthodox element in religion is manifested in the stories of *Tirunilakanda Yalpanar* and *Nandanar* which the orthodox attitudes are emphasized and at the same time an imagined equality is established through *bahkti.* Such attempts at creating an equality in the religious sphere led to the emergence of a Śaiva community, redrawing the social boundaries with the exclusion of the Jainas and Buddhists. The temple functioned as the centre of this community.

Notes

1. A.M. Paramasivanandam, *Historical Study of the Thevaram Hymns,* Madras 1982, p. 129.
2. R. Gopalakrishnan, *Religion and Mysticism in the Periyapuranam,* Madras 1990, p. 63.
3. A.M. Paramasivanandam, *op. cit.,* p. 29.
4. Gopalakrishnan, *op. cit.,* p. 20.
5. Ibid., p. 106.
6. Ibid., p. 106.
7. T.K. Venkatasubramanian, 'Social Roots of Tamilian Religious Ideology,' *Proceedings of the Indian History Congress,* 1984, p. 183.
8. George. L. Hart, 'The Theory of Reincarnation among the Tamils,' in Wendy Doinger O'Flaherty (ed.), *Karma and Rebirth in Classical Indian Tradition,* California 1960, p. 133.
9. Vidya Dehejia, *Slaves of The Lord – The Path of the Tamil Saints,* Delhi 1998, p. 1.

10. D. Dayalan, *Early Temples of Tamilnadu*, Delhi, 1992, p. 17.
11. Nicholas Dirks, 'Political Authority and Structural Change in Early South Indian History, *The Indian Economic and Social History Review*, 1979, p. 132.
12. George. W. Spencer, 'Religious Networks and Royal Influences in 11th Century South India,' *Journal of Economic and Social History of Orient*, XII 1969, p. 46.
13. R.N. Nandi, 'Origin and Nature of Saivaite Monasticism: The Case of *Kālamukhas*' in R.S. Sharma (ed.), *Indian Society: Historical Probings*, Delhi, 1976, p. 191.
14. *Appar Tēvāram*, 5.100.2.
15. R. Gopalakrishnan, *op. cit.*, p. 30.
16. Ibid., p. 70.
17. Vidya Dehejia, *op. cit.*, p. 45.
18. *Appar Tēvāram*, 5.11.6.
19. *Sambandar Tēvāram*, 3.72.2.
20. *Sambandar Tēvāram*, 1.7.3
21. *Sambandar Tēvāram*, 1.130.5.
22. *South Indian Inscriptions (S.I.I.)*, Vol. XIX, No. 171.
23. *Sambandar Tēvāram*, 3.72.4.
24. *Appar Tēvāram*, 4.90.7.
25. Dorai Rangaswamy, *The Religion And Philosophy of The Tēvāram*, Madras, 1958, p. 97.
26. R. Gopalakrishnan, *op.cit.*, p. 92.
27. Kinsley David, *The Divine Player: A Study of Kṛṣṇa Lilā*, Delhi, 1979, p. 51-55.
28. F. Hardy, *Viraha Bhakti The Early History of Kṛṣṇa Devotion In South India*, Delhi, 1983, p. 45.
29. Dorai Rangaswamy, *op. cit.*, p. 67.
30. *Sambandar Tēvāram*, 2.187.9.
31. *Sambandar Tēvāram*, 1.130.1.
32. R. Nagaswamy, 'South Indian Temple as an Employer,' *The Indian Economic and Social History Review*, 1965, p. 370.
33. *S.I.I*, Vol. XIII, No. 88.
34. D. Shulman, *Tamil Temple Myths*, Princeton, 1980, p. 13.
35. K. Sivathamby, *Literary History In Tamil*, Thanjavur, 1986, p. 38.
36. Maraisusai Dhavamony, *Love of God according to Śaiva Siddhanta*, Oxford 1971, pp. 29-30.
37. F. Hardy, *op. cit.*, p. 433.
38. Kamil Veith Zvelebil, *A History of Indian Literature – Tamil Literature*, ed. Jan Gonda, Otto Harrasowig Weisbaden, Vol. X,

1974, p. 95.

39. Ibid., p. 94.
40. Susmita Pande, *Birth of Bhakti in Indian Religions and Art*, Delhi 1990, p. 134.
41. *Sambandar Tēvāram*, 1.66.10.
42. D. Shulman, *op. cit.*, p. 317
43. Maraisusai Dhavamony, *op. cit.*, pp. 24-28.
44. *Appar Tēvāram*, 4.113.4.
45. Rangaswamy, Dorai, *op. cit.*, p. 535.
46. Ibid., p. 1007.
47. F. Hardy, *op. cit.*, p. 236.
48. R. Champakalakshmi, 'Religion and Social Change in Tamilnadu (CE 600-1300),' in N.N. Bhattacharya (ed.), *Medieval Bhakti Movements in India*, Delhi, 1989, p. 165.
49. *Appar Tēvāram*, 4.43.8.
50. *Appar Tēvāram*, 4.60.3.
51. *Appar Tēvāram*, 6.89.2.
52. *Appar Tēvāram*, 5.18.4, 4.75.4, 5.64.10.
53. *Sambandar Tēvāram*, 1.24.5.
54. Dorai Rangaswamy, *op. cit.*, p. 252.
55. S.R. Balasubramanyam, *Early Chola Temples*, Faridabad, 1971, p. 81.
56. M.A. Mohan Ram, 'Famines and Relief Measures under the Imperial Cholas (850-1279),' *Proceedings of Indian History Congress*, 1984, p. 185.
57. S.R. Balasubramanyam, *Middle Chola Temples*, Faridabad 1975, pp. 293-299.
58. Dorai Rangaswamy, *op. cit.*, p. 59.
59. C.V. Narayana Ayyar, *Origin and Early History of Saivism in South India*, Madras 1974, p. 312.
60. A.M. Paramasivanandam, *op. cit.*, p. 151.
61. Ibid.
62. Ibid.
63. Ibid
64. *Appar Tēvāram*, 5.99.8.
65. Venkatasubramaniam, *op. cit.*, pp. 182-184.
66. C.V. Narayana Ayyar, *op. cit.*, p. 156.
67. D. Shulman, 'Poets and Patrons in Tamil Literature and Literary Legend,' in Barbara Stoler Miller (ed.), *Powers of Art: Patronage in Indian Culture*, Delhi 1992, p. 122.
68. Ibid., p. 96.
69. Ibid.

70. C.V. Narayana Ayyar, *op. cit.*, p. 146.
71. Ibid., p. 126.
72. Ibid., p. 324.
73. D. Shulman, *Tamil Temple Myths, Princeton*, 1980, p. 14., 1980, p. 14. Also see *Tēvāram* 6.4.8.
74. *Appar Tēvāram*, 6.74.8.
75. Dorai Rangaswamy, *op. cit.*, p. 196.
76. *Appar Tēvāram*, 6.96.5,6.50.5,5.21.9.
77. *Appar Tēvāram*, 4.4.4.
78. *Sambandar Tēvāram*, 2.183.2.
79. *Sambandar Tēvāram*, 2.183.3.
80. *Appar Tēvāram*, 6.45.5.
81. *Sambandar Tēvāram*, 2.183.4.
82. *Appar Tēvāram*, 6.75.10.
83. *S.I.I.* Vol. XIX, No. 316.
84. *Appar Tēvāram*, 4.89.7.
85. R.N. Nandi, *op. cit.*, p. 191.
86. R. Champakalakshmi, *op. cit.*, p. 168.
87. *Appar Tēvāram*, 4.33.5,4.72.6, 5.17.5.
88. *S.I.I.* Vol. XIII, No. 146.
89. *Sambandar Tēvāram*, 1.61.4.
90. Arjun Appadurrai & Carol Breckenridge Appadurrai, 'The South Indian Temple: Authority Honour and Redistribution,' *Contributions to Indian Sociology*, Vol. 10, No. 2, 1976, pp. 191-193.
91. S. Arulsamy, *Saivism – A Perspective of Grace*, p. 101.
92. Dorai Rangaswamy, *op. cit.*, p. 233.
93. Ibid., p. 255.
94. Ibid., p. 441.

8

THE SACRED GEOGRAPHY OF MEDIEVAL TAMILAKAM
A Study of Distribution Pattern of Śaiva and Vaiṣṇava Temples

S. JEEVANANDAM

Introduction

It has been noted that the knowledge of the sacred geography and astronomy were the domains of religious specialists.[1] One group was replaced by another over the last several centuries and these locations continued to be recognized as sacred locales and to operate within a system of ethno astronomical and mythological beliefs. The transference of such traditions took place between groups that differed in language, religion, economic focus and area of origin.[2] A particular group entered into the new territories and they gradually adapted their belief and systems to their new physical environments. This often involved adopting many of the traditions of earlier occupants of the area. The development of a sacred landscape thus was a process of transferring old mythic locales to new points on the landscape and incorporating new beliefs borrowed from groups with whom they were coming into contact.[3] In India's Great Tradition many regional and local sub- cultures coexist and all are related directly or indirectly to one another, and to the Sanskritic culture of the pan-Indian Brahmanical tradition activities.

Sacred geography is primarily associated with the places of pilgrimage, which bring the traditions of the gods and goddesses, heroes, heroines and sages to a living embodiment in a particular geographical locale.

This paper seeks to study the evolution of distribution pattern of temples in medieval Tamilakam, by analyzing the devotional literature of Tamil *Bhakti* movements, in the backdrop of socio-economic changes.

To define the exact geographical boundaries of Tamilakam is tough. According to the *Cilappadikārama* (one of the earliest epics of Tamil literature), Tamilakam extended form Veṅkata hills in the north to Cape Comorin in the south and form the Bay of Bengal in the east to the Arabian Sea in the west.[4] According to Subramanian, 'the Tamil country called Tamilnadu or Tamilakam lies to the south of the Mysore plateau in the north and northwest and the Tirupati hills in the northeast, it is bounded on the west by the Arabian Sea, on the south by the Indian Ocean and on the east by the Bay of Bengal.'[5] *Vaiṣṇava* literature of medieval Tamilnadu treats Veṅkata hills area as part of Tamilnadu. So our study covers the area from Veṅkata hills in the north to Cape Comorin in the south. It also includes parts of modern Kerala.

Śaiva and Vaiṣṇava temples in medieval Tamilakam

The process of growth and proliferation of temples in the Tamil country and the travels of the saints and singing of their hymns were reinforced by one another. The temples which were eulogized by the *Śaiva* saints for a particular shrine are known as *pādal petra ṣtalam* or *vaippu stalam*.[6] According to the Tamil *Śaiva* tradition there were 274 *Śaiva* shrines in India.[7] Temples which were extolled by *Ālvārs* were known as *maṇgala cācanam petra stalam*. They were collectively called as *tirupadikal*. As per Tamil Ā*lvār* tradition, there were 108 such temples.[8] The importance of temples which were *pādal petra stalam* or *maṇgala cācanam petra stalam* can be easily understood from the fact that even in modern days a rich and pious moneylender of *Nagaratār* community would never consider to renovate any temple which was not sanctified in the songs of a saint.[9]

A particular temple or sacred place was not necessarily, and equally, popular with all saint singers. Some sacred places were eulogized by only one of the saints and others were praised by two or more than two. Among the 274 *Śaiva* shrines the Tevāram trio *Appar, Campantar* and *Cuntarar* eulogized only 223, 231 and 138 shrines respectively. In *Vaiṣṇava* sect, *Madurakaviālvār* was one among the twelve *Ālvārs* who did not compile songs on any of the *Vaiṣṇava* shrines or deities.[10] Table 1 lists the *Vaiṣṇava t*emples, which were eulogized by eleven *Ālvārs*.

Table 1

Name of the Ālvār	*Maṇgala cācanam Petra Stalams*
Poigaiālvār	6
Pudattālvār	13
Pey ālvār	15
Tirumalic ālvār	17
Namm ālvār	37
Kulacekar ālvār	9
Periy ālvār	18
Aṇḍāl	11
Tondaradipodiy ālvār	1
Tiruppan ālvār	3
Tirumangai ālvār	86

Among the sacred centers only few shrines were frequently mentioned and popular in the hymns of the saints. For example, Piramapuram or Brahmapuram shrine in Cikali *tāluk* of Thanjavur district is repeatedly referred to in the hymns under a dozen of synonymous names.[11] Yet the name

Piramapuram is mentioned only in the hymns of *Campantar* and not in the hymns of any other saint. In contrast the famous sacred centre of Tiruvārur, which is located only about eight miles south of Piramapuram, is repeatedly eulogized in the hymns of all three saints.[12] Among the *Vaiṣṇava* temples, centers like Srirangam and Tirumalai (Modern Tirupathi) were especially famous, and they were eulogized by eleven and ten *Ālvār*s respectively. The position of the deity in the sanctum was special in *Vaiṣṇava* traditions. The posture differed from shrines to shrines. The 67 idols of *Viṣṇu,* in the 108 sacred temples were postured in a standing manner, 17 idols were on sitting posture and 10 idols were in a lying down posture.[13]

Distribution pattern of Temples

The medieval Tamilakam was divided into a number of smaller divisions for the administrative purposes. These divisions were called *kurram* (divisions). The political units of Pallavas were noted as *kottam, nāḍu* and *ūr* or villages.[14] The larger section of the land was called as *Valanādu* or *Maṇḍalama.* During the Pallava period the term *rāṣtra*[15] was also used instead of *maṇḍalamas. Tondaimaṇḍalama, Cholamaṇḍalama, Pāṇḍyamaṇḍalama, Nāḍumaṇḍalama, Ceramaṇḍalama,* which was later known as *Malaimaṇḍalama*[16] and *Koṅgumaṇḍalama* were important divisions in medieval records.[17]

Sacred geography played a major role in the distribution of temples. The sacred shrines of Saivism and Vaishnavism were not confined to a single geographical place but the overwhelming majority of places are located within these *maṇḍalamas.* Out of 274 *Śaiva* scared shrines 269 were situated in South India and remaining few were in the Himalayan regions.[18] As far as *Vaiṣṇava* shrines are concerned, 95 shrines were placed in Tamilakam and remaining 13 sacred shrines were spread over North India. Tamil *Śaiva* saints concentrated their travels in the Chola country by singing hymns at 190 shrines in this segment of Tamil region. The rest were in *Pāṇḍyamaṇḍalama, Tondaimaṇḍalama, Nāḍumaṇḍalama, Koṅgumaṇḍalama, Malaimandalam, Īlam* and *Tirukkokarnama* or *Tulunāḍu.*[19] Like *Śaiva* shrines, *Vaiṣṇava* shrines also show heavy concentration in *Cholamaṇḍalama*, which had 40 shrines, and the rest were in *Tondaimaṇḍalama*, *Pāṇḍyamaṇḍalama*, *Malaimaṇḍalama* and *Nāḍumaṇḍalama*.[20]

Tondaimaṇḍalama

The medieval *Tondaimaṇḍalama* included the modern districts of Chennai, Tiruvallur, Kanchipuram, Vellore, Tiruvannamalai and Vilupuram. During the period of Cholas the province was denoted as *Jayankonda Cholamaṇḍalama*.[21] It had 32 Śaiva Shrines and 22 Vaiṣṇava shrines. The capital of this territory was Kanchipuram. Out of 22 *Vaiṣṇava* temples in *Tondaimaṇḍalama*, the capital town itself had 14 *Vaiṣṇava* shrines. The *Vaiṣṇava* saints *Poigaiālvār*, *Pudattālvār*, *Peyālvār* and *Tirumalicaiālvār* were born here and they propagated their ideology in this territory. Brahmanical centers in *Tondaimaṇḍalama* were committed to learning, as well as to propagate the resurgence of the Vedic religion. It was a direct outgrowth of the previous importance from Buddhist and Jain intellectual and religious activities against which the subsequent enthusiastic sponsorship of Brahmanical learning and religion by the Pallavas of *Simhaviṣṇu* line were directed.

Pāṇḍyamaṇḍalama

The present districts of Madurai, Virudhunagar, Ramanadapuram, Pudukkottai, Sivagangai and Tirunelveli constituted medieval *Pāṇḍyamaṇḍalama*. Cholas captured this territory from Pāṇḍyas and made it their stronghold. *Pāṇḍyamaṇḍalama* was also named as *Rājarājamaṇḍalama* or *Rājarājavalanāḍu*.[22] *Periyālvār*, *Aṇḍāl*, *Nammālvār* and *Madurakaviālvār* belonged to this region. Initially this region was under the influence of Jainas. The Pāṇḍya queen requested *Campantar* to propagate Saivism in this territory. *Campantar* agreed and he converted the king Ninracir Nedumaran and wiped out the Jaina influence over Pāṇḍyas land. Under the influence Saivism, 14 *Śaiva* shrines came up in this region. There were already 18 *Vaiṣṇava* temples in existence in this region.

Cholamaṇḍalama

In the distributions of temples, *Cholamaṇḍalama* had a large number of temples. Both the devotional zeal of the saints and the "publicity" value of their hymns had a profound influence upon the styles of religious devotion in later times, especially in the Kaveri delta. The program of temple construction, which was encouraged by the imperial Cholas, who dominated the Kaveri delta from the 9th century CE through the 12th century CE, drew much of its inspiration from the earlier *bhakti* movement of the Pallava period. The Kaveri placed the temples into two geographical areas. The first one was to the north of river Kaveri and the second to the south of the same river. The north and south carried 63 and 190 *Śaiva* temples respectively. 40 *Vaiṣṇava* shrines were also established in this area. The districts of Ariyalur, Cuddalore, Nagapattinam, Thanjavur and Tiruchirappalli were in the northern part of river Kaveri. The southern portion had the districts of Tiruvarur, Karaikkal, Karur, Nagapattinam, Thanjavur and Tiruchirappalli. Places like Karur, Nagapattinam, Thanjavur and Tiruchirappalli were put in more than one category, due to the course of river flowing through different parts.

Nāḍumaṇḍalama

Nāḍumaṇḍalama was situated in between Koṅgumaṇḍalama and Cholamaṇḍalama. It was ruled by Malaiyamans. It consisted of modern districts of Vilupuram, Cuddalore and Tiruvannamalai. It had 2 *Vaiṣṇava* and 22 *Śaiva* temples. Tiruvadikai, Tirukkovalur and Tiruvannamalai were prominent Śaiva temples.

Koṅgumaṇḍalama

Koṅgumaṇḍalama flourished by the rivers of Kaveri and Ciruvani. The land was surrounded by the hilly tracts of Udagamaṇḍalama, Javvadu hill, Kolli hill and Serveroys hills. This *maṇḍalama* comprised of the areas of modern districts of Coimbatore, Erode, Salem, Namakkal and Karur. According to the Tamil *Śaiva* tradition there were 14 temples placed in this *maṇḍalama*.

In contrast to *Koṅgumaṇḍalama* and *Nāḍumaṇḍalama*, *Malaimaṇḍalama* had only one *Śaiva* shrine but 13 Vaiṣṇava shrines. Kulacekara was the ruler and one of the prominent Ālvār saints of *Malaimaṇḍalama*. He influenced the *Vaiṣṇava* zeal and initiated the construction of temples. Apart from Tamilakam, *Īlam* (modern Srilanka) and Tulu country had one Śiva temple each.

There are many reasons, which can be attributed for the spread to temples in Tamilakam. The process of Brahmanization influenced the indigenous Tamils and emphasized the Brahmanical ideology in their society. Brahmanical ideology created its own mythology and legends in Tamil soil. Brahmanical ideology linked kings and Brahmins together. Kings and the Brahmins were interdependent for their social and economic status. The construction of temples and establishment of *Brahmadeya*s satisfied both the economic needs and consolidation of the vast empire. Hence kings and royal officials encouraged the construction of temples. The tireless propagation of the saint singers and their pilgrimage towards those centers made it popular. Their pilgrimages interlinked the temples with one another and also associated the lives of the saints with one another as they were all seeking the blessings of the same God.

Pilgrimage

The geographical principles illuminate the nature of the pilgrimage and pilgrimages become important for the principles of the geography.[23] The sacred places are consecrated as a crossing place between heaven and earth.[24] So pilgrimages are generally considered as sacred journeys with earthly and spiritual pathways. Ideally, it involves a comforting or enlightening transformation of the self. An important element of pilgrimage is leaving behind the mundane or familiar as pilgrims approach the divine to embrace an alien cosmos.[25] Generally pilgrimages are much older than any of the particular myths and deities which are attached to it.[26] Diana. L Eck said that the phenomenon of pilgrimage to such charged places was firmly grounded in the ancient locative folk traditions and only later do we find the Brahmanical traditions of pilgrimage.[27]

The Cultural Mediators

In Tamilakam, *bhakti* saints propagated the ideas, themes and symbols from one level to another. Their activities vividly illustrated how significant ideas and symbols of the Indic tradition could be translated and transformed into themes which were more directly reflective of local or regional practices.[28] They acted as cultural mediators and it is difficult to exaggerate the importance of oral tradition as a medium for the dissemination of ideas in traditional India.[29] Raghavan has rightly pointed that the significant of the words for "knowledge" in Sanskrit (*śruta*) and in Tamil (*kelvi*) both mean literally "that which is heard."[30] The modes of communicating were the significant cultural themes and values and its "cultural performances." It structured the events ranging from religious rituals to plays, concerts, and lectures. [31] They are linked in a cultural continuum "which includes village and town, Brahmin and non- Brahmin, north and south, the modern mass- media culture and the traditional folk and classic cultures, the little and the great traditions.'[32] Public singing of devotional hymns by specialists or laymen has developed directly out of this oral tradition.[33]

The Tamil *bhakti* saints deemed some centres as holy and introduced the practice of visiting the sites and singing about them and thereby the concept of pilgrimage emerged and, thus, creates a sacred geography. The *Śaiva* and *Vaiṣṇava* saints traveled through the countryside and praised the deity and of the shrines believed to be sacred to them. Each hymn is said to have been composed at a particular place and either the name of that place or the name under which the god was worshipped there was usually mentioned in the text of the hymns. It is a detailed study of these references which allows us to reconstruct the sacred geography of medieval Tamil *Śaiva* and *Vaiṣṇava* traditions.

Distribution pattern of temples in *Cholamaṇḍalama* is striking. George. W Spencer is surprised to see the heavy concentration of temples on the banks of the rivers particularly in the Kaveri delta [34] and, to a lesser degree, in the Pennai, Vaigai, and Tamraparani river valleys. The connection between the sacred geography of Tamil Saivism and the early agricultural development of Tamilakam is, thus, evident.[35] A large number of hymns focused on these places. Next to fertility, political conditions. played prominent role in the distributions of the temples in a particular geography area. The imperial Cholas, who dominated the Kaveri delta encouraged the temple construction from ninth through twelfth centuries, drew much inspiration from the earlier *bhakti* movement of the Pallava period.[36] The delta regions of the Kaveri were one of the most densely populated parts of Tamilakam.[37] In medieval period *Cholamaṇḍalama* and *Tondaimaṇḍalama* witnessed a great concentration of Brahmanical settlements. There were 646 *brahmadeyas* in Tamilakam. Out of that, *Tondaimaṇḍalama* had 307, *Cholamaṇḍalama* had 300, *Pāṇḍyamaṇḍalama* had 25, and *Kongumaṇḍalama* had 14.[38]

To conclude, the propagation of the *bhakti* ideology by Tamil saints and the patronage by the kings and nobles increased the construction of temples. Distribution of temples over different *maṇḍalamas* of Tamilnadu was not uniform. As our analysis of Tamil *bhakti* literature has revealed, 269 *Śaiva* and 95 *Vaiṣṇava* shrines were unevenly distributed. The fertile *Cholamaṇḍalama* had 190 *Śaiva* and 40 *Vaiṣṇava* shrines. *Pāṇḍyamaṇḍalama* had 14 *Śaiva* and 18 *Vaiṣṇava* shrines, *Tondaimaṇḍalama* had 32 *Śaiva* and 22 *Vaiṣṇava* shrines, *Nāḍumaṇḍalama* had 22 *Śaiva,* and 2 *Vaiṣṇava* shrines, *Koṅgumaṇḍalama* had 14 *Śaiva* shrines, and *Malaimaṇḍalama* had only one *Śaiva* shrine and 13 *Vaiṣṇava* shrines. There was no *Vaiṣṇava* shrine in *Koṅgumaṇḍalama, Īlam* and *Tulunāḍu.*

An analysis of the distribution pattern of the temple clearly points out the heavy concentration of temples in *Cholamaṇḍalama* and on the banks of the rivers particularly the Kaveri and a lesser degree in Pennai, Vaigai, and Tamraparni.

This clearly points the connection between the Tamil temples and the early agricultural development. As these were the areas where first agricultural expansion took place and people settled in large numbers, more and more temples were concentrated in these regions. A number of hymns also speak of these places. Hence the first and foremost condition for the expansion and location of temples was the availability of fertile regions. Next to fertility, the political condition of the country played prominent role in the distributions of the temples in a particular geographical precinct. Pilgrimages linked the temples in different regions and over a period of time trade and craft production integrated the Tamil society.

Notes

1. Linea Sundstrom, 'Mirror of Heaven: Cross-Cultural Transference of the Sacred Geography of the Black Hills,' *World Archaeology*, Vol. 28, No. 2, 1996, p. 187.
2. Ibid., p. 187.
3. Ibid., pp. 187-188.
4. V. Kanakasabhai, *The Tamils 1800 Years Ago,* New Delhi, 1904, p. 10.
5. N. Subramanian, *History of Tamilnadu*, Madurai, 1978, p. 1.
6. K.K. Pillai, *Thamizhaga Varalaru Makkalum Panpadum* (in Tamil), Chennai, 2002, p. 233.
7. Indira Viswanathan Peterson, *Poems to Siva*, Delhi, 1989, p. 12.
8. K.K. Pillai, *op. cit.*, p. 233.
9. C.M. Ramachandra Chettiar, 'Geographical Distribution of Religious Places in Tamilnad,' *Indian Geographical Journal*, Vol. XVI, 1941, p. 45.
10. A. Etiraj, *Vaishnava Divya Stala Varalaru* (in Tamil), Karaikudi, 2006, p. 23.
11. It should be noted that a single place is often referred to in the hymns by more than one name.
12. George. W Spencer, 'The Sacred Geography of the Tamil Saivite Hymns,' *Numen*, Vol. 17, No. 3, p. 239.
13. A. Etiraj, *op. cit.*, pp. 25-26.
14. Kuram Plates, *South Indian Inscriptions* (*SII*), Vol. I, p. 144.
15. Tamil Portion, *SII*, Lines, 57-58.

16. Indira Viswanathan Peterson, *op. cit.*, p. 13.
17. C.M. Ramachandra Chettiar, *op. cit.*, pp. 42-50.
18. Indira Viswanathan Peterson, *op. cit.*, p. 12.
19. Ibid., p. 13.
20. A. Etiraj, *op. cit.*, p. 23.
21. *South Indian Inscriptions (SII)*, Vol. II, Part I and II, p. 27.
22. *SII*, Vol. II, Part I and II, p. 28.
23. R.M. Stoddard, Hans Aldskogius, A. Morinis, 'Sacred Places, Sacred Spaces, The Geography of Pilgrimage,' *Human Geography*, Vol. 80, No. 3, 1998, p. 178.
24. Diana, L. Eck, 'India's Tirthas: Crossings in Sacred Geography,' *History of Religion*, Vol. 20, No. 4, 1981, p. 325.
25. Barbara, A Weightman, 'Sacred Landscapes and the Phenomenon of Light,' *Geographical Review*, Vol. 86, No. 1, 1996, p. 68.
26. Diana, L. Eck, *op. cit.*, p. 323.
27. Ibid., p. 326
28. George. W. Spencer, *op. cit.*, p. 241.
29. Ibid., p. 242.
30. V. Raghavan, *'Methods of Popular Religious Instruction in South India,'* in Haridas Bhattacharyya (ed.), *The Cultural Heritage of India*, Vol. IV, Calcutta, I956, pp. 503- 5I4.
31. Milton Singer, 'The Cultural Pattern of Indian Civilization,' *Far Eastern Quarterly*, Vol. XV, No. I, I955, pp. 23-36.
32. Ibid., pp. 32-33.
33. George, W. Spencer, *op. cit.*, p. 243.
34. Ibid., p. 236.
35. Ibid., p. 236.
36. Ibid., p. 239.
37. T.B. Ranganatha Davey, 'The Historical Geography of the Cauveri Delta with Special Reference to the Tanjore District,' *Journal of Madras Geographical Association*, Vol. 12, No. 2, 1987, pp. 83-94.
38. Burton Stein, *Peasant State and Society in Medieval South India*, Oxford, 1985, p. 290.

9

THE TEMPLE AND TEMPLE DANCING GIRLS OF MEDIEVAL DECCAN

REKHA PANDE

Introduction

An important institution that continued to play a very important role in the religious and cultural life of Deccan from the medieval times is the institution of the temple dancing girls. Emerging from the concept of divine fecundity as an integral part of agrarian societies, this institution continued to flourish and is in existence even in the 21st century. Unfortunately such an important institution has not been very central to our understanding of history of pre- Colonial Deccan, primarily due to the neglect of women's history. In the present paper our endeavour is to see the temples and the institution of temple dancing girls as corollary to the feudal set up of medieval Deccan.

The Deccan region is an amalgam of many ecozones, from the arid rocky plateau of the Rayalseema to the bountiful coastal plains flanked by the Eastern and Western Ghats to the vast hinterlands. It has agricultural plains and forests such as Coorg and Dandakaranya. It had varied social formations; and agrarian, pastoral, hunting-gathering, artisans and other forms of production. This region in the medieval period witnessed many transformations in the politico-economic and socio-cultural spheres. Politically, the state gradually transformed into a multi-centered power structure, fragmented and segmented at different levels, owing to the extensive growth of socio-religious, philanthropic and service tenures, which operated within the matrix of tax- tribute –plunder. The *dharmic* kingship of ancient times transcended into ritual kingship, further legitimized by the performance of *Dana, dakshina, tirtha, darshana* etc. Deforestation and land reclamation during the Kakatiya (1000-1323 CE) and Vijaynagara times (1327-1600 CE) contributed to the growth of Brahmanical institutions-*brahmadeyas* and *devabhogas*-on the one hand and the growth of industries and agricultural expansion on the other. This resulted in the consolidation of not only the peasant and non-peasant groups like the merchants and artisans into guilds (the caste-cum-professional organizations) but also the temple as an institution that controlled a significant part of the power structure of state and society. Hence in the feudal set up of medieval Deccan it was the temple that became a manifestation of this feudal set up and a link between the agrarian hinterland and the urban context, between the king and the masses.

During this period we find that there was a mutual exchange of honours between the kings and the pontiffs of religious institutions, the former for legitimization of their ritual status and the latter for protection of their tenures. The sectarian religions (Saivism and Vaisnavism), their leaders and institutions like temples, *pithas* and *maṭhas*, tried to consolidate the political base of the state, through the propagation of the ideology of *bhakti*. In other words the temple became a centre of power that gradually transformed the part of the temple, which gradually institutionalized into a professional organization.

A study of the institution of the temple girls becomes very important in this context because it helps us in understanding the role of women in perpetuating a particular ideology and understanding the complexity of the women's situation in terms of oppression within a patriarchal structure. These temple girls commonly referred to as Devadasis in popular literature and dedicated to the temple and performing sacred duties have become an object of reminiscences of the past. They were employed in temples as dancers, singers, musicians and for offering certain services to the deities. Often they were not allowed to marry a mortal man. Some of them were responsible for the smooth functioning of the temple administration. They have been regarded as *nitya sumangali* ('an ever auspicious one'), an entire tradition as part of the *sacer ludus* of Hinduism and investigated as an example of traditional arts.[1]

There has been a lot of controversy about the role of the temple dancers and if they practiced prostitution or not. B.R. Patel states that the dedication of the Devadasi to the temple signified virginity and chastity.[2] Putali Krishnamurthi depicts them as virgin devotee initially and it was only later that they degenerated into prostitution.[3] Tarachand also states that Devadasi custom had its own status, roles and functions to play and it had its own rules. The decline of the Hindu rule in south India resulted into the loss of sacredness of the system. During colonial period it degenerated into prostitution.[4] Priyadarshini Vijaisri sees this as a sacred prostitution which is linked to the cultural hegemony and caste oriented feudal economy.[5] Other researches represent the temple girls either as performer-cum prostitutes or performers, echoing their indexical status in the society, despite their professional scholarship.[6]

The institution of temple girls is viewed as an isolated entity, but not as an associated component of sacred complexes which were one of the power loci of the state and society. The transformation of *Sanis* into *Devadasis* is not highlighted in terms of changes in the status of temple as an institution. In this paper, we will make an attempt to look at the institution of temple girls in a historical perspective and trace their emergence and decline. Some of the aspects that we touch upon are: relation between the state and religious institutions like temples; factors behind the emergence of the institution of the temple girls; institutionalization of the *Sanis* and their categories; the organizations of the *Sanis*; their accomplishments; their ritualistic and non ritualistic functions; and customs and obligations on the part of temple and other power groups.

Sources

We have a variety of sources, which provide a lot of information about the temple girls and help us in situating them within the political and socio-economic milieu of medieval Deccan. The sources for our study are inscriptions, literature and travelogues of the Portuguese, Venetian and Muslim travellers. We have a number of inscriptions recording the endowment made by these women or the gifts they received and the services performed by them. We have a large number of votive inscriptions, which consist of the records of gifts made to the temple and public works such as tanks, *choultries*(rest houses for the travellers and pilgrims) and *satras* (monastic settlements). They provide a rich source of information in understanding the role of the temple and the dancing girls in medieval times. Inscriptions published in *South Indian Inscriptions*, Vol. 4,5,6.9 parts I and II, 16, Inscriptions of Warangal, Nalgonda, Karimnagar Districts, *Tirumala Tirupati Devsthanam inscriptions*, *Epigraphica Indica*, *Epigraphica Andhrica*, *Epigraphica Carnatika*, Vijaynagara Inscriptions, *Inscriptions of Andhra Desa* etc. are consulted.

The indigenous literature of the period, *Andhra Mahabaratam* of Nannaya and Tikkana *Kumar Sambhavam* of Nannechoda, *Basava Puranam* and *Sri Panditaradhya Charitra* of Palkuriki Somnatha, *Prataprudra Yashobhusanam* of Vidyanath *Kridabhiramam* of Vallabhacharya and *Amuktamalyada* of Krishnadevraya give a vivid picture of the court life, temple festivities of the dancing girls in the Vijaynagara period. *Kasikandama*, *Palanativiracharitra*, *Sivaratrimahatmyam* of Srinatha, *Simhasana dvatrimsika* of Koravi Goparaju, *Vijnanesvarama* of Ketana throw a flood of light on different aspects of the lives of the temple girls and prostitutes. The accounts of the Portuguese writers (Domingo Paes and Fernao Nuniz) and Abdur Razzak, a Persian ambassador who was sent to Zamorin on an important mission, is also very useful. Duarte Barbossa, a Portuguese traveler, has also left a rich narrative of the Vijaynagara Empire. *Futuh-us Salatin* of Isami also touches upon the Vijaynagara rulers. Huighen Van Linschoten, a Dutch traveler, who visited Deccan around 1583, also provides some information.

Geo-political milieu of medieval Deccan

The medieval period in Deccan was a period of the rise of various feudatories to power. In order to secure legitimacy for their power they endeavoured to have the support of the Brahmin priests, temples and the tribals. The situation was no different in Andhra. The Andhra region can be defined as an area extending from Mahendragiri in the north to Kalahasti in the south, and from the Bay of Bengal in the east to Sri Sailam in the west.[7] Prior to the emergence of the Kakatiyas, the Andhra region, especially its deltaic strip, formed a peripheral part of Karnataka or Tamilnadu based empires. This was the case under Karnataka- based Western Chalukyas, or Tamilnadu-based Cholas.

The upland region was seldom incorporated as it was sparsely settled. When the Kakatiyas came to power with their base in Telangana, we find a shift in the political, economic and cultural activity from the coastal region to interior Andhra. The Eastern and Western Ghat regions of the Kakatiya kingdom were covered with deciduous forests and hilly areas. Three major rivers and their tributaries— Godavari, Krishna and Pennar —flowed through the region. The soil was red loamy, and it provided a lot of arable land. These areas, in short, provided important avenues for agrarian expansion. The Kakatiyas realized the agrarian potentials of these tracts and tried to clear the forests by donating land to their officials and Brahmins. As a result many new villages were established and several thousands acres of land were brought under the plough. By digging many new tanks, irrigation facilities were extended in this area. An undated inscription of Upputuru in Bapatla taluk, Gundur District, records the grant of Lavanapura or the modern Upputuru by Trilochana Pallava (his identity is not established) to one thousand brahmins who were said to have come from Ahichchatrapura, situated on the banks of Ganges. This is confirmed by a copper plate grant of the time of Kakatiyas.[8] Virchoda near Pithapuram was granted to about 536 Brahmins.[9] This was a continuation of the practices of the earlier period.

It may be pointed out that in the early medieval period, when the archaeological data is corroborated with the inscriptional evidences; we find that land grants were given in a large scale to priests and the temples. Most of these land grants, between the 5th to 7th century CE, were concentrated in the tribal areas of Bengal, Assam, Orissa, Madhya Pradesh, Maharashtra and Andhra Pradesh.[10] As a result, we see a large number of tribal and Sudras coming into the fold of Brahmanism. The spread of Brahmanical ideology in new areas was an important factor in securing legitimacy to the state. The Brahmins, by advocating *Varnashrama Dhrama* and respect to the king, were instrumental in ensuring stability to the empire and removing any dissenting voice. In fact the medieval period saw a gradual establishment of a process started much earlier in early medieval times with the clearance of forests, system of land grants to Brahmins and monastic establishments, recruitment of Sudras as artisans and agricultural laborers and contact with different forest dwelling communities.[11] Kingship assumed a dualistic sovereignty incorporating both the political and ritualistic aspect. While the kings stabilized their political power by coercion, they established their ritualistic power by conciliation and giving gifts. The earlier Vedic sacrifices were now replaced by *dana* and *dakshina* as legitimizing factors for kingship. This reveals a shift from *dharmic* to ritual kinship. Gifts giving included land grants to the temple, Brahmins, monastic establishments and the construction activities under the ideology of Saptasanta.[12] The example of the ruler was followed by the ruled. Thus the state polity backed by the *dharmic* ideology fostered temple building activities.

Temple as a supra-religious and supra-local Institution

During the medieval times the temple slowly emerged as supra-religious and supra-local institution bringing the people under the ambit of its power and influence. Temples were expected to confer on the builder several merits and benefits such as longevity, health, wealth and prosperity in this world and religious merit. We see kings building temples in token of gratitude for victories.[13] Sometimes temples were raised in the name of the dead person.[14] Many a times vassals erected temples in the names of their overlords.[15] Temples were built for the merit of parents and preceptors.[16] We also have instances of temples being built for self-merit or to establish the religious merit of their *gotras*.[17]

The various economic functions of the temple made it an important centre of economic power, enjoying a status almost equal to that of the state. Temples directed agricultural development, through the endowments it received. Endowments were made in order to provide income for temple maintenance, for festivals honoring the deities and for food offerings to the deities. The endowments involved provisions for a perpetual service for the merit of the donor or someone designated by the donor. Of the land endowments, which the temple received, it did not have ownership rights but had a major share in the income. The money investments received by the temple were frequently loaned to the village assemblies and commercial firms for a perpetual interest and these added to the income of the temples.[18] Temple became one of the nuclei of socio-economic activities of the people. It was the nucleus around which village, towns and commerce flourished. The temple was closely associated with the territorial and communal bodies in the administration of local areas. It was both a landlord and an employer. Its treasury was a bank, which received deposits and lent money.

Thus there was a great institutionalization of the temple. These temples flourished because the ruling warrior groups provided them support and protection.[19] A vast range of officials and warlords came to exercise a lot of control over the temple functioning. Besides these functionaries, there was also a substantial participation by pilgrims. There was now a perfect homologisation of God and the king. Along with the growth in the number of temples there was a growth in the number of rituals performed therein. It now became necessary to employ a number of specialized priests to perform daily rituals. They were supported by a large group of people belonging to various professions. These included weavers, potters, carpenters, musicians and a large number of temple girls. These temple girls were, thus, a necessary and integral part of the socio- economic and political set up of medieval times.

The temple firmly established the agrarian feudal order. The rise of the devotional *bhakti* literature also supported this process. There were a number of attempts to authenticate and legitimize the new feudal polity of the period through a parallelism between the deity and the king.[20] In fact the deity in the temple is equated with the king and a parallel world of authority is reconstructed on the spiritual plane. Ritual worship in the temple is conceived on the same lines as ritual services offered to the king. Since the temple and the God were homologous with the royal court and the king respectively, the *Devasthana* had to maintain the same bureaucracy as that of the *Rajasthana*. Elaborate temple rituals were developed. These were of two kinds: *Angabhoga*- the general worship services; and *Rangabhoga*, which were special services performed at the *Rangamantapa*, which were constructed for this purpose, either daily or on festive occasions.

All these services meant that god was an earthly king and like the king in the court his daily needs had to be taken care of right from the beginning of the day to the mid night service. In both these places the temple and the court women were employed in large numbers. In fact we often find the distinction between the Devas and the kings court diminishing with certain inscriptions hinting at interchangeability of women in the temple services with those of the courts of kings. An inscription in the 18th year of Kulottunga Chola) from Sri Kalahasti temple (Kalahasti Temple is at Kalahasti, Chandragiri taluk, Chittor district, Andhra Pradesh) records the orders of the king transferring dancing girls and their descendants from his service to that of the temple.[21] A record from Mukhalingam temple (Muhalingam temple is at Ganjam district in Orissa) mentions that Vasama the *Gudisani* (a dancer in the temple) of Madhukisvara temple was also the *Lanjya* (prostitute) of Doddapanayaka, an officer of the Velanaduchoda king Rajendra Choda.[22] An epigraph of 1531CE from Tirumala states that Muddukuppayi, who was originally attached to the palace of Achuta Raya, was ordered to proceed to the temple.[23]

A major corollary to the process of increase in temple building activity between 10th and 20th century was an increasing demand for the services of the Śudra artisan castes. It was these groups, which constituted the hereditary and customary source of supplying temple prostitutes.[24]

The Temple Girls

Therefore the temple girls were one of the links between God and the king and served to establish the power of the king and give it legitimacy in the eyes of the people by being a part of the temple. These girls could easily occupy both the spaces in the temple as well as in the kings' court granting legitimacy to both. Unlike the traditional wife who was tied to a single man and was expected to be a *pativrata,* these girls were not tied to one man but to an immortal God and the temple. All these girls were regarded as *"Nityasumangali"* – the ever auspicious women – because these women were married to the immortal God, there was no chance of their ever becoming a widow and being deprived of their marital status and the toe ring, which was a symbol of this status.

The elaboration of temple ritual and homologisation of God and the king necessitated the expansion of the temple hierarchy, especially of the *Sani*s or dancing girls. Most of the temples in medieval Deccan had 300 to 500 such girls, depending on the location and importance of the temple. These girls were employed to perform dance and play music before the deity, sing *mangaalgitas* and *namasankirtanas,* wave fly whisks in the presence of the God, carry on administrative responsibilities and clean and decorate the temple premises.

Some of the temple girls were donated by the kings, nobles, vassals, and generals. Nearly thirty daughters from the Nayaka family of Kalinga *mandala* were donated to the temple of Mukhalingam by an officer of the Eastern Ganga kingdom to execute various deeds specified in the records.[25] General Jaya donated 300 girls in the age group of eight years to the temple at Chebrolu in 1215 CE.[26] A record of 1390 CE records that the king Achyuta Raya ordered Muddukuppayi, daughter of Vidvatsabharaya Ranjakam Kuppasani, to serve as a dancer in the temple of Sri Venkatesa at Tirumalai in the year 1531.[27] One of the damsels residing in Tirupati, sent by Achyuta Ray to serve Sri Venkatesvara was also sent by the king Achyuta Raya to serve in the temple at Sri Venkatesa.[28] Another epigraph indicates the donation of a girl – Bhanaramu (Bhandaramu) Akkama— as *Sani* to the temple at Velpuru by Kota Ganapatidevra), son of Kota Bayyaladevi.[29] He also donated lands and gardens as *vritti* to her.[30]

Rangabhoga became so customary that musicians were brought from long distances like Kashmir as in the Sri Visvesvara temple at Malkapuram (Guntur taluk, Guntur district, Andhra Pradesh), built by Visvesvara Siva.[31] (Visvesara was the *Rajaguru* of Kakatiya king Ganapatideva and his daughter Rudramahadevi, who ruled in 1261 AD). Many a times parents donated their own daughters as an act of religiosity. A merchant of Elesvaram donated his two granddaughters to the temple. An inscription (dated: 1271 CE) from Elesvaram (now submerged in Nagarjunasagar) states that certain Manikisetti made a gift of his two granddaughters as *sanis* to the god Elesvaradeva.[32] Many a times women entered the temple to seek employment and they were often given a portion of the *prasadam* in lieu of their services. This enables us to infer that the profession of *Sanis* was respected by society and its sacrality was honoured.

Nomenclature

In the records of medieval period the temple girls are hardly referred to as Devadasis, a name which became synonymous with them in the later period. The temple girls are referred to as *Sanulu, Sani, Sampradayamuvuru,* and *Gadisanulu*. Some times they are referred to as *Munuti Sanulu, Pedamunnuti, Sanulu, Sani* or *Munnuri,* indicating numeric status.[33] The males employed in the temple were designated as *Manyulu* or *Manulu* irrespective of their posts; whereas female employees are known by different names. An inscription (1172 CE) from Srikakulam refers to *Munnuru Sanulu* or *Sani vada,* stating that a gift of certain grants was made to the *Sanis* of *Sani vada,* probably residing in that area.[34] The Tirumala Tirupati inscription (1486 CE) mentions the temple dancer as *Tiruvidhisani*. The inscription states that *Tiruvidhisanis* were women attached to the temple accompanied the procession of deities through the streets, with their set of pipers, drummers, dancers and dancing masters and exhibited their skills in dancing in the streets and before the deities.[35] A medieval Andhra inscription of 14th century CE refers to the term *Sampradaya* for those temple girls who rendered the *Vinjamara* service i.e. the fanning service.[36] A gift of cash, was deposited for the *sampradaya* of those who rendered the service of recitation of *Kirtanas*.[37]

Domingo Paes, the Portuguese traveller who visited the court of Vijaynagara in 1520 CE, refers to *"Bayaders," (bayhadeiras)* as the dancing girls of the temple and palace. He differentiates between the courtesans and the *bayaders* who danced infront of the temple.[38] We also come across the term *basavi* for few temple girls,[39] besides *patri*[40] and *devara sule*.[41] In fact, in most of Karnataka inscriptions *Devadasis* of the Saivite shrines are denoted as *basavis*. We come across many categories of *basavis* such as *gudi basavi* (principal wife of the village deity), *jati basavi* (dedicated by the caste group to the caste deity), *balagada basavi* (born to a couple who had no male children and use one of their daughters to propagate their progeny), *nandikola basavi* (dedicated to the flag post of *nandi*, the sacred vehicle of Siva), *Yade basavi* (who made food offerings to the deity) and *Gurudag ambada dasi* (who worshipped the flag post erected for Guruda, the vehicle of Vishnu).[42] Hence in medieval period these dancing women were very much a part of the feudal structure. Through this institution women who were outside the domestic sphere were regulated in accordance with the patriarchal control of the temple authority.

It was primarily in the Colonial period that these dancing women of the temple received a distinct identity as Devadasis. Today we use the blanket term *'Devadasi'* for all girls attached to the temples. By the beginning of the Colonial period, most of these women had taken up prostitution as the temples had lost royal patronage and were no longer able to support them. In fact, as per 1891 Census report, Madras alone had 20,154 *Bhogams*.[43] By 1921, their number had increased to 26,957.[44] In the dominion of the Nizam, the temple dancing girls numbered 26,932.[45] The lack of temple patronage and increasing economic pressures resulted in their cultural marginalization. Many of these girls were forced to migrate to urban areas as commercial sex workers and many others worked as labourers and coolies in factories.[46] This system continued till it was abolished by the Madras Devadasis (Prevention of Dedication) Act, 1947. This Act abolished the dedication of women as *Devadas*is to Hindu deities, idols and objects of worship in the temple and the religious institutions because it stated that such a practice, however ancient and pure in its origin, leads many of the women so dedicated to the life of prostitution.[47] Hence by 1947, most of the Devadasis or temple girls were leading a life of a common prostitution, though it cannot be denied that most of these women did practice prostitution serving the king and priests in medieval times.

Social background of the temple girls

In old Hindu texts we have seven categories of women who serve the temple as Devadasis under the *Rudraganika* or *Gopika* category.[48] They are:

1. *Datta*: one who gave herself as a gift to the temple
2. *Vikrita*: one who sells herself for the same purpose.

3. *Bhritya*: who offers herself as a temple servant for the prosperity of the family.
4. *Bhakta*: one who joins the temple out of devotion.
5. *Hrita*: one who is enticed away and presented to the temple.
6. *Alanka*: one who is well trained in her profession and is decked and presented to the temple by kings or noblemen.
7. *Rudraganika*: one who receives regular wages from a temple and is employed to sing and dance.[49]

In medieval times the temple girls came from different social backgrounds, each having to perform a different ritual and they had a different status. Some of these girls participated in charities, public utilities work and were also involved in elaborate ritualistic services. Some of them were the honored ones because the king himself appointed them. Probably their public appearances were restricted to certain ceremonial occasions. These girls represented the hereditary class namely, *sampradayamuvaru* or *kanya sampradayamuvaru*. They came from elite and royal families and attached themselves to the service of the temple and the deity. Prostitution by this class is doubtful or false as we do not have much evidence for the same.

Next to these were the *Sanis*, who have been described as *nartakis*(dancers) or *gayaki* (singers). These were followed by the fan -bearing *Sanis*. Besides, there was a large number of temple girls, who did menial jobs and came from lower sections of society. They performed duties like supplying flowers and decorating the floor. Sometimes to supply flowers to the deity, flower gardens were raised and temple girls were in charge of maintaining such temple gardens.

Another important category of temple girls, often coming from menial castes, were those who were offered or dedicated to female deities in temples or to the village goddesses. There are a number of inscriptional references to Vishnu and Shiva temples but references to the temples of local deities are very rare. A 16th century inscription referrers to the performance of *tirthas* and *jataras* (rituals and fairs or village festival where the goddess is taken out on a procession) conducted once in a year.[50] In spite of rare inscriptional references to the village cults and beliefs, oral traditions may be considered to be helpful in knowing about the village cults in Andhra. The worshipers of village deities or goddesses belonged to the lower orders of society. The Brahmins helped in directing some parts of this worship by standing at a distance because these goddesses were considered to be very powerful and could not be neglected. There were gods belonging to the family (*Kul deva*), those belonging to the place (*Ur Deva*) and lineage (*Kula*). There were both dangerous goddesses and friendly goddesses who had the power to either bles or harm the worshipper due to their power. The modes of worship differed from deity to deity and place to place as per the fierceness of the deity. The fierce village goddesses were called *Śakti.*

The worship of *Śakti* consisted of sacrificial procedures. The worship of *peys* (demons, devils, and ghosts) was attended by the *Bhutavaidyudu* ('demon doctors') because demons were in the form of possessions. A woman was usually engaged to tell which ghost or demon possessed the deceased person or the patient. Then the doctor treated the patient. The ritual followed in this regard was very lengthy and consisted of sacrifices, offerings of rice, lamp and drawing of sacred diagrams, called *muggus*.[51] Often the story tellers were from the *Asadi* caste. They were outcastes. They married *Madiga* girls and dined with them. The *Asadi* girls never married and they were dedicated to the goddess as *Basavi,* a type of the Devadasis. Usually a Madiga woman was supposed to be possessed by the spirit of *mathamma,* the tutelary goddesses of Madigas, and was called a *Matangi.* The other name for a *Matangi* was *Basavi.* Even today, the system of dedicating girls to village goddesses for the vows made or for the bodily cure of parents exists in several parts of Andhra, at places such as Bapatala, Tenali, Bodhan, Chebrolu, Sattenpally, and Narasaraopet.[52]

Ritual of initiation

The dedication of girls to temple involved an elaborate ceremony. Their rituals were similar to the ones performed in human marriages, and they were performed in the presence of a large audience. In order to legitimize this system elaborate ceremonies were performed and, depending on the class of the Devadasi, kings, nobility, and other sections of population participated in the same. The girls who were dedicated to the temples were a very important part of the social milieu and elaborate rules and regulations were laid down for their qualification and performance of their duties. The initiation ceremony was held in the precincts of the temple to give it an aura of religious sanctity. Through this act, the community, the priest and the noble men all became a part and parcel of the system, granting it legitimacy.

The temple girls that were dedicated to the temple were dedicated with a vow and with the approval of the deity, the priest and the community at large. It was necessary that at the time of initiation the girl should not have attained puberty. Before her retirement her caste group was expected to designate her successor from among their families. The family members hardly refused for this brought in a lot of socio-religious and financial advantages to the family.[53] Often these were the daughters of the Devadasis. So a typical Devadasi was young, charming, beautiful and accomplished women in singing, dancing and public relations.

An elaborate ceremony of initiation was performed. The procedure began with a senior Devadasi of the first *kudi* (house), presenting the girl's application to the *Yogakkar* (the head priest). The application took the form of request for being enrolled as one of the Devadasis and being granted a *kudi* (house) and *padi* (allowance for temple service). The *Yogakkar* took into account the number of girls admitted in that particular year and the status of the applicant's family and then accepted or rejected the application. If the application was approved a document was executed with the mother or the nearest kin- woman of the girl and this was considered as the *Jataka* ceremony.[54] After this, the marriage or *tallikettu* ceremony of the girl with the deity took place on a stipulated day. All the ceremonies of an orthodox Hindu marriage were gone through and the priest officiated on behalf of the deity.

He tied the *tali* (a symbol of married status like the *Mangal sutra),* consisting of a *triangulat bottu* (a small triangular shaped symbol) bearing the image of Ganesha with a gold bead on either side around the girl's neck.[55] She was also initiated into the act of dancing. For two days celebrations of marriage like feasting and merriment took place. The girl was also taken in procession through out the streets of the village or town.

Functions of the temple girls

The functions of the temple girls were both ritualistic and non-ritualistic in nature. The former was customary and the latter was obligatory. The temple girls were expected to entertain their patrons with dance and music. Besides, they also performed certain assigned duties. They sometimes acted as priestesses for a few castes, especially the lower ones, who were not permitted by tradition to have priests of their own.[56] They rendered services like *vijamara seva* (fan-service). In 1376 CE a gift was made to a woman for waving the *chamar* at the time of *Chandanalagi* (after *sandhana dhoopa* deities changed their clothes and are anointed with sandal paste mixed with chamber, keshar and kasturi. This ritual was called *Chandanalagi.* This still prevail in temples) in Simhachalam temple.[57] An endowment for *Chamarseva* was made in 1389 CE by the *Sanis* of Kodepa of the Sampradaya (tradition).[58] They had to accompany the deity (*Utsav Vijrahas*) whenever it was taken around the village in a procession during festive occasions. Among the various services rendered by these dancing girls, they were also assigned duties of decorating the floor of the temple with various designs of coloured powders. A provision was made by the Durka Devi, wife of Suresvarajiyana, who was a well known noble of the province in 1381CE for the maintenance of women who decorated the floor with designs before the deity at Simhachalam. (Sri Lakhsminarasimha temple, Simhachalam, Vizagapatnam taluk, Vizagapatnam district).[59]

Another inscription, dated 1376 CE, speaks of the appointment of a woman for the purpose of decorating the temple front yard before the god with *kolamu* or colored designs once a week.[60] Duties like cleaning the premises, cleaning the cooked vessels, husking the paddy, cutting the vegetables and other sundry works were also done by the temple girls.[61] Most of the temple girls probably belonged to the lower sections of society. The temple girls therefore performed a variety of duties. They were in charge of maintaining temple properties, supervising grants or other endowments to the temple, mobilizing temple resources through leasing out lands and cattle, and performing various tasks connected with the day to day running of the temple.

Each temple had to arrange for the recitation of religious and sacred texts like the *Vedas* the *Puranas, Visnustotas, purusasukta, Gajendra-moksamslokas, Venkatachalammahatmyam* and *srinivasakalyanam*. Many a times temple girls were appointed to recite these *sanskritanas* (the religious songs). In 1359 CE, one Naramsimha Bharati made provision for keeping two florist and eight women singers to form two batches which did the *sanskritanam* at the time of *dhupa* in the Simhachalam temple.[62] Many a times these women played musical instruments. An inscription of 1356 CE made a provision to maintain two women to play the *veena*.[63]

These women played a very important role in the temple administration. Various donations made by them to many temples show their rich economic status. About 300 such *Sanis*, along with *sltanapati* (a male appointed in the temple), were made *nibandhakaras* and were authorized to see that the gifts were properly administered.[64]

We come across a number of donations made by the Devadasis to temples. Sometimes they got dilapidated temples repaired by their own resources. The Devadasis of Suchindram temple constructed a *vasanta mandapa* and the *natakasala* of Siva temple at Suchindaram.[65] Some of the temple dancers were honored and conferred with certain privileges for their services. Tiru Venkata Manikkam, a dancer in the temple of Sri Venkateswara or Tirumala, was permitted to use a palanquin for her conveyance by the temple authorities during Achyuta Raya's time.[66] In Kannada region, a dancing girl, named Mangayi of Belagula, was bestowed with the title of

"Raya patra Chudamani," meaning the 'crest- jewel of royal dancing girls.' She was a lay disciple of Charukirti Pandita Acharya.[67] Kuppasani (1531 CE) mother of Muddukuppayi, was honored with the title of *Vidvatsabharaya Ranjaka*, meaning 'one in the court of scholars.'[68]

Since the services of the temple girls were frequently required, we find that they were often provided with quarters in the vicinity of the temple. In temples like those at Srikurmam, Juttiga, Ghantasala, Chebrolu there were separate quarters built for the dancing girls.[69] Chebrolu inscription of General Jayapa (1215 CE) records the construction of two rows of double storied buildings for 16 women attendants to the temple.[70] The Pillamarri inscription of the Recherla chief Namireddy (1195 CE) records the construction of houses for the temple girls attached to the temple of Erkesvara in the fort of Pillalamarri.[71]

Indeed such was the prestige and status of these dancing girls, especially the ones who came from elite sections, that the kings and noblemen had no hesitation in marrying them. Velanti Gonka II (later half of the 12th century CE) married Kamidevi, the daughter of Sokkara, who was a dancer in the temple of Pandisvara at Tsandavolu.[72] Virasekhara Varma, who ruled Venad around 1225 CE, married Kandiyar Tevadici Unni Kaltram, a *Sani*.[73] The temple dancing girls interacted with the wives of the king in equal terms and they could spend some time with them and eat beetle leaf, a privilege not bestowed on any other person, no matter what their rank was.[74]

Most of the functions performed by the temple girls took on a hereditary character by 12th century. Those temple girls, who served the temple on a hereditary basis, were called *Sampradaya Sanulu*. They were permanent employees of the temple. At Sri Kurmam temple (in the Andhra region in Srikakulam), we have references to the presence of *thirty Sampradaya Sanulu*.[75]

Income and Wealth

The temple girls were paid generally in kind, with a share in temple property. They were often given a part of the *prasada* offered to the deity. Occasionally they were also paid in cash. Many a times the donors specified the manner of enjoying share in temple lands by the temple girls and deposited certain amount in the temple treasury for their maintenance. The temple dancers acquired a lot of wealth as can be seen from the numerous grants made to the temples. They also paid taxes to the State. An epigraph of1547 CE records the remission of taxes paid by the dancing women to the villages of Kommuru, Voruganti, Ravipadu, and Gomgulamudi belonging to the God Agastyeswara of Kommuru.[76] They were entitled to receive monetary benefits, lands, share of *prasadam* towards their remuneration. An important inscription dated 1250 CE and coming from the Srikurmam temple gives us the details of the *Sanis* and musicians employed and the wages paid to them in both cash and kind. It gives us the details of the payment made to these girls. These girls were employed to render *rangabhoga* (worship) to the god *Srikurmanatha*. The employees and the wages paid are as follows,

Sanis=30, Drummers=6,
Dance teachers =1,
Mukhariplayers =1,
Avajakadu =1,
Karadakadu =1
Melinayakadu =1.

The same inscription gives details of the wages to be paid both in cash and kind to the members of the above troupe as follows, To the *Sanis*= 42 *putti*s of paddy per year, 2 *tambula*s daily to each, 3 *appams* daily to each, to the dance teacher= 4 *mada*s (coins), 8 *Chinna*s per year, 4 *Kuncha*s of *prasadama* and 1 *tambul*a daily besides 4 *appams* per month. To the *mukhari* player 3 *mada*s per year, 2 *kuncha* and 1 *adda prasadam* and 1 *tambula* daily besides 4 *appams* per month. To each of the *mrudanga avajakarada* conch and *Kahali* players, 2 *kunchas* of *prasadama*, ´*tambulla* every day and 3 *appams* per year.[77] Thus they are paid in cash, kind and have shares in the *prasadma* of the temple.

Besides getting grants of cash and kind the Devadasis were often provided with free housing. A number of records of medieval Deccan refer to the provision of maintenance of houses for the Devadasis around the temple.[78] Therefore these girls were very well off. Abdur Razzaq, who visited the Vijaynagara kingdom, remarks that prostitution by dancing girls was a great source of revenue to the kingdom and out of the income of the dancing girls the entire upkeep of the police was paid.[79] It is really not clear from his writings if these were girls attached to the temples or they practiced independently. There is enough evidence to show that the institution of prostitution was legalized under the Vijaynagara kings and they levied a tax on it. By and large through out the feudal set up of medieval Deccan while there was exploitation of women under the guise of religion, the temple girls were given legitimacy through gifts, involvement in temple functions and rituals, and various honourable titles. Thus both the temple girls and the kings gave legitimacy to each other and were mutually supportive to each other.[80]

Conclusion

To conclude, the medieval period in Deccan, Andhra being no exception, is a period of the rise of feudatories. The Kakatiyas came to power with their base in Telangana and it heralded a shift in the political, economic and cultural activities from the coastal region to the interiors of Andhra. Many forested areas are cleared by donating land to the officials and Brahmins. Many new villages are established by bringing land under the plough. Grant of lands to the Brahmins, who propagated *bhakti* and *varnashramadharma*, was one of the means for securing royal legitimacy. The spread of Brahmanical ideology into such areas was one of the factors in consolidating the political and ideological base of the state. Kingship now assumed dual sovereignty: political and ritualistic. While the kings stabilized their political power by coercion, they establish their ritualistic sovereignty by conciliation and giving gifts. The earlier Vedic sacrifices were now replaced by *dana* and *dakshina* as instruments of securing legitimacy for kingship. *Dāna* included land grants to temples, Brahmins and monastic establishments. Between the thirteenth and the sixteenth centuries, number of land grants to temples increased greatly.

Since the temple and the God were homologous with the royal court and the king respectively, the *Devasthana* had to maintain the same bureaucracy as was the case with the *Raja-sthana*. Development of the institution of temple girls was a natural corollary. Women were employed in large numbers in the temples. These temple girls were the link between God and the king. In the feudal milieu of the medieval Deccan, it was these girls who crossed from one boundary to another with ease, and were the objects of ritualistic exchange between the courts of kings and the temple. Elaborate initiation ceremonies were designed and the king and nobility also participated in such ceremonies. We can see three distinct categories of temple girls: elite temple girls; girls performing menial tasks; and those dedicated to village goddesses and local deities. This institution in the garb of religion served the interest of king, various feudal lords and the temple priests. The Devadasi was given a status much above the normal woman, who was tied to domesticity and one man. By not being tied to one man and being a *Nitya sumangali*, the Devadasi arose much above the domestic women. Hence the institution of the temple girl was a corollary to the temples and the feudal set up of medieval Deccan.

Notes

1. Saskia C. Kersenboom-Story, *Nityasumangalī, Devdasi Tradition in South India*, Delhi, 1987, pp. 1-2.
2. B.R. Patil, 'The *Devdasis*,' *Indian Journal of Social Work*, Vol. XXXV, No. 4, 1975, pp. 377-89.
3. Krishnamurthi N. Putali, *The Changing Conditions of Women in Andhra from the Middle of 19th Century to the Middle of 20th Century*, Hyderabad, 1987 pp. 202-203.
4. K.C. Tarachand, *Devdasi Custom: Rural Social Structure and Flesh Market*, New Delhi, 1972, p. 3.
5. Priyadarshini Vijaysri, *Recasting the Devadasi-Patterns of Sacred Prostitution in Colonial South India*, New Delhi, 2004, pp. 10- 22.

6. A.K. Singh, *Devadasi System in Ancient India*, New Delhi, 1990, p. 12.
7. K. Sundaram, *Studies in Social and Economic conditions in Medieval Andhra Desa (1000-1500 AD)*, Warangal, 1968, p. 9.
8. K. Satyanarayana, *A Study in the History and Culture of the Andhras*, Vol. II, *Consolidation of Feudalism*, Peoples Publishing House, 1983, p. 25.
9. *Epigraphia Indica*, Vol. V, p. 96.
10. R.S. Shrama (ed.), *Indian Society: Historical Probings*, New Delhi, 1974, pp. 177-79.
11. Ibid., pp. 105-123.
12. There were seven pious deeds known as *Sapta Santanas*. They were: having one's own son, adopting a son, composing a literary work, and gifting an *agrahara*, a garden, a tank or construction of a temple. See P.V. Parabrahma Sastri, *The Kakatiyas of Warangal*, Hyderabad, 1978, p. 281.
13. Kakatiya king Rudradeva (she was a female ruler, Rudramba Devi by name, but ruled as king Rudra Deva) built shrines around 13th century CE for Surya, Rudra and Vasudeva at Hanamkonda after defeating several chieftains. M. Rama Rao. (ed.), *Kakatiya Sanchika Inscriptions*, No. 18, pamphlet, Hyderabad, 1991(reprint edition), p. 389.
14. The Kota queen Ganapamba constructed a temple for god Betesvara in the name of her father in 1172 CE. *Epigraphia Indica*, Vol. III, pp. 94- 103.
15. In 1153 CE, Jaya, the General of the Kakatiya king Ganapati Deva, built a temple at Dvipa, and installed in it Ganapeswara, named after the king. *Epigraphia Indica*, Vol. III, p. 82.
16. In 1059 CE, a Reddy of the Kondapamati country built a temple of Somesvara at Goniyapundi for the merit of his parents. *Tirumal Tirupati Devsthanam Inscriptions*, Vol. III, Madras, 1935, pp. 73-74.
17. In 1176AD. Hacalamba the daughter of king Allugi, the lord of the town of Morata, founded the shrine of Hacalesvara, after her own name, *Pushpagiri*.
18. Burton Stein, 'The State, The temple and Agricultural Development,' in Burton Stein (ed.), *All the Kings' Mana: Papers in Medieval South Indian History*, Madras, 1984, pp. 162- 163.
19. Burton Stein, 'Social Mobility and Medieval South Indian Hindu Sects,' in Burton Stein (ed.), *All the Kings' Mana: Papers in Medieval South Indian History*, Madras, 1984, pp. 282- 301.
20. M.G.S. Narayanan and K. Veluthat, 'The Bhakti Movement in

Medieval South India,' in D. N. Jha (ed.), *Feudal Social Formations in Early India*, Delhi, 1987, pp. 348- 373.
21. J. Ramyya Rao (ed.), *Inscriptions of Andhra Desa*, Madras, 1949, Vol. 11, part, 1, No 669.
22. Ibid.
23. Soma Reddy, *History of Religious Institutions in Andhra Desa (1300-1600 AD)*, Madras, 1984, p. 260.
24. Priyadarshini Vijaysri, *Recasting the Devdasi: Patterns of Sacred Prostitution in Colonial South India*, New Delhi, 2004, p. 72.
25. Rao Bahadur H.K. Krishna Sastri (ed.), *South Indian Inscriptions*, Mysore, 1986(reprint), Vol. V. No. 1083.
26. Ramson N. Mukunda Rao (ed.), *Temple Inscriptions of Andhra Pradesh*, Hyderabad, 1980, Vol. I, No. 264, Srikakulam District.
27. *Tirumala Tirupati Devasthanam Inscriptions*, Vol. IV, No. 11, p. 23.
28. *Tirumala Tirupati Devasthanam Inscriptions*, Vol. IV, No. 142, p. 262.
29. P. V. Parabrahma Sastri, *The Kakatiyas of Warangal*, Hyderabad, 1978, p. 286.
30. V. Yasoda Devi, 'A History of Andhra Country,' *Journal of Andhra Historical Research Society*, Vol. XXV, p. 147.
31. J. Ramayya Pantulu (ed.), *South Indian Inscriptions*, Madras, 1948, reprint, Mysore, 1986 (reprint), Vol. X, No. 344. Visvesara was the *Rajaguru* of Kakatiya king Ganapatideva and his daughter Rudramahadevi, who ruled in 1261 CE.
32. Abdul Waheed Khan, *A Monograph on Yalesvaram Excavation*, Hyderabad, p. 63. Quoted in P.V. Parabrahma Sastri, *The Kakatiyas of Warangal*, Government of Andhra Pradesh, Hyderabad, 1978, p. 286.
33. Abdul Waheed Khan, *A Monograph on Yalesvaram Excavation*, Hyderabad, 1963, No. 25, p. 62.
34. *South Indian Inscriptions*, Vol. IV. Gen. No. 989, A.R. No. 164 of 1893.
35. *Tirumala Tirupati Devasthanam Inscriptions*, Vol. II, No. 86, p. 167.
36. *South Indian Inscriptions*, Vol. VI, No. 818, STI No. 59, p. 105.
37. Ibid., No. 722, STI No. 59, p. 105.
38. Paes, "*Chronicles of Paes and Nuniz*," in Robert Sewell, *A Forgotten Empire-Vijaynagara, A Contribution to the History of India*, New Delhi, 1985(reprint), p. 267.
39. *Vijaynagara Inscriptions*, Vol. III, K.N. 2164, p. 411.
40. Ibid., p. 411.

41. *'Sule'* means prostitute in Kannada language. Rev. F. Kittel, *A Kannada English Dictionary*, p. 1586.
42. For details, see K.C. Tarachand, *op. cit.*, p. 12-16.
43. *Census of India*, 1891, Vol. XIII, Madras, p. 29.
44. *Census of India*, 1921, Vol. XIII, Madras, part II, p. 110.
45. *Census of India, 1891*, Vol. XXIII: His Highness the Nizam Dominion, part II, p. 183.
46. Edgar Thruston and K. Rangachari, *Castes and Tribes of South India*, Madras, 1909, Vol. IV, p. 309.
47. *The Madras Devadasis (Prevention of Dedication) Act*, The Government of Madras Law, Legislative Department, January, 26, 1948.
48. Manjulatha, 'Devdasis Inams: A Case Study of Chittoor District,' *Ithihas*, Vol. XIV, 1988, pp. 116-7.
49. *Madras Census Report*, 1901.
50. Saskia C. Kersenboom-Story, *op. cit.*, pp. 50-53.
51. Ibid., pp. 55-56.
52. Krishn Kumari, *Studies in Medieval Andhra History and Culture*, New Delhi, 1994, p. 120.
53. K.C. Tarachand, *op. cit.*, p. 17.
54. K.K. Pillai, *The Caste System in Tamilnadu*, Madras, 1977, p. 281. The details of these procedures are learnt from a palm leaf record in the Vattapalli *matha.*
55. Edgar Thurston and K. Rangachari, *Castes and Tribes in South India*, Vol. II, New Delhi, 1987, pp. 143-4.
56. K.C. Tarachand, *op. cit.*, p.23.
57. K.V. Subrahmanya Aiyar (ed.), *South Indian Inscriptions*, Delhi, 1986 (reprint), Vol. VI. No 751, Simhachalam.
58. Ibid., No. 764, Simhachalam.
59. Ibid., No. 738, Simhachalam.
60. Ibid., No. 1128, Simhachalam.
61. K.V. Raman, *The Varadarajaswamy Temple: Kanchi*, New Delhi, 1975, p. 135.
62. K.V. Subrahmanya Aiyar (ed.), *South Indian Inscriptions*, Delhi, 1986 (reprint), Vol. VI. No. 890, Simhachalam.
63. Ibid., No. 955, Simhachalam.
64. J. Ramayya Pantulu (ed.), *South Indian Inscriptions*, Mysore, 1986, Vol. X. No. 110, Simhachalam.
65. *Mysore Epigraphical Reports*, 1914, No. 354.
66. V. Vijay Raghavcharya (ed.), *Tirumala Tirupati Devasthanam Inscriptions*, Vol. II, Madras, 1933, p. 259.
67. B.A. Salatore, *Social and Political life in Vijaynagar Empire*, Vol.

II, Madras, 1934, p. 409.

68. *Tirumala Tirupati Devasthanam Inscriptions*, Vol. IV, No. 11, p. 23.
69. *South Indian Inscriptions*, Vol. V. No. 989.
70. Ibid., Vol. X, No. 107, 110, 115.
71. V. Yasoda Devi, 'A History of Andhra Country,' *Journal of Andhra Historical Research Society*, Vol. XXV, p. 147.
72. A.R.E. (1915- 17), No. 99 of 1916.
73. P.N. Elamkulam Kunjanpallai, *Studies in Kerala History*, Trivandrum, 1970, p. 279.
74. Paes, "*Chronicles of Paes and Nuniz*," in Robert Sewell, *A Forgotten Empire-Vijaynagara, A Contribution to the History of India*, New Delhi, 1985 (reprint) p. 253.
75. *South Indian Inscriptions*, Vol. V, No. 1188.
76. Ibid., Vol. XVI, No. 160.
77. Ibid., Vol. V, No. 1183, Sri Kurmam.
78. Rekha Pande, 'Devdasis,' in J.S. Grewal (ed.), *Religious Movements and Institutions in Medieval India*, Vol. VII, Part 2, in D.P. Chattopadhyay (general editor), *History of Science, Philosophy and Culture in Indian Civilization*, New Delhi, 2006, p. 500.
79. E.M. Elliot, *History of India as told by its own Historians*, Vol. IV, Allahabad, 1964, p. 112.
80. Rekha Pande, 'At the Service of the Lord-Temple Girls in Medieval Deccan (11th to 17th centuries),' *Deccan Studies*, Vol. II, No. 2, 2004, pp. 25-43.

10

SURVIVAL OF THE LIṄGARĀJA TEMPLE
A Study of Spatial Context, Linkage and Patronage

SUBASH KHAMARI

Introduction

The temple in Orissa originated as a place of worship or a cult centre in the centuries immediately before and after the beginning of the Christian era. Gradually, it was systematically built up as an institution, an eminent focus of multifarious human activities: social, economic and cultural. The institutionalization of temple began with the donation of gifts to temples, which ultimately integrated a diverse section of people with the temple. Temple was not meant for one period or time. Continuation to enlive its reputation of drawing allegiance from people constantly, required a shift and alteration in the temple plans and elevations. Structural elaboration and addition were adopted in temple precincts to cater to the needs of the correspondingly growing requirements of devotees. This can be seen not only within the precincts of the temple, but also in its spatial context.

Though the work and duty of architects, sculptors and artisans was over with the construction of temple, but then only the functional life of temple began. Its ability to continue as a living institution depended on a regular supply of goods and services from its patrons, as well as on its ability to fulfill the requirements of the devotees.

In the Orissan context, the temple never functioned in a unilinear evolutionary pattern for survival. Rather, its networks were diverse- both horizontally and vertically. It is important to recognize at the outset that many regional, tribal, and Brahmanical religious groups made their presence felt through temple. Temple was serving as a nodal point for their proliferation and survival, though the temple was also drawing some utility from them also. An imagined community from diverse strata and sects were actively involved in the pilgrimage. This community consisted of people out for pilgrimage, which transcended the socially acclaimed caste limits, but for a limited period of journey, it served on humane affiliation. We have seen a variety of linkages among them, which facilitated their continual function and survival, most of the cases, through cumulative variables. Thus, the sacred temple-scape of Orissa represented a pluralistic pattern, through hierarchies and multiplicity, which may be better understood through the extant example of the Liṅgarāja temple.

Construction

Epitome of *Kaliṅgān* type of temple architecture,[1] the Liṅgarāja temple was built in the eleventh century[2] in fine grained khondalite stone displaying impeccable proportion compatibly blended with adorned embellishments. The main temple consists of a *rekhā deula* and *piḍhā jagamohana, nāṭamandira* and *bhogamaṇḍapa,* the last two being subsequent additions,[3] within an enclosure dotted with 127 religious and secular edifices. The palm leaf manuscript and the Jagannātha temple chronicle, *Mādalāpānji*[4] records that the Liṇgarāja temple or the temple of Kirttivasa at Bhuvaneswar was constructed by three generations (*e deula tinipāṭare nirmāṇa helā*) of Somavamsi kings – Yayati Kesari, Anantakesari and Lalatendu Kesari. The structure was started by Yayati (*bhuvaneúwara deulaku śubha dele*), continued by Ananta (*ethi utāru anantakeúari e deula tolāithile*), and completed by Lalatendu (*e raja deula pratisṭhā kale*). In some of the copies of the *Mādalāpānji* a fourth king is also added as the builder-Suryakesari (*e rājā bhuvaneúwara deula tolāithile*). Of these only Yayati is found in the genealogical table whereas others are unknown. Possibly, Ananta and Lalata are two other names of Udyota, hence the building as a stupendous structure, began by Yayati (CE1020-1040) and finished by his son Udyota (CE1040-1065).[5]

It infers that the temple was built by royalty but acclaimed through a much later text of *Mādalāpānji* with a fictitious king. It refers to a weak central or royal hold over the temple institution. Besides, the survival of a grand temple like Liṇgarāja did not solely rest with the patronage of kings, otherwise it might have vanished with the royalty. It is obvious that through the centuries, Liṅgarāja employed multiple strategies for its survival, accompanied by varieties of reciprocal networks. It not only dominated the temple town, but also expanded its horizon to other parts of India, through pilgrimage network.

A. Linkages

No temple can stand as an isolated entity. No ritual or temple complex can be understood as an isolated phenomenon. Temples form part of a socio-religious matrix, connecting people in different geographical regions in a series of complex symbolic networks. Each individual temple is a nexus of ritual activity, which radiates outwards and interlinks with other temples through a series of myths and rites. Economic and social ties, which forge a set of permanent bounds and make the system durable and fluid, also connect these temple institutions. Each temple fits into the network in its proper hierarchical position. Thus, the linkages among the temples are not only horizontal but also vertical. Ultimately, such linkages connect the most obscure way-side shrines to the large all- India pilgrimage centre. Though, in many cases; such linkages may be indirect or remote.

The Liṅgarāja temple manifests different forms of linkages. At one level, these linkages are made possible by the non-exclusivity of the sacred space or structure. So the first network of the linkage, exercised by the temple, was through architecture. It was consciously chosen since the inception of the plan and the execution of the elevation. This was operating at two levels: macro or pan Indian level, and micro or intra-regional level. However, in spite of having this binary schism between them, they essentially did not distract from the unitary character of temple as a whole. Broadly, the Liṅgarāja temple, the culmination of *Kaliṅgān* type of temple architecture, is classified as a subtype of *Nāgara* variety.[6] Moreover it has close affinity with north Indian typology in the plan and elevation along with theme and spatial allocation to sculptural representations. Notwithstanding this affinity, the *Kaliṅgān* type preserved its uniqueness through utilizing a different set of terminology and having its own set of *Śilpaśāstras*[7] though codified in later period, moreover by maintaining a name (*Kaliṅgān* type) and a strict geographical limitation to its expanse. Its individual characteristics were so conspicuous that a 12th century inscription found at Amriteswar temple at Holal, classified it as a type along with *Nāgara, Veśara* and *Drāviḍa*.[8] Nepalese manuscript *Pratisṭhā Laksaṇa Sāra Samuccaya* figures it as one of the *prāsāda* type with five others. Thus, on one hand, the Liṅgarāja temple maintained structural affinity with *Nāgara,* on the other hand it secured its features to stand out.

In the temple complex of the Liṅgarāja, the number of temples around the main shrine multiplied corresponding to the multiplication of religious affiliation. The sacred landscape within its enclosure is dotted with temples of *Pārvatī, Kārttikeya, Narasimha, Gaṇeśa, Śani, Santoṣimā* etc. with a wide range of cross-sectorial religious affiliation. Thus, the clustering is represented on inter-sectarian basis depending on their dispersal, angular characteristics, stylistic variation and quantitative representation.

Temple with diverse typological structures and sects,

within an enclosure wall, symbolize the importance of main or the central shrine, which is the largest and the most embellished structure. Other temples, which surround the main shrine, are smaller and usually have no equal footing with the central deity. Though it presents a dynamic form of sectarian dispersion and co-existence, their mutual relationship is hierarchically ordered. In other words, in ritual stratification, central deity tops the list followed by others, symbolizing its superiority over others and drawing allegiance.

To sum up, the Liṅgarāja temple is linked through architecture with the *Nāgara* variety of north Indian temples. Śiva is the presiding deity in the form of a *liṅgama;* through other temples in the precincts making the pattern a complex one.

B. Diversity and pluralism

With the proliferation of structural activities within the enclosure, there was an increasing multiplication of deities and plurality of beliefs. It resulted into the evolution of a heterogeneous tradition within the temple complex. Contrary to this integrative role of temple, it also envisaged sectarianism. Sectarianism characterized the medieval *bhakti* movement, with the temple as their focus, aimed at building their respective Puranic religious traditions and social bases.[9] In Orissa, various sects associated with Saivism – *Mattamayuras, Kāpālikas, Pāśupatas* etc. – consolidated their organizations through association with the temple institution. However, these sects served across the Brahmanical caste divisions and create a sense of community among the devotees on the basis of equality, placing community above caste divisions as criteria of social acceptance. It meant emergence of parallel and counter structures, leading to *mokṣa* for all irrespective of social status.[10] Thus, sects succumbed to the ideology of the temple institution. In the network of interaction between temple and sects, multifaceted linkages are evident. The temple endorsed pluralism, consisting of diverse groups with varied interests, many of which were involved in close interaction, and were often in conflict as well. From one perspective, the sects or groups were hierarchically ordered. Largest temple was constructed for Saivism, which symbolized the dominant position of this sect. On the other hand, different forms of access to the deity by other groups continuously challenged this hierarchy. Though it seems to be a relation between domination and subordination, in actuality it was more or less subdued with the negotiation of their status with the temple, when temple devotees in itself became a community, beyond sectarian and caste limits. Thus, temple provided a physical and ideological space for assimilation of diverse groups. Pattern of assimilation is unique to each temple, but that holds the key to its survival.

Diversity and pluralism are more pronounced in inter-sectarian linkages. Largest numbers of temples were constructed for Brahmanical deities, but other pantheons including local deities also shared the sacred space. Temples were constructed for *Nāgas, Grāmadevas* and autochthonous deities. Nonetheless, there was a unified endeavour, emerged out of pluralism, to shape the Kaliṅgān type of temple architecture.

Diversity is also found in iconographic programmes, both on the surface of the temple and independent of it. Numerous figures appear on the exterior of the temple. Most of them are related to the deity in the sanctum. Many of them are also related to other deities. This does not present a uniform style and in most of the cases, the pattern is specific to a particular temple. In the Liṅgarāja temple, many *Śaiva* and *Vaiṣṇava* themes, *Yakṣas, Śārdulas, Nāgas, Gajalakṣmī, Saptamatṛkās, Yoginis* etc. are depicted along with Buddhist and Jaina images. Even *Lakuliṣa* adopted the form of *vyākhyāna mudrā* of the Buddha. Thus, it was a process of interaction between important deities like *Viṣṇu, Śiva* and *Śakti* with local and popular forms of worship. In one way these 'others' were mere incrustation to the surface and the iconographic programme of the temple. It must also be mentioned that these very local cults survived in the very Brahmanical structure. The images and icons in the temple walls did not merely represent the different forms of the deities to whom the temple was dedicated, but also reflect religious syncretism, rivalry and synthesis. This was accomplished in the form of images combining two deities (Harihara) or subordinating one to the other (*liṅgodbhava*) or incorporating a rival deity (Buddha) in the pantheon of dominant deity. Further, the temple narratives are quite conspicuous of diversified elements. Themes of the *Rāmāyaṇa*, the *Mahābhārata* and *Purāṇas* are though popular, others themes were also vigorously represented such as stories from the *Panchatantra*, war, hunting, local practices, worship etc.[11] This represents a fusion of sacred and profane elements. It testifies that the temple was providing its functional utility to a diverse range of people. Thus, the temple and images were meant to convey different levels of meanings through design, organization, orientation of structure and sculpture. But the process that entwined these elements in a holistic fabric is specific to each temple.

C. Hierarchy

Multi-layered ritual networks support a hierarchy in the classificatory scheme of the temple. To understand the relation between various components within this categorization, it is important to define the variables first. It is easier in the case of ethnographic studies; but very difficult for historical ones. This is primarily because of paucity and alteration in the ritual practices, non-identification of the temple or due to lack of cultic distinguishing feature in temples, and lack of textual evidences. In many cases, the hierarchy among the living temples only has been attempted (and that is the only way available). That provides a partial understanding of the temple institution and proves to be a major handicap in analyzing temple-scape as a whole during the period of its inception. However, an attempt is made here by scrutinizing polyvalent criteria for ordering each temple. In the reconstruction of this hierarchy, we will take into account such variables as architectural elaboration, sectarian affiliation, temple's scope for geographic influence, its ritual pattern, typology of worshippers (if possible) and its relative position in the overall pattern of ritual network such as pilgrimage. However, many variables are overlapping, and they are, thus, not meant for exclusivity in our classification.

The temples in the sacred precincts may be placed in a three-level hierarchy.

1. Pan Indian: Liṅgarāja temple attracted pilgrims from all India, mentioned in the texts, dominated the sacred landscape of Orissa, architecturally and sectorally.
2. Regional: it attracted pilgrims from a limited region and hence having regional affinity. Examples are the temples of Śiva, Viṣṇu, Śakti etc.
3. Local: it attracted many people from the locality, across sects and limited number of people, 27 numbers of unknown religious edifices is examples of it.

Though this classification is not exclusive and leaves many details to speculation, it will surely help to place temples in the Liṅgarāja complex within this context. Further, it offers intermediary zones between categories.

In Bhuvaneswar, growth of religious architecture is inseparably linked with the growth of town, both developing simultaneously or in tandem. The temple formed the nucleus of organized ritual space, physical space and functional space for various social groups in the settlement.

D. Pilgrimage

One of the most important mechanisms of survival of the Liṅgarāja temple is pilgrimage. Many sacred *kṣetras* of Orissa attracted pilgrims from all over India, among which *Ekāmra* grew into an important centre of pilgrimage. This is evident from a copper plate grant of Santikaradeva, who was probably a feudatory ruler of *Yamagartta Maṇḍala*, under the Bhaumakaras.[12] The grant, issued in the 9th 10th centuries CE, states that Santikaradeva came to *Ekāmra* on pilgrimage in his second regnal year. Verse 12 of Brahmeswar temple inscription mentions *Ekāmra* as *Siddhatīrtha*.[13] It is possible that after the conquest of the coastal tract of Utkala, Yayati I visited this *kṣetra*. The sacrality of Bhuvaneswar is also envisaged in various classical Sanskrit texts. In the *Vanaparva* of *the Mahābhārata*, it has been referred to as *Swayambhuvana*, the seat of Viśvakarmā's penance. In the *Skandapurāṣa*, it has been referred to as *Sambhava kṣetra* with its great temple being called Kotiliṇgeśwara.[14] In some other texts, it is referred to as *Dvitiya Kāśī* (second Kāśī) or Vārāṇasi.[15] Majority of its extant examples are dedicated to Śiva, which also suggests that it was a Śaiva *kṣetra*. The greatest eulogy of the site is found in *Utkalakhaṇḍa* of the *Skandapurāṇa* (composed between 9th to 12th century), where Brahma himself declares that *Ekāmra* is as auspicious and splendid as Vārāṇasi. He describes the beauty of *Ekāmra*, its splendid streets, lofty mansions, its many temples, its gardens, which were comparable to *Nandana* garden of heaven and its perpetual festivities. As mentioned in this text, it covered an area of two and half *yojanas* or about fifteen kilometers.[16] Later, some *Sthalapurāṇas* like *Ekāmra Purāṇa, Ekāmra Chandrikā, Kapila Samhitā, Swarṇādri Mahodaya* eulogized the sacredness of the area.[17] In the *Ekāmra Chandrikā*, a Sanskrit text dealing with the Liṅgarāja temple, it has been stated that the Gaud king Sasanka, a staunch devotee of Śiva, built the first Śiva temple at the site of Tribhuvaneswara in the first quarter of 7th century CE.[18] Gradually, the number of temples increased. The total number of temples included in this area at one time, as recorded in a hyperbolic tone in *Ekāmra Purāṇa*, was a 'hundred thousands' whereas *liṇgas* numbered 'ten millions.'[19] Famous as *Dwitiya Kāśī*, it emerged as a pan-Indian pilgrimage centre and attracted a large number of pilgrims.

In addition to Bhuvaneswar being known as a *Śaiva kṣetra*, chapter 22 of the *Matsya Purāṇa* glorifies it as a *devītīrtha* of *Kirttīmati*, which is corroborated in the *Devī Bhāgavata Purāṇa* also.[20] Many Tantric texts glorify Ekāmra as a *śākta pītha* as well: in the *Jnanārāava tantra*, Ekāmra is on Number 5 among 50 Tantric *pīthas*. In the *Brihannanlā Tantra*, the presiding deity of this area is Ekā. In the *Namastottarasata* and the *Praṇatosani Tantra*, the presiding deity of this area is named *Kirttīmati*. In the *Tantrasara*, Ekāmra is *pītha* number 12 and the presiding deity is *Bhagavaha*. In the *Brahmāṇḍa Purāṇa* Ekāmra is *pītha* number 10.[21] So, in Tantric pilgrimage also, Bhuvaneswar was well linked to other *pīthas* of India.

The information being scanty, we are handicapped to know the networks of linkages, routes followed, or the interactions the devotees had with the deity or among themselves. Possibly, a multi-layered network was ensued upon with the context and the sect. At one level at local or village or regional, people might gain a sense of uniqueness by identifying with the local deities symbolizing a widely followed variety of social system and belief pattern. At another level, on pan- Indian scenario, their uniqueness is dissolved into a larger religious whole. Pilgrimage to this famed sacred centre, which was also eulogized in the traditional Sanskrit literature, is tantamount to reasserting the validity of a pan – Indian belief system and religious space. That, thereby, transcends the linguistic and regional diversity of India. So, it is not simply the question of universal communitas versus status quo, rather it is having multiple levels of functional zones, ascribing polymorphic meaning to hierarchy and context. At the same time, diversity is reinforced, perpetuated and dissolved in the hierarchy. The network of temple is sustained and perpetuated because it provides avenues for maximum diversity.

One of the most conspicuous elements to attract pilgrims was celebration of festivals, which differs in *jalatīrtha* and *mandiratīrtha*. In the *Aśokāṣṭami* festival, *utsavas* were parts of ceremonies with *nṛtya, gīta* and *vādya* during the 11th century CE. Here, pilgrims participated regardless of their caste and sex. It implied a significant change in the Brahmanical attitude towards women and lower caste group which had hitherto been denied the right of ritual participation.[22]

Purposes of undertaking pilgrimage were manifold. In the inscriptions, we are informed that merely visiting the Liṅgarāja temple ensured *puṇya* for the pilgrim. However, this could be much more. What is apparent that the contexts ranged from *samskārika* (connected to life crises) to *paramārthika* (dealing with spiritual aspiration) and *vyavahārika* (pertained to more worldly desire), for children (*putreṣṇā*) and wealth (*vitteṣṇā*) as well as other material gains (*lokeṣṇā*).

In the *Brahma Purāṇa, tīrthas* are placed into fourfold

division comprising *Daivatīrthas* (which had been created by gods), *Asuratīrthas* (which were associated with the killing of Asuras by gods), *Ārṣatīrthas* (which were established by sages) and *Manuṣatīrthas* (which were created by kings and other men).[23] As recorded in the *Ekāmra Purāṇa*, the Liṅgarāja is an example of *Daivatīrtha*, pilgrim age centre of highest order where god revealed himself as a *liṅgama*. Hence it was called *Swayambhu*.[24]

E. Texts

Ekāmra Śaiva *kṣetra* or the Liṅgarāja managed to survive through a three stages operation by literature –

I. The temple had a Pan-Indian patronage and found in pilgrim route, mentioned eulogically in the epics (the *Mahābhārata*) and the *Purāṇas* (*Matsya, Vāyu, Brahmāṇḍa* etc.). However the earlier texts devote very little space to *Ekāmra kṣetra*, which is not more than a cursory glance. This indicates an incipient form of ensuring pilgrimage for *Ekāmra*.
II. In later *Purāṇas*, the site is more frequently mentioned. A chapter entitled *"Ekāmra Kṣetra Mahātmya"* enumerates the sacrality of the site in the *Brahma Purāṇa*. It is eulogized in a whole section called *Utkala Khaṇḍa* in *Skandapurāṇa*, by Brahma himself. This indicates an increasing sacrality of the site at a pan-India level.
III. But the most important factor is the support from the local populace with regional affiliation, which was extended in the form of *Mahātmyas* and *Sthalapurāṇas*. Around 15th –16th centuries CE, many such texts were composed such as *Ekāmra Purāṇa, Ekāmra Chandrikā, Kapila Samhitā* and *Swarṇādri Mahodaya*.[25] They extol and praise *Ekāmra*, employ local myths and legends to amplify the greatness and glory of the place, in the context of a wider vision in which *Tīrthas* and *Mahātmyas* are entwined compatibly. They give a new origin to the holiness of the shrine and new meaning

to its sacredness. *Ekāmra Purāṇa*[26] records that the deity was originally under a mango tree and it was not seen as a *liṇgama* in the first two ages – *Satya* and *Tretā* – but in *Dvāpara* and *Kali* ages, it revealed itself as a *liṅgama* but it had no temple. The story, apart from appropriating worship of tree and stone, also indicates the extreme local nature of the deity. The same *Purāṇa* mentions that the Gauḍa king Sasanka, a staunch devotee of *Śiva*, built the first *Śiva* temple at the site called Tribhuvaneswara[27] denoting its regional nature. It became a dominant temple till the present Liṅgarāja temple replaced it. However, by the 14th century, *Ekāmra* was renamed as Bhuvaneswar, an abridged form of Tribhuvaneswara.[28] It exemplifies how literature assimilated many levels from local to regional to pan-Indian. That is an important factor behind its survival.

F. Architectural alterations as a survival strategy.

To fulfill the changing requirements of laity; the Liṅgarāja temple adopts two architectural means:

I. Addition

When the temple was constructed; it was only a *rekhā vimāna* with a *piḍhā jagamohana*. However, with increasing rituals, *bhogamaṇḍapa* and *nāṭamandira* were added to the facade. Besides, many other structure – religious and secular – were gradually added into the precincts, catering to the needs of the visitors. Examples of such buildings are shrines dedicated to *Pārvatī, Viṣṇu, Gaṇeśa, Kārttikeya, Nṛsimha, Devī* etc. They are around one hundred in number and they too have *manḍapas*, wells, kitchen, *prākāra*, gates etc. This represents a proliferation of sects as well as shared nature of sacred space and shared faiths to accommodate diverse sectarian communities.

II. Alteration

Gradually we notice modification in the temple structure as well as in allied structures. Side windows and one of the side doors were closed; many doors and window of *nāṭamandira* and *bhogamaṇḍapa* were closed, possibly for regulation of space and movement of human body in the sacred space, and for security concerns.

In term of architecture, what is important about the sacred complex is its plurality and multiplicity. This feature developed over a period of time. Within sacred precincts, now 127 (see table 1 and fig. 1) structures exist of which 115 and 12 are earmarked for religious and non- religious purpose respectively. Though it is predominantly a Śaiva *kṣetra* with 79 Śaiva temples, the space is split and shared with other pantheons: Viṣṇu – 8, Śakti-8, Gaṇeśa-3, Sūrya-1, Yama-1 and unknown–15. However, all these deities conform to the festivities and rituals of the Liṅgarāja, acknowledging his supremacy. Regarding exteriors of these temples, 56 are having curvilinear *rekhā* tower followed by 55 pyramidal *piḍhā* roof whereas *khākhrā* vaulted roof are found only at 2 places. In addition, 11 *manḍapas*, 1 *stambha* and 2 wells are also located there. Majority of the temples (79) conform to the main shrine in their *ratha* projections being *pancharatha* whereas 30 *triratha* shrines are also constructed. Majority of the temples (73) are facing east including the Liṅgāraja, but temples were constructed facing all directions – to north 15, to south 7 and to west 18. Thus the Liṅgarāja complex presents an exemplary account of multiplicity and pluralism, which is key to its survival.

G. Rituals

Traditionally, it is believed that originally the presiding deity (Liṅgaraja) was worshipped by the *Śavaras* in *Ekāmravana* and it gradually assimilated *Vedic* and Tanitric features.[29] In the pre- Jagannātha temple period, Liṅgarāja was the most respected and most powerful deity. After winning over Orissa with the help of Vāsudeva Vāhinipati, Chodaganga expressed his gratitude to lord *Kruttivasa*. But after that, several changes were incorporated into the rituals of the Liṅgarāja temple, particularly to accommodate the rising Vaisnavism in Orissa. Strictly speaking, now the Liṅgarāja is worshipped as Harihara, a composite form of Viṣṇu and Śiva. The deity is offered both *bela* (aegleus marmalus) and *tulasi* (ocimum sanctum) leaves, which were favourites to Śiva and Viṣṇu respectively. Both Nandī and Garuḍa, the respective mounts of Śiva and Viṣṇu, surmount the pillar erected in front of the *bhogamaṇḍapa*. The flag on the temple spire is fixed to a *Pināka* bow instead of a trident, usually found in Śiva temples. Vaiṣṇava themes are also carved on the temple: Yaśodā, *kāliyadalana*, Nanda etc. Many Vaisnavite fairs and festivals were also added to the Liṅgarāja temple. The swing festival (*dola*) and sun worship (*Sūrya pūjā*), which are generally performed in Viṣṇu temples are also observed here. These changes had repercussions on the priests of the Liṅgarāja temple also. The high caste Vaisnavite Brahmins generally do not take the *Mahāprasāda* of *Śiva* temple, but in the Liṅgarāja, they do. The sacred marks of the priests serving the deity have also changed. The Saivites who marked their foreheads with sandal paste in horizontal lines with a big dot in the middle, afterwards added a big 'U' with the dot in its middle on the horizontal lines, which signifies the sacred marks of both Śiva and Viṣṇu. Thus, Liṅgarāja assumed a dual nature, representing a syncretism of Śiva and Viṣṇu cult and the *kṣetra* is equally sacred to Saivites and Vaisnavites. Further diversification of rituals in the premises is achieved through the worship of *Sūrya, Gaṇeśa, Śani, Santoṣīmā, Yogini, Mātṛkās* etc.

H. Sacred Space

As noted in the *Brahma Purāṇa*, the sacred area of *Ekāmra* extended two and a half *yojanas* or about fifteen kilometers. But this area expanded gradually. The boundaries of this *tīrtha*, as noted in the later texts like *Ekāmra Purāṅa, Ekāmra Chandrikā, Kapila Samhitā, Swarṇādri Mahodaya* etc., extended over an area of 16 to 20 kilometers (three *yojanas*), with the temple of Liṅgarāja at the centre, from Khandagiri in the west to god

Kundaleswar in village Tankapani in east and goddess Balaha in Miyapalli in north to temple of Bahirangeswar and Dhauli hill in the south.[30] The Śaiva *kṣetra* was dotted with 'hundred thousand temples and ten million *liṅgas.*'

Though the extant temples speak of a predominant *Śaiva kṣetra,* the space was shared by other pantheons also. The *Brahmāṇḍa Purāṇa, Matsya Purāṇa, Devī Bhāgavata Purāṇa* and many Tantric texts glorify *Ekāmra* as a *Śākta pītha.* Many *khākhrā* shrines for *Devīs* are found- Vaitāla, Gaurī, Mohinī etc. – along with Chausath Yogini temple at Hirapur and many scattered and detached images strewn all over Bhuvaneswar: *Chāmuṇḍdā, Mahiṣamardinī, Chaṇḍī, Matṛkās* etc. During the period when the Liṅgarāja temple was constructed by Kesaris, they mentioned in their records that their tutelary deity was *Pancāmvari Bhadrāmbikā.* They also carved Jaina images in the Navamuni caves of Khandagiri. Buddhist images are also found carved in many temples of Bhuvaneswar. It represents a polyreligious nature of the landscape. Though it was predominantly a Śaiva *kṣetra,* the sacred space was shared by other pantheons. The concept of split space thus emerged within a sacralized boundary, represented in three ways:

I. When the images of other sects are carved on the temple walls, the religion of the temple dominated over other sects.
II. When smaller temples were constructed for other sects around the main shrine, the pantheon of main temple dominated.
III. When two or more temples of same size and same embellishment were built on the same podium, it represented equal sharing of the split space and coexistence of various sects, as represented by Gandharadi temples or by the rituals of the Liṅgarāja temple.

But this shared space and shared faith led to a common purpose of attracting a diverse group of devotees, whose constant participation and patronage support the life of temple for a longer period.

I. Temple Community

The Liṅgarāja temple utilized the services of a diverse group of people, who are classified as *bhītara* and *bāhāra sevakas*. 36 types of services are performed in the Liṅgarāja by people from all castes, ranging from Brahmins to Sudras.[31] The temple rather than suppressing and opposing non-Brahmanic elements, tend to assimilate them under an elaborate set of overarching myths and rites. Tradition reinforces their assimilation by providing a broad range of local themes woven into the Liṅgarāja, which can be elaborated further. They are involved in daily or periodic rituals, providing a link to their works as well as interaction with others, so, people from other communities apart from Brahmins are also linked to the temple intimately as their caste groups were involved in the rituals of temple, thus drawing a support from the non-Brahmin community for the Liṅgarāja temple, the linkage which was important for increase in devotees as well as maintenance of rituals services in the temple.

J. Patronage

The temple survived for a thousand years not due to its dependence on royal support but due to support of a diverse community. Patronage is required for the maintenance of the structure as well as for the continuation of the rituals. In the post-11th century CE period, many donations were made to the temple for performance of various types of services. These donations – money, land, gold, animals and other assets – came from a diverse group of donors. That increased the resource base of the temple and provided constant material support for elaborate rituals, which were performed within the temple.[32] Through performance of elaborate ceremonies, pilgrims gathered here and extended their support to the temple institution. It led to a huge accumulation of property for the deity and its management is instrumental in providing life support to the Liṅgarāja temple and deity. In the 13th century alone, 8 votive inscriptions are found in the Liṅgarāja recording gifts of land, *naivedya*, lamp, gold, *pārijātaka*, *tāmbula* etc. Donors range from kings to common men, which reflect its continual importance in the society and increasing societal support.[33] In subsequent periods as well many donations were made in a wide range of materials land, village, gold, lamp, paddy, oil, coins etc., for the performance of many rituals i.e. *pūjā, dīpama, naivedya, utsava,* provision of water, repairs etc. by a host of patrons across the social strata such as kings, queens, members of the royal family, *Senāpati, Śaivaguru,* disciple of *Śaiva ācārya,* common men and women.[34] The gifts are recorded in the walls of temple in various languages like Sanskrit, Oriya and Telugu recording an expanding base for the deity Liṅgarāja.

K. Relation with other Temples

With most of the temples of Bhuvaneswar, the Liṅgarāja has either sectarian relation or the relation of shared space. With few of them, the deity has close affinity in two ways:

I. Consanguinity or official relation with some of them.
II. Establishing a network of pilgrimage with some of them.

In the temple precincts, the Liṅgarāja lives with his family members and relatives. His parents live in an open shrine to the southeast of the temple compound. Separate temples are constructed for his consort *Pārvatī,* sons *Kārttikeya and Gaṇeśa.* His sister *Kāmākṣī* lives in the premises of the Bhārati *maṭha* whereas his maternal uncle *Mitreśwara* lives in the temple of *Mitreśwara.* Lord *Kapilanātha* lives in Kapileśwara temple and *Ananta Vāsudeva* in *Ananta Vāsudeva* temple. They are his minister and wise elder (*Bhadraloka*) respectively. Both of them accompany him during the festive processions.

The deity visits his relatives and other temples on festive occasions. In *Prathamāṣṭami,* he visits his maternal uncle, at *Mitreśwara* temple. On *Māgha Saptami,* the mobile images of the Liṅgarāja, Pārvatī, Durgā and Vāsudeva were taken to Bhāṣkareśwara temple and on the way of returning, they convoy moves to Kedārgaurī temple. *Aśokāṣṭami* is the car festival when the procession is taken to Rāmeúwara temple.

On *Damaṇaka Chaturdaśī*, Liṅgarāja visits the Tīrtheśwara temple; whereas on *Parṣurāma Aṣṭamī*, he is taken to *Parṣurāmeśwara* temple. On *Yama Dwitiyā*, he visits to Yameśwara temple as well as Kāmākṣī temple, the residence of his sister.

L. Cult of the Liṅgarāja, the king

The concept of the Liṅgarāja was not there till the 11th century CE. It is basically a later formulation. Liṅgarāja is the king of temple community, temple is his palace and temple estate is his kingdom. Liṅgarāja is seen wielding both ritual and secular authority and performing other roles through kinship, kingship and property institutions among gods and men in his *Ekāmra kṣetra*.[35] *Chhatisa Nijoga* serves the Liṅgarāja. He also has his courtiers and officials such as *Parākaraṇa, Panchāyata, Parichhā, Panchadi* etc. Lord *Kapilnātha* and lord *Ananta Vāsudeva* are his minister and wise elder (*Bhadralok*) respectively, who accompany him in his processions. When he goes in procession, he is followed by a retinue holding royal insignia such as umbrella, fan etc. along with musical instruments. Every year, a ceremony corresponding to *rājyābhiṣeka* is held in the temple where all the procedures followed in royal palace are observed. Not only that, the lord holds his royal court on *Suniyān* day (Oriya new year) in the month of *Bhādra* when his servants and subjects (temple servants, peasants and other holders of temple lands) offer him loyalty and tribute as a token of their subservience.[36] This also marks the beginning of an indigenous royal calendar in Orissa. When the deity falls ill for three months, from *āayana Chaturdaśī* to *Sthāpana Chaturdaśī*, lord *Parṣurāma* of *Parṣurāmeśwara* temple is appointed as regent to look after the kingdom.[37] Though this cult is a later addition, and it closely resembles the same at the Jagannātha temple at Puri. Nonetheless, the local *liṅga* was raised to the status of a great all India deity, which significantly contributed to its survival. As apparent from its network of royalty, it was established only after all those deities and temples were constructed and organized in the ritual scene of Bhuvaneswar, which was a much later phenomenon.

What is apparent from the above discussion is that multilevel networks coalesced with the diversities. It is this process which keeps the life of the Liṅgarāja temple ever expanding. Beginning of this linkage in a polymorphic way has its antecedent in the 11th century CE. In this period Kesari kings constructed Liṅgarāja, Jagannātha and Sūrya temples, worshipped their tutelary deity as *Pancāmvari Bhadrāmbikā*, dedicated *Saptamatṛkās*, carved Jaina *Tirthankaras*, performed *Aśvamedha* sacrifices, brought *Veda* knowing Brahmins from Kānyakubja and Dravidian Brahmins from southern India to the Liṅgarāja temple, and thus followed a diverse range of rituals. But it established the multiplicity of sects and coexistence in a shared space to accommodate other pantheons. It did not offer schism but integration through interactional network to bind them together, for the survival of the Liṅgarāja temple. At present, the Jagannātha temple outshines the Liṅgarāja temple in popularity, but Liṅgarāja's fame and reputation is not much less either.

It will be unreasonable to assume that the survival strategy of the Liṅgarāja temple was the only model for other Orissan temples. Many temples differ from it substantially. For instance, Viraja temple survives without its monumentality. Its ability to attract pilgrims did not depend on its architectural monumentality. This temple managed itself in an alternative way. It basically entwined with the local myths and legends through sacred literature. It was eulogized in various *Purāṅas*. Later, in the *Brahma Purāṅa*, a whole section is devoted to it. Subsequently, it attained great fame and managed to devote a *Mahātmya – Viraja Mahātmya* – to the *kṣetra*. In many other cases, neither monumentality nor literature helped the temple to survive. Similarly, numerous small temples, which are scattered in many villages of Orissa and remain largely unnoticed by outsiders, survive due to exclusive support of the local population. The local support network is basically community based.

Thus, various processes involved in the survival of the temple through the centuries suggest that temple is not a static entity, but a multi-layered polymorphic structure. Basically, its networks were operative in three levels – pan-Indian, regional and local – and based on architecture, sculpture, religion, hierarchy and pilgrimage. Effective linkages among those strata are vital for the survival of any temple as exemplified by the Liṅgarāja. However, this is not the only pattern available for survival of temples of Orissa, as temples are different, so are their survival strategies. Each temple invented a distinct process of sharing and negotiation, hence followed a changing repositioning and reinvention, which corresponded to the requirements of patrons, priests and laity. These patterns intersperse and they support non-exclusivity. Thus, temple represented multiple identities and pluralism accommodating regional diversities. At the same time, they postulated a unified notion in a holistic mode.

Notes

1. R.P. Chanda, 'The Lingaraja or Great Temple of Bhubaneswar,' *Annual Report of the Archaeological Survey of India*, 1923-24, New Delhi, 1926, pp. 119-122.
2. P. Acarya, 'Date of the Lingaraja Temple at Bhubaneswar and the Jagannath Temple at Puri,' *Studies in Orissan History, Archaeology and Archives*, Baripada, 1969, pp. 292-296.
3. K.S. Behera, 'Brahmanical Temples of Orissa,' *Orissa Review, Monument Special*, Cuttack, 1976, pp. 53-80.
4. A.B. Mohanty, *Mādalāpanji*, Cuttack, 1940, pp. 6-8.
5. K.C. Panigrahi, *Archaeological Remains at Bhubaneswar*, Cuttack, 1981, pp. 164-166.
6. Krishnadeva, *Temples of India*, Vol. 1, New Delhi, 1995, pp. 67-83; Percy Brown, *Indian Architecture(Buddhist and Hindu Period)*, Bombay, 1959; K.C. Panigrahi, *Archaeological Remains at Bhubaneswar*, Cuttack, 1981.
7. R.P. Das, 'The Study of Śilpaśāstras,' in A.N. Tiwari (ed.), *Reference Orissa*, Bhubaneswar, 1999, pp. 174-181.
8. M.A. Dhaky, *The Indian Temple Forms*, New Delhi, 1977.
9. R. Champaklakshmi, *The Hindu Temple*, London, 2001, p. 100.
10. Ibid., p. 100.
11. K.N. Mahapatra, 'Puranic Stories in the Early Records and

Sculptures of Orissa,' *Orissa Historical Research Journal (OHRJ)*, 1962, Vol. X, No. 4, pp. 59-74.
12. Snigdha Tripathy, 'Ekāmra-Bhuvaneswar,' *Orissa Historical Research Journal (OHRJ)*, Vol. 33, No. 1-2, 1987, p. 141.
13. S.N. Rajguru, 'Brahmeswar Temple Stone Inscription of the Time of Udyotakesari,' *Inscriptions of Orissa* (*IO*), Vol. 4, Bhubaneswar, 1966, pp. 244-252.
14. V.S. Sukhthankar (ed.), *Mahābhārata* (11:II:12.8-10), Poona, 1942.
15. Snigdha Tripathy, *op. cit.*, p. 144.
16. J.L. Sethi (ed.), *Brahmapurāṇa*, Delhi, 1985-86, pp. 140-145,230-240.
17. K.N. Mahapatra, 'Puranic Literature of Orissa,' *OHRJ*, Vol. XI, No. 1, 1962, pp. 21-31.
18. M.M. Mahapatra, *Traditional Structure and Change in an Orissan Temple*, Calcutta, 1981, p. 6.
19. R.L. Mitra, *The Antiquities of Orissa*, Vol. II, Calcutta, 1880, pp. 105-108, 165.
20. Swami Vijnanananda (tr.), *Devī Bhāgavata Purāṇa* (7.30.53-102) Allahabad, 1974.
21. G.V. Tagore (tr.), *Brahmāṇḍa Purāṇa* (LM,44:93-100), Delhi, 1983-84.
22. Vijaya Nath, *Puranas and Acculturation, an Anthropological Perspective*, New Delhi, 2001, p. 126.
23. *Brahmapurāṇa* (70.16.9).
24. U.N. Dhal, *Ekāmra Purāṇa*, New Delhi, 1986.
25. For an analysis of such references, see K.N. Mahapatra, 'Puranic Literature of Orissa,' *OHRJ*, Vol. XI, No. 1, 1962, pp. 21-31.
26. U.N. Dhal, *Ekāmra Purāṇa*, New Delhi, 1986.
27. M.M. Mahapatra, *op. cit.*, pp. 5-6.
28. T.E. Donaldson, 'Bhuvaneswar (*Ekāmra Kṣetra*):Temple Town and Cultural Centre,' *Marg*, Vol. 52, No. 3, 2001, pp. 12-27.
29. K.S. Behera, *The Lingaraja Temple of Bhubaneswar, Art and Cultural Legacy*, New Delhi, 2008, p. 126.
30. R.D. Banerjee, *History of Orissa: From the Earliest Times to the British Period*, Vol. 1 and 2, Delhi, 1931, p. 7.
31. N.K. Bose, Nityananda Patnaik and Ajit Kishore Ray, 'Organization of Services in the Temple of Lingaraja in Bhubaneswara,' *Journal of the Asiatic Society, Letters*, Vol. XXIV, No. 2, 1958, pp. 85-129.
32. S.N. Das, 'The Votive Inscriptions in the Lingaraja Temple of

Bhubaneswar,' *OHRJ*, Vol. 1, No. 4, 1953, pp. 301-305.

33. S.N. Rajguru, *Inscriptions of Orissa*, Vol. V, Pt. I, 3-4, 96, 97, 117, 118, 124, 128 and 157, Bhuvaneswar, 1975.
34. K.S. Behera, *op. cit.*, pp. 132-156.
35. L.K. Mahapatra, 'Gods, Kings and Caste System in India,' in Bhavagrahi Mishra and James J. Preston (ed.), *Community, Self and Identity*, The Hague, 1978, pp. 7-26.
36. Ibid., pp. 7-26.
37. M.M. Mahapatra, *Traditional Structure and Change in an Orissan Temple*, Calcutta, 1981, pp. 19-20.

Table 1
Structural Analysis of Liṅgarāja Complex

	Usage	*Status*	*Orientation*	*Pantheon*	*Temple type*	*Ratha*
Religious	115					
Secular	12					
Living		98				
Dead		29				
North			15			
South			7			
East			73			
West			18			
Open			14			
Śiva				79		
Viṣṇu,				8		
Śakti				8		
Gaṇeśa				3		
Sūrya				1		
Yama				1		
Unknown				27		
Rekhā					56	
Piḍhā					55	
Khakhra					2	
Mandapa					11	
Well					2	
Stambha					1	
Triratha						30
Pancharatha						79
Others						18

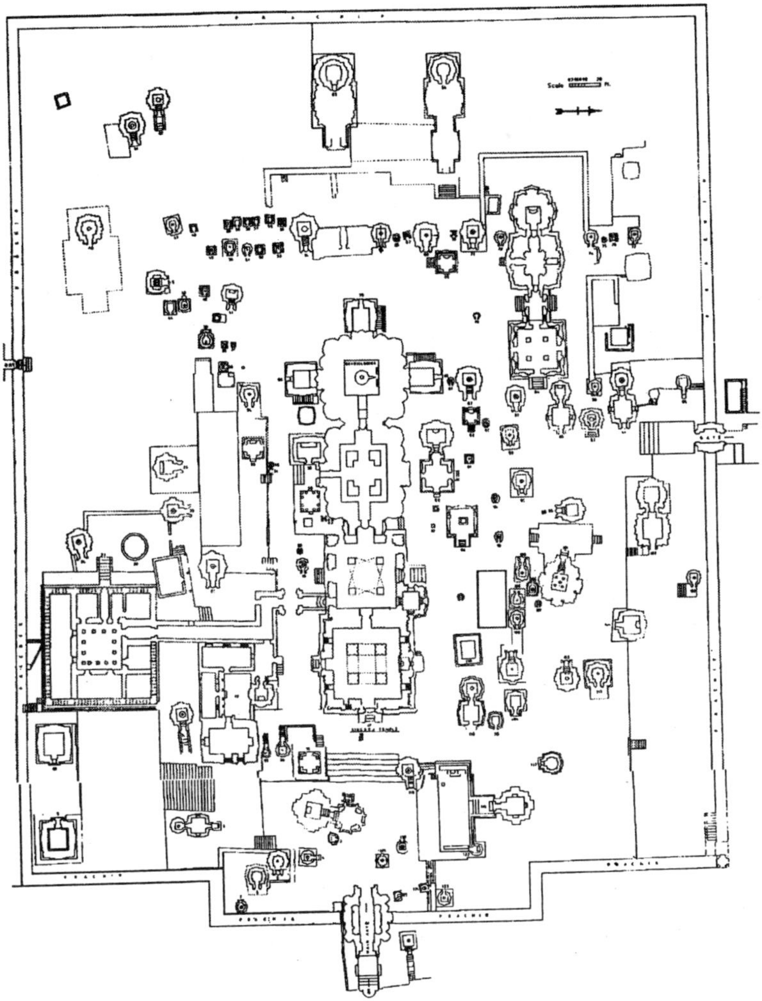

Ground plan of Lingaraj temple with subsidiary shrines

BIBLIOGRAPHY

Aboshi, Yoshinor, *et al.* 1999. 'Excavations at Saheth Maheth 1986-1996,' *East and West*, Vol.49,1-4,pp.119-173.

Agrawal, V.S. 1963. *Devi Mahatmyam: The Glorification of the Great Goddess*. Varanasi: All India Kashiraj Trust.

Ahir, D.C. 2005. *Buddhism Declined in India: How and Why*. Delhi: BR Publishers.

Ahmed, N. 1984. *Discover the Monuments of Bangladesh.* Dhaka: University Press Limited.

Alam, A.K.M. Shamshul. 1982. *Mainamati.* Dacca: Department of Archaeology and Museums.

Ali, Daud. 1988. 'Technologies of the Self: Courtly Artifice and Monastic Discipline in Early India,' *Journal of Economic and Social History of the Orient*, 41, pp. 159-184.

Allen, M.R. 1973. 'Buddhism without Monks: The Vajrayana Religion of the Newars of the Kathmandu Valley,' *South Asia*, 2, pp. 1-14.

Allen, J. 1991. 'An Inscribed Tablet from Kedah, Malaysia, Comparison with Earlier Finds,' *Asian Perspectives*, 27(1), pp. 35–57.

Almond, Philip. 1988. *The British Discovery of Buddhism.*

Cambridge: Cambridge University Press.

Anita R. 2004. 'An Archaeological Study of Temples in Eastern Deccan' in H.P. Ray, Carla Sinopoly (eds.), *Archaeology as History in Early South Asia*, pp. 426-463. Delhi: Aryan Books International.

Appadurai Arjun & Carol Breckenridge. 1976. 'The South Indian Temple: Authority Honour and Redistribution,' *Contributions To Indian Sociology*, Vol. 10, No. 2, pp. 191-193.

Appadurai, Arjun. 1977. 'Kings, Sects and Temples in South India, 1350-1700 AD,' *The Indian Economic and Social History Review*, XIV (1), pp. 47- 73.

Aṅguttara Nikāya. 1917. *The Books of Kindred Sayings* tr. By C.A. F. Rhys Davids. London: Oxford University Press.

Arulsamy, S. 1987. *Saivism – A Perspective of Grace*. Delhi: Sterling Publishers.

Balasubramaniyam, S.R. 1944. 'The Oldest Chidambaram Inscriptions,' *Journal of Annamalai University*, XII, pp. 55-91.

Balasubramaniyam, S.R. 1971. *Early Cola Temples: Parantaka I to Rajaraja I (A.D. 907 – 985)*. New Delhi: Orient Longman.

Balasubramaniyam, S.R. 1975. *Middle Cola Temples: Rajaraja I to Kulottunga I (A.D. 985 – 1070)*. Faridabad: Thomson Press.

Balasubramaniyam, S.R. 1979. *Later Cola Temples: Kulottunga I to Rajendra III (A.D. 1070–1280)*. Faridabad: Thomson Press.

Banerjee, J.N. 1956. *Development of the Hindu Iconography*. Calcutta: University of Calcutta.

Banerjee, R.D. 1931. *History of Orissa: From the Earliest Times to the British Period*, Vol. 1 and 2. Delhi: Bharatiya Publishing House.

Banerji, RD. [1933] 1988. *Eastern Indian School of Medieval Sculpture*. Delhi: Archaeological Survey of India.

Bapat, P.V. 1972. *2500 Years of Buddhism*. Delhi: Publications Division, Govt.of India.

Barpujari, H.K. 1977. *Political History of Assam*. Guwahati: Department for the Preparation of Political History of Assam, Government of Assam.

Barpujari, H.K. (Ed.) 1992. *Comprehensive History of Assam*, Vol. I. Guwahati: Assam Publication Board.

Barua, K.L. 1966. *Early History of Kamrupa*. Gauhati: Lawyers Book Stall.

Barua, B.K. 1969. *A Cultural History of Assam (Early Period)*. Gauhati: Lawyers Bok Stall.

Barua, Dimbeswar. 1981. *Kāmārūpaśāsanāvalī*. Guwahati: Publication Board, Assam.

Beal, S. 1958 (reprint). *Si- Yu-ki or Buddhist Records of the Western World*. London: Kegan Paul.

Behera, K.S. 1976. 'Brahmanical Temples of Orissa,' *Orissa Review, Monument Special*, pp. 53-80. Cuttack: Government of Orissa.

Behera, K.S. 2008. *The Lingaraja Temple of Bhubaneswar, Art and Cultural Legacy*. New Delhi: IGNCA and Aryan Books International.

Benestie, M. 1981. *Contribution a l'etude du stupa bouddhique indien: Les stupas mineurs de Bodh-Gaya et Ratnagiri*, 2 vols. Paris.

Bernard, F. 1967. 'Zur Entstehung erner Dharani,' *Zeitschrift der Deuschen Morgen Landischen Gesellschaft*, 117, pp. 162-63.

Beyer, S. 1973. *The Cult of Tara: Magic and Ritual in Tibet*. Berkley: University of California Press.

Bharathi, Srirama. 2000. *The Sacred Book of Four Thousand*. Chennai: Sri Sadagopan Tirunarayanaswami Divya Prabandha Pathassala.

Bhaskara Reddy, G V. 1991. *Erotic Sculptures of Ancient India*. Delhi: Inter-India Publications.

Bhatia, M.L. 2002. 'Identifying Buddhism in Early Islamic Sources of Sindh,' *Buddhist Studies Review*, 19(2), pp. 143-163.

Bhattacharjee, A. 1976. *Icons and Sculptures of Medieval Assam*. Delhi: Ashish Pub. House.

Bhattacharya, A. 1998. 'Trade Routes of Ancient Bengal' in A. Dutta (ed.), *History and Archaeology of Eastern India*, pp. 200-212. Delhi: Books and Books.

Bhattacharyya, B. [1925] 1928. (ed.). *The Sādhanamālā*, 2 parts.

Baroda: Gaikwad Oriental Series 26 & 41.

Bhattacharyya, B. 1968. *The Indian Buddhist Iconography*. Calcutta: Firma KLM.

Bhattacharyya, B. 1972 (ed.). *The Niṣpannayogāvalī of Mahāpaṇḍita Abhayākara*. Baroda: Gaikwad Oriental Series 109.

Bhattacharya, G. 1993. 'An Inscribed Metal Vase, Most Probably from Chittagong,' in A.J. Gail & G.J.R.Mevissena (ed.), *South Asian Archaeology 1991, Proceedings of the Eleventh International Conference of the Association of South Asian Archaeologists in Western Europe held in Berlin 1-5 July 1991*, pp. 323-338. Stuttgart: Verlag.

Bhattacharya, G. 1996. 'A Preliminary Note on the Inscribed Metal Vase from the National Museum of Bangladesh,' in D. Mitra (ed.), *Explorations in the Art and Archaeology of South Asia: Essays Dedicated to N.G. Majumdar*, pp. 237-246. Calcutta: Directorate of Archaeology and Museums, Govt. of West Bengal.

Bhattacharya, N.N. 1981. *History of Researches on Indian Buddhism*. Delhi: Munshiram Manoharlal.

Bhattacharya, N.N. [1987]1993. *Buddhism in the History of India Ideas*. Delhi: Manohar.

Bhattacharya, N.N. 1995. *Religious Culture of North Eastern India*. Delhi: Manohar.

Bhattasali, N.K. 1945. 'New Light on the History of Assam,' *Indian Historical Quarterly*, XXI, pp. 20-35.

Blake, Kevin S. 2001. 'In Search of a Navajo Sacred Geography,' *Geographical Review*, Vol. 91, No. 4, pp. 715-724.

Bluck, Robert 2002. ' The Path of the Householder: Buddhist Lay Disciple in the Pali Canon,' *Buddhist Studies Review*, 19,(1),pp. 1-18.

Bopardikar, B.P. 1996. *Excavations at Tuljapur Garhi 1984-85 (Vidarbha, Maharashtra)*. New Delhi: Archaeological Survey of India.

Bose, N.K., Nityananda Patnaik and Ajit Kishore Ray. 1958. 'Organization of Services in the Temple of Lingaraja in Bhubaneswara,' *Journal of the Asiatic Society Letters*, Vol. XXIV, No. 2, pp. 85-129.

Brahmāṇḍa Purāṇa (5 Vols), 1983-84, Trans. by G.V. Tagore. Delhi: Motilal Banarsidass.

Brahma Purāṇa (4 Vols), 1985-86. Translated by A Board of Scholars, Ed., J.L. Sethi. Delhi: Motilal Banarsidass.

Brown, Percy, 1959. *Indian Architecture (Buddhist and Hindu Period)*. Bombay: Taraporewala Sons and Co.

Carr, E.H., 1980. *What is History?* Harmondsworth: Penguin.

Carrithers, Michael. 1983. *The Forest Monks of Sri Lanka: An Anthropological and Historical Study*. Delhi: Oxford University Press.

Chakrabarti, D.K. 1987. 'Pakbir: A Jaina Site in Purulia District, West Bengal,' in B.D. Chattopadhyaya, B.M. Pandey (ed.), *Archaeology and History: Essay in Honour of A.Ghosh*, pp.335-45. Delhi: Agam Kala Prakashana.

Chakrabarti, D.K. 1995. 'Location of Buddhist Sites as Influenced by Political and Economic Factors,' *World Archaeology*, 27(2), pp. 185-202.

Chakrabarti, D.K. 1995. *The Archaeology of Ancient Indian Cities*. Delhi: Oxford University Press.

Chakrabarti, D.K.1998. *Issues in East Indian Archaeology*. Delhi: Munshiram Manoharlal.

Chakrabarti, D.K. 1999. *India-An Archaeological History, Paleolithic Beginnings to Early Historical Foundations*. New Delhi: Oxford University Press.

Chakrabarti, D.K. 2001. *Archaeological Geography of the Ganga Plains; The Lower and the Middle Ganga*. Delhi: Permanent Black.

Chakravarti, Kunal. 2001. *Religious Process: The Puranas and the Making of A Regional Tradition*. New Delhi: Oxford University Press.

Chakravarti, Ranabir. 1990.'Monarchs, Merchants and a *Maṭha* in Northern Konkan,c.900-1053AD,' *The Indian Economic and Social History Review*, 27, 2, pp. 189-208.

Chakravarti, Ranabir. 2002. '*Vaṅgasāgarsaṁbhāṇḍāriyaka*: A Riverine Trade Centre in Early Medieval Bengal,' in his *Trade and Traders in Early Indian Society*, pp. 142-169. Delhi: Manohar.

Chakravarty, Uma. 1996. *The Social Dimensions of Early*

Buddhism. Delhi: Munshiram Manoharlal.

Champakalakshmi, R. 1989. 'Religion and Social Change in Tamilnadu (A.D. 600-1300)' in N.N. Bhattacharya (ed.), *Medieval Bhakti Movements in India*. Delhi: Munshiram Manoharlal.

Champakalakshmi, R. 1998. 'Buddhism in Tamilnadu: Patterns of Patronage,' in *Buddhism in Tamilnadu, Collected Papers*, pp. 69-96. Chennai: Institute of Asian Studies.

Champaklakshmi, R. 2001. *The Hindu Temple*. London: Greenwich.

Chanda, R.P. 1926. 'The Lingaraja or Great Temple of Bhubaneswar,' *Annual Report of the Archaeological Survey of India*: 1923-24, pp. 119-122. New Delhi: Archaeological Survey of India.

Chandra, Lokesh. 1987. *Buddhist Iconography*, 2 Vols., Sata-Pitaka Series 342. New Delhi: Aditya Prakashan.

Chandra Lokesh. 1988. *One Thousand forms of Avalokiteśvara*. Delhi: IGNCA and Ahinav Prakashan.

Chandrapur District Gazetteers. 1973 (2nd revised edition). Mumbai: Govt.of Maharashtra.

Chapekar, B.N. 1969. *Report on the Excavation at Ter (1958)*. Poona: Shrisaraswati Mudranalaya.

Chatterji, Rama. 1985. *Religion in Bengal during Pala and Sena Times*. Calcutta: Punthi Pustaka.

Chattopadhyaya, B.D. 1990. *Aspects of Rural Settlements and Rural Society in Early Medieval India*. Calcutta: KP Bagchee.

Chattopadhyaya, B.D. 1994.*The Making of Early Medieval India*. Delhi: Oxford University Press.

Chattopadhyaya, B.D. 1993. 'Historiography, History and Religious Centres: Early Medieval North India, circa AD 700-1200.' In Visakha N. Desai and D. Mason (eds.), *Gods, Guardians and Lovers: Temple Sculptures from North India, AD 700- 1200*, pp. 33-47. Ahmedabad: Mapin Publishing Company.

Chattopadhyaya, B.D. 2003. *Studying Early India*. Delhi: Permanent Black.

Chattopadhyaya, B.D. 2004. "State Perception of the 'Forest' and the 'Forest' as State in Early Medieval India" in B.B.

Chaudhury, Arun Bandopadhyaya (eds.), *Tribes, Forests and Social Formations in Indian History*, pp. 23-37. Delhi: Manohar.

Chaudhury, P.D. 1959. *Ancient Treasures of Assam through Assam State Museum*. Gauhati: Government of Assam.

Chaudhury, R.K. 1975. *The University of Vikramashila*. Patna: Bihar Puravid Parishad.

Chaudhury, Sukomal. 1982. *Contemporary Buddhism in Bangladesh*. Calcutta: Atisha Memorial Publishing Society.

Choudhury, N.D. 1985. *Historical Archaeology of Central Assam*. Delhi: Agam Kala Prakashan.

Choudhury, Pratap Chandra. 1966. *The History of Civilization of the People of Assam to the Twelfth Century A.D.* Gauhati: Department of Historical and Antiquarian Studies, Govt of Assam.

Choudhury, P. D. & Das, M.C. 1959. *Ancient Treasures of Assam*. Gauhati: Assam State Museum.

Choudhury, R. D. 1985. *Historical Archaeology of the Brahmaputra Valley of Assam (Pre-Ahom Period)*. Delhi: Agam Kala Prakashan.

Chettiar, Ramachandra, C. M. 1941. 'Geographical Distribution of Religious Places in Tamilnad,' *Indian Geographical Journal*, Vol. XVI.

Clarke, Shayne. 2004. '*Vinaya Mātṛkā*: Mother of All Monastic Codes or Just another Set of Lists? A Response to Frauwallner's Handling of the Mahāsaṅghika Vinaya,' *Indo-Iranian Journal*, 47, pp. 77-120.

Cohen, Richard S. 1998. 'Naga, Yakshini, the Buddha: Local Deities and Local Buddhism at Ajanta,' *History of Religions*, 37 (4), pp. 360-400.

Coninghum, Robin A.E. 1995. 'Monks, Caves and Kings: A Reassessment of the Nature of Early Buddhism in Sri Lanka,' *World Archaeology*, 27(2), pp. 222-242.

Conze, Edward. [1951] 1957. *Buddhism: Its Essence and Development*. Oxford: Bruno Cassirer.

Cunningham, A. 1879. *Stupa of Bharhut*. London: W.H. Allen & Co.

Das, R.P. 1999. *'The Study of śilpaśāstras,'* in A.N. Tiwari (ed.),

Reference Orissa, pp. 174-181. Bhubaneswar: Enterprising Publishers.

Das, S.N., 1953, 'The Votive Inscriptions in the Lingaraj Temple of Bhubaneswar,' *Orissa Historical Research Journal*, Vol. 1, No. 4, pp. 301-305.

Das, S.R. 1967. *An Interim Report on Excavations at Rajabadidanga and Terracotta Seals and Sealings*. Calcutta: Asiatic Society.

Davey, Ranganatha, T.B. 1987. 'The Historical Geography of the Cauveri Delta with Special Reference to the Tanjore District,' *Journal of Madras Geographical Association*, Vol. 12, No. 2, pp. 83-94.

Davidson, Ronald M. 2004. *Indian Esoteric Buddhism: A Social History of the Tantric Movement*. Delhi: Motilal Banarsidass.

Davis, Winston. 1989. 'Buddhism and the Modernization of Japan,' *History of Religions*, 28 (4), pp. 304 –339.

Dayalan, D. 1992. *Early Temples of Tamilnadu: Their Role in Socio-Economic life (c. A.D. 550-925)*. Delhi: Harman Pub. House.

De, Gokuldas. 1955. *Democracy in the Buddhist Sangha*. Calcutta: University of Calcutta Publication.

Decoroli, Robert. 2004. *Haunting the Buddha: Indian Popular Religions and the Formation of Buddhism*. New York: Oxford University Press.

Dehejia, Vidya. 1992. 'The Collective and Popular Basis of Early Buddhist Patronage: Sacred Monuments, BC 100-AD 250,' in Barabara S. Miller (ed.), *The Powers of Art: Patronage in Indian Culture*, pp. 35- 50. Delhi: Oxford University Press.

Dehejia, Vidya (ed.). 1997. *Representing the Body*. New Delhi: Kali for Women.

Dehejia, Vidya. 1998. *Slaves of The Lord – The Path of the Tamil Saints*. Delhi: Munshiram Manoharlal.

Deo, S.B. and M.K. Dhavalikar 1968. 'Report of Paunar Excavation (1967),' in *Nagpur University Journal (Humanities)*, Vol. XVIII. Nos. 3 & 3. Nagpur: Nagpur University Vidyapeeth Mudranalay.

Deo, S.B. and J.P. Joshi 1972. *Pauni Excavation (1969-70)*. Nagpur: Nagpur University Vidyapeeth Mudranalay.

Deo, S.B. 1970. *Excavations at Takalaghat and Khapa*. Nagpur: Nagpur University.

Deo, S.B. 1973. *Mahurjhari Excavations 1970-72*. Nagpur: Nagpur University.

Deo, S.B. 1973. 'New Evidence of Hinayana Buddhism in Vidarbha,' *Puratattva* 1972-73, 6, pp. 84-86.

Deo, S.B. and A.P. Jamkhedkar. 1982. *Excavations at Naikund 1978-80*. Bombay: Department of Archaeology and Museums, Government of Maharashtra.

Deo, S.B. 1982. *Recent Researches on the Chalcolithic and Megalithic Cultures of the Deccan*. Madras: Madras University Archaeological Series No. 5.

Deo, S.B. 2000. *Indian Beads: A Cultural and Technological Study*. Pune: Deccan College Post-graduate and Research Institute.

Deotare, B.C., Gurudas Shete, Reshma Sawant, Vaishali Kathale and S. Naik. 2007. 'Discovery of Structural Stupa at Bhon, District Buldana, Maharashtra,' *Puratattva* 37, pp. 177-185.

Deotare, B.C. 2007. 'Preliminary Report on the Excavations at Bhon and Paturda, Buldana District, Maharashtra,' *Bulletin of Deccan College Research Institute* 64-65 (2004-05), pp. 87-105.

Deotare, B.C. 2008. 'Excavations at Kholapur, District Amravati, Maharashtra,' *Annual Report of Deccan College Research Institute* (2007-08). Pune: Deccan College.

Deotare, B.C., Gurudas Shete, Reshma Sawant and S. Naik. 2008. 'Ancient Irrigation Canal: Evidence from the Purna Basin, Vidarbha Region of Maharashtra,' *Puratattva*, 38,pp. 210-216.

Desai, D. 1975. *Erotic Sculptures of Ancient India: A Socio-Cultural Study*. New Delhi: Tata McGraw-Hill Pub. Co.

Deshpande-Mukherjee, Arati 2002. 'Marine Shell Utilization by the Chalcolithic Societies of Western Deccan Region of India,' in Daniella E. Bar, Yoser Mayer (eds.), *Archaeomalacology*, Proceedings of the 9th Conference of the International Council of Archaeozoology, Durham, August 2002, pp. 174-184.

Deshpande-Mukherjee, Arati 2005. 'Archaeomalacological Research in India with Special Reference to Early Historic

Exploitation of the Sacred Conch Shell (*Turbinella pyrum*) in Western Deccan,' paper presented in the Conference '*Early Human Impact on Megamollusks*,' September 26th - 28th 2005, at Isla de Margarita, Venezuela.

Devi Bhāgavata Purāṇa. 1974. Translated by Swami Vijnanananda. Allahabad: SBH.

Dhaky, M.A. 1977. *The Indian Temple Forms*. New Delhi: Abhinav Publications.

Dhal, U.N. 1986. *Ekāmra Purāṇa*. New Delhi.

Dhavalikar, M.K. 1999. *Historical Archaeology of India*. New Delhi: Books and Books.

Dhavamony, Maraisusai. 1971. *Love of God according to Śaiva Siddhānta*. Oxford: Oxford University Press.

Dikshit, M.G. 1968. *Excavations at Kaundinyapur*. Bombay: Government Central Press.

Dikshitar, V.R. [1955] 1995. *The Purana Index*, Vol. I-III. Delhi: Motilal Banarsidass.

Dirks, Nicholas. 1976. 'Political Authority and Structural Change in Early South Indian History,' *The Indian Economic and Social History Review*, 13(2), pp. 125-157.

Diskalkar, D.B. 1949. 'Excavations at Kasrawad,' *Indian Historical Quarterly*, 25, pp. 1-18.

Doinger O'Flaherty (ed.). 1960. *Karma and Rebirth in Classical Indian Tradition*. California: California University Press.

Donaldson, T.E. 2001, 'Bhuvaneswar (Ekāmra Kṣetra):Temple Town and Cultural Centre,' *Marg*, Vol. 52, No. 3, pp. 12-27.

Donaldson, T.E. 2001. *Iconography of the Buddhist Sculptures of Orissa*, Vol. 2, Delhi: IGNCA/Aryan Books International.

Dumont, L. [1966].1980. *Homo Hierarchicus: The Caste System and Its Implications*. Chicago: University of Chicago Press.

Dutt, S. 1962. *Buddhist Monks and Monasteries in India: Their History and their Contribution to the Indian Culture*. London: George Allen and Unwin.

Dutt, S. [1924]1984. *Early Buddhist Monachism*, Delhi: Munshiram Manoharlal.

Dutta, Pramatta Nath. 1985.*Glimpses into the History of Assam*. Shillong.

Fleet, J.F. 1970. *Corpus Inscriptionum Indicarum*, Vol. III.

Eaton, Richard M. 1984. 'Conversion to Christianity among the Nagas, 1870-1971,' *The Indian Economic and Social History Review*, 21, 2, pp. 1–44.

Eaton, Richard M. 1994. *The Rise of Islam and Bengal Frontier*. Delhi: Oxford University Press.

Eaton, Richard M. 2001. 'Who are the Bengal Muslims? Conversions and Islamisation in Bengal' in R. Ahmed (ed.), *Understanding Bengal Muslims*, pp. 26-51. Delhi: Oxford University Press.

Eck, Diana, L. 1981. "India's Tīrthas: 'Crossings' in Sacred Geography," *History of Religions*, Vol. 20, No. 4, pp. 323-344.

Ekāmra Chandrikā. 1933. Edited by R. Gargavatu. Cuttack

Ekāmra Purāṇa. 1931. Edited by R. Gargavatu. Cuttack

Elliot, E.M. 1964. *History of India as told by its own Historians*, Vol. IV. Allahabad : Kitab Mahal Pvt. Ltd.

Erdosy, G. 1987. 'Early Historical Cities of North India,' *South Asian Studies*, 3, pp. 1-23.

Erdosy, G. 1988. *Urbanisation in Early Historic India*. Oxford: BAR International Series.

Etiraj, A. 2006. *Vaishnava Divya Stala Varalaru* (in Tamil). Karaikudi: Sri Vaishnava Siddhanta Nurpatippu Kazhakam.

Frauwallner, E. 1956. *The Earliest Vinaya and the Beginnings of the Vinaya Literature*. Rome: Instituto Italiano per Il Medio ed Estremo Oriente.

Fogelin, Lars. 2004. 'Sacred Architecture, Sacred Landscape: Early Buddhism in North Coastal Andhra Pradesh,' in H.P. Ray & Carla M. Sinopaly (ed.), *Archaeology as History in Early South Asia*, pp. 376-391. New Delhi: Aryan Books International.

Gait, Edward. 1897. *Report on the Progress of Historical Research in Assam*. Shillong: Assam Secretariat.

Gait, Edward. 1926. *A History of Assam*. Calcutta: Thacker, Spink & Co.

Ganguli, K.M. 1992. *The Mahābhārata*. Vol. IV. New Delhi: Munshiram Manoharlal Publishers.

Gangopadhyaya, Jayeeta. 1986. *Uposatha Ceremony: The Earliest Traditions and Later Developments, Mainly from the Vinaya Traditions Preserved in Chinese*. Varanasi and Delhi: Bharatiya Vidya Prakashana.

Geddes, Arthur. 1982. 'Some Geographical Factors in Indian History,' in A.T.A. Learmonth *et al.* (ed.), *Man and Land in South Asia*, pp. 91-112. Delhi: Concept Publishing Company and Indian Council for Social Science Research.

Gellner, D. N. 1996. *Monk, Householder, and Tantric Priest: Newar Buddhism and its Hierarchy of Rituals*. Delhi: Cambridge University Press.

Gellner, David N. 2003. 'The Newar Buddhist Monastery: an Anthropological and Historical Typology,' in his *The Anthropology of Buddhism and Hinduism*, pp.134-138. Delhi: Oxford University Press.

Gellner, David N. 2003. 'What Is Anthropology of Buddhism About,' in his *The Anthropology of Buddhism and Hinduism, Weberian Themes*, 45-60. Delhi: Oxford University Press.

Gernet, Jacques. 1995. *Buddhism in Chinese Society: An Economic History from the 5th to 10th Centuries AD*. English translation by Franciscus Verrelen. New York: Columbia University Press.

Getty, A. 1978. *Gods of Northern Buddhism*. Oxford: Clarendon Press.

Ghosh M. 1980. *Development of Buddhist Iconography in Eastern India: A Study of Tārā, Prajñās of Five Tathāgatas and Bhṛkuṭī*. Delhi: Munshiram Manoharlal.

Gilchrist, Roberta. 1994. *Gender and Material Culture: The Archaeology of Religious Women*. London: Routledge.

Gogte, V.D., V.N. Bhoraskar and P.S. Lahoti 1984. '14 MeV Neutron Activation Analysis of Megalithic Iron Objects,' *Bulletin of Deccan College Research Institute*, 43, pp. 49-52.

Gokhale, B.G. 1976. *Buddhism in Maharashtra*. Bombay: Popular Prakashan.

Gokhale, B.G. 1994. 'Early Buddhism and Urban Revolution,' in his *New Light on Early Buddhism*, pp. 43-57. Bombay: Popular Prakashana.

Gokhale, B.G. 1994. 'The *Saṅgha* and the Laity,' in his *New*

Light on Early Buddhism, pp. 13-24. Bombay: Popular Prakashana.

Gombrich, Richard. 1988. *Theravada Buddhism: A Social History from Ancient Benaras to Modern Colombo*. London: Routledge.

Gombrich, Richard. 2002. *How Buddhism Began: The Conditioned Genesis of Early Teachings*. Delhi: Munshiram Manoharlal.

Gopalakrishnan, R. 1990. *Religion and Mysticism in the Periyapuranam*. Madras: University of Madras.

Gordon, A.K. 1967. *The Iconography of Tibetan Lamaism*. Delhi: Oxford and IBH Publishing Co.

Gunawardana, R.A.L.H. 1979. *Robe and Plough: Monasticism and Economic Interest in Early Medieval Sri Lanka*. Tucson: University of Arizona Press.

Gupta, P.L. 1963. *The Amaravati Hoard of Silver Punch-marked Coins*. Hyderabad: Government of Andhra Pradesh.

Haladhar, S.M. 2004. 'The Robe and the Throne: An Analysis of the Symbiotic Relationship between Buddhism and the State in Ancient Sri Lanka,' *Indian Historical Review*, XXXI (1-2), pp. 18-30.

Hall, Kenneth R. 1992. 'The Temple-based Political Economy of Angkor Cambodia' in Nicholas Tarling (ed.), *Cambridge History of Southeast Asia*, Vol. 1, pp. 229-239. Cambridge: Cambridge University Press.

Hall, Kenneth R. 1992. 'Buddhism as an Economic Force in Pagan Burma,' in Nicholas Tarling (ed.), *Cambridge History of Southeast Asia*, Vol. 1, pp. 240-245. Cambridge: Cambridge University Press.

Hardy, F. 1983. *Viraha Bhakti: The Early History of Kṛṣṇa Devotion in South India*. Delhi: Oxford University Press.

Hardy, R. Spence. [1860] 1989. *Eastern Monachism: An Account of the Origin, Laws, Discipline, Sacred Writings, Mysterious Rites, Religious Ceremonies and Present Circumstances of the Order of Mendicants Founded by the Buddha*. Delhi: Sri Satguru Publications.

Harris, Ian. 2001. 'Buddhist *Saṅgha* Groupings in Cambodia,' *Buddhist Studies Review*, 18 (1), pp. 73-106.

Hart, George L. 1980. *'The Theory of Reincarnation among the*

Tamils' in Donige Wendy (ed.), *Karma and Rebirth in Classical Indian Traditions*, pp. 116-133. Berkley: University of California Pres.

Hawkes, Jason. 2009. 'The Wider Archaeological Contexts of the Buddhist Stupa Site of Bharhut,' in Hawkes, Jason and Shimada, Akira (ed.), *Buddhist Stupas in South Asia: Recent Archaeological, Art-Historical and Historical Perspective*, pp. 146-176. Delhi: Oxford University Press.

Hazra, K.L. 1983. *Buddhism in India as Described by Chinese Pilgrims, A.D. 399-689.* New Delhi: Munshiram Manoharlal.

Heitzman, J. 1984. 'Early Buddhism, Trade and Empire,' in G.L. Possel & K. Kennedy (ed.), *Studies in Archaeology and Palaeoanthropology of South Asia*, pp. 121-132. Delhi: Oxford University Press.

Henn, Matt & Weinstein, Nick Ford. 2006. *A Short Introduction To Social Research*. New Delhi: Vistaar Publications.

Hiralal. 1909-10. 'Kuruspal Stone Inscription of Somesvaradeva,' *Epigraphia Indica*, Vol. X, pp. 25-28.

Hoque, M.M. & Hoque, Seema. 1997. 'Ancient Human Settlement Pattern of Bangladesh: A Preliminary Study,' *Journal of Bengal Art*, Vol. 2. Dhaka, pp. 283-300.

Huntington, Susan L. 1984. *The " Pala-Sena" Schools of Sculpture*. Leiden: E.J. Brill.

Huntington, S. 1992. 'Aniconism and the Multivalence of Emblems: Another Look,' *Ars Orientalis*, 22, pp. 111-56.

Hussain, ABM (ed.). 1997. *Mainamati-Devaparvata*. Dhaka: Asiatic Society.

IAR (*Indian Archaeology: A Review*). 1979-80, 1981-82, 1982-83, 1983-84, 1984-85, 1984-85, 1989-90, 1990-91, 1991-92, 1992-93, 1994-95. New Delhi: Archaeological Survey of India.

Imam, Abu. 2002. 'Samatata- Mainamati: Some Observations' in G. Sengupta & S. Panja(ed.), *Archaeology of Eastern India: New Perspectives*, pp. 613-629. Kolkata: Centre for Archaeological Studies and Training, Eastern India.

Jaini, P.S. 2001. 'The Disappearance of Buddhism and the Survival of Jainism in India: A Study in Contrast,' in his *Collected Papers on Buddhist Studies*, pp.139-154. Delhi:

Motilal Banarsidass.

Jayaswal, K.P. and R.D. Banerji. 1925. 'Bhaṭṭaswāmin's Commentary on the Arthaśāstra,' *The Journal of the Bihar and Orissa Research Society*, Vol. XI, Part 1.

Jayaswal, K.P. and R.D. Banerji. 1933. 'The Hathigumpha Inscription of Kharavela,' *Epigraphica Indica*, XX (1929-30), pp. 71-89.

Jayaswal, K.P. 1967. *Hindu Polity* (4th edition). Bangalore: Banglore Print &Publishing Company.

Jha, D.N. 2004. *Early India, A Concise History*. New Delhi: Manohar.

Jha, D.N. 2000. *The Feudal Order: State, Society and Ideology in Early Medieval India*. Delhi: Manohar.

Joshi, J.P. and Sharma, A.K. 2000. 'Excavation at Mansar, District Nagpur, Maharashtra – 1997-2000,' *Puratattva* 30, pp. 127- 131.

Joshi, J.P. and Sharma, A.K. 2005. 'Mansar Excavation 1998-2004: The Discovery of Pravarapur,' *Puramanthan* (Pravarapur special) 3, pp. 1-26.

Joshi, L.M. 1967. *Studies in the Buddhist Culture of India during the Seventh and Eight Centuries A.D.* Delhi: Motilal Banarsidass.

Joshi, P.S. 1993. *The Vidarbha Megaliths: A Cultural Study*. Unpublished Ph.D. Thesis submitted to University of Poona, Department of Archaeology.

Kajale, M.D. 1989. 'Archaeobotanical Investigation on Megalithic Bhagimohari and its Significance for Ancient Indian Agricultural System,' *Man and Environment*, Vol. XIII, pp. 87-100.

Kajale, M.D. 1994. 'Archaeobotanical Investigations on a Multicultural Site at Adam, Maharashtra, with Special Reference to the Development of Tropical Agriculture in Parts of India,' in J.G. Hather (ed.), *Tropical Archaeobotany: Applications and New Developments*, pp. 34-50.

Kane, P.V. 1917. 'Ancient Geography and Civilization of Maharashtra,' *Journal of Bombay Branch of Royal Asiatic Society*, Vol. XXIV (1914-17), pp. 613-657.

Kangle, R.P. 1963. *The Kautiliya Arthaśāstra*, Part II. Bombay:

University of Bombay.

Kangle, R.P. 1986. *The Kautilya Arthaśāstra*. Delhi: Motilal Banarsidass.

Khan, Abdul Waheed. 1963. *A Monograph on Yalesvaram Excavation*. Hyderabad.

Khan, Akabar Ali. 2001. *Discovery of Bangladesh: Explorations in the Dynamics of a Hidden Nation*. Dhaka: University Press Limited.

Khan, A.M. 1999. *The Maghs: A Buddhist Community in Bangladesh*. Dhaka: University Press Limited.

Khan, F.A. 1963. *Mainamati*. Karachi: Deptt. of Archaeology, Ministry of Education and Information, Govt. of Pakistan.

Kenoyer, J.M. 1985. 'Shell Working at Mohenjo-daro Pakistan,' in J. Schotsmans and M. Toddei (eds.), *South Asian Archaeology 1983*, pp. 297-344. Naples: Istituto Universitario Orientale.

Kern, J.H.C. [1896]. 1989. *Manual of Indian Buddhism*. Delhi: Motilal Banarsidass.

Kinsley, David, R. 1979. *The Divine Player: A Study of Kṛṣṇa Līlā*. Delhi: Motilal Banarsidass.

Kosambi, D.D. 1986. 'The Decline of Buddhism in India,' in his *Exasperating Essays: Exercises in the Dialectical Method*. Pune: Peoples' Book House.

Kittel, Rev. F. 1984. *A Kannada English Dictionary*. Mangalore: Basil Press.

Krishnadeva. 1955. *Temples of India*, 2 Vols. New Delhi: Aryan Books International.

Krishna Kumari M. 1994. *Studies in Medieval Andhra History and Culture*. New Delhi: Kanishka Publishers.

Kramrisch, Stella. 1933. *Indian Sculpture*. London: Oxford University Press.

Kulkarni, P. 2005. 'Coins of Vidarbha, *Aśmaka* and *Chedi Janapada*,' *Numismatic Studies*, Vol. 7, pp. 19-36.

Kulke, Hermann. 1995. 'The Early and Imperial Kingdom: A Processual Model for Integrative State Formation in Early Medieval India,' in Hermann Kulke (ed.), *The State in India 1000-1700*, pp. 233-262. Delhi: Oxford University Press.

Kulke, Hermann. 1999. 'Rivalry and Competition in the Bay of Bengal in the Eleventh Century and its Bearing on Indian Ocean Studies' in Om Prakash and Denys Lombard (ed.), *Commerce and Culture in the Bay of Bengal 1500-1800*, pp. 17-35. Delhi: Manohar.

Kumar, B.M. 1987. *Archaeology of Pataliputra and Nalanda*. Delhi: Ramanand Vidyabhavan.

Kunjan Pillai, Elamkulam. 1970. *Studies in Kerala History*. Trivandrum: National Book Stall.

Lahiri, Nayanjot. 1986. *Pre-Ahom Assam*. Delhi: Munshiram Mahoharlal.

Lamotte, E. 1988. *History of Indian Buddhism; From the Origins to the Saka Era*. English translation by S.Webb Boin. Louvain-la-neuve: Publications De L'institut Orientaliste De Louvain.

Lawson, D. 1982. *A Catalogue of Indian Buddhist Clay Sealings in British Museums*, Ph.D. Thesis, University of Oxford, Oxford.

Levi, S. 1905. *Le Nepal: Etude Historique d'un Royaume Hindou*, 3 vols. Paris: Leroux.

Ling, Trevor O. 1973. *The Buddha: Buddhist Civilisation in India and Ceylon*. London: Temple Smith.

Ling, Trevor O. 1979. *Buddha, Marx and God: Some Aspects of Religion in the Modern World*. Second edition, London: Macmillan.

Liu, Xin Riu. 1988. *Ancient India and Ancient China: Trade and Religious Exchange, A.D. 1-600*. Delhi: Oxford University Press.

Liu, Xin Riu. 1996. *Silk and Religion: an Exploration in to the Material Life and Thought of the People, AD 600-1200*. Delhi: Oxford University Press.

Lopez, Donald S. (ed.). 1995. *Buddhism in Practice*. New Jersey: Princeton University Press.

Mabbett, Ian & Bailey, Greg. 2003. *The Sociology of Early Buddhism*. Cambridge: Cambridge University Press.

Macdonell A.A. and Keith, A.B. 1912. *Vedic Index of Names and Subjects*. Vol. 1-2. London: John Murray, Albemarle Street, W.

Mahapatra, K.N. 1962, 'Puranic Literature of Orissa,' *Orissa Historical Research Journal*, Vol. XI, No. 1, pp. 21-31.

Mahapatra, K.N. 1962. 'Puranic Stories in the Early Records and Sculptures of Orissa,' *Orissa Historical Research Journal*, Vol. X, No. 4, pp. 59-74.

Mahapatra, L.K. 1978. 'Gods, Kings and Caste System in India,' in Bhavagrahi Mishra and James J. Preston (ed.), *Community, Self and Identity*, pp. 7-26. The Hague: Mouton Publishers.

Mahapatra, M.M. 1981. *Traditional Structure and Change in an Orissan Temple*. Calcutta: Punthi Pustak.

Mahāvairocana Sutra. Translated by Chikyo Yamamoto. Sata Pitaka Series, Vol. 359. Delhi: International Academy of Indian Culture.

Mallman, M.T. de. 1975. *Introduction a l' iconographie du Tantrisime boudhique*. Paris: CNRS.

Manjulatha. 1988. 'Devdasis Inams: A Case Study of the Chittoor District,' *Ithihas*, Vol.XIV, pp. 116-7.

Matsya Purāṇa. 1972. Translated by Various Scholars, Ed. J.D. Akhtar. Delhi, Oriental Publishers.

McMohan, David. 1998. 'Orality, Writing and Authority in South Asian Buddhism: Visionary Literature and the Struggle for Legitimacy in Mahayana,' *History of Religions*, 37 (3), pp. 249-274.

Meshram, Pradeep. 1993. *Vidarbhatil Buddha Dharmacha Itihaas*. Nagpur: Sanket Prakashan.

Meshram, Pradeep. 1994. *Vidarbhatil Bauddha Dharmakshetra-Pauni*. Yavatmal.

Meshram, Pradeep. 1996. 'Vidarbhat Alikade Milalele Kahi Bauddha Puravashesha,' *Vidarbha Samshodhana Mandal* 1995, 38, pp. 155-166.

Meshram, Pradeep, Khobragade, P., and Naranje, M. 2005. *Kshitij Vaidarbhiya Paryatanache, Bhatala – Ek Upekshit Shilpgram*. Nagpur: Sanket Prakashan.

Meister, M.W., Dhaky, M.A., Deva, Krishna (ed.). 1989. *Encyclopedia of Temple Architecture (North India): Foundations of North Indian Style, c.250 B.C.-A.D.1100*, Vol. II, Pt. I. New Delhi: Oxford University Press.

Miller, Robert James. 1959. *Monasteries and Cultural Change in Inner Mongolia.* Wiesbaden: Otto Harrassowitz Press.

Mirashi, V.V. 1968. 'New Light on Deotek Inscriptions,' in *Studies in Indology,* Vol. I, pp. 125-134. Nagpur: Vidarbha Samshodhan Mandal.

Mishra, B.N. 1998. *Nalanda,* Vol. I-III. Delhi: DK Printworld.

Mishra, S., Shete, G. and Deotare, B.C. 2005. '2000-2001 Excavations at Kaundinyapur, Wardha Valley,' Proccedings of National seminar on *Megalithic Tradition in Ethnography and Archaeology in India,* held by Indira Gandhi Rashtriya Manav Sangrahalaya, Bhopal during 28th-30th Nov. 2005.

Mishra, Umakant. 2005. *Buddhism and Maritime Networks in Early Medieval Orissa.* PhD Thesis, Centre for Historical Studies, Jawaharlal Nehru University, New Delhi.

Mitra, Debala. 1978. *Bronzes from Achutarajpur.* Delhi: Agam Kala Prakashan.

Mitra, Debala. 1983. *Ratnagiri* (1958-1961), Memoir of Archaeological Survey of India, No. 80, Vol. 1-2. New Delhi: Director General of Archaeology, Archaeological Survey of India.

Mitra, R.L, 1880, *The Antiquities of Orissa,* Vol. II. Calcutta: Mukhopadhyaya.

Mitra, R. L. [1882]. 1981. *The Sanskrit Buddhist Literature of Nepal.* Delhi: Cosmo Publications.

Mohan Ram, M.A., 1984. 'Famines and Relief Measures under the Imperial Cholas (850-1279),' *Proceedings of the Indian History Congress.*

Mohanty, A.B. 1940. *Madalapanji,* Prachi edition. Cuttack: Orissa Sahitya Academy.

Monier-Williams, Monier. 1889. *Buddhism, in its Connections with Hinduism and in Its Context with Christianity.* New York: MacMillan.

Morrison, B.M. 1974. *Lalmai: A Cultural Centre in Early Bengal.* Seattle: University of Washington Press.

Morrison, B.M. [1970]1980. *Political Centres and Cultural Regions in Early Bengal.* Jaipur: Vikash Publishers (Indian edition).

Morrison, K.D. 1995. 'Trade, Urbanism and Agrarian

Expansion: Buddhist Monastic Institutions and the State in the Early Historic Western Deccan,' *World Archaeology*, 27.2, pp. 203-221.

Mukherjee, B.N. 1980. *East Indian Art Style: A Study in Parallel Trends*. Calcutta: K.P. Bagchee.

Mukherjee, B.N. 1992. *Trade of Early North-Eastern India*. New Delhi: Har Anand Publications.

Mukharjee, Rila. 2004. 'Rice Culture of Divine Right in a Celestially Ordered Zone: A Case Study of South Asian and South-East Asian Ideologies and Hegemonies from c.2000 BC. to c.1800 AD with Specific Reference to Bengal,' *Revista Lusofona de Ciencias Sociais*, Lisbon, 1, pp. 49-58.

Mukharjee, Rila. 2006. *Strange Riches: Bengal in the Mercantile Map of South Asia*. Delhi: Foundation Books.

Nagaraju, S. 1996. 'From Spirituality to Power: A Millennium of Buddhist Monastic Architecture as a Mirror of Social History,' in K. Sankaranasayan, *et. al.* (ed.), *Buddhism in India and Abroad: An Integrated influence in Vedic and Post-Vedic Perspective*, pp. 301-314. Mumbai and New Delhi: Sommaiya Publishers.

Nagaswamy, R. 1965. 'South Indian Temple as an Employer,' *The Indian Economic and Social History Review*, 2, 1965, pp. 367-72.

Naiṣadhacarita. 1965. Translated and edited by K.K. Handique. Poona: Deccan College.

Nakamura, H. 1987. *Indian Buddhism, A Survey with Bibliographical Notes*. Delhi: Motilal Banarsidass.

Nandi, R.N. 1976. 'Origin and Nature of Saivaite Monasticism: The Case of Kālamukhas' in R.S. Sharma (ed.), *Indian Society: Historical Probings*, 190-201. Delhi: Peoples' Publication House.

Narayana Ayyar, C.V. 1974. *Origin and Early History of Saivism in South India*. Madras: University of Madras.

Narayanan M.G.S. and Veluthat, K. 1987. 'The Bhakti Movement in Medieval South India,' in D.N. Jha (ed.), *Feudal Social Formations in Early India*, pp. 348-373. Delhi: Chankya Publishers.

Nath, A. 1989. 'Archaeology of the Wardha Wainganga

Divide,' *Puratattva*, 20, pp. 93-98.

Nath, A. 1992. 'Adam – an Index to Vidarbha Archaeology,' in Nayak B.U. and N.C. Ghosh (ed.), *New Trends in Indian Art and Archaeology*, Vol. I, pp. 69-79. New Delhi: Aditya Prakashan.

Nath, A. 1998. *Further Excavations at Pauni*. New Delhi: Archaeological Survey of India.

Nath, R.M. 1948. *Background of Assamese Culture*. Shillong: A. K. Nath publishers.

Nath, Vijaya. 2001. *Puranas and Acculturation*. Delhi: Munshiram Manoharlal.

Neog, Dimbeswar. 1947. *Introduction to Assam*. Bombay: Vera.

Neog, Maheswar and Barpujari, H.K. (eds.). 1966. *Professor Suryya Kumar Bhuyan Commemoration Volume*. Gauhati: All India Oriental Conference.

Neog, Maheswar (ed). 1973. *Studies in the Early History of Assam (A Collection of Papers Published in various Journals by K.L. Barua)*. Gauhati.

Neog, M. 1984. *Religions of North East India*. Delhi: Munshiram Manoharlal.

Nicholas, Ralph. 2001. 'Vaisanvism and Islam in the Environs of Rural Bengal,' in Rafiuddin Ahmed (ed.), *Understanding Bengal Muslims*. Delhi: Oxford University Press.

Niyogi, Pushpa. 1967. *Buddhism in Ancient Bengal*. Calcutta: Jijnasa.

O'Connor, Richard A. 1993, 'Interpreting the Thai Religious Change: Temples, Sangha Reform and Social Change,' *Journal of South East Asian Studies*, 24 (2), pp. 330-339.

Oddie, G.A. 1998. *Religious Transformations in South Asia: Interactions and Change*. Surrey: Curzon Press.

Omvedt, Gail. 2003. *Buddhism in India: Challenging Brahmanism and Caste*. Delhi: Sage.

Paes, [1901]. 1985. 'Chronicles of Paes and Nuniz' in *A Forgotten empire-Vijaynagara, A Contribution to the History of India by Robert Sewell*. New Delhi: Asia Educational Services.

Panashikar, V.L. and K. Gore. 1925. *Aitareya Brāhmaṇa*. Bombay: Nirnaya Sagar.

Panigrahi, K.C. [1961]1981. *Archaeological Remains at*

Bhubaneswar. Cuttack: Kitab Mahal.

Pande, G.C. 1957. *Studies in the Origins of Buddhism*. Allahabad: University of Allahabad.

Pande, Rekha. 2004. 'At the Service of the Lord: Temple girls in Medieval Deccan (11th to 17th centuries),' *Deccan Studies*, Vol. II, No. 2, pp. 25-43.

Pande, Rekha. 2006. 'Devdasis,' in J.S. Grewal (ed.), 'Religious Movements and Institutions in Medieval India,' Vol. VII, Part, 2. in D.P. Chattopadhyaya (general editor), *History of Science, Philosophy and Culture in Indian Civilization*. New Delhi: Oxford University Press.

Pande, Susmita. 1990. *Birth of Bhakti in Indian Religions and Art*. Delhi: Books and Books on behalf of Indian History and Culture Society.

Paramasivanandam, A.M. 1982. *Historical Study of the Thevaram Hymns*. Madras: Tamilkalai Pub. House.

Patil, B.R. 1975. 'The Devdasis,' *Indian Journal of Social Work*, Vol. XXXV, No. 4, pp. 377-89.

Patra, Chitaranjan. 1998. 'Spread of Buddhism in Bengal' in A. Dutta (ed.), *History and Archaeology of Eastern India*, pp. 200-212. Delhi: Books and Books.

Peterson, Indira Viswanathan. 1989. *Poems to Siva*. Delhi: Motilal Banarsidass.

Pillay, K.K. 1977. *The Caste system in Tamilnadu*. Madras: University of Madras.

Pillai, K.K. 2002. *Thamizhaga Varalaru Makkalum Panpadum* (in Tamil). Chennai: International Institute of Tamil Studies.

Parabrahma Sastri, P.V. 1978. *The Kakatiyas of Warangal*. Hyderabad: Government of Andhra Pradesh.

Prasad, Birendra Nath. 2006. 'Cultural Communications in Early Medieval India: Some Preliminary Observations,' *Prajna Bharati*, Journal of K.P. Jayaswal Research Institute, Patna, Vol. 12, pp. 27-49.

Prasad, Birendra Nath. 2006. 'Dilemmas of Revival of Buddhism in India,' *Indian International Journal of Buddhist Studies*, Vol. 7, Varanasi, pp.171-75.

Prasad, Birendra Nath. 2006. 'Tantric Buddhism as Sacralised *Samanta* Feudalism in Early Medieval India,' a Review of

Ronald M. Davidson's *Indian Esoteric Buddhism: A Social History of the Tantric Movement, Social Science Probings*, Vol. 18 (2) pp. 147-149. New Delhi: Manak Publishers.

Prasad, Birendra Nath. 2007. 'Trajectories of Urbanisation: A Study of Seals and Sealings from Early Historic Vaiśālī,' *Prajna Bharati*, Journal of K.P. Jayaswal Research Institute, Patna, Vol. XIII, pp. 7-22.

Prasad, Birendra Nath. 2008. 'Monarchs, Monasteries and Trade on an "Agrarian Frontier": Early Medieval Samataṭa-Harikela Region, Bangladesh,' *South and Southeast Asia: Culture and Religion*, Journal of South and South-East Asian Association for the Study of Culture and Religion, Vol. 3, pp. 160-177.

Prasad, Birendra Nath. 2008. 'Major Trends and Perspectives in Studies in the Functional Dimensions of Indian Monastic Buddhism in the Past One Hundred Years: A Historiographical Survey,' *Buddhist Studies Review*, Journal of the UK Association for Buddhist Studies, London, Vol. 25, No. 1, pp. 54-89.

Prasad, Birendra Nath. 2009. 'Urbanisation at Early Historic Vaiśālī,' *Social Science Probings*, Vol. 21, number 1, pp. 21-46. New Delhi: Manak Publishers.

Prasad, Birendra Nath, *et al*. 2009. 'Bārā: A Recently Discovered Site in Nalanda District and its Bearings on the Decline of Indian Buddhism' in B.Labh (ed.), *The Ocean of Buddhist Wisdom*, Vol. IV, pp. 225-234. Delhi: New Bharatiya Book Corporation.

Prasad, Birendra Nath. "Nalanda – 'the Greatest Centre for Buddhist Learning' – in a Poly-religious Landscape: An Interpretation of Archaeology of Religious Transformation in Early Medieval Bihar," forthcoming.

Prasert, Sanit Wongs. 1988. 'Impact of the Dhammacarika Bhikku's Programme on the Hill Tribes of Thailand,' in K.M. Desilva *et al.* (ed.), *Ethnic Conflict in the Buddhist Societies: Sri Lanka, Burma and Thailand*, pp. 126-137. London: Pinter Publications.

Prebish, Charles S. [1975] 2002. *Buddhist Monastic Discipline*. Delhi: Motilal Banarsidass.

Preston, James J. 1980. *Cult of the Goddess: Social and Religious Change in a Hindu Temple.* Delhi: Vikash.

Preston, James J. 1992. 'Sacred Centres and Symbolic Networks in India,' in S. Mahapatra (ed.), *The Realm of the Sacred*, pp. 79-112. Delhi: Oxford University Press.

Puri, B.N. 1968. *Studies in Early History and Administration in Assam.* Guwahati: Dept. of Publication, Gauhati University.

Putli, Krishnamurthy, V. 1987. *The Changing Conditions of Women in Andhra from the middle of 19th Century to the Middle of 20th Century.* Hyderabad: Navayug Publishers.

Raghavan, V. I956. 'Methods of Popular Religious Instruction in South India,' in Haridas Bhattacharyya (ed.), *The Cultural Heritage of India*, Vol. IV, pp. 503-5I4. Calcutta: R.K.M. Institute of Culture.

Rajaguru, S.N. 1962. 'Jayarampur Copper-Plate Inscription of the time of Gopacandra,' *Orissa Historical Research Journal*, Vol. 11, pp. 206-29.

Rajguru, S.N. 1966. 'Brahmeswar Temple Stone Inscription of the Time of Udyotakesari,' *Inscriptions of Orissa*, Vol. 4, Orissa State Museum, Bhubaneswar: 244-252.

Rajguru, S.N. 1975. *Inscriptions of Orissa*, Vol. V, Pt. I. Bhuvaneswar: Orissa State Museum.

Rajgor, D. 2001. *Punch-marked Coins of Early Historic India.* California: Reesha Books International.

Raman, K.V. 1975. *The Varadarajaswamy Temple: Kanchi.* New Delhi: Abinav Publications.

Ramteke, A. 2006. 'Coins of Vidarbha *Janapada*: A Revolutionary Discovery,' *Indian Coin Society Newsletter*, No. 40 (July-sept 2006): 68-87.

Rangaswamy, Dorai. 1958. *The Religion And Philosophy of The Tēvāram.* Madras: University of Madras.

Ray, Amita 1983. *Life and Art of Early Andhradesa.* Delhi: Agam Kala Prakashan.

Ray, H.P. 1986. *Monastery and Guild: Commerce under the Satavahanas.* Delhi: Oxford University Press.

Ray, H.P. 1987. 'Bharahut and Sanchi: Nodal Points in Commercial Exchange,' in B.M. Pande, & B.D.

Chattopadhyaya (ed.), *Archaeology and History, Essays in Honour of A. Ghosh*, pp. 621-629. Delhi: Agam Kala Prakashana.

Ray, H.P. 1994. *The Winds of Change: Buddhism and the Maritime Links of Early South Asia.* Delhi: Oxford University Press.

Ray, H.P. 1994. 'Kanheri: The Archaeology of an Early Buddhist Pilgrimage Site in Western India,' *World Archaeology*, 26(1): 35-46.

Ray, H.P. 2003. *The Archaeology of Sea Faring in Ancient South Asia.* Cambridge: Cambridge University Press.

Ray, N.R. 1994. *History of the Bengali People.* Translated by J.W. Hood. Calcutta: Orient Longman.

Ray, Reginald A. 1994. *Buddhist Saints in India: A Study in Buddhist Values and Orientations.* New York: Oxford University Press.

Raychaudhury, H. 1950. *Political History of Ancient India.* Calcutta: University of Calcutta.

Rea, A. 1894. *South Indian Buddhist Antiquities.* Madras: The Superintendent, Government Press.

Reddy, Soma. 1984. *History of Religious Institutions in Andhra Desa* (1300-1600 A.D.). Madras: New Era Publications.

Rhys Davids, C.A.F. 1931. *Sakya or Buddhist Origins.* London: Kegan Paul.

Rhys Davids, T.W. [1903] 2005.*Buddhist India.* Delhi: Motilal Banarsidass.

Rhys Davids, T.W. [1932] 1978. *Manual of Buddhism.* Delhi: Munshiram Manoharlal.

Rhys Davids, T.W. 1934. *Outlines of Buddhism: A Historical Sketch.* London: Methuen & Company.

Sahu, N.K. 1958. *Buddhism in Orissa*, Bhubaneswar: Utkal University.

Salatore, B.A. 1934. *Social and Political life in Vijaynagar Empire*, Vol. II. Madras: B.G. Paual and Co.

Sali, Chetan. 1998. 'Vakataka Culture: Archaeological Perspective,' *Sanshodhak*, March 1998 (year 66), pp. 3-38.

Sankalia, H.D., S. Subbarao and S.B. Deo. 1955. *The Excavations at Maheshwar and Navdatoli 1952-53.* Pune: Deccan College and Baroda: M.S. University, Publication No. 1.

Sarkar, H.B. 1971. *Corpus of the Inscriptions of Java*, 2 vols. Calcutta: Firma KLM.

Sarkar, H. 1987. 'Emergence and Growth of Urban Centres in Early Historic Andhradesa,' in B.M. Pande & B.D. Chattopadhyaya (ed.), *Archaeology and History, Essays in Honour of A.Ghosh*, pp. 631-641. Delhi: Agam Kala Prakashana.

Sarao, K.T.S.1990. *Urban Centres and Urbanisation as Reflected in the Pali Vinaya and Sutta Pitakas*. Delhi: Vidyanidhi Publishers.

Saskia C. Kersen. 1987. *Boom – Story, Nityasumangali*. Delhi: Motilal Banarsidass.

Sastri, Hara Prasad. 1897. *Discovery of Living Buddhism in Bengal*. Calcutta: Sanskrit Press Depository.

Satyanarayana, K. 1983. *A Study in the History and Culture of the Andhras*, Vol. II, *Consolidation of Feudalism*. New Delhi: Peoples Publishing House.

Sawant, Reshma 2003. '*Aśmaka Mahājanapada*: A New Perspective,' *Man and Environment*, XXVII (2), pp. 9-20.

Sawant, Reshma. 2006. *Vidarbha: An Archaeo-Historical Approach*. Unpublished Ph.D. thesis submitted to Deccan College, Pune.

Sawant, Reshma (In press). *Historical Archaeology of Vidarbha*. Nashik: Indian Institute of Research in Numismatic Studies.

Schoff, W.H. 1912. *Periplus of the Erytharean Sea*. London: Longmans, Green and Co.

Schopen, Gregory. 1991. 'Archaeology and Protestant Presuppositions in the Study of Indian Buddhism,' *History of Religions*, 31 (1), pp. 1-23.

Schopen, Gregory. 1994. 'Doing Business for the Lord: Lending on Interest and Written Loan Contracts in the *Mūlasarvāstivādina Vinaya*,' *Journal of American Oriental Society*, 114 (4),pp. 527-554.

Schopen, Gregory. 1995. 'Monastic Law Meets the Real World: A Monk's Continuous Right to Inherit Family Property in Classical India,' *History of Religions*, 35 (2), pp.101-123.

Schopen, Gregory. 1995. 'Deaths, Funerals and Division of

Property in a Monastic Code' in Donald S. Lopez (ed.), *Buddhism in Practice*, pp. 473-502. New Jersey: Princeton University Press.

Schopen, Gregory. 1997. *Bones, Stones and Tools: Collected Papers on the Archaeology, Epigraphy and Text of Monastic Buddhism in India*. Honolulu: University of Hawaii Press.

Scott, David. 1995. 'Buddhist Functionalism: Instrumentality Reaffirmed,' *Asian Philosophy*, 5 (2), pp.127-149.

Sen, Tanasen. 2004. *Buddhism, Diplomacy and Trade; Realignment of Sino-Indian Relations, 600-1400*. Delhi: Manohar.

Seneviratne, S. 1978. 'The Mauryan State,' H.J.M. Claessen and P. Skalnìk (ed.), *The Early State*, pp. 381-402. The Hague: Mouton.

Seneviratne, S. 1981. 'Kalinga and Andhra: the Process of Secondary State Formation in Early India,' *The Indian Historical Review*.. VII, pp. 54-69.

Sengupta, R. 1955-57. 'A Sculptural Representation of the Buddhist Litany to Tara at Ellora,' *Bulletin of the Prince of Wales of Museum of Western India*, No. 5, pp. 12–15.

Shamashastry 1929. *Kautilya's Arthśāstra*. Mysore: Wesleyan Mission Press.

Sharma, M.M. 1979. *Inscriptions of Ancient Assam*. Guwahati: Gauhati University.

Sharma, P. 1988. *Architecture of Assam*. New Delhi: Agam Kala Prakashan.

Sharma, R.S. 1967. *Indian Feudalism*. Calcutta: University of Calcutta.

Sharma, R.S. 1983. *Material Culture and Social Formation in Ancient India*. Delhi: Macmillan.

Sharma, R.S. 1987. *Urban Decay*. Delhi: Munshiram Manoharlal.

Sharma, R.S. 2001. *Early Medieval Indian Society: A Study in Feudalisation*. Hyderabad: Orient Longman.

Sharma, Shanta. 2003. 'Rulers, Urban Milieu and Temple Patronage: Shifting Contours in Rajasthan, c. AD 700-1000,' *History Today*, Vol. 4, pp. 9-21.

Shashibala. 1989. *Comparative Iconography of the Vajradhātu-Maṇḍala and the Tattva Saṅgraha*, Sata Pitaka series 344. Delhi: International Academy for Indian Culture.

Shastri, A.M. 1965. *An Outline of Early Buddhism*. Varanasi: Indological Book House.

Shastri, A.M. 1969. *India As Seen in the Bṛhatsamhitā of Varāhamihira*. Delhi: Motilal Banarsidass.

Shastri, A.M. 1978. 'Mandhal Utkhanan' (in Hindi), *Vidarbha Sanshodhan Mandal Varshik,* Vol. 20, pp. 142-174.

Shastri, H. P. (ed.). 1927. *Advayavajrasamgraha*. Baroda: Gaikwad Oriental Series, 90.

Shaw, Julia, & Suitclif, J. 2000. ' Sanchi and its Archaeological Landscape; Buddhist Monasteries, Settlements and Irrigation Work in Central India,' *Antiquity*, 74, pp. 775-796.

Shaw, Julia, & Suitclif, J. 2001. 'Ancient Irrigation Works in the Sanchi Area: An Archaeological and Hydrological Investigation,' *South Asian Studies*, 17,pp. 55-75.

Shaw, Julia, & Suitclif, J. 2003. 'Water Management, Patronage Networks and Religious Change: New Evidence from the Sanchi Dam Complex and Counterparts in Gujarat and Sri Lanka,' *South Asian Studies*, 19, pp.73-104.

Shimada, Akira. 2009. 'Amaravati and Dhanyakataka: Typologies of Monastic Spaces in Ancient Indian Cities' in Jason Hawkes and Akira Shimada (ed.), *Buddhist Stupas in South Asia: Recent Archaeological, Art-Historical and Historical Perspective*, pp.216-234. Delhi: Oxford University Press.

Shulman, David D. 1980. *Tamil Temple Myths*. Princeton: Princeton University Press.

Shulman, David. 1992. 'Poets and Patrons in Tamil Literature and Literary Legend' in Barbara Stoler Miller (ed.), *Powers of Art: Patronage in Indian Culture*. Delhi: Oxford University Press.

Singer, Milton, November, I955. 'The Cultural Pattern of Indian Civilization,' *Far Eastern Quarterly*; Vol. XV, No. I, pp. 23-36.

Sircar, D.C. 1971. *Studies in the Geography of Ancient and Medieval India*. Delhi: Motilal Banarassidas.

Singh, A.K. 1990. *Devadasi System in Ancient India*. New Delhi: H.K.Publishers and Distributors.

Singh, Upinder. 1996. 'Sanchi: The History of Patronage of an Ancient Buddhist Establishment,' *The Indian Economic and Social History Review*, 33(1),pp.1-35.

Singh, Yogendra.2003. 'Influence of Naga Worship in Buddhist Art,' in R.C.Sharma (ed.), *Interactions between Buddhist and Brahmanical Art*, pp. 30-35. New Delhi: D.K.Printworld.

Sinha, Nandini. 2001. 'Early Maitrakas, Land grant Charters and Regional State Formation in Early Medieval Gujarat,' *Studies in History*, n.s. 17 (2), pp.151-163.

Śivathamby, K. 1986. *Literary History In Tamil*. Thanjavur: Tamil University Press.

Snellgrove, D. 1959. *The Hevajra Tantra: A Critical Study*, 2 vols. London Oriental Series 6. London: Oxford University Press.

Snellgrove, D. L. 1987. *Indo-Tibetan Buddhism: Indian Buddhists and Their Tibetan Successors*. London: Serindia.

Spencer, George W. 1969. 'Religious Networks and Royal Influences in 11th Century South India,' *Journal of Economic and Social History of Orient*, XII, pp. 42-56.

Spencer, George. W. 1970. 'The Sacred Geography of the Tamil Shaivite Hymns,' *Numen*, Vol. 17, No. 3, pp. 232-44.

Sontheimer, G.D. 1993. *Pastoral Deities in Western India*. Delhi: Oxford University Press.

Sontheimer, G.D, 1994. 'The *Vana* and the *Kṣetra*: The Tribal Background of some famous cults, in G.C. Tripathy & H.Kulke (ed.), *Religion and Society in Eastern India*,, pp.117-64. Delhi: Manohar Publishers.

Southwold, M. 1983. *Buddhism in Life: The Anthropological Study of Religion and the Sinhalese Practice*. Manchester: Manchester United Press.

Spink, Walter M., 1992. 'Before the Fall: Pride and Pity at Ajanta,' in Barbara S. Miller(ed.), *The Powers of Art: Patronage in Indian Culture*, pp. 65-77. Delhi: Oxford University Press.

Spiro, Melford E. 1971. *Buddhism and Society: A Great Tradition and its Burmese Vicissitudes*. London: George Allen and Unwin.

Stein, Burton. 1985. *Peasant State and Society in Medieval South*

India. Oxford: Oxford University Press.

Stoddard, R, M, and Aldskogius, Hans, Morinis, A. 1998. 'Sacred Places, Sacred Spaces, the Geography of Pilgrimage,' *Human Geography*, Vol. 80, No. 3.

Subrahmanian, N.S. 1985. *Encyclopaedia of the Upniṣadas*. New Delhi: Sterling Publishers.

Sukhthankar, V.S. (ed.) 1942. *Mahābharata, Vanaparva* (Book 3). Poona: Baroda Oriental Research Institute.

Suksamran, S. 1977. (edited with an Introduction by Trevor O. Ling). *Political Buddhism in South East Asia: The Role of the Sangha in the Modernization of Thailand*. London: C. Hurst & Company.

Sundaram, K. 1968.*Studies in Social and Economic Conditions in Medieval Andhra Desa (1000-1500 AD)*. Warangal

Sundstrom, Linea. 1996. 'Mirror of Heaven: Cross-Cultural Transference of the Sacred Geography of the Black Hills,' *World Archaeology*, Vol. 28, No. 2, pp. 177-189.

Svarnadri Mahodaya. 1912. Edited by R. Gargabatu. Calcutta.

Takakusu, J (1966). *A Record of the Buddhist Religion as Practiced in India and Malay Archipelago (671-695) by I-tsing*. Delhi: Munshiram Manoharlal.

Talbott, Cynthia. 2001. *Precolonial India in Practice: Society, Religion and Identity in Medieval Andhra*. Delhi: Oxford University Press.

Tambiah, S.J. 1976. *The World Conqueror and the World Renouncer: A Study of Buddhism and Polity in Thailand against a Historical Background*. Cambridge: Cambridge University Press.

Tambiah, S.J. 1984. *Buddhist Saints of Forests and the Cult of Amulets*. Cambridge: Cambridge University Press.

Tarachand, K.C. 1972. *Devdasi Custom: Rural Social Structure and Flesh Market*. New Delhi: Reliance Publishing House.

Tarafdar,M.R. 1995. *Trade, Technology and Society in Medieval Bengal*. Dhaka: University Press Limited.

Thakur, Laxman S. 2001. *Buddhism in the Western Himalaya: A Study of Tabo Monastery*. Delhi: Oxford University Press.

Thapar, Romila. 1966. *A History of India*. Delhi: Penguin Books.

Thapar, Romila. 1992. 'Patronage and Community,' in Barbara S. Miller (ed.), *The Powers of Art: Patronage in Indian Culture*, pp. 19-34.Delhi: Oxford University Press.

Thapar, Romila (2000) 2002. *Cultural Past - Essays in Early Indian History*. New Delhi: Oxford University Press.

Thomas, E.J. 1927 [1983]. *Life of the Buddha as Legend and History*. Delhi: Motilal Banarsidass.

Thomas, E. J. 1933. *The History of Buddhist Thought*. London: Kegan Paul.

Thruston, Edgar and Rangachari, K. 1909. *Castes and Tribes of South India*, Vol. IV. Madras: Government press.

Tieken, Herman. 2000. 'Aśoka and the Buddhist Saṅgha: A Study of Aśoka's Schism Edicts and Minor Rock Edicts,' *Bulletin of School of Oriental and African Studies*, London, 63(1),pp. 1-30.

Tripathi, R.S. 1942. *History of Ancient India*. Delhi: Motilal Banarsidass.

Tripathi,R.K. 1987. *Social and Religious Aspects of Bengal Inscriptions*. Calcutta: Firma KLM.

Tripathy, Snigdha. 1987. 'Ekāmra-Bhuvaneswar' *Orissa Historical Research Journal*, Vol.33,No 1-2, pp. 133-155.

Tsuda, S. 1974. *The Samvarodaya-Tantra: Select Chapters*. Tokyo: Yokuseido Press.

Upadhyay, S.C.1961. *Kāmasūtra of Vātsāyana*. Bombay: Taraporevala.

Utkalakhandam of SkandaPurāṇāa. 1905. Edited ms. Panchanana Tarkaratna. Calcutta: Sanskrit Parishad.

Van kooji, K. R. 1977. 'The Iconography of the Buddhist Wood Carvings in a Newar Buddhist Monastery in Kathmandu (Chusya- Baha),' *Journal of the Nepal Research Centre*, Vol 1, pp. 39-82.

Varma, V.P. 1972. *Early Buddhism and its Origins*. New Delhi: Munshiram Manoharlal.

Vasu, N.N. [1911]1981. *Archaeological Survey of Mayurbhanja*. Delhi: Rare Reprints Publications.

Vasu, N.N. 1922. *A Social History of Assam*, Vol. 1. Calcutta: Vishwakosh Press.

Venkatasubramanian,T.K. 1984. 'Social Roots of Tamilian Religious Ideology,' *Proceedings of the Indian History Congress*.

Verma, Susan. 2004. 'The Archaeology of Early Temples of Saurashtra,' in H.P.Ray, Carla Sinopoly (ed.), *Archaeology as History in Early South Asia*, pp. 411-425. Delhi: Aryan Books International.

Vijaysri, Priyadarshini. 2004. *Recasting the Devadasi: Patterns of Sacred Prostitution in Colonial South India*. New Delhi: Kanishka Publishers and Distributors.

Wagle, Narendra. 1995. *Society at the Time of The Buddha*. Second revised edition, Bombay: Popular Prakashan.

Waley, Arthur. 1931-32. 'New Light on Buddhism in Medieval India,' *Melanges Chinols et bouddhiques*. (Full text downloaded from http/ccbs.ntu/edu.tw/FULLTEXT/JR-MEL/Weale.htm).

Walimbe, S.R. 2003. 'Excavations at the Early Historic Site of Kahali-Bramhapuri,' *Annual Report* (2001-2002), pp 39-40. Pune: Deccan College.

Watters, T. [1904-05] 1961. *On Yuan-chwang's Travels in India*. Delhi: Munshiram Manoharlal.

Wayman, A. and Tajima, R. 1992. *The Enlightenment of Vairocana*, 2 parts, Sata Pitaka Series. Delhi: International Academy for Indian Culture.

Weber, Max. [1921]1992. *The Religion of India: The Sociology of Hinduism and Buddhism*. Edited and translated by H.H. Gerth & D. Martindale. Delhi: Munshiram Manoharlal.

Wedemeyer, Christian K. 2001. 'Tropes, Typologies and Turnarounds: A Brief Genealogy of Tantric Buddhism,' *History of Religions*, Vol. 41, pp. 223- 259.

Weightman, Barbara. A. 1996. 'Sacred Landscapes and the Phenomenon of Light,' *Geographical Review*, Vol. 86, No. 1, pp. 59-71.

Welch, David J. 1997. 'Archaeological Evidence of Khmer State Political and Economic Organisation,' *Bulletin of Indo – Pacific Prehistory Association*, Chiangmai Papers, Vol. 3, pp. 69-78.

Wink, Andre. 1999. *Al-Hind: The Making of the Indo-Islamic World*, Vol. II. Delhi: Oxford University Press.

Winternitz, M. [1933] 1983. *History of Indian Literature*, 2 Vols. Delhi: Motilal Banarsidass.

Wolf, Thom. 2007. 'Buddhism in the 21st Century: Three Challenges,' in B. Mungekar (ed.), *Buddhism and the Contemporary World: An Ambedkarian Perspective*, pp. 29-48. Delhi: Bookwell Publishers.

Yasoda Devi, Y. 'A History of Andhra Country,' *Journal of Andhra Historical Research Society*, Vol. XXV.

Zelliot, E. 1992. *From Untouchable to Dalit: Essays on the Ambedkar Movement*. Delhi: Manohar.

Zysk, G. 1991. *Asceticism and Healing in Ancient India: Medicine in the Buddhist Monastery*. Delhi: Oxford University Press.

INDEX